DISCARDED,

AMERICAN GUIDE SERIES

U.S. One:

MAINE to FLORIDA

*Compiled and written by the Federal Writers' Project
of the Works Progress Administration*

WITH 30 PHOTOGRAPHS

SPONSORED BY THE U. S. NO. 1 HIGHWAY ASSOCIATION

and published by

MODERN AGE BOOKS, INC.   NEW YORK

Republished 1972
SOMERSET PUBLISHERS – a Division of Scholarly Press, Inc.
22929 Industrial Drive East, St. Clair Shores, Michigan 48080

COPYRIGHT 1938 BY U. S. NO. 1 HIGHWAY ASSOCIATION, INC.

PUBLISHED BY MODERN AGE BOOKS, INC.

[BMG · UOPWA, 18]

All rights in this book are reserved, and it may not be reproduced in whole or in part without written permission from the holder of these rights. For information address the publishers.

Library of Congress Cataloging in Publication Data

Federal Writers' Project.
  U. S. one: Maine to Florida.

  "Sponsored by the U. S. No. 1 Highway Association."
  Reprint of the 1938 ed., issued in series: American guide series.
  1. Atlantic States--Description and travel--Guidebooks. 2. Automobiles--Road guides--Atlantic States. 3. United States Highway 1. I. Title. II. Series: American guide series.
F106.F45 1972   917.4   72-84519
ISBN 0-403-02208-8

FOREWORD

U. S. ONE is a publication of the Federal Writers' Project of the Works Progress Administration. Under this project, organized to give useful work to unemployed writers, an ambitious and pioneering task has been undertaken — a written description of the most important sections of the United States. The Federal Writers' publications are of many types. This volume is part of the American Guide Series of regional, State and local guidebooks, and second in a series of interstate route guides. The entire series of guides, when completed, will highlight the history, resources and points of interest in an area of more than three million square miles. Although collated, rechecked and edited in the central office in Washington, the materials for the book were collected in the States and the book was written by the state workers on the Federal Writers' Project. To insure its accuracy authorities have checked statements of fact, and to give it all possible scope many public spirited persons have given their services freely. They share with us the hope that those who use this volume will through it gain a better knowledge and greater understanding of America and American life.

The Federal Writers' Project, directed by Henry G. Alsberg, is administered by Ellen S. Woodward, WPA Assistant Administrator.

Harry L. Hopkins
Administrator

CONTENTS

Foreword	iii
Notes on Use of Book	ix
Introduction	xi
Special Foods from Maine to Florida	xvii

MAINE — 1
Section 1. Calais to Ellsworth — 2
Section 2. Ellsworth to Belfast — 15
Section 3. Belfast to Brunswick — 20
Section 4. Brunswick to New Hampshire Line — 33

NEW HAMPSHIRE
Section 5. Maine Line to Massachusetts Line — 47

MASSACHUSETTS
Section 6. New Hampshire Line to Rhode Island Line — 55

RHODE ISLAND
Section 7. Massachusetts Line to Connecticut Line — 65

CONNECTICUT
Section 8. Rhode Island Line to New Haven — 89
Section 9. New Haven to New York Line — 105

NEW YORK
Section 10. Connecticut Line to New Jersey Line — 114

NEW JERSEY
Section 11. New York Line to Pennsylvania Line — 124

PENNSYLVANIA
Section 12. New Jersey Line to Maryland Line — 135

MARYLAND
Section 13. Pennsylvania Line to Baltimore — 151
Section 14. Baltimore to Washington — 168

CONTENTS

DISTRICT OF COLUMBIA	184
VIRGINIA	
Section 15. Washington to Richmond	185
Section 16. Richmond to North Carolina Line	202
NORTH CAROLINA	
Section 17. Virginia Line to Raleigh	210
Section 18. Raleigh to South Carolina Line	220
SOUTH CAROLINA	
Section 19. North Carolina Line to Columbia	231
Section 20. Columbia to Georgia Line	235
GEORGIA	
Section 21. South Carolina Line to Florida Line	240
FLORIDA	
Section 22. Georgia Line to Jacksonville	252
Section 23. Jacksonville to New Smyrna	255
Section 24. New Smyrna to Miami	264
Section 25. Miami to Key West	282
MAINE	
Side Route 1. Perry to Eastport	296
Side Route 2. Whiting to Lubec	299
VIRGINIA	
Side Route 3. Richmond to Westover	301
GEORGIA	
Side Route 4. Folkston to Okefenokee Swamp	305
Annual Events	311

Map of US 1

ILLUSTRATIONS

		Following page
Eastport, Maine	*Highton*	xxviii
Fort Knox, Maine	*Highton*	xxviii
Shiloh, Maine		32
"Wedding Cake House," Maine		32
New Hampshire Coast	*Highton*	48
Ironworks House, Saugus, Mass.		48
Providence Harbor, R. I.	*Highton*	48
Hannah Robinson House, Narragansett, R. I.		48
Congregational Church, Old Lyme, Conn.		96
New Haven Green, Conn.	*Highton*	96
Hutchinson River Parkway, Saxon Woods, N. Y.		112
Bush Homestead, Port Chester, N. Y.		112
George Washington Bridge, New York City		112
Stretch of US 1, N. J.		112
Bayonne Bridge, N. J.		128
State House, Trenton, N. J.	*Highton*	128
City Hall, Philadelphia, Pa.	*Highton*	160
Brandywine Baptist Church, Pa.	*Highton*	160
Jerusalem Mills, Md.	*Shriver*	192
House at Greenbelt, Md.	*Rothstein*	192
State Capitol, Raleigh, N. C.		224
State House, Columbia, S. C.		224
Presbyterian Church, Camden, S. C.		240
Turpentine Distillery, Ga.		240

ILLUSTRATIONS

Following page

Old Slave Market, Louisville, Ga.		240
Southern Georgia Plains	*Highton*	240
On a Florida Beach	*Miami News Service*	256
Biscayne Bay, Miami, Fla.	*Miami News Service*	256
Gates at Westover, Va.	*Va. Cons. & Dev. Com.*	272
Okefenokee Swamp, Ga.		272

NOTE: *The illustrations referred to on pages* 47, 121, 138, 167, 184, *and* 188 *have been omitted*

NOTES ON USE OF BOOK

THIS is a mile-by-mile description of US 1 and most of the short routes branching from it. Descriptions of the more important side and cross routes and large cities have been omitted for lack of space; readers are referred to the State guide books of the American Guide Series for this material. The description of the main route, written north to south, is of course valid in the reverse direction. For the convenience of those entering the route at midway points the description of US 1 has been broken into short sections, cumulative mileage being started afresh at the beginning of each. Mileages on the side routes are also cumulative, being counted from the junctions with the main route. Those using this guide book on the road are reminded that cumulative mileages depend on the manner in which a car is driven; if curves are rounded on the inside, if many other cars are passed, if the road is left even briefly for stops at filling stations, if an alternate to the indicated route is used in going through a city or town, total mileages will differ from those given here.

Travelers are advised to read in advance the descriptions of sections they expect to travel and to mark the points of interest they particularly wish to view.

Great effort has been expended to make this book as accurate as possible, but it is realized that no volume covering such a wide range of material, some of it inadequately documented, can be free of mistakes; if those who find errors will report them to the Federal Writers' Project in Washington, corrections will gladly be made in future editions.

KATHARINE A. KELLOCK
Tours Editor

INTRODUCTION

THE HISTORY OF US 1, which runs from the Canadian Boundary of Maine to southern Florida, reflects the history of the Atlantic Seaboard States. North of Baltimore the route approximates the Old Post Road, first official intercolonial highway of the country connecting the leading cities of all the thirteen Colonies but Delaware. The cities of this northern section maintained their primacy as settlement spread inland. South of Baltimore, however, the early commercial and cultural centers along the coast gradually lost leadership to cities that developed inland along the geologic fall line; the main north-and-south highway connecting the States veered inland with the shift of power. It is significant that when Federal highway numbering began in 1925 this old route became US 1. It remains as it was in Colonial and early Federal days the chief line of communication between the centers of the Atlantic Seaboard States.

With increasing congestion of metropolitan areas, US 1 has in many places been rerouted to bypass the centers of the cities it formerly traversed. It still, however, runs through country intimately bound up with important events. In Maine the route runs close to the sites of the first two settlements attempted in New England; in Florida it passes through St. Augustine, the oldest settlement in the present United States. Many of the New England towns through which it runs were "little hornets' nests" during the Revolutionary War. Over a part of the route Paul Revere in 1773 spurred his horse on his dash to Philadelphia with news of the Boston Tea Party. Fort Washington in New York City is where three thousand Americans surrendered to General Howe in 1776, completing the abandonment of the city. Across the river in New Jersey the route passes the site of old Fort Lee, from which Washington watched the attack and surrender of his Fort Washington garrison. Lafayette and his troops in 1781 hurried along this road to oppose the British invasion of Richmond.

This highway was likewise closely bound up with the Civil War. In Pennsylvania US 1 traverses the territory in which first rose the opposition to the institution of slavery that was to culminate in the bitterest internal struggle of the nation. The highway crosses the Mason-Dixon line, which marked the division between the free and slave States in this war. In Virginia it runs close to the bloody battlefield from which in 1864 Grant sent the words that became the slogan of the final days of the Civil War: "I intend to fight it out on this line if it takes all summer." South of Fredericksburg is a hundred-mile stretch of land that bore the brunt of the four-year drive of the Federal armies to capture the Confederate capital; the route here traverses an area that has seen more bloodshed than has any other on the North American Continent.

In Maine the highway runs close to the house prepared for the reception of Marie Antoinette if her friends should rescue her; in Massachusetts, to the house in which lived the Scottish prisoners captured by Cromwell at the Battle of Dunbar and indentured for seven years to the Saugus iron works; in Virginia, to the site of the home of Margaret Brent, who before 1634 had demanded "voyce & vote allso"; in North Carolina, to the place where lived for a time the lovely Flora MacDonald of Scottish history; in the same State, to the house in which the Governor of North Carolina made his famous complaint to the Governor of South Carolina: "It's a damned long time between drinks"; in Georgia, to an area that is an untamed wilderness.

The chronicle of US 1 is directly related to the history of transportation in America. In the early seventeenth century the colonists blazed trails or made use of the Pequot Path, the Potomac Path, and other Indian traces along the general line of the present route to establish an artery of communication between isolated settlements. According to Madam Knight, who made the trip between Boston and New York on horseback in 1704, "the Rodes all along this way were very bad. Incumbered with Rocks and mountainos passages, which were very disagreeable to my tried carcass. In going over a Bridge, under which the River Run very swift, my hors stumbled and very narrowly 'scaped falling over into the water." A "cannoo" in which she crossed the Thames River was so unstable that she kept her "eyes stedy, not daring so much as to lodg' my tongue a hair's breadth more on one side of my mouth than tother, nor so much as think of Lott's wife, for a wry thought would have upset our whery."

Travel south of the Potomac was even more difficult. Several ferries from Virginia to the Maryland shore were early established along the Potomac as short-cuts to Baltimore and Philadelphia. Diaries and travel books written by those who used the route through Virginia in the days when it was known as the King's Highway record many near-disastrous adventures on it. Even at the end of the eighteenth

INTRODUCTION xiii

century Dr. Coke, an Englishman, nearly perished in fording Accotink Creek during a freshet; John Marshall spoke feelingly of miring his horse; and Thomas Jefferson bemoaned the fact that the best speed he could make was three miles an hour.

The development and expansion of the Colonies in the eighteenth century created commercial transportation needs, and various types of vehicles came upon the scene. The first common carrier service in America was established under a franchise granted by the Governor of New Jersey, over a part of what was to become US 1, with the use of a crude sort of cart for carrying freight. About 1725 the stage wagon, of English origin, appeared in the Colonies. Until 1870, when the first transcontinental railroad was completed, the modified stagecoach remained the chief transport agency in America, though the conditions of land travel were far from uniform. The Old Post Road between Boston and New York ran through New London, Newport, and Providence; stagecoach fare was ten dollars. Regular passenger service between New York and Philadelphia, largely by boat, was inaugurated in 1732; the trip required five days, though by the end of the century the time had been reduced to a day and a half. During the stagecoach era, when passengers were for a time charged according to their weight, competition between rival stages reached such a fantastic peak that in Massachusetts passengers were carried free by one stage line, until the alert rival company offered not only free passage but dinner as well. Ownership of taverns and stagecoaches was frequently combined. The sound of the coachman's horn became familiar throughout the countryside not only serving advance notice to would-be passengers, but also by the number of toots indicating to the landlord how many passengers planned to eat at his inn.

The appearance of the first wheeled vehicles brought about the transformation of tote-paths and pack-train routes into wagon roads; even then a "middling good road" was one in which the mud did not come up over the traveler's boot tops. The introduction of stages necessitated improvement of the dirt roads, which were maintained by the various communities. Some of the turnpike companies attempted to lay permanent stone surfaces, financing and building them according to English precedent; the corporations charged tolls not only for the cost and maintenance of the roads but also for the profit of stockholders. Part of the Old Post Road near Greenwich,

Connecticut, was built by the third turnpike company chartered in the United States, and within a few years many other sections of the route were improved in the same way. But the turnpikes proved unprofitable, particularly after the advent of the railroad, most of the roads soon reverting to public control, though the last toll gate on US 1 was not removed until little more than a decade ago.

Roads south of Washington were slow to develop. In 1804 Thomas Moore, the Irish poet, while traveling in Virginia, wrote home: "Such a road I have come and in such a conveyance. The mail takes twelve passengers which generally consist of squalling children . . . and stinking republicans smoking cigars." During the War of 1812 communication by means of sailing packets, which had formerly united the New England States and the southern seaboard, was almost entirely cut off. For a time the only commercial intercourse possible was by means of trains of Conestoga wagons, which departed daily from the North with commodities. This long interruption of water transportation stimulated the development of movement by land between the two sections, despite the mire, difficult fords, and other obstacles that drew the curses of travelers, and increased the use of the stagecoach and the improvement of roads.

After the war the coastal packets never fully recovered their trade. Turnpikes and plank roads were built between the fall-line cities as an inland north-and-south route, which became increasingly more popular than the post route nearer the coast.

The coming of the railroad led to the disappearance of the stagecoach and thus marked the end of one of the most adventurous aspects of early American life. US 1 connects points at which the earliest railroad experiments were made. In 1805 Thomas Leiper of Philadelphia constructed the first "rail road" with horse-drawn cars that hauled stone from his quarry to the river landing nearly a mile away. Twenty-five years later the first section of the Baltimore & Ohio Railroad was opened between Baltimore and Ellicott Mills, fourteen miles away. At a number of points US 1 bore the shock of the railroad advance. Stages were unable to compete with the superior steam-powered rivals, and the route fell into general disuse for half a century.

By the end of the nineteenth century a need for better and more extensive roads had developed in the thickly populated northeastern States. In 1890 New Jersey passed the first State highway law;

INTRODUCTION

Massachusetts, New York, and other States followed suit. But it was the extensive development of motor transportation that inaugurated a new period in the history of the route. State roadbuilding aid had been extended to counties through which the principal highways passed. Eventually the Federal Government began to interest itself, and the Federal Aid Act of 1916 led to active participation in the financing and construction of roads in all States. A condition of the Act was the creation of State highway departments to cooperate in establishing uniform standards for building roads partly financed by the Government. Five of the States through which US 1 passes were among the first seven to establish such departments, and to benefit from the more scientific engineering methods prescribed.

Though US 1 runs through many attractive areas, its roadside for long sections, as on other express highways of the country, is depressingly ugly, being characterized by hideous shacks, enormous signs, dumps, and raw cuts. A group of far-sighted businessmen who profit by the traffic on US 1 has organized a committee to remedy this condition, but it is unlikely that any real progress will be made until the States take control of the situation, because indifference or lack of cooperation on the part of a few can nullify the efforts of the many, or can force them into screaming competition. Today there are more than three million miles of roads and highways in the United States, used by some twenty-six million motor vehicles. What can be done toward beautifying U. S. highways is briefly though admirably illustrated by the Mount Vernon Memorial Highway, a parkway that serves as an alternate to US 1 for about twenty miles south of Washington. In some States, notably in Connecticut, advances have been made in the control of roadside advertising and in roadway beautification; Virginia clubwomen have persuaded a number of national manufacturers to cease billboard advertising in the State.

SPECIAL FOODS FROM MAINE TO FLORIDA

While traveling speed and comfort have reached heights undreamed of a century ago, meals available to travelers have declined steadily in quality because the American is no longer the gourmet he once was. Nowhere are the democratic processes more evident than in the food-catering business; the restaurant keeper is up for reelection three times a day and must continually respond to the will of the majority if he is to avoid bankruptcy. If his constituents demand elaborate dining room furnishings and pantalets on the chop-bones rather than high-priced cuts of meat, if they prefer quick service in place of cooked-to-order dishes, or if they order a limited range of foods and ignore new ones, the restaurant keeper must fill the demands.

America has native foodstuffs in variety and of qualities unsurpassed in any other country, and American colonists early devised a large number of savory dishes. Delegates to the first Continental Congress were offered meals Lucullus would not have scorned. Even the austere John Adams, deeply engrossed in the affairs of the Colonies, found time to comment in detail on them. Up until the middle of the nineteenth century no account of an entertainment or meeting was complete without some mention of the menu.

There are many reasons for the decline in food standards. The sedentary occupations of city-dwellers have lessened the keenness of their appetites, and the tempo of modern life has left little time for them to test the quality of individual dishes, and even less time to wait for the preparation of special orders. More important in the decline has been the domestic revolution. Women have seldom had as great an interest in food as men have had, but when housekeeping was the only career open to them and compliments on satisfying meals were the chief rewards for service, they spent much of their time in shopping for choice foodstuffs, mixing, beating, paring, boiling, and baking. When new careers were opened to women and they were no longer dependent on cooking for their living, they and the manufacturers united to make the preparation of meals a short process. Today a pre-cooked dinner, from soup to nuts, can be bought and placed on the table in half an hour. The difference between a dinner created by mass-production processes and one prepared at home is as great as the difference between a ready-made suit and one tailored to order, but an eating public gradually accustomed to the ready-made meal has lost appreciation of the finer product.

While the fine old American dishes have in many places disappeared from restaurant menus because of the lack of demand for them, there are still restaurant keepers here and there who cater to the discriminating minority. For the benefit of those interested in the food specialties of the areas through which US 1 runs, the following lists have been compiled. Some of the dishes are offered in restaurants along the route, occasionally prepared according to the best traditions, more often in debased forms; others, relics of a more leisurely way of life, are found only in private homes. Fortunately, the art of preparation has not been completely lost, and food purveyors will be quick to respond to a demand for their revival.

MAINE

Apple Fritters: sweet milk, eggs, sugar, and salt, with slices of apple stirred into the batter; dropped into hot fat and fried until brown. Served with sugar and cream.

Apple Slump: cored and sliced apples, seasoned with sugar and cinnamon. Dough is dropped on in separate spoonfuls. Baked and served with butter sauce.

Old-Fashioned Pan Dowdy: alternating layers of sugar, molasses, cinnamon, salt pork, and sliced apples, topped with thin crust. Baked in slow oven and served with thin cream.

Steamed Suet Pudding: flour, milk, molasses, sugar, seasoning, spices, suet, raisins, citron, currants, and almonds. Steamed and served with soft sauce.

Baked Indian Pudding: scalded milk, corn meal, and molasses, cooked until thick; sugar, egg, butter, and spices are added, and the mixture is baked. Served either hot or cold with whipped cream or hard sauce.

Woods-Style Planked Game Fish: fish is placed, skin side in, on live hardwood tree from which bark is stripped; salt pork or bacon strips are pegged just above fish for basting; cooked until brown with fire built two feet from tree. Served with drawn butter.

Woods-Style Baked Game Fish: dressed fish is covered with an inch of wet clay and baked overnight in hot ashes of campfire; when clay is broken open, the fish meat comes out steaming. Served with butter.

1743 Poloe: fowl, rice, onion, and seasoning stewed together and served hot.

Red Flannel Hash: cooked beets, potatoes, carrots, turnips, and left-over corned beef or spare ribs, chopped, seasoned, and pan fried.

Soused Clams: freshly shucked clams stewed in vinegar. Served either hot or cold.

Clam Bake: clams, lobsters, crabs, green corn, sweet potatoes, and eggs cooked in rockweed on ledges heated by outdoor fire.

Boiled Pies: cider applesauce mixed with fritter batter and fried in deep fat.

Eggs Canadian: eggs scrambled with maple syrup.

Roast Venison: leg or saddle of venison thoroughly larded with pork, basted with claret while baking; served with gravy made from pan drippings, also with currant, barberry, or wild plum jelly.

NEW HAMPSHIRE

Blanc Mange: sea moss (picked up along the ocean beaches), milk, salt, and vanilla cooked until thick.

LOBSTER ROLL: roll filled with lobster, lettuce, and salad dressing.
PEPPER STEAK SANDWICHES: small steak and pepper relish filling.
FRIED CLAMS: dipped in batter of bread crumbs and fried in deep fat.
FISH AND CLAM CHOWDER: made with milk and no vegetables.
CODFISH BALLS: codfish mixed with potatoes and fried.
CRANBERRY TURNOVERS: biscuit dough fried in deep fat, then filled with cranberry sauce.

MASSACHUSETTS

BOSTON BAKED BEANS: pea or kidney beans, salt pork, black molasses, sugar, and dry mustard, baked six to twelve hours.
BOSTON BROWN BREAD: yellow cornmeal, rye meal, soda, salt, molasses, and milk steamed for several hours.
NEW ENGLAND CHOWDER: clams, potatoes, onion, pork, and milk.
SUCCOTASH: corn stewed with green beans.
BAKED INDIAN PUDDING: cornmeal, molasses, sugar, egg, butter, milk, salt, ginger, and cinnamon baked in slow oven.
PARKER HOUSE ROLLS: flour, milk, salt, sugar, butter, and yeast; dough cut into circles, each of which is folded. These originated in the old Parker House, one of the famous hotels of Boston.

RHODE ISLAND

JOHNNY CAKE: white corn meal, well scalded, sugar, salt, milk, fried on a griddle.
CLAM CAKES: chopped clams, milk, flour, egg, and seasoning fried brown in deep lard.
CLAM CHOWDER: chopped clams, milk, butter, diced pork or bacon, fried sliced onion, seasoning, thickened with flour and served over soda or oyster crackers.
WHITPOT PUDDING: Indian meal, molasses, milk, and salt baked one hour. Served cool.
BROWN BREAD: yellow or white corn meal, milk, molasses, soda, flour, and salt steamed for three hours in crock.
INDIAN APPLE PUDDING: white meal, cut apples, sugar, salt, hot skimmed milk, and molasses baked for one hour; cold milk is then added and baking is continued four hours more.
OLD-FASHIONED MOLASSES COOKIES: molasses, granulated sugar, eggs, lard, and saleratus dissolved in sour milk or water.
CLAM BAKE: clams in shells, fish, sweet potatoes, Irish potatoes, onions, and sweet corn, separated by layers of rockweed, steamed half an hour over hot stones in barrel or trench.

CONNECTICUT

BROILED LOBSTER: broiled over live coals; served with butter sauce.

SHORE DINNER: all available seafoods (clams, fish, lobsters, oysters, crabs) prepared in various ways.

CLAM BAKES: clams steamed on hot stones beneath a seaweed blanket.

SQUASH PIE: open face; made with baked squash (usually Hubbard).

MINCE PIE: double crust; home-made mincemeat moistened with cider.

COWSLIP OR DANDELION GREENS: picked before ready to bloom; cooked slowly with salt pork. Dandelion greens have been a standard "spring tonic" for generations, folk-medicine having recognized the signs of a marked vitamin-A deficiency without knowing anything about vitamins. The deficiency occurs less frequently today because green vegetables are available in winter.

BAKING POWDER BISCUITS: the Yankee "quick biscuit" is made only on individual recipes.

CLAM CHOWDER: hard clam stew made without tomatoes; tastes better the second day.

PUMPKIN PIE: open face, made with small, sugar pumpkins and smooth, flaky crust crinkled on the edge.

BAKED WOODCHUCK: special delicacy, particularly in early autumn when Johnny Chuck has rounded out by feeding on sweet clover.

ROAST RACCOON: available only after a hunt for the little washing bear.

RHUBARB PIE: either open face or double crust. Served with venison or turkey.

POVERTY RELISH: chopped cabbage, salt, and a dash of vinegar.

BAKED SPARE RIBS: served cold or hot with brown gravy.

NEW ENGLAND BOILED DINNER: corned beef and cabbage.

NEW YORK

OYSTER STEW: oysters steamed only until edges curl; served in own liquid mixed with milk heated below the boiling point; salt, pepper and butter added before serving.

SOFT-SHELL CLAMS: powdered lightly with flour and fried in hot bacon fat. Never dipped in batter before frying.

CAMP FIRE SWEET POTATOES: sweet potatoes mashed with egg, topped with marshmallows, and browned in oven.

BLUSHING BUNNY: cheese, egg and tomato puree, made as in Welsh Rarebit, served on crackers or toast.

POST ROAD PUDDING: sliced sponge cake sprinkled with sherry in which apricots and prunes have been placed; covered with a mixture of beaten eggs, sugar, milk, and vanilla, thickened over slow fire. Served cold with whipped cream, decorated with glacéd cherries.

UPSIDE DOWN CAKE: bottom of iron skillet is covered with melted butter, then with brown sugar and pieces of fruit such as pineapples, pears, peaches, apricots, and finally with cake batter. Baked in moderate oven. Served upside down with whipped cream.

BROILED T-BONE STEAK: broiled close to flame; after first searing on each side it is basted with melted butter well peppered and salted.

NEW JERSEY

SUCCOTASH: corn and lima beans stewed together, a dish adopted from the Indians.

BEACH PLUM JAM: plums that grow wild on Sandy Hook; equal quantities of fruit and sugar.

NEW JERSEY CLAM CHOWDER: chopped clams, onions, carrots, potatoes; seasoned with thyme and a small amount of salt pork.

BULLY CLAM CHOWDER: large juicy clams, ground ripe tomatoes, green peppers, onions, parsley, spices, salt, and pepper.

CAPE MAY CLAM CHOWDER: clams drained and chopped fine, diced potatoes, onions, and lean salt pork; simmered for an hour after potatoes are soft.

SNAPPER SOUP: ground snapper, boiled slowly in salt water; crab meat, green peppers, thyme, parsley, small cubes of Jersey red-skin potatoes, garlic, salt, and red pepper.

SNAPPER STEW: snapper cut in small cubes cooked slowly; hard-boiled egg yolk, butter, cream, salt, nutmeg, and paprika are added. Served on toast.

Lowlands of south Jersey abound with snapping turtles, popularly known as snappers. It is a difficult job to get at the meat. The snapper is tickled on the nose with a stout stick. When he grabs it, the stick is pulled until he has fully unfolded his long neck. Then his head is chopped off behind the ears, after which he relaxes. A sharp knife is then inserted between the interstices in the side bridges that tie the lower and upper shells.

PLANKED SHAD: whole roe or buck shad split down back and placed on a hickory or white pine plank slightly larger than the fish; the plank is heated to the charring point, then propped upright before fire of hot coals.

PICKLED EELS AND MUSSELS: soaked in brine 48 hours, with spices and vinegar, served with lemon and chopped parsley.

THE LARGEST HOT DOG IN THE WORLD: a New Jersey invention.

PENNSYLVANIA

The "Pennsylvania Dutch" tradition of "seven sweets and seven sours" on the table at each meal is still evident in eastern Pennsylvania restaurants;

MARYLAND

in no other place are so many kinds of jelly and pickles routinely placed on the table along with the salt, pepper, sugar and catsup.

KARTUFFLE GLACE: boiled potatoes put through meat grinder, and added to flour, eggs, and melted butter; formed into balls the size of large marbles.

LENTIL SOUP: lentils with beef or pork and often potatoes.

FAGGOTS: pork *pluch*, consisting of the liver, heart, and lungs of a pig, chopped up and baked.

FROIS OR WELSH PANCAKES: giant pancakes sprinkled with currants and sugar, stacked high and cut across in quarters. Served piping hot with jelly.

SOUSE: pigs' feet; eaten cold or hot with vinegar.

SCHNITZ UN KNEPP: dried apples and dumplings cooked with or without a ham shoulder.

PORK FRITTERS: slices of pork tenderloin dipped in corn meal batter and fried.

APPLE BUTTER: sweet apples and sweet cider boiled into a rich paste, then cooled.

PHILADELPHIA SCRAPPLE: corn meal and ground pork, boiled and allowed to cool; it is then sliced and fried.

PHILADELPHIA PEPPER POT: white honeycomb tripe, veal, potatoes, onion, peppers, seasonings, and dumplings.

SAUERKRAUT AND DUMPLINGS: dumplings covered over with sauerkraut.

PIGS' KNUCKLES WITH SAUERKRAUT AND DUMPLINGS: dumplings made of flour and melted butter; pig's knuckles added and covered with sauerkraut.

SHOO-FLY: crumb pie made with molasses and sprinkled with sugar and cinnamon.

MARYLAND

MARYLAND BISCUITS: stiff dough beaten with a hatchet and baked in small hard cakes pricked with a fork.

MARYLAND FRIED CHICKEN: young chicken cut in pieces, dipped in light batter, floured, fried in deep fat. Served with cream gravy and waffles or with corn fritters and bacon.

TIPSY PARSON: loaf of sponge cake stuck full of blanched almonds and saturated with sherry. Served with boiled custard, topped with whipped cream.

EGGNOG: yolks and whites of eggs beaten separately, with sugar, brandy, milk, and rich cream. Served particularly during the holidays.

SOFT CRABS: cleaned by removing sand bag, dead men and eyes; dipped in batter and cracker crumbs and fried in deep fat.

CREAMED HOMINY: soaked overnight, simmered for six hours, and creamed with butter, salt, and milk.

LADY BALTIMORE CAKE: white layer cake with filling of soft icing and chopped fruits and nuts.

PLANKED SHAD: boned, baked on hickory or other hardwood plank, and served on plank with trimmings of lemon and potato chips.

SALLY LUNN: unsweetened cake dough, raised with yeast; baked brown in deep dish.

STUFFED HAM: parboiled ham cut in even slices, alternated with chopped greens and spring onions; sewed in clean white cloth and boiled. When sliced, it reveals stripes of pink and green. Served particularly at Easter.

BRAISED MUSKRAT: boiled until tender, cut small, and baked with thick brown crust. Known to the trade as "marsh rabbit."

SWEET POTATO SOUTHERN: boiled Maryland sweet potatoes, mashed, mixed with beaten egg, cinnamon, cream, and brown sugar, topped with marshmallows, and baked in casserole.

KOSSUTH CAKE: a rich cake served with chocolate and whipped cream; by a Baltimore baker and first served at a reception given to Louis Kossuth, the Hungarian patriot, in the winter of 1851–52.

DIAMOND-BACK TERRAPIN: boiled, skinned, and cut fine, blended with butter and sherry.

At hotels individual portions range from $3.00 to $5.00. There was a time when terrapin were so plentiful that indentures stipulated that the servant should not be fed the food oftener than twice a week. H. L. Mencken pronounces terrapin the noblest of all victuals but warns against its desecration by the addition of sauces or condiments. Some Maryland gourmets decry the use of sherry as a flavoring but drink sherry (or Madeira) while eating it.

VIRGINIA

CORN PONE: yellow corn meal, water, salt, and shortening, baked.

CORN DODGER: meal, water, salt, and shortening, fried.

ASH CAKE: corn bread cooked in ashes near the coals of an open fireplace.

CRACKLING BREAD: corn bread with crisp bits of fat.

SPOON AND BATTER BREADS: thin mixtures of corn meal, eggs, milk, and shortening, baked.

BRUNSWICK STEW: squirrel, rabbit (the old recipes began "First catch your hare") or chicken, tomatoes, onions, okra, carrots, celery, cabbage, potatoes, butter beans, bacon, red pepper, corn, and salt. Originated in Brunswick County, Virginia; hence the name.

TURNIP GREENS AND COLLARDS: usually cooked with hog jowl.

FRIED HERRING: rolled in corn meal and fried till crisp; a breakfast dish.

HERRING CAKES: herring flakes mixed with eggs, potatoes, flour, or corn meal.

FRIED APPLE PIE: sliced apples mixed with sugar and spices and placed in a half moon of short pastry; fried in deep fat.

SMITHFIELD HAM: may or may not be peanut-fed; cured by months of exposure to the smoke of hardwoods. Soaked overnight and simmered half an hour for every pound of ham. Slashed, prepared with a paste made of brown sugar and sherry, dotted with cloves, and covered with cracker crumbs. Baked and served cold; sliced very thin.

NORTH CAROLINA

CHICKEN BRUNSWICK STEW: chicken, lima beans, corn, and tomatoes.

BARBECUED CHICKEN: while roasting, basted with sauce made of butter, lemon juice, Worcestershire sauce, red pepper, and other seasoning.

BEATEN BISCUITS: made from flour, lard, salt, and sweet milk, beaten for half an hour, preferably on a marble slab; baked in a hot oven, and served cold.

SWEET POTATO BISCUITS: boiled mashed sweet potatoes added to regular buttermilk biscuit dough.

BAKED HAM: country cured from peanut-fed hogs; baked with a wine sauce.

SUCCOTASH: corn and lima or string beans; okra and tomatoes often added.

PEACH AND OTHER SHORTCAKES: made with a short unsweetened biscuit dough.

TIPSY CAKE: sponge cake, blanched almonds, and syllabub flavored with brandy, in layers, the whole moistened with scuppernong or Concord wine.

SALLY WHITE CAKE: pound cake batter, sherry, citron, coconut, blanched almonds, rose water, and mace; sometimes moistened with peach brandy.

SWEET PICKLED PEACHES: peaches cooked whole in a thick spiced syrup.

BRANDIED PEACHES: heavily sugared peaches fermented in a stone crock that is sometimes buried for a time.

WINE JELLY: jelly flavored with home-made scuppernong, blackberry, or Concord wine. Served with whipped cream.

SOUTH CAROLINA

SCRAPPLE: corn meal cooked in pork broth to consistency of thick mush, added to tender pieces of pork, seasoned with salt, pepper, and onion juice. When cold and firm, the moisture is sliced and browned in a hot skillet.

PERSIMMON PUDDING: fresh fruit, egg whites, sugar, milk, and corn starch, baked in a crust.

SWEET POTATOES: potatoes boiled, sliced, and baked in a butter and sugar syrup.

SWEET POTATO BISCUITS: boiled mashed potatoes added to biscuit dough.

SWEET POTATO PONE: grated raw potatoes mixed with sugar, molasses, milk, and ginger, then baked.

SWEET POTATO PUDDING: parboiled potatoes grated, mixed with butter, sugar, powdered cinnamon, lemon juice, and eggs, then baked.

JELLY PIE: blackberry or scuppernong grape jelly, butter, sugar, and eggs, baked in a crust.

CAROLINA OPOSSUM: meat cut in small pieces, soaked in salted water, stewed, and seasoned with lemon juice and currant jelly.

CAROLINA OPOSSUM AND SWEET POTATOES: opossum boiled whole, surrounded with baked yellow sweet potatoes, and basted with grease in which possum was boiled; baked until brown.

DEVILED BAKED HAM: soaked 18 hours in vinegar, sherry, and mustard; boiled in this sauce, then baked in quick oven.

FISH STEW: fresh-water fish stewed in large quantity of water seasoned with fat-back bacon, onions, tomato catsup, Worcestershire sauce.

HOMINY WAFFLES: cooked hominy, flour, milk, and melted butter.

CRACKLING CORNBREAD: meal, salt, boiling water, cracklings (crisp bits of pork left after lard rendering), molded into small oblong cakes and baked until brown.

GEORGIA

'POSSOM AND 'TATERS: opossum, parboiled in salt water; highly seasoned and baked; served with sweet potatoes.

SOUSE MEAT: hog's head, ears, and feet stewed, mashed, seasoned, pressed, and sliced when cold.

TURNIP GREENS: fresh and tender turnip tops, boiled with salt pork or smoked bacon.

CORN PONE: stiff dough of meal, water, and salt, baked in oblong pones.

SORGHUM PUDDING: pudding made with sorghum syrup and ginger, baked in a loaf, and sliced.

LEATHER BREECHES: dried green snap beans, soaked overnight and boiled with salt bacon.

BARBECUE: pork, beef, lamb, or chicken, turned frequently and basted with a sauce of vinegar, pepper, salt, and butter.

BRUNSWICK STEW: chopped beef, pork, tomatoes, corn, onion, peppers, and high seasonings.

FRIED PIES: pastry filled with dried or fresh fruit and fried in hot fat.

BOILED PEANUTS: Spanish peanuts in shell boiled in salt water until soft.

FLORIDA

WAMPUS OR HUSH PUPPIES: corn meal scalded in milk, mixed with egg, baking powder, and onion, and cooked in the grease of frying fish. In early Florida days when fish were fried in large pans out of doors, the savory odor caused the family's pack of hounds to whine and yelp with hunger. As a means of quieting the dogs, the cook would hastily scald corn meal, pat it into cakes without salt or shortening, and cook it in the grease of frying fish.

FLORIDA

When done, it was thrown to the dogs, after which silence prevailed; hence the name, hush puppies.

SWAMP SALAD: the raw bud of a palmetto tree (which has the taste of a green chestnut) served with salad dressing.

SWAMP CABBAGE: the sliced bud of a palmetto tree boiled with salt pork until tender.

COMPTIE: the powdered root of a wild plant in south Florida; used as flour for making cakes or bread.

RATTLESNAKE SNACKS: meat of skinned snake cut into thin slices, salted, and smoked over hickory. Served as hors-d'oeuvres.

RATTLESNAKE ENTREE: meat boiled and served with supreme sauce.

FROMAJARDIS: ring-shaped baked cheese cakes with cinnamon; a cross is cut in rim of cake.

SEA TURTLE: sliced into steaks and fried.

FLORIDA GOPHER: sliced into steaks and fried over a low fire. (In Florida a gopher is a land turtle.)

GUAVA JELLY: made from ripe fruit and prepared as other jellies.

STONE CRAB: boiled in salted water until claws are salmon pink; meat is extracted and dipped in melted butter.

COQUINA COCKTAIL: chilled coquina broth, to which lemon juice and Tabasco are added; mixture churned in a cocktail shaker and served immediately. Coquina is an ocean shellfish about the size of a coffee bean.

CRAWFISH ENCHILADO: green and red peppers added to meat of crawfish and fried in olive oil.

ARROZ CON POLLO: rice colored and flavored with saffron, then boiled in pot with chicken.

NOTE

In the above list a few dishes appear in more than one State. Succotash, for example, is made of corn with any kind of fresh beans in one State; in a second it is made of corn with lima beans only; and in a third of corn with beans, okra and tomatoes. It will be observed that most of the dishes are made of foods native to America; the best dishes of every land are those developed by native cooks from local products. Few American cooks are entirely successful in following French recipes and few French cooks can cook a typical American meal. A blighting influence on American cooking has been the attempt to impose French menus on the American people without an understanding of French cooking methods and the use of French ingredients.

EASTPORT, MAINE

FORT KNOX, MAINE

MAINE

Calais — Ellsworth — Bangor — Belfast — Brunswick — Portland — N.H. Line, **341.4 m.** US 1.

Bangor & Aroostook R.R. parallels route between Bangor and Searsport; Maine Central R.R. between Calais, Bangor, and Bucksport and between Rockland and Portland; and Boston & Maine R.R. between Portland and Portsmouth.
Hard-surfaced roadbed, three lanes wide between Portland and Portsmouth. Accommodations principally in cities.

US 1 in Maine runs close to the coast from one end of the State to the other. It runs through resort areas, rolling and rocky farmlands, and along the banks of broad rivers; it crosses high hills — locally called mountains — and blueberry plains. It connects the two ends of the 2,500-mile coast line, which are but 225 miles apart by air line. The southern part of the route is more frequented, but the whole of the broken and jagged coast has a picturesque charm that makes it a favorite with summer travelers. South of Maine, land and sea have few rigid boundaries; the waves encroach and retreat, the land is washed away and built up. But on the Maine shore they meet abruptly; that old devil sea at times comes dashing in as though it had been gathering force halfway around the earth to break the stubborn, granite headlands; it attacks with a roar, retreats, and returns to attack again.

There are two coasts of Maine. The coast known to most visitors has spruce-tipped hills and hard beaches dappled with the red, orange, green, blue, and white raiment of visitors, blue-green waters broken by tilting sails and the wakes of speeding motorboats, and a brilliant blue sky. The inhabitants of this land work night and day running hotels, boarding houses, tourist camps, and lunch stands, piloting fishing and sightseeing boats, trying in a brief season to earn the money for house repairs, heavy shoes and overcoats, medicines, school books, and other 12-month needs.

The second coast of Maine is for four or five months muffled in snow; travel is at times difficult and most hotels and many of the rooms in homes are closed. But this Maine has its own charm. The rural inhabitants, even though striving to add to their limited incomes, have time to relax and they accept the comparatively few visitors as members of their families, telling them long stories of grandfathers and uncles who never returned from the sea, of the great-aunts who heard voices, and other tales characteristic of a country that part of the year has almost pioneer isolation. There are other rewards for those who visit this coast out of season. The chowder and baked beans, made in family quantities and eaten after strenuous climbs over snowy hills, have a finer flavor than those of summer; the headlands, snow-crowned, take on an icy glaze that sharpens their strange silhouettes; and the sea in acrobatic assaults causes the very rocks to tremble. But the glory of this Maine is its sky, unreal saffron after the gray light that comes before the dawn, blue as Persian tiles for a brief time at midday, and an unearthly pale green streaked with rose in the late afternoon, turning the snow pale heliotrope with purple shadows.

Section 1. Calais to Ellsworth, *123.9 m.*

US 1 between Calais and Ellsworth passes through the old hunting grounds of the Passamaquoddy Indians, which still provide good sport in season. Broad blueberry plains stretch out to the W., and numerous rivers and streams along the route provide excellent fishing.

CALAIS (*pron. Kal' is*), **0 m.** (82 alt., 5,470 pop.), the "international city" of Maine, is the only city in the State on the Canadian Border. It is a port of entry and many of its citizens came from the Canadian Provinces. The city spreads out on a hilly terrain along the western bank of the St. Croix River, directly opposite St. Stephen, N.B. The mile-long main street, a wide thoroughfare lined with fine old elm trees, runs from the end of the International Bridge to the St. Croix Country Club at the southern end of the city. The business district is at the northern end, close to the river; from the bridge are visible the docks that once played an important part in the city's industrial history. Around the business district are quiet streets with attractive houses surrounded by trees, broad lawns, and well-trimmed shrubbery. Handsome churches and modern schools add to the air of prosperity. The municipal affairs of Calais and St. Stephen are allied to the extent that the fire engines of the two communities clang back and forth across the International Bridge to answer alarms in what to each community is technically a foreign land. The Calais water supply comes from St. Stephen, being piped across the river. United States and Canadian currencies are accepted in both cities.

MAINE

The first settlers, who arrived in 1779, were attracted to Calais by the wealth of timber, the fertile soil, and the abundance of fish and game.

Calais early became an important lumbering center. The launching in 1801 of the *Liberty*, the first vessel built in the community, marked the beginning of a profitable industry that lasted till the end of the era of tall ships. In 1809 the Massachusetts Legislature named the settlement for the French port of Calais, as a compliment to France because of the aid rendered to the struggling Colonies during the Revolution. After 1820 the primitive backwoods settlement began to expand rapidly. Roads and bridges were built; churches and homes sprang up along the highways. In 1850, with a population of 4,749, it was incorporated as a city.

The MASON HOUSE (*private*), at the point (R) where Main St. turns toward the customhouse, was the home of Noah Smith, Jr. (1800–68). Smith, paternal grandfather of the writer, Kate Douglas Wiggin, is said to have been one of the last people who had official business with President Lincoln before his assassination; at that time he received the President's signature to a pardon granted to a young Calais soldier who had been convicted of treason.

RED BEACH, **8.9 m.** (90 alt.; Ward 9, City of Calais), takes its name from the color of the granite outcrop along the shore. The village lies along the main highway in a pleasant wooded area from which the wide island-dotted St. Croix is visible.

Opposite Red Beach, in the St. Croix River, is DOCHET ISLAND (40 alt.), which is reached by rowboat.

In 1603 Pierre du Guast, the Sieur de Monts, received the trading concession for Acadia, which, in the grand manner of the times, was defined as a territory extending from Cape Breton Island to a point well below the present New York City. In the following spring he set sail with his lieutenant, Samuel de Champlain, and four score colonists, including a Huguenot minister and a Catholic priest, landing on June 26, 1604, on this island, which he called St. Croix, and on which he expected to establish a trading post and settlement. So sketchy was knowledge of the New World at the time, that the settlers brought with them part of the timber used in the erection of their buildings. Before winter arrived the island held a storehouse, dining hall, kitchen, barracks, a blacksmith shop, and carefully laid out gardens. An unusually severe winter and scurvy wrought such discouragement that in the spring of 1605 de Monts and Champlain sailed off S. to find a more suitable place for the colony; in August they decided to move it to the spot that is now Annapolis Royal, in Nova Scotia. Dochet Island was not entirely abandoned, however; the French used it for a garrison at intervals for some years.

This early settlement played an important part in the adjustment of the boundary question after the Revolutionary War; both the United States and Great Britain acknowledged the River St. Croix as the point of departure in drawing the line, but Britain disputed the American claim as to what river bore this name. Discovery of Champlain's map and subsequent examination of the ruins of the early settlement decided the matter; had the British won their point eastern Maine would probably now be Canadian territory.

ROBBINSTON, 12.4 m. (60 alt.; Robbinston Town, 582 pop.), is a village whose main street parallels the St. Croix River (*ferry service to St. Andrews, N.B.*). The smokestack of a sardine-canning factory that burned down sometime in the past is a landmark here. Fishing, supplemented by sardine canning, is the principal industry of the town. In the spring when the herring are running, the fish weirs offshore can be seen from the road.

At **18.4 m.** is a granite boulder placed by the National Geographic Society to mark the 45TH PARALLEL OF LATITUDE, which is exactly midway between the Equator and the North Pole.

PERRY, **20.3 m.** (40 alt.; Perry Town, 992 pop.), lies on a double bend of US 1 where it crosses Boyden Stream. The houses are few and scattered.

At Perry is the junction with State 190 (*see Side Route 1*).

PEMBROKE, **26.2 m.** (80 alt.; Pembroke Town, 965 pop.), is a village of pleasant homes along the bank of the Pennamaquam River. While the principal industries are now the packing of blueberries and sardines, the substantial, well-built houses recall the prosperity of the wooden-hull era, when extensive shipbuilding activities were carried on in the area.

The large, square, stone building of the OLD IRONWORKS here resembles a fort. The plant was established in 1828 with machinery brought from Wales. Much of the ore used came from bogs in the vicinity.

At WEST PEMBROKE, **27.2 m.** (50 alt., Pembroke Town), which seems part of Pembroke village rather than a separate community, are a number of sturdy old homes. H. Styles Bridges, Governor of New Hampshire (1935-1936) and U.S. Senator (1937-   ), was born here on September 9, 1896.

Right from West Pembroke on State 214, an improved gravel road, is MEDDYBEMPS LAKE, **10 m.**, with excellent fishing (*boats and canoes for hire*) and a good bathing beach.

This is one of the many hunting regions where the illegal practice of "deer jacking," less frequent today, was popular. The bright light of a hooded lantern or of a flashlight fascinates the fleet-footed animal, making him a target for the huntsman's bullet. When shot, the deer seldom drops immediately, but runs sometimes for hours, the hunter in hot pursuit. This phase, known as "deer running," develops fleet runners, particularly in deer-jacking expeditions when the law is pursuing the hunters as swiftly as the hunters are pursuing the deer.

A story is told of a Washington County stripling who, left unwarned on sentry duty at Cedar Creek, Va., when a retreat was ordered, found himself alone facing the advancing enemy. He made his solitary retreat from Cedar Creek with the speed he had acquired in deer jacking in the Meddybemps region. He is said to have reported at Harpers Ferry, W. Va., 19 miles from his post, in advance of the dispatch bearer, who was on horseback.

DENNYSVILLE, 32.4 m. (30 alt.; Dennysville Town, 443 pop.), took its name from Dennys River, which in turn was named for an Indian chief whose hunting grounds were in this region. Swift Dennys River parallels the main street, over which tall trees form an arch.

In 1786 the township land was granted to Gen. Benjamin Lincoln of Hingham, Mass., who, at the surrender of Yorktown, was selected to conduct the British to the spot where their arms were deposited.

There is a fine SALMON-FISHING POOL near the center of the village.

The LINCOLN HOME (*private*), half a mile N. of the center and facing the river, was erected in 1787 by artisans from Hingham, Mass., under the direction of General Lincoln's son, Theodore. It is a two-story yellow structure. Theodore, who occupied the house, had large lumber interests and employed many Indians of the district. James Audubon, the artist and naturalist, was a friend of Theodore's son, Thomas, who assisted Audubon in making arrangements for an expedition to Labrador in 1833. Members of the Lincoln family still own and occupy the house, which contains many of the early furnishings, as well as old books and documents.

In the store of I. K. Kilby in the village is a COLLECTION OF INDIAN RELICS (*open*) found in the neighborhood.

WHITING, 41.7 m. (60 alt.; Whiting Town, 327 pop.), a village formerly called Orangetown, is in an area where extensive lumbering operations are still carried on; the town is recognized by the large piles of lumber near its center along the road. The route passes a lumber mill on the Orange River, which has been dammed at this point to provide water power.

In this area are long stretches of forests, broken occasionally by small scrubby farms. In spite of the extensive lumbering operations that have been carried on in what is now the State of Maine, the forests have not been seriously depleted. The country is full of game. Many rabbits are caught here and shipped to other parts of Maine, as well as to other States, for stocking game preserves.

At the rear of a small white church (R) is the GRAVE OF COL. JOHN CRANE, the first white settler. He was a member of the Boston Tea Party, and during the Revolution commanded one of the batteries whose fire diverted the attention of the British from the American forces in their capture of Dorchester Heights in March 1776.

At Whiting is the junction with State 189 (*see Side Route 2*).

INDIAN LAKE (*fishing and boating facilities*), **47.3 m.** (R), lies along the road, the blue of its waters enhanced by the dark green foliage of the dense forest surrounding it.

At **50.9 m.** (R) is the graveled entrance to the SUMMER SURVEYING SCHOOL of the Massachusetts Institute of Technology, on the shore of Gardner Lake; the neighborhood provides a variety of surveying problems.

EAST MACHIAS, **54.3 m.** (60 alt.; East Machias Town, 1,253 pop.), is bisected by the East Machias River, the residential area and the business districts being on opposite sides of the stream.

On top of a hill across the river (L) is WASHINGTON ACADEMY. A general interest in having a local school was shown as early as 1790–1791, and a petition for help from the Government in the undertaking was transmitted to the General Court of Massachusetts in that year. The petition was granted and Township 11, since known as Cutler, was given as an endowment for an academy, but it was not until September 1823 that Washington Academy was opened.

In the LIBRARY (L), a brick building with two old millstones from an early gristmill set strikingly in the front wall, one on either side of the entrance, is a canvas showing a panorama of the community in the prosperous lumbering and shipbuilding days.

At **55.9 m.** is the junction with a local road.

Left on this road is MACHIASPORT, **4 m.** (80 alt.; Machiasport Town, 825 pop.), a typical Maine coast village where lumber shipping is now the chief activity.

When news of the battle of Lexington reached this part of Maine in early May 1775, Ichabod Jones, who had left Massachusetts because of the increasing disturbance to business, caused in part by the Boston Port Bill, hastily left for Boston, to secure his personal property. The Boston Port commander refused, however, to allow him to take his boat out of the harbor except to return to

MAINE

Maine for lumber to be used in building barracks for the increasing number of British soldiers. The armed schooner *Margaretta* was sent along as a convoy to enforce the order. Meanwhile, public opinion in Machias had been inflamed and Captain Moore of the *Margaretta* found a Liberty Pole in the little frontier coast town and citizens incensed at the idea of providing supplies for the armies to be used against them. Led by Benjamin Foster and the fiery Irishman, Jeremiah O'Brien, the local citizens commandeered two boats, one of which, however, became stranded; on June 12, 1775, they closed in on the *Margaretta*. In the fight that followed the British officer was mortally wounded and his boat captured. The following month the Machias men captured a British schooner from Nova Scotia. The British sent Sir George Collier with the *Ranger* and three other boats to punish the rebels; Collier routed the local force from the breastworks they had hastily thrown up along the river and burned several buildings before his fleet moved on. The capture of the *Margaretta* has been called the "first naval battle of the Revolution"; the battle itself was not important but it provided the Revolutionary leaders in Philadelphia with a talking point in urging the establishment of a navy.

Machiasport was the terminus of the narrow-gage Machias-Whitneyville R.R., built in 1841 to carry lumber from Whitneyville to Machiasport for shipping, and operated for 50 years by the Sullivan family of Whitneyville. One of the locomotives used on this railroad is now at the Crosby Laboratory, University of Maine, Orono.

From WRIGHT'S LOOKOUT, a bold rock at the top of Corn Hill, a few hundred yards back from the main street, is a splendid view of the Machias headlands and the western end of the Bay of Fundy.

At the southern end of the village, on the western bank of the Machias River, is the State reservation holding the EARTHWORKS OF FORT MACHIAS, or Fort O'Brien as it is locally called because it was erected in part through the activities of the O'Briens. After the Collier raid Washington ordered a regiment of militia recruited and sent to protect the settlement. In 1781 Fort Machias was made part of the national defense. The British, however, did not return to the little town until 1814, when they took the fort and burned the barracks. The place was again fortified in 1863, during the Civil War, but was not attacked.

At CLARK'S POINT, 7 m. (L), are the so-called PICTURE ROCKS. Figures somewhat resembling men, animals, and landscapes can be seen on a slanting ledge below the high-water mark. Some authorities who have examined the formations believe they are geologic, others that they are hieroglyphics.

MACHIAS (Ind., *bad little falls*), **58.8 m.** (80 alt.; Machias Town, 1,853 pop.), seat of Washington Co., lies along the Machias River; the town formerly included what is now the town of Machiasport (*see above*). The gristmill in the center of the bridge across the river looks down on the narrow gorge through which the waters tumble and roar ceaselessly. From the bridge are seen the buildings of the WASHINGTON STATE NORMAL SCHOOL on a high hill overlooking the town.

After the destruction of the Plymouth Colony trading post at Pentagoet by the French, the English in 1633 established under command of Richard Vines, another post here, in a spot much closer to the French headquarters; La Tour, French Governor of Acadia, wiped it out almost at once. In 1675 Rhodes, the pirate, used the site as a base for repairs and supplies; a few decades later another pirate, Samuel Bellamy, came here for the same purpose, and, liking the place and deciding that it offered him security, determined to establish a permanent stronghold. Piracy was rampant along the Atlantic seaboard at this time, partly because of English and Spanish trade restrictions, designed to force colonists to buy from the mother country alone; this created a good market for stolen goods in the Colonies. Privateering served as excellent training for piracy, as Cotton Mather warned in 1704 in one of his "hanging sermons," and many men who started out to prey on shipping for their governments soon decided to keep the booty for themselves. Bellamy, from all reports, developed a Robin Hood philosophy on the matter; when he had captured a ship he would harangue its crew and invite them to join him, arguing that the men had as much right to rob as had the shipowners, who were merely powerful bandits protected by law.

When Bellamy determined to settle on the site of the present Machias, he erected breastworks and a crude fort before leaving for another expedition with three objectives — recruits, loot, and women. He had left the mouth of the river and was plundering along the Nova Scotian banks when, by mistake, he attacked a French naval vessel. His vessel, the *Whidaw*, was almost captured before he managed to escape. Sailing south, he had further bad luck; he captured a New Bedford whaler, whose captain pretended to join him and agreed to act as a navigator through the dangerous reefs and shoals. The whaling captain did his part for a time and then deliberately ran his ship aground on a sandbar near Eastham, Mass. The pirates, following the lead of the whaler, went on the rocks, and Bellamy and most of his crew drowned.

In 1763 the first permanent English colony was established by settlers from Scarboro near Portland.

The Machias River has played an important part in the town's development as a commercial lumber and shipbuilding center. One of the few remaining "long lumber" log drives in Maine takes place on the Machias River each spring. Logs are hauled over the snow to the landings, and when the ice goes out of the river they are shoved into the fast-moving water, which hurtles them downstream. When one of the numerous jams occurs, a daring river driver walks out on it to pry loose the key log; if this does not succeed the jam is blasted.

BURNHAM TAVERN, High and Free Sts. (*open Sat. aft., June 1–Oct. 1; adm. 10¢*), a plain two-story gambrel-roofed structure with the lower section of the roof broken back to a vertical wall with five windows, was built in 1770 by Joe Burnham. Beneath each of the four cornerstones of the building the owner placed a box containing a slip of paper inscribed with the words "hospitality," "cheer," "hope," and "courage." Over the door hangs the original sign, which reads: "Drink for the thirsty, food for the hungry, lodging for the weary, and good keeping for horses." Beneath the roof the townspsople gathered to plan their movements against the British and to discuss the exciting events of the day. Here Jeremiah O'Brien and his comrades devised the capture of the *Margaretta* (*see above*).

In the O'Brien Cemetery here is the GRAVE OF CAPTAIN O'BRIEN. Just beyond the cemetery is a marker indicating the site of his home.

Also on Elm St., half a mile from the center, is a small stream called FOSTER'S RUBICON; the men of Machias met on its banks in June 1775 to discuss the demands that they furnish lumber to be sent back to Boston and used in building barracks for the British troops. After a long debate, during which part of the townsmen advocated compliance and others resistance, Benjamin Foster, a church leader as well as a rebel, sprang across the stream, inviting those who shared his views to follow him. The rebels went first, then those who had been wavering, and finally those who had advocated compliance; the settlement as a whole was committed to the Revolution.

At Machias is the junction with State 1A.

Right on State 1A is WHITNEYVILLE, **4.5 m.** (70 alt.; Whitneyville Town, 229 pop.), a small farming community on the western bank of the Machias River that is the terminus of an annual spring log drive. A marker near the river indicates the spot where the *Margaretta* was beached, after being towed up the river following her capture, and concealed from the British by leafy boughs.

State 1A runs through wide blueberry plains and rejoins US 1 at Jonesboro.

JONESBORO, **66.3 m.** (60 alt.; Jonesboro Town, 468 pop.), a small Chandler River farming community, had a Revolutionary

War heroine in the person of Hannah Weston, a descendant of Hannah Dustin, who became famous in the Indian massacre at Haverhill, Mass., in 1697. With a younger sister, Hannah Weston carried 50 pounds of lead and powder, collected from neighbors, through the woods from Jonesboro to Machias for use during the *Margaretta* episode (*see above*) in June 1775. The GRAVE OF HANNAH WESTON is near the highway on the Charles Fish farm at the northern end of the village.

At 73.7 m. is a junction with State 187.

Left on State 187, which cuts through the deep stillness of the woods and runs along the western shore of Englishman's Bay for several miles, presenting many attractive scenes, is JONESPORT, **12.7 m.** (40 alt.; Jonesport Town, 1,634 pop.). Although it derives considerable income from summer visitors, Jonesport's principal means of livelihood are fishing and sardine packing. Jonesport became famous as the background of Phillip Lord's radio program, *Sunday Night at Seth Parker's*. Island views, camp sites, fishing, and beaches are its resort attractions.

In the harbor is BEALS ISLAND, reached from Jonesport by ferry. Separated from its larger but much less populous neighbor, Great Wass Island, by the FLYING PLACE, a narrow strait, Beals Island affords views of surrounding islands and curious sea-wrought rock formations. Play of surf is most spectacular on stormy days in the Flying Place.

BEALS (40 alt.; Beals Town, 524 pop.) is a fishing community on Beals Island, as well as a summer resort, where the popular sport is deep-sea fishing.

There is a faithful congregation of the Church of Jesus Christ of Latter-Day Saints at Beals. In 1865 G. J. Adams, a Mormon missionary from Philadelphia, succeeded despite local opposition in recruiting followers here. Prevailing upon many to sell their worldly goods, he organized the Palestine Emigration Association, issuing a religious publication, *The Sword of Truth and the Harbinger of Peace*. After arrangements had been made with the Turkish Government, through the American consul, 175 members left on a 52-day voyage to Palestine in the barkentine, *Nellie Chapin*, and settled near Jaffa. Beset by internal dissensions, misunderstandings with the natives, and disease caused by poor sanitary conditions, the colony was disbanded within a year and the survivors returned to the United States.

BARNEY's POINT, on the island, was named for Barney Beal, a son of Manwaring Beal, the first settler. The most colorful of the island legends are woven around the bold exploits and feats of strength of "Tall Barney," who always wore a butcher's coat and whose 6 ft. 7 in. of brawn earned him fame as "cock of the walk" from Quoddy Head to Cape Elizabeth; it was said that when he sat in a chair his hands touched the floor. Once while he was fishing off Black's Island, armed sailors, objecting to his proximity to English territory, boarded his sloop, intent on capture at gun point. Barney relieved the sailors of their guns, which he promptly broke over his knee and tossed back into the British boat. When the Canadian guards unwisely persisted in their intimidations, Barney twisted the arm of one until he broke the bone. In Rockland, Barney was said to have felled a horse with his fist, when a truckman drove too close to him. In a Portland saloon, without argument or assistance, he proved to 15 men the folly of deriding a "down-easter."

PERIO'S POINT, near the Freeman West Beal Wharf, was named for Perio Checkers, an Indian, who is the only man known to have scaled the perpendicular side of the steep cliff that still challenges climbers at this point.

In the past, shipwrecks in this vicinity were frequent. Companies were formed on the mainland to salvage boats and cargoes.

The GRAVE OF AUNT PEGGY BEAL, in the cemetery near the public square, reminds natives of how Aunt Peggy exorcised the powers of a witch, a Mrs. Thomas Hicks. Mrs. Hicks had the habit of borrowing from Aunt Peggy; if Aunt Peggy refused to lend what Mrs. Hicks wanted, it either died or disappeared. The last thing refused was a sheep, which died the following day. A Salem sailor, who claimed to know all about the handling of witches, told Aunt Peggy to build a hot fire and to hold the sheep over it until it was scorched all over. This was done. "Now," he said, "a boat will come over for something three times, and you must refuse each time, even though the witch tells you where the article is." It all came about as the sailor predicted, so the story goes, and the day following the refusal of the third article, Mrs. Hicks was dead.

GREAT WASS ISLAND COAST GUARD STATION is notable for its equipment and drills. The SEACOAST MISSION SHIP regularly visits the island lighthouse.

In this area US 1 continues through blueberry plains; the homes show few evidences of prosperity, being weather-beaten and unpainted.

COLUMBIA FALLS, 75 m. (60 alt.; Columbia Falls Town, 583 pop.), was once a thriving lumber and shipbuilding center. Today the inhabitants depend on general farming and the blueberry industry for a livelihood. The prosperity that the town once knew is revealed by the many fine old homes in the vicinity.

The RUGGLES HOUSE (*open*), constructed in 1820 after a design by Aaron Sherman of Duxbury, Mass., who planned a number of homes in Washington County, was built for Judge Thomas Ruggles, a wealthy lumber dealer. The house is notable for the delicate detail of its exterior trim. The interior woodwork, executed by an unknown English artisan, is unusually fine. In the drawing-room are rope beadings on the cornices of the fireplace, done with great skill, exquisite carvings on the molding, and delicate indentures on the chair rail of the wainscoting and on the frames and sills of the wide-shuttered windows. The house is in the process of restoration, and workmen have uncovered rich mahogany-inlaid panels. Of particular interest is the swastika design, carved with a common penknife, below the mantel in the dining room. It is said that the villagers were so impressed by the delicacy of the work that they believed the carver's knife was guided by the hand of an angel.

Arthur Train used the Ruggles house as the setting for his short story, *The House that Tutt Built.*

The MAUDE BUCKNAM HOUSE, opposite the post office, a yellow Cape-Cod style dwelling with a wing, was built about 1820. It is notable for its woodwork.

The LIPPINCOTT HOUSE, opposite the Bucknam House, is a square hip-roofed building with interesting interior details, including old-fashioned rope moldings and many fireplaces.

At **76.8 m.** is the junction with a dirt road, known locally as the Jeff Davis Trail, which was cut in 1858 to enable members of the U.S. Coast Survey to transport supplies and heavy instruments to the top of Humpback, or Lead Mountain. Jefferson Davis, a close friend of Alexander Bache, Superintendent of the Coast Survey, was a guest at the survey camp during the summer when the trail was cut.

Right on this road is COLUMBIA, **1.5 m.** (60 alt.; Columbia Town, 409 pop.), settled soon after the Revolutionary War.

The road continues in a northwesterly direction onto a 200-sq.-m. plateau, where nearly 90 percent of the country's blueberries are raised. Small brooks meander through acres of the low bushes, which in mid-June are covered with inverted bell blossoms. Blueberry packing begins in August and lasts through September. Men in large straw hats, women in sunbonnets, and barefoot children work from dawn to sundown raking, winnowing, and boxing the berries to be trucked to the canning factories.

The blueberry industry has grown up in the wake of lumbering; the plants quickly cover the thin sandy soil after the trees are cut, and they need little cultivation. The land is burned over every third year to stimulate new growth. The spruce in this area was removed in the first quarter of the 19th century to provide masts and spars for ships built in the nearby yards. Blueberry plains are privately owned but protected by the State. "Bootleg berries," those stolen by night pickers, are not as common as they once were.

HARRINGTON, **79.8 m.** (40 alt.; Harrington Town, 862 pop.), was settled about 1765 and incorporated in 1797. Like many other villages along the route, its air of comfort and prosperity depends largely on the money derived from the summer tourist trade. Pleasant Bay is a favorite spot for deep-sea fishing.

CHERRYFIELD, **86.1 m.** (50 alt.; Cherryfield Town, 1,111 pop.), lies on both sides of the Narraguagus River. The *Belgrade*, full-rigged bark that carried 56 local men around Cape Horn to California in the days of the gold rush, was built in this formerly active

MAINE 13

shipbuilding community. Today lumbering and blueberry packing are the chief industries of the town.

MILBRIDGE, 91.6 m. (20 alt.; Milbridge Town, 1,207 pop.), lies at the mouth of the Narraguagus, its main street, which US 1 follows, paralleling the river. From the highway at the southern end of the village there is a fine view of the offshore islands (*boats and guides for deep-sea fishing*). Lumbering, lobster fishing, and farming are the main sources of livelihood. A knitting mill is also in operation.

A boat once frequently seen along the Maine coast and still occasionally found in some of the fishing villages of Nova Scotia is the pinky (Prov. Eng., *small*). These boats, pointed at both ends, have wide gunwales rising to meet in a stern overhang. In 1927 Howard L. Chapelle, naval architect and author of *The History of American Sailing Ships*, revived the building of this type of craft in the Milbridge yard.

GOULDSBORO, 101.9 m. (80 alt.; Gouldsboro Town, 1,115 pop.), is principally a summer resort and small trading center for the Grindstone Neck area. David Cobb made his home here from 1796 to 1808. During those years he was one of the most influential citizens of Maine. In 1795 he was appointed agent of the great Bingham estate (*see below*); the following year he moved to Gouldsboro, and in 1802 was sent to the Massachusetts Legislature to represent eastern Maine.

SULLIVAN, 111.6 m. (60 alt.; Sullivan Town, 873 pop.), a small hamlet, is the corporate center of a township whose many summer homes are spread out along US 1.

The STONE STORE (*not open*), in the center of the village, is a two-story gabled building, constructed of heavy blocks of stone.

At 112.1 m. is a striking view of Mt. Desert Island and its hills.

HANCOCK, 114.8 m. (Hancock Town, 760 pop.), was settled in 1764 and incorporated in 1828. In 1890 the township had a population of 1,190; the decrease has been gradual.

At 120.3 m. is a magnificent view of the Schoodic Hills and Cadillac Mountain, also various other hills rising from and around Frenchman's Bay.

The region through which US 1 passes here has small farms that look fairly prosperous, and much wooded land.

ELLSWORTH, 123.9 m. (100 alt., 3,557 pop.), the seat and the only city in Hancock Co., was settled in 1763. The community has seen extensive lumbering operations, a period of shipbuilding, and an industrial era brought about by the development of its water power. A large part of the business district and many of the old buildings were destroyed by fire in 1933, but the center has been rebuilt. Today the town is a happy combination of gracious old homes and attractive modern business buildings. An example of this is the new CITY HALL, showing a Scandinavian influence and standing near the old white CONGREGATIONAL CHURCH, which dominates the business district from the E. side of State Street Hill. The latter, built in 1812, has a portico with delicately fluted columns, and a slender spire.

The sparkling Union River flows through the center of the city, and from the bridge (L) 60-foot falls are visible.

The BLACK MANSION, on W. Main St. (*open May 30–Nov. 1; adm. 50¢*), built about 1802, was the home of Col. John Black, land agent for William Bingham, who owned very large tracts of land E. of the Penobscot River. Colonel Black's predecessor in the agency was his father-in-law, Col. David Cobb, an aide-de-camp of General Washington. The two-story brick house, an elegant structure in the tiny frontier settlement, is of modified Georgian design, with one-story wings that may have been added after the main structure was built. An ornamental cornice and balustrade surround the low roof. The main structure has no front entrance; four triple-hung, shuttered windows open out on a low porch with five Ionic columns, that runs the length of the main building and is surmounted with a balustrade. A notable feature of the interior is the graceful curving staircase rising from the spacious hall that divides the house and parallels its front. Many of Colonel Black's possessions and those his wife inherited from her father are in the house; other articles have been added since the house became public property in 1928. Among the valued relics are a miniature of Washington by one of the Peales, a rare volume of the Colonial laws of Massachusetts, and a high-backed Dutch chair with a hinged seat that can be lengthened to form a couch or bed.

The furnishings include fine Duncan Phyfe, Sheraton, and Chippendale pieces, as well as Spode and Royal Dresden china.

The PUBLIC LIBRARY (*open 2–5 p.m.*), State St., once the Tisdale house, built before 1820, retains many of its original features, such as arched doorways and deep fireplaces.

MAINE

Section 2. *Ellsworth to Belfast, 61.3 m.*

From Ellsworth US 1 cuts sharply NW. to Bangor, traversing placid farmlands that contrast with the wooded hills; south of Bangor the route follows the west bank of the Penobscot River, running through scenic country to Belfast.

LUCERNE-IN-MAINE, 14.7 m. (440 alt.; Dedham Town, 279 pop.), is a resort on the shores of LAKE LUCERNE, drawing winter sports enthusiasts as well as summer visitors. The CLUBHOUSE (L), just off the highway, was the halfway house on the old Bangor-Ellsworth stagecoach route; it has been much remodeled. Thick woods nearly conceal (R) the huge log tourist lodge and tennis courts and (L) a golf course, bridle paths, hiking trails, and a bathing beach. This resort was carefully planned by the head of a lumbering firm, who did not wish to see the natural beauty of the lakeshore and hills spoiled.

At 14.9 m. is a beautiful view of Lake Lucerne.

EAST HOLDEN, 17.8 m. (100 alt., Holden Town), is at a crossroads where overnight cabins outnumber the handful of residences.

At 19.1 m. is HOLDEN (190 alt.; Holden Town, 543 pop.). The TOWN HALL and GRANGE HALL (L) mark the corporate and social center of the township. The National Grange of the Patrons of Husbandry, of which the local lodges are members, was organized in 1867 by Oliver H. Kelley, an employee of the U. S. Department of Agriculture who felt the need of a fraternal organization to unite the farmers for social and educational purposes. The lodges became politically important, serving as local forums; they are still very active in Maine. Grange suppers and meetings are open to the public and visitors who want to study the State are advised to attend the meetings, which are always advertised. The suppers are standardized and usually include baked beans, ham, cole slaw, pie, and cake.

At 23.2 m. is a sweeping view across valleys and mountains.

BREWER, 25.8 m. (100 alt., 6,329 pop.), is a city somewhat overshadowed by Bangor, across the Penobscot River. It was named for Col. John Brewer, who was one of the first settlers, as well as the first postmaster. Once famous for the wooden ships built in its yards, the city depends for its present prosperity on the activity of pulp and paper mills.

U. S. ONE

CHILLICOTE HOUSE, now an antique shop, corner of State and N. Main Sts., is a conspicuous landmark standing at the crest of a short hill that drops sharply to the E. approach of the Bangor-Brewer bridge.

At 80 Chamberlain St. is the JOSHUA CHAMBERLAIN HOUSE (*private*). General Chamberlain, noted for his gallantry during the Civil War, received the Congressional Medal of Honor for his part in the defense of Little Round Top at Gettysburg; as a further reward for his military activity he was delegated to review and receive the arms and colors of the Confederate Army at Appomattox in 1865. In spite of repeated injuries received while in active service, he was able to serve as Governor of the State (1867–1871) and as president of Bowdoin College (1871–1883).

BANGOR, **26.5 m.** (100 alt., 28,749 pop.), manufacturing city (*see MAINE GUIDE*).

Points of Interest. Salmon Pool, Veazie House, Old City Hall, and others.

HAMPDEN, **31.5 m.** (80 alt.; Hampden Town, 2,417 pop.), on the banks of the Penobscot River, a suburban village flanked by farms, was settled in 1767, two years before Bangor, and for a long time rivaled that town in importance. During the War of 1812 the British drove the out-numbered militia from the settlement.

Huge piles of pulp wood are seen in the Penobscot (L) as the route passes through the outskirts of Bangor.

HAMPDEN HIGHLANDS, **32.7 m.** (150 alt., Hampden Town), has blue-green river vistas. In the latter part of May the numerous orchards in the township and in Orrington across the Penobscot blanket the countryside with translucent pink and white beauty and send forth a delicate scent that permeates the whole area.

The DOROTHEA LYNDE DIX MEMORIAL PARK (L) is on the site of the Isaac Hopkins farm, on which in 1802 the prison and almshouse reformer, for whom the park is named, was born. When Miss Dix went to Boston as a young girl, she was so shocked by conditions in public institutions that she began a campaign that carried her all over the country and resulted in marked reforms.

WINTERPORT, **39.8 m.** (80 alt.; Winterport Town, 1,437 pop.), whose name was derived from its position at the head of winter navigation on the Penobscot River, at one time had some importance as a port and shipbuilding community. In the 1936 State election

Winterport was the first and only town in Maine to use voting machines.

At **40.4 m.** (R) is the BLAISDELL HOUSE (*not open*), built in 1798, a two-and-a-half-story yellow structure with a gable roof and two dormer windows.

FRANKFORT, **42.5 m.** (180 alt.; Frankfort Town, 468 pop.), a village shaded by huge century-old elms, belies its history of industrial prosperity. Log cabins first appeared here in 1756, and a permanent settlement was made in 1760. Shipbuilding began early and, by the time of the Revolution, Frankfort was important enough to draw the attention of the British Navy. Many of the 33 ships destroyed along the Penobscot in 1779 were tied up, or under construction, in this port. The English bombarded the settlement in 1814, subsequently occupying it.

In the vicinity of Frankfort, the road, which is very hilly and winding, affords many panoramas of the valley. Small farms cling to the hillsides.

At **43.9 m.** along both sides of the road are the buildings of the MT. WALDO GRANITE CORPORATION (*open*); nearby are the deep clefts from which countless tons of fine granite have been quarried.

The FLATS here bordering the river are among several points on the Maine coast where Captain Kidd is said to have buried a part of his treasure. A tinker who lived on the spot refused to allow searchers on the property; after his death a number of attempts were made to find the supposedly hidden jewels and gold. Legend has it that the hunters were frightened away by mysterious noises from the earth; no treasure has ever been found here.

MOUNT WALDO (1,062 alt.), highest of several small peaks in this region, can be seen (R) at intervals. Mt. Waldo granite has been used in many public buildings.

The granite ledges of MOSQUITO MOUNTAIN, **44.7 m.**, rise sharply (R).

At **46.7 m.** is PROSPECT (90 alt.; Prospect Town, 388 pop.).

Left from Prospect on State 174 is FORT KNOX (*see illustration*), **2.5 m.**, now a State reservation. The site for this fort was selected during the days of the heated boundary disputes with Great Britain, but work was not begun until 1846; the fort was never entirely completed, though troops were trained here during the Civil War. This massive structure was built of Mt. Waldo granite and commands one of the most beautiful views on the Penobscot River.

A short distance beyond Fort Knox is the western approach to the WALDO-HANCOCK BRIDGE (*toll 50¢*) on State 3.

STOCKTON SPRINGS, 51.2 m. (150 alt.; Stockton Springs Town, 877 pop.), has become relatively prosperous because of its fish canneries and fertilizer factories. In 1890 an attempt was made to exploit the spring for which the town was named, but failed when it was found that sediment settled in the bottles when the water was ready to market.

At 55.1 m. (L) stands the HOME OF LINCOLN COLCORD, a writer and the son of a sea captain; he was born off Cape Horn. His home, for several generations the snug haven to which his adventurous forebears retired at the end of their voyages, is beautifully situated above the bay.

In this area US 1 passes many estates as well as farms that have achieved prosperity by catering to the needs of their summer neighbors.

SEARSPORT, 55.4 m. (50 alt.; Searsport Town, 1,414 pop.), has a small, compact business district on its main street (US 1). The rest of the village stretches along the highway, which affords many vistas of Penobscot Bay. In the heyday of New England shipping, Searsport was known as the home of expert seamen, and it has been the birthplace of many United States naval officers. As a terminus of the Bangor & Aroostook R.R., it ships much of the annual potato crop of Aroostook Co.

In an old brick house that was built in the village during the days of the town's prosperity is housed the PENOBSCOT MARINE MUSEUM, containing an unusually fine collection of relics and papers connected with the ships, shipowners, and captains of the days when the Penobscot was one of the most important shipbuilding centers of the Nation.

At 59.4 m. (R) is STEPHENSON TAVERN (*private*), a story-and-a-half house of simple lines, built in 1800; there is a well sweep in the front yard. The old pine sign, bearing a black horse and the name Jerome Stephenson, is so weather-beaten that the painted horse and lettering stand out a quarter of an inch.

On the northern outskirts of Belfast the route crosses Passagassawakeag River on the BELFAST MEMORIAL BRIDGE, which is dedicated to Waldo County's enlisted men of the World War. From a hill beyond the bridge can be seen the dark red warehouses of Belfast's

MAINE

waterfront. From US 1 between this point and Belfast are a succession of views of the waters of the Penobscot and its islands.

BELFAST, 61.3 m. (160 alt., 4,993 pop.), a popular tourist center and seat of Waldo Co., has parallel streets that follow a rolling terrain, which rises in a majestic sweep from the banks of the Passagassawakeag. Its highest points command views of the island-sprinkled waters of Penobscot Bay.

The town was named for Belfast, Ireland, by a group of Scotch-Irish settlers who came to the place in 1770, after having tried settlement at Londonderry, N.H. Belfast was harassed by the British in 1779 and its settlers were driven away, but they successfully reestablished themselves five years later. The city has achieved prosperity by catering to the many summer residents and visitors.

Reminiscent of an earlier prosperity are the many fine old houses, whose chief interest lies in their variation on the standard 19th century architecture.

The JAMES P. WHITE HOUSE (*private*), 30 Church St., is a simple white structure built in 1825. Fine old elms shade the broad lawn, which is surrounded by a picket fence.

The CLAY HOUSE (*private*), 130 Main St., was built in 1825. It is an attractive structure of the Greek Revival type with Doric columns.

The old JOHNSON HOUSE, 100 High St., set in beautiful grounds, is a hip-roof structure with a lookout, built in 1812. The Corinthian columns on the front and sides may be later additions. Its shutters were the first used in Belfast.

The BEN FIELD HOUSE (*private*), 137 High St., is a large, square, hip-roof structure with a dentiled cornice, built in 1807.

The old BLAISDELL HOUSE (*private*), a third of a mile S. of the center on High St., on spacious grounds, has a portico with four Ionic columns and an elaborately carved pediment.

1. Right from Belfast on Main St.; R. at **0.2 m.** on Waldo Ave. to the junction with Poor Mills Rd. at **1.4 m.**; L. here to the old JOSEPH MILLER TAVERN, **2.4 m.** (R). It has the only salt-box roof left in Belfast, tiny panes in the windows, and no eaves, a characteristic of early building in the vicinity.

2. Straight ahead from the center on High St. at **1.2 m.** (R) is the OTIS HOUSE (*private*), a one-and-a-half-story gable-end house on Nickerson Hill, overlooking the river; it was built in 1800.

3. Visible from Belfast's waterfront, and lying about 6 miles offshore in Penobscot Bay, is ISLESBORO, a long, low, tree-clad island that can be reached from Belfast.

U. S. ONE

Section 3. Belfast to Brunswick, 79.3 m.

Between Belfast and Brunswick US 1 follows the western edge of Penobscot Bay, then gradually swings SW. to cross the Kennebec River. The countryside is fairly open, with distant views of the ocean. Houses belong chiefly to the 19th century, and there are few signs of recent prosperity. The area around Camden is particularly beautiful, the hills being covered with evergreens, though these grow thinner toward the south.

At **1 m.** (L) is the BELFAST CITY PARK with excellent camping and trailer facilities.

At **7.6 m.** is a junction with a gravel road.

Left on this road is NORTHPORT, **0.5 m.** (140 alt.; Northport Town, 413 pop.), near Saturday Cove, an arm of Penobscot Bay; many delightful woodland walks lead from the village to the shore.

CAMDEN, **18.3 m.** (100 alt.; Camden Town, 3,606 pop.), one of Maine's loveliest towns, lies "under the high mountains of the Penobscot, against whose feet the sea doth beat," as Capt. John Smith described the site. Champlain, who visited the Penobscot in 1605, named the Camden Hills the "mountains of Bedabedec" on his map; so steeply do they rise from the blue waters of Penobscot Bay that the magnificent yachts dropping anchor all summer long in the harbor seem from a distance to ride in the heart of the business district.

The town has developed rapidly as a small summer resort in recent years, the estate valuation now being more than half that of Bar Harbor. It has also become a winter sport center. The summer residents have taken particular interest in the landscaping of the town, a project that is stimulated by annual contests in which prizes are awarded.

Behind the CAMDEN PUBLIC LIBRARY, Main St., is an AMPHITHEATER with a seating capacity of 1,500, landscaped with native trees, shrubs, and plants.

The old CAMDEN OPERA HOUSE, corner Elm and Washington Sts., has been remodeled into a modern auditorium with elaborate interior decorations. Mrs. Mary Louise Bok, daughter of the late Cyrus H. K. Curtis, a summer resident for many years, has been a leader in carrying out many municipal improvements. A notable group of musicians, including Josef Hoffman, pianist, summer here.

MAINE   21

1. Right from Camden on Mechanic St., the southern section of State 137; straight ahead (R) from State 137 at **1 m.**; L. at **1.5 m.**, passing a lake at **3.4 m.**; L. at **3.5 m.** and again at **3.7 m.** to the CAMDEN BOWL, in which carnivals and competitive sports events are held in summer and winter.

2. Right from Camden on Mountain St., which enters the northern section of State 137, at **1 m.** is the junction with a trail leading to the summit of MOUNT BATTIE (800 alt.). From this height, occupied by cannon during the War of 1812, are beautiful views of Penobscot Bay and the surrounding hills. An area of approximately 6,000 acres between Lake Megunticook and the seashore, including part of Mt. Megunticook, Mt. Battie, and Bald Mountain, is being proposed for park development.

ROCKPORT, **19.9 m.** (100 alt.; Rockport Town, 1,651 pop.), a town with a diminishing population, was set off from Camden in 1891. From the bridge at the S. end of the village is a remarkable view of the harbor and the white lighthouse jutting out on the point. Goose River forms a V-shaped waterfront that has been landscaped by Mrs. Mary Louise Bok (*see above*). Unusually interesting are the OLD LIME KILNS nearby.

SPITE HOUSE (L), on Deadman's Point, was moved in 1925 over land and water from Phippsburg, 85 miles away, by Donald W. Dodge of Philadelphia. James McCobb, a prominent Phippsburg citizen of his time, built the so-called Minott House in Phippsburg for his second wife. Some time after his third marriage, the elder McCobb died while his son Thomas was at sea. The third Mrs. McCobb, who had also been previously married, arranged a marriage between her son by her first husband and her stepdaughter, the sister of Thomas McCobb, thereby obtaining practical control of one of the largest estates in the section. When Thomas McCobb returned and learned of the marriage and its consequences, he became incensed, declared he would build himself a mansion large enough and sufficiently grand to overshadow the residence occupied by his stepmother, and in 1806 built this beautiful structure which, from the day of its completion, has borne its present name.

At **25 m.** is the junction with Waldo Ave.

Left on Waldo Ave. to the ROCKLAND BREAKWATER, which extends from Jameson Point nearly a mile across the harbor entrance and makes an excellent point from which to survey the city and environs. There is a LIGHTHOUSE at the end of the breakwater.

ROCKLAND, **26.3 m.** (40 alt., 9,075 pop.), separated from Thomaston and incorporated in 1848 as East Thomaston, is a trading center and shire town for Knox Co. The many summer residents and visitors have been a good source of trade. The city fronts on the fine harbor that the Indians called Catawamkeag (*great landing place*). Fishing, shipping, shipbuilding, and limestone quarrying have been the chief industries of the past.

The BIRTHPLACE (1892) OF EDNA ST. VINCENT MILLAY, the poet, is at 200 Broadway.

The COMMUNITY YACHT CLUB and PUBLIC LANDING, Main and Pleasant Sts., have floats, docks, and clubhouses for visitors.

1. Left from Rockland on Main St.; at **2 m.** L. on a tarred road; at **2.1 m.** L. to large triangular RANGE BEACONS, **3.7 m.** These open structures are used by vessels of the U.S. Navy in sighting their positions on the measured trial course off Rockland, which is marked by six buoys. New vessels and old ones that have been reconditioned are sent here for tests of speed and engine efficiency.

OWL'S HEAD, **4.6 m.** (40 alt.; Owl's Head Town, 574 pop.), a summer resort, lies on the far end of a tree-sheltered cape. Visited by Champlain in 1605, it was then called Bedabedec Point (Ind., *cape of the waters*). The town was the scene of a bloody encounter in 1755 when Captain Cargyle, famous Indian fighter employing Indian tactics, killed and scalped nine braves, receiving a bounty of 200 pounds sterling each. During the Revolution and the War of 1812, British and American privateers were active in nearby waters.

Left from Owl's Head to the heavily wooded U.S. LIGHTHOUSE RESERVATION, **5.3 m.** (L).

OWL'S HEAD LIGHT (*open 9–11:30 a.m. all year; 1–5 p.m. July–Aug.; 1–3 p.m. remainder of year*), was built in 1826, during the administration of President John Quincy Adams. The old white tower is only 26 ft. high; but because of its situation the light can be seen 16 miles at sea. In summer, yachts cruising in these waters are welcomed by three strokes of a bell. Snowshoeing parties from Rockland visit the snow-clad headland in winter.

At **5.7 m.** the road ends. From this point it is but a short walk to the shore, where the red and yellow quartz-streaked face of the headland, worn smooth by the pounding of the surf, rears itself nearly 100 ft. above sea level. Tall spruces, their roots clinging tenaciously to the few inches of soil, crown the summit.

2. Left from Rockland, in Penobscot Bay and to the E. of it in the Atlantic Ocean, are North Haven and Vinalhaven Islands, Deer Isle, and Isle au Haut, to all of which there is steamship service from Rockland.

NORTH HAVEN (476 pop.), about **12 m.** from Rockland, at the mouth of Penobscot Bay, is a fashionable area with a number of summer estates. There is a flying field here.

VINALHAVEN (1,843 pop.) is S. of North Haven, with which it is connected by ferry. It also has many large summer homes. The town was settled in 1789 and when incorporated 14 years later was named for John Vinal of Boston. It has a larger permanent population than North Haven because of its active granite quarries, from which came the 51- to 55-foot monoliths of the Cathedral of St. John the Divine in New York City.

DEER ISLE (1,226 pop.), on the eastern side of Penobscot Bay, is an hourglass-

MAINE

shaped area, about 12 miles in length. It has much charm but has received little development, which is a satisfaction to those who cherish its primitive character. Its permanent inhabitants are skilled boatmen, some of them having manned yachts in the international races.

ISLE AU HAUT (89 pop.), presenting a headland to the Atlantic some miles S. of Deer Isle, is the administrative headquarters of Isle au Haut Township, which contains about a dozen smaller islands. It is chiefly visited by the more hardy summer visitors. The nearby waters have been the scene of a number of wrecks.

At **29.1 m.** (L) is the LAWRENCE PORTLAND CEMENT CO. PLANT (*not open to visitors*), one of the largest of its kind in New England. The quarry is between the highway and the plant.

At **29.7 m.** (L) is a junction with State 131. On a hill close to the junction and entered from State 131 is MONTPELIER (*open daily, 10 a.m.–6 p.m., June 1–Nov. 1; adm. 50¢*), a recent reproduction of the home built in 1795 by Gen. Henry Knox (*see below*). This large, imposing two-story-and-basement structure has a low roof surrounded by a balustrade and surmounted with a monitor that rises between the four inside chimneys. The central third of the façade is elliptical and ornamented by four engaged columns; the pedimented doorway is reached by a stairway leading to a wide roofless piazza. The 18 rooms of the house are furnished with old pieces, many of them from the original structure; they also contain many relics of the general and a portrait of him by Gilbert Stuart.

THOMASTON, **30.6 m.** (100 alt.; Thomaston Town, 2,214 pop.), lying at the head of the long narrow fiord into which St. George River drains, is a favorite port of call of yachtsmen. Its main street has many attractive old homes with notable doorways. A trading post stood here in 1630 and occupation of the site was fairly continuous in spite of Indian attacks, though actual settlement did not begin until more than a hundred years later. Real development began after the Revolutionary War; Henry Knox, who had made a name for himself at the Battle of Bunker Hill, who became a trusted adviser of Washington, and who was Secretary of War both under the Confederation and during Washington's first term as President, had married a granddaughter of Samuel Waldo, proprietor of the enormous Waldo Patent (*see below*); through purchase and marriage he came into control of a large part of the patent and, at the close of his cabinet career, came to live in Thomaston, which had been incorporated in 1777. Knox made many plans for the development of his holdings, trying shipbuilding, brick making, lime burning, farming, lumbering, and many other industries, but, though an able military man, he was a poor business man. His extensive hospitality contributed to his failure to amass a fortune.

The community prospered, however, and was at one time active in shipbuilding, reaching its peak of prosperity and population about 1840, when its population was three times as large as it is today.

The plain frame CILLEY HOUSE (*private*), 25 Main St., was the home of Jonathan Cilley, a Congressional Representative from Maine when he was killed in a duel in February 1838 on the old Bladensberg duelling ground, close to the District of Columbia Line. Cilley had risen in Congress to denounce an article with a charge of immorality against another Congressman, which had appeared in an anonymous gossip column of a New York newspaper. He fastened the blame for the article on a Virginian, was challenged to a duel by William Graves, a Representative of Kentucky, and fell at the third shot.

From Thomaston there is steamship service to other coastal points as well as to Monhegan and other islands.

MAINE STATE PRISON (*visiting hours Tues. and Fri., 2:30–4 p.m.*), **31.1 m.**, on Limestone Hill and surrounded by high gray walls of field stone, has accommodations for 300 prisoners. The first, and possibly the only, military execution in Maine took place on this site when Jeremiah Braun was hanged on the charge of having guided a British raiding party that in 1780 captured Gen. Peleg Wadsworth, a grandfather of Henry Wadsworth Longfellow.

The prison site was sold to the State in 1824 by William King, Governor of Maine.

Capital punishment was abolished in Maine in 1876, reestablished in 1883, and finally abolished in 1887 at the request of the Governor, who said that it had not deterred crime.

At **31.6 m.** is a junction with State 131.

Right on State 131 is the entrance (L) to the KNOX STATE ARBORETUM and the ACADEMY OF ARTS AND SCIENCES, **1.1 m.** (*adm. free*). In the arboretum are specimen trees, shrubs, and wild flowers native to Maine. The museum, a two-story brick building, contains a collection of Maine minerals, Red Paint Indian artifacts, two fine American bird collections, and a collection of sea shells and marine life indigenous to Maine.

At **35.7 m.** is a junction with State 137.

MAINE 25

Right on State 137 is WARREN, **1.3 m.** (37 alt.; Warren Town, 1,429 pop.). In 1864, after the recovery of Mrs. Mary Baker Eddy — then Mrs. Patterson — from a serious illness under the guidance of P. P. Quimby of Portland, Me., she came to this village with another Quimby pupil, who had become much attached to her. While here she gave a number of public lectures, which she reported to the Portland healer in a series of charming letters. The title of one lecture she wrote was publicly advertised as *P. P. Quimby's Spiritual Science Healing Disease — as opposed to Deism or Rochester — Rapping Spiritualism*. Her work here is considered by some as the beginning of her career as the founder of Christian Science.

At **42.5 m.** is the junction with State 220.

Left on State 220 to WALDOBORO, **0.7 m.** (120 alt.; Waldoboro Town, 2,311 pop.), at the head of navigation on the Medomak River. It was named for Gen. Samuel Waldo, proprietor of the Waldo Patent, which included this township and many hundred thousand other acres. The settlers, who arrived in 1748, were Germans who had received special encouragement from Governor Waldo. The town at one time had considerable prestige as a shipbuilding center, the first five-masted steamer, the *Governor Ames*, having been built here.

A seasonal local industry is the catching, packing, and shipping of alewives, commonly called herring. The village also has a pearl button factory and derives considerable income from the summer tourist trade. Many local boats are hired for deep-sea fishing, the catch including cod, cusk, hake, and halibut. Fly-fishing for mackerel and pollock is popular with visitors in this area. Occasionally gamey striped bass and very large tunas are caught in nearby waters.

The GERMAN MEETING HOUSE (*open for services once a year*), on the west side of the river, was built between 1770 and 1773. The 36- by 46-foot building has a large entrance porch. Inside, a gallery overlooks a hand-made communion table and contribution boxes. The pews are unpainted. A cabinet contains a collection of old German books and mementos.

Nearby is the old GERMAN CEMETERY, with many unusual and interesting inscriptions on grave markers. One bears the following: "This town was settled in 1738 by Germans who immigrated to this place with the promise and expectation of finding a prosperous city, instead of which they found nothing but wilderness."

FRIENDSHIP, **10.1 m.** (90 alt.; Friendship Town, 742 pop.), a fishing village of small neat homes, is at the end of a peninsula. Local travel here being generally by boat, small floats or wharves appear at the ends of the side streets, which slope sharply down to the shore. Pride in the building and care of small boats is traditional in Friendship, as evidenced by the large number of well-painted craft in the bay.

In a small building on the grounds of Dr. William H. Hahn (L) is an extensive COLLECTION OF GLASSWARE (*seen at convenience of owner*), consisting of about a thousand pieces, most of which are early American lamps. Dr. Hahn also has a collection of ruby glassware and some old Roman and Turkish metal lamps.

Salt-water fishing, from both sail and motor boats, is the chief pastime in the vicinity of Friendship, the coastal waters offering many kinds of fish. Casting for mackerel has become popular, but heavy catches are often made by trolling in the early morning and in the evening; these fish are as lively and agile as trout. Cunners, excellent pan fish 12 to 15 inches in length and up to 1½ pounds in weight, are usually caught on the incoming tides, with sharp hooks on straight poles baited with worms, clams, or periwinkles. Pollock, gamey as salmon, are caught with a fly rod, by trolling bright flies in a swift current, or with herring attached to a colored spinner. The silver hake, which when fresh is one of the most satisfying foods for a hungry fisherman, can be caught from small boats near the shore.

As at other points on the Maine coast the skipper who takes parties out for deep-sea fishing is generally an entertaining fellow who knows the fish runs, as well as many fish stories; he furnishes tackle and good advice, and cooks a tasty chowder.

Clambakes, another popular diversion, can be arranged at reasonable rates, if assistance is wanted. A driftwood fire, built between granite boulders and reduced to embers, is used to steam lobsters, clams, and crabs in pails of seaweed; potatoes and corn, also cooked in seaweed, complete the menu.

GARRISON ISLAND (20 alt., Friendship Town), off the extreme southern end of the peninsula but connected with the mainland at low tide, is the site of a fort that was built about 1755.

NOBLEBORO, 48 m. (170 alt.; Nobleboro Town, 599 pop.), was part of the Pemaquid Patent and named, when incorporated in 1788, for Arthur Noble, one of the heirs of the proprietor.

Between a white house and a barn at **50.9 m.** is the junction with a dirt road.

Right on this road, which runs through a pasture to SHELL HEAPS, 0.5 m., which have been explored, leaving the strata exposed. Between the bottom layer and the second, which is approximately 6 ft. thick, is a layer of soil; in this second layer the shells are mixed with the bones of animals. The top layer, containing smaller shells, is covered with earth holding good-sized trees. The age of the heap is unknown but the bottom layer was undoubtedly deposited many centuries ago. The top deposit was made by the Abnaki Indians, who came to this region in summer to catch fish and smoke them for winter use.

DAMARISCOTTA, **52.4 m.** (30 alt.; Damariscotta Town, 825 pop.), is a tiny village on low land in a bend of the Damariscotta River.

The digging of clams, which are served extensively in the many nearby summer hotels and eating places, and are shipped away in refrigerated cars, is an important local industry. The clammers, who live in shacks near the salt water during the summer, tap along the beaches at low tide, causing the clams, disturbed by the vibrations, to spout out tiny streams of water that betray their hiding places in the mud.

MAINE

NEWCASTLE, **52.6 m.** (60 alt.; Newcastle Town, 914 pop.), is a pleasant little community with tree-shaded streets on the bank of the Damariscotta River at a point where it widens considerably. Like many southern Maine towns, Newcastle was settled early in the 17th century but the settlers, harassed by Indians, left their new homes repeatedly.

Right from Newcastle on a local road is (R), atop a hill, the KAVANAUGH MANSION (*private*), **2.6 m.**, built in 1803 and once owned by Edward Kavanaugh, acting Governor of Maine in 1843. The two-story white building has an octagonal cupola, a balustraded roof, and a fine doorway with fanlight and side lights under a semicircular portico. Although slightly altered from its original form, it retains an old-fashioned charm.

ST. PATRICK'S ROMAN CATHOLIC CHURCH (*open*), **2.8 m.** (R), was built 1803–1808 and dedicated by Father Jean de Cheverus (1768–1836), who in 1808 became the first Roman Catholic bishop of New England. Bishop Cheverus came to America from France in 1796 and did some work among the Indians of the Maine coast. In the final year of his life, after his return to France, he was made a cardinal.

This thick-walled old church has a 250-year-old altarpiece from France. Some of its paintings were taken from a Mexican convent during the Mexican War. The present altar is of the sarcophagus type, unusual in the United States; in the chancel is the original altar.

WISCASSET (Ind., *meeting of three rivers*), **60 m.** (50 alt.; Wiscasset Town, 1,186 pop.), seat of Lincoln Co., is a ghost town with little more than half the population it had in 1850, when it was still a fairly important port on the west bank of the wide Sheepscot River. Its beautiful old homes, most of which were built by shipping merchants and sea captains, are now occupied in part by artists and writers who have been attracted by the distinctive charm of the place. Until 1802 the town, formerly much larger in area than it now is, was called Pownalborough in honor of Royal Governor Pownal. Settlement began here in the middle of the 17th century but the place was abandoned during King Philip's War and was not again occupied until 1730.

Open House Day is held annually in August, the funds going to the support of the town library. On this day the beautifully furnished old homes, some occupied by descendants of the original owners and others by summer residents, are opened to the public (*adm. $2*), and collections of old and new craft work are displayed.

The WILLIAM NICKELS HOUSE (1807–08), corner of Main and Fort Sts., one of the largest mansions of its period in Wiscasset, is a massive three-story structure with a one-story entrance portico, Corinthian pilasters, a long central Palladian window in the second story, and a large semicircular window above it interpolated between the square windows on each side in the third story. This unfortunate arrangement of windows is a characteristic central motif of the façade in houses on the Maine coast. The inharmonious railing above the portico is a later addition (c. 1890). An interesting variation in the detail of the main cornice is the omission of the modillions and the use of a double row of dentils in their place. The main portal with its elliptical fan light and elaborately mullioned side lights is particularly notable for slender pilasters and delicately carved transom rail and architrave. The face of the pilasters is carved in herringbone pattern.

The ABIEL WOOD HOUSE (1812), corner of High and Lee Sts., is almost a duplicate of the Nickels House. The Wood House, however, has greater distinction because of the more pleasing proportions of its Palladian window, and the lack of such superficial embellishments as the Corinthian pilasters.

The CLAPP HOUSE, or Lilac Cottage, on US 1 opposite the Common, is an old story-and-a-half structure of unknown date, now painted white with green shutters. The front yard, which is fragrant with lilacs in the spring, is enclosed by a picket fence.

The LINCOLN COUNTY COURTHOUSE (1824), on the Common, contains a jail that was at one time a State prison. This building, the oldest in which court is still held in Maine, at one time resounded with the rolling periods of Daniel Webster.

The LEE-PAYSON-SMITH HOUSE, High St. opposite the library, is still owned by the descendants of Samuel E. Smith, Governor of Maine (1831–34). It was erected in the early 19th century and admirably illustrates the skill of the carpenter-architects of the day and their sensitive appreciation of classic detail executed in wood. The distinctive charm of this square, two-story frame house, with its clapboard front, brick ends, hip-roof topped with a captain's walk, and low service wings, is found in its refinement of detail and its subtle proportions, which attain an almost monumental quality. Perhaps the most notable feature of the exterior is the fine modillioned and dentiled cornices, both on the main section of the house and on the ells at the side; its thin acute-angle profile, combined with the low pitch of the roof, gives an effect of singular grace and delicacy. The

Ionic pilasters, placed at some distance from the corners of the main façade, are carved in somewhat heavier detail. The open railing around the captain's walk, suggesting a Chippendale pattern, is well proportioned to the mass of the house.

In the TOWN LIBRARY (*open weekdays 2–5:30 p.m.*), High St., is a very old piece of fire apparatus, a hand-drawn affair, equipped with two leather buckets, two cotton bags for use in carrying small articles from burning buildings, and a bed key for unfastening beds preparatory to their removal. The Wiscasset Fire Society, organized in 1801, though no longer active in a fire-fighting capacity, has maintained many of its old-time rules and regulations, and members are still fined 10¢ if they are absent from meetings.

The TUCKER MANSION, or Tucker Castle, E. end of High St., built in 1807, is of curious architecture; it is said to be a copy of a castle in Dunbar, Scotland. The piazza was added in 1860. Inside, a slender spiral staircase with mahogany balustrades rises in the center of the hall. Patience Tucker Stapleton, daughter of a sea captain and author of *Trailing Yew* and other stories, lived here in her youth.

1. From the eastern end of Wiscasset an improved, unnumbered road branches S. NORTH EDGECOMB, **0.8 m.** (50 alt., Edgecomb Town), is a small settlement of white houses, with lawns extending to the tree-shaded bank of the Sheepscot.

Opposite the post office, on the high riverbank is (L) the MARIE ANTOINETTE HOUSE (*visited at convenience of owner*). This structure, built in 1774 by Capt. Joseph Decker on Squam Island, from which it was much later brought to this spot, was inherited by Decker's daughter, the wife of Samuel Clough, captain of a merchantman that frequently visited France. In 1793 the captain became engaged in an enterprise, the details of which are somewhat obscure. According to tradition, he was moved by the unfortunate situation of the imprisoned Queen of France to attempt her rescue with the aid of her friends; it seems clear, however, that he was merely hired by them to carry her to America on the *Sally* when they had managed to effect her release. Some of her personal belongings and various articles that her friends thought might make her home in exile more comfortable and furnish it in a style befitting her rank, were smuggled aboard the Yankee ship. The plan, however, like others with the same purpose, failed; the Queen was beheaded and Captain Clough set sail hastily to escape possible punishment for his share in the enterprise.

In the meantime the captain had written to his wife to give her warning of the guest she might expect to have for a time, carefully trying to reconcile her to the dismaying idea of sheltering royalty. He doubtless found his home polished and shining when he at last arrived — without the Queen. The captain stored the Queen's possessions in his home; some thought this was because of a personal devotion to her, but it seems more likely that his Yankee conscience made him uneasy about his right to dispose of the goods that had come into his possession in such an irregular manner. Gradually, as time passed and no one came to claim the cargo, the furnishings came into use in the large, plain, square house, now standing in North Edgecomb. Many stories are told of their later uses and wanderings. It is said that a satin robe, worn by the King of France on state occasions, was in time made into a dress by Mrs. Clough. A Wiscasset clockmaker discovered in the interior of an old clock a plate inscribed in French indicating that the timepiece had been presented by the maker to the Queen on the Dauphin's birthday. Other mementos are at the Metropolitan Museum of Art in New York; a few articles still remain in the Clough house.

There is a legend that Talleyrand and Marie Antoinette's son, the Dauphin of France, were passengers on the return voyage of the *Sally* and that both were guests at the Clough house for some time.

2. Right from Wiscasset on State 218 to (L) the old ALNA MEETING HOUSE 7.1 m. (*apply at Walker House, next door, for admission*). The original hand-hewn shingles are in place on two of the weather-beaten sides of this old structure, which was built in 1789, and on the north side are the original clapboards, shiplapped at the northeastern corner against the storms. Curiously designed handwrought foot scrapers grace the sides of the doorstep. The interior woodwork is very well preserved; the box pews, with carved spindles, seated nearly five hundred people. The raised hourglass pulpit, with a winding flight of steps and finely molded handrail, is paneled in contrasting dark and light wood; above the pulpit is an octagonal bell-shaped canopy and sounding board, and behind it a long arched window flanked by fluted pilasters. The pulpit, with an arrangement for accommodating ministers of different heights, has been used by many men of varying oratorical talents since Parson Wood, the first minister, preached of fire and brimstone and fought in vain against the introduction of instrumental music.

HEAD TIDE, 10 m. (40 alt., Alna Town), a tiny village consisting of a few homes, one store, a church, and a sawmill, lies on both sides of the bridge that crosses the Sheepscot River. The second house (L) on the road beyond the store is the BIRTHPLACE OF EDWIN ARLINGTON ROBINSON (1869–1935).

At **64.6 m.** is the junction with Montsweag Road, which is unmarked and in poor condition.

Left on this road, at **4.4 m.**, is a view of HOCKOMOCK BAY with its several islands.

At PHIPPS POINT, **4.8 m.** (R), on a private estate, is the SITE OF SIR WILLIAM PHIPS' HOME. Phips was born in Maine in 1651 of a poverty-stricken family and worked as a shepherd and ship carpenter until he was 25, when he went to sea; he learned to read and write in Boston and decided to make his fortune by treasure hunting, managing in 1683 to receive a commission from the English Crown for the recovery of treasure in a ship sunk off the Bahamas. He was successful in this enterprise, receiving 16,000 pounds sterling and a knighthood as his reward. He next commanded an expedition that captured Port Royal without difficulty but his second expedition to Canada failed. Through the wirepulling of Cotton

Mather he was appointed Royal Governor of Massachusetts; he lacked, however, the tact and education to enable him to cope with the problems that confronted him and became involved in difficulties resulting in his recall to England. He died there in 1695 during an investigation of the charges against him.

NEQUASSET MEETING HOUSE, **67.7 m.** (R), the oldest meeting house E. of the Kennebec River, was built in 1757. Here Josiah Winship, the first permanent pastor, was ordained in 1765, when there were but 20 families and only two frame houses in the settlement.

WOOLWICH, **69.1 m.** (30 alt.; Woolwich Town, 671 pop.), is on the east bank of the Kennebec River opposite the city of Bath. Shipbuilding and fishing for shad and sturgeon were the early industries, now replaced by farming, dairying, and orcharding. The canning of corn, peas, and beans is here rapidly increasing in volume.

Right from Woolwich on State 127 to the APPLETON DAY HOUSE, **3 m.** (R), built in 1777 on the site of the Samuel Harnden blockhouse. It is a two-and-a-half-story frame house with a fireplace in each room. The chimneys and fireplaces are constructed of locally made bricks. There are three cellars under this house; legend has it that an underground passageway extending from the cellars to the river was built for use in times of Indian attack.

US 1 crosses CARLTON BRIDGE (*toll 50¢*), built in 1927, which spans the Kennebec River. The bridge commands a sweeping view of the river, waterfront, and city.

The Kennebec is one of the historic rivers of America. It was one of the earliest explored routes on the coast of North America; various adventurers had made fragmentary reports on it before 1600, and Champlain and Weymouth had explored it to some extent before 1606. It was named as one of the boundaries of various large land grants in the race between the French and the British for control of the continent. In the middle of August 1607 George Popham and Raieigh Gilbert, commanding the expedition prompted by Sir Fernando Gorges and Sir John Popham, sailed up the river, passing the place now spanned by the bridge in their search for a site for the colony that was to send fur, sassafras, and other commodities back to England to make fortunes for the London investors. Two decades later it saw a steady stream of traffic to and from the trading settlement on the site of the present Augusta conducted by the "Undertakers" of Plymouth; the rich cargoes that came down its waters saved the Massachusetts settlement from extinction. Since that time the river has been the scene of continuous activity, of log-drives, ship launchings, commercial travel, power development, and, not least important, hunters' and fishermen's treks.

BATH, **70.3 m.** (50 alt., 9,110 pop.), named for the ancient city of Bath, England, has a history of almost two centuries of shipbuilding, though its yards turn out comparatively few vessels today. Its heyday was in the wooden-ship era, though the first steel sailing vessel, a four-master, was built here. Naturally, many of its inhabitants have been shipmasters and shipowners, and the older homes are filled with souvenirs from distant parts of the earth — printed Indian linens, teakwood chests, blue and white ginger jars from Canton, and strangely shaped sea shells — and still have a faint odor of sandalwood, camphor, and spice. During the World War the local yards were active again, attracting several thousand workmen, but the revival was temporary. The chief event in local life, however, is still the launching of a new craft; and the townspeople follow the histories of Bath ships with pride.

BATH IRONWORKS (*visited by permit*), in the center of the city at Union and Water Sts. below the Carlton Bridge, was founded by Gen. Thomas Hyde after his return from the Civil War. Some fairly large and many small Government vessels have been built here, including the battleship *Georgia*, cruisers, and lighthouse tenders. Many fine yachts have also come from this plant.

Nearby are other shipbuilding works that can make any but the largest vessels.

The new DAVENPORT MEMORIAL BUILDING, Front St., housing the Bath municipal offices, has in its tower a bell cast in 1805 at the Paul Revere foundry. The DAVENPORT MEMORIAL MUSEUM in the building contains ship paintings, original half-models from which were built famous Kennebec merchantmen and vessels launched in other Maine ports, and many exhibits of importance in Maine marine history.

In the beautifully landscaped CITY PARK, on Front St., is a cannon taken from the British man-of-war *Somerset*, which was "swinging wide at her moorings" in Boston Harbor when Paul Revere made his ride. The cannon was used for the firing of salutes at Bath until the latter part of the 19th century.

The APARTMENT HOUSE, 3 North St., corner of Front St., formerly a rather pretentious old home, was between 1915 and 1924 occupied by Madame Emma Eames (1867), the operatic star, and her husband, Emilio de Gogorza, the baritone.

SHILOH, MAINE

"WEDDING CAKE HOUSE," MAINE

MAINE 33

The home of Herbert L. Spinney (*open*), 75 Court St., houses a COLLECTION OF NATIVE FLORA AND FAUNA. Mr. Spinney was associated with the Smithsonian Institution for many years.

Right from Bath on Washington St., at **1.6 m.** and opposite Harward St., is the old PETERSON HOUSE, on the river bank. The place is an architectural curiosity that was built (1770) by ship carpenters for the King's timber agent. The mass of the building is broad at the base and narrow at the top; the door jambs, windows, and window frames follow the lines of the house. The front lawn is the site of the dock at which were loaded the tree trunks that had been marked with a "broad arrow," indicating that they were sacred to the Royal Navy. These trees were intended for masts and were at least 24 inches in diameter. The resentment of the people of Maine against the commandeering of their best mast pines was one of the causes of the revolt that became a revolution.

Right from Washington St. on Harward St.; at **1.8 m.** is the junction with High St.; L. here to Whiskeag Rd.; R. on the latter to (R) the STONE HOUSE **2.1 m.** (*private*), a structure with cathedral-like doors and windows that was erected in 1805 and became the home of Maine's first Governor (1820), William King. It is said to have been built as a hunting lodge by some Englishmen.

BRUNSWICK, **79.3 m.** (30 alt.; Brunswick Town, 6,144 pop.), old port (*see MAINE GUIDE*).

Points of Interest. Gilman Mansion, Emmons House, Pejepscot Historical Museum, Bowdoin College, and others.

Section 4. Brunswick to New Hampshire Line, 76.9 m.

South of Brunswick US 1 runs through pleasant farmlands broken occasionally by pine groves, with open ocean (L) never far distant and often visible across wide stretches of marshland. Side routes branch (L) to historic and scenic spots on coastal peninsulas where the inhabitants are for the most part descendants of early fishermen and seamen, gaining their livelihoods by catering to the summer colonists and tourists.

At **8 m.** is the junction with a dirt road.

Right on this road is SHILOH, **10 m.**, which has received national attention from time to time as the home of the Holy Ghost and Us Society, a religious sect with Adventist beliefs, founded by the Reverend Frank W. Sandford, the Elijah of the early 1900's.

Sandford's cult brought converts from many parts of the world to pour their money into a common fund. Men and women sold their worldly possessions and turned the proceeds over to him. The colony flourished for a time, practicing various crafts. When the world did not end as he had predicted after ordering a ceaseless night-and-day vigil of prayer in the high tower on the main building,

Sandford announced that the Almighty had commissioned him to go forth and convert the heathen. When he prayed for means to accomplish this, a $10,000 check appeared; he purchased a 150-ton sailing vessel, the *Coronet*, and set sail from Portland Harbor with a flowing beard, purple robe, sailor hat, and Bible. Several voyages were made without noticeable results. During the last voyage, in 1912, after many hardships and privations, eight members of the party died of scurvy; when the ship returned to Portland Harbor, Sandford had trouble with the authorities. When he came back to Shiloh two years later he found his old power gone and his people scattered; he subsequently dropped from sight. The buildings (*services at noon Sun.*), on a high, windswept hill, are unusual. The square, hip-roof three-story MAIN STRUCTURE (*see illustration*), on a high foundation, has a large five-story tower on its front, each story of the tower containing a large room and the top floor having protruding bay windows on each side; the tower is surmounted with a high-domed cupola supported by very slender columns. Between the main building and two-story, towered wings are three-story ornamental gateways with arched doors. Broad piazzas with balustrades on the roofs surround the three buildings.

In 1936, after many years of neglect, the place was repaired and the towers regilded. A small group of cultists lives here but does not welcome curious visitors. When rumors reached Portland of renewed activities under the leadership of Sandford's son and of the reconditioning of the *Coronet*, reporters were sent to investigate; the residents refused to answer questions.

Services are held in a well-carpeted room seating 200. During prayer all persons kneel with elbows on chairs, various members introducing the prayers as called upon by the speaker. While visitors are now invited to these services, none can inspect other buildings on the grounds at any time.

FREEPORT, **8.9 m.** (140 alt.; Freeport Town, 2,184 pop.), a pleasant, tree-shaded old village, is often referred to as the Birthplace of Maine, because the final papers for the separation of Maine from Massachusetts, which established it in 1820 as an independent State, were signed here by commissioners from Massachusetts and the Province of Maine, probably in JAMESON'S TAVERN (1779), just N. of the post office (R).

When Freeport was incorporated in 1789 it was named for Sir Andrew Freeport, the character in Addison's *Spectator Papers* who represented the London merchant class. There was a time when Freeport had a prosperous shipbuilding business, but it is now engaged in shoemaking, crabbing, and crab-meat packing. The crab meat, picked from the shells by groups of young women, is shipped in iced cartons.

Freeport, like almost every other old town along this coast, has its story of an Indian attack. In 1756 Thomas Means, living near Flying Point, was surprised in his bed and scalped; his wife and infant son were killed by a single bullet; two other children crept into hiding and escaped. The Indians took Mrs. Means' sister Mary with them to Canada, where she became a housemaid in the home of one of the French feudal lords. She was later rescued by William McLellan, whom she married.

Left from Freeport on a dirt road to an old CEMETERY, **0.6 m.**, the burial place of many sea captains and seamen of the area.

PORTER'S LANDING, **1.2 m.**, the commercial center in Freeport's shipping days, is now a dignified residential section in which the old homes have been entirely modernized.

At **2.7 m.** is a four corners in SOUTH FREEPORT, the street (L) leading to the village center. South Freeport, at the mouth of Harraseeket River on Freeport Harbor, which is navigable throughout the year, has been a fishing center from its earliest day, assuming its greatest importance between 1825 and 1830, when as many as 12,000 barrels of mackerel were packed and shipped annually. Of late it has specialized in crab-meat packing. In 1878 the *John A. Briggs*, one of the largest wooden vessels built on the Maine coast up to that time, was launched here.

Beyond the four corners are the RUINS OF CASCO CASTLE, once a picturesque summer hotel modeled after a medieval stronghold. The tower, all that remains of the hotel, which was burned in 1904, is a round solid structure of field stone about 80 ft. high with walls 3 ft. thick. Standing on an eminence overlooking the bay, it has long been a landmark for fishermen.

At **10.1 m.** is the junction with a local road.

Right on this road to the DESERT OF MAINE (*adm. 25¢*), **2 m.**, covering 300 acres and surrounded by forests and green farmlands. This miniature Sahara, not unusual in coastal areas, is an example of the worst type of soil erosion.

The first patch of sand, noticed in the latter part of the 19th century, was about 30 ft. sq. The sand stratum is present around the 300-acre (1937) area for a radius of six miles. In this circle a top layer of loam is either being covered or worn by frequent sandstorms. Some geologists believe the spot covers the bed of an ancient lake, perhaps formed by glacial deposits, for a glint of mica is apparent in the sand, which is very fine in texture. Sandstorms constantly raise and lower the desert level as the erosion creeps outward, the sand covering everything in its path, creating 30-ft. gullies and high dunes. The tops of trees once 70 ft. high appear as bushes, and strangely enough are still alive. Among them is an apple tree that still blossoms and bears fruit.

At **14.6 m.** is the junction with State 115.

Right on this road is YARMOUTH, **0.4 m.** (80 alt.; Yarmouth Town, 2,125 pop.). This seaport town on Casco Bay was settled in 1658, laid waste by Indians in 1673, and resettled in 1713. Fishing and crab-meat packing are the major industries, which have supplanted the shipping and shipbuilding of the 19th century.

NORTH YARMOUTH ACADEMY, on Main St., was founded in 1810.

At **15.5 m.** (L) in the Westcustogo neighborhood (Ind., *clear tidal river*) is a BURIAL GROUND dating back to 1732. Just beyond is a group of three large old houses. The most southerly of the houses is on the SITE OF THE ROYALL GARRISON HOUSE, part of the property purchased by William Royall in 1643. The house behind it stands on the SITE OF THE FIRST CHURCH OF YARMOUTH, built in 1729. The third house (1769) is on the SITE OF THE LORING GARRISON of the 17th century.

FALMOUTH FORESIDE, **19.8 m.** (100 alt.; Falmouth Town, 2,041 pop.), is a residential section of fine homes in an agricultural town on the shores of Casco Bay.

UNDERWOOD SPRING (L), now exploited as a private commercial enterprise, is a natural curiosity, for though it has no perceptible source, it has a large flow of pure water unaffected by drought or freshet. The Abnaki Indians maintained a permanent settlement here, and Waymouth, the English explorer, wrote in his journal that the Indians allowed him to fill his casks at this spring.

Along the route here is an exceptional panoramic view (L) of Casco Bay and its islands.

At **21.8 m.** (R) is a marker indicating the nearby SITE OF FORT NEW CASCO, which, erected in 1698, was also a trading post. The Indians of Maine had at first been very friendly with the English; it was only after they had been repeatedly betrayed, insulted, cheated, and assaulted that they became hostile and vengeful. The French, who managed their relations more amicably, soon won the friendship of the Indians and determined to use them in their efforts to drive the English from American shores. Maine, part of the territory that the French claimed longest, was particularly subject to attack. In 1703 a conference was held with the Indians at Fort New Casco and the settlers hoped for safer times; but within two months another attack came and the fort was the center of defense for the settlements of Casco Bay. The attack of a large force of Frenchmen and Indians was repulsed only by the arrival of an armed vessel. The fort was abandoned in 1716, when Massachusetts thought it was no longer necessary to maintain a garrison here.

The attractive castellated stone edifice (L) is the Episcopal CHURCH OF ST. MARY THE VIRGIN; directly opposite is FALMOUTH TOWN FOREST, a well-kept grove of old pine trees.

MAINE

PORTLAND, **27.7 m.** (80 alt., 70,810 pop.), largest city in Maine (*see MAINE GUIDE*).

Points of Interest. Longfellow Birthplace, Sweat Memorial Art Museum, City Hall with Municipal Organ, Wadsworth House, and others.

From Portland there are steamer trips to the various islands of CASCO BAY (Ind., *place of herons*), on which the city lies. The bay was visited by most of the explorers who came along this coast shortly after 1600; all were attracted to it because of the safe anchorage offered by its deep waters and because the islands gave them places to land where they felt reasonably safe from the inhabitants of the country, on whom they looked with some fear. The islands are now frequented by summer visitors. Some are fairly large, some mere dots on the water. On them hang countless legends of castaways, buried treasures, shipwrecks, and Indian gods. Many of the islands bear homely names given by the pioneers, who displayed considerable imagination in finding resemblances to objects and animals in the rough profiles — Ram, Horse, Sow and Pigs, the Goslings, Turnip, and Whaleboat are among them. Others have names derived from events that took place on them, or from animals inhabiting them.

The first settlement in the bay took place in 1623, when Capt. Christopher Levett erected a stone house, probably on YORK ISLAND, formerly known as House Island.

JEWELL ISLAND, one of the outermost, acquired by George Jewell in 1636, has the usual legend of treasure buried on it by Captain Kidd. Treasure seekers, ignorant of the fact that Kidd never visited this part of the coast, tried every possible device to find the gold and jewels they believed to be there, sacrificing animals, using divining rods, and invoking the help of demented people they believed to have second sight. Legends have grown up about the activities of the persistent diggers; one concerns a mysterious stranger who appeared, asking for the help of a skipper residing there. The visitor disappeared without anyone's having seen him leave the island and shortly afterward the captain showed evidence of great wealth; curious neighbors announced that they had seen the imprints of a large chest near a newly dug hole and a later treasure hunter reported the finding of a buried skeleton nearby.

CLIFF ISLAND was the home of men who were accused of luring ships onto the rocks, in order to wreck them.

ORR'S ISLAND, accessible from State 24, S. of Brunswick, was the scene of Harriet Beecher Stowe's story *The Pearl of Orr's Island;* Mrs. Stowe's former home stands on a hill near the ferry landing.

EAGLE ISLAND, on the outer rim of the bay, was owned by Admiral Robert E. Peary, who made his home on its stony acres for many years.

Large PEAKS ISLAND, near Portland and a favorite resort of residents of that city, has various amusement devices; a number of Portland people have year-round homes here.

BAILEY ISLAND, S. of Orr's Island, was the summer home of Clara Louise Burnham of Chicago, who wrote a number of stories about the area.

At **29.3 m.** US 1 crosses Fore River, the southern boundary of Portland, on Vaughan's Bridge. Here huge oil and gas tanks line the highway on both sides of the river, which separates Portland and South Portland.

The NONESUCH RIVER, **32 m.**, so named for its remarkably crooked course to the sea, figured prominently in the affairs of Scarboro settlers and is mentioned in many early histories. Because it was impossible to bring boats of any size up this sharply winding tidal river, a canal was constructed, to follow the general course of the river. Instead of digging the entire canal by hand, the workers made a narrow ditch along the proposed course. The action of the tides carried away the loose soil, finally completing a project that would have required much back-breaking toil. Near the highway bridge, fishermen congregate in May for the annual run of alewives.

At **32.6 m.** is the old PLUMMER HOUSE (*private*), set back with its side facing the street. It is a one-and-a-half-story, gable-end house with a central chimney.

At **33.7 m.** is OAK HILL (100 alt., Scarboro Town).

Left from Oak Hill on State 207 to (R) the HUNNEWELL HOUSE (1684), **0.7 m.** (*private*), known as the Old Red House. It stands in a "heater piece", a triangular plot of ground at a junction of roads, so called in early days when snow-removal equipment, which included a heater, was stored there. The timbers of this small one-and-a-half-story lean-to dwelling are hand-hewn and wooden pegged. A trap door in the living room floor leads to the shallow dugout used as a hiding place during Indian raids.

At **1.2 m.** is SCARBORO (20 alt.; Scarboro Town, 2,445 pop.). Most of the houses in this small village were built and are inhabited by seafaring men. The FIRST PARISH CONGREGATIONAL CHURCH (R), on the site of one built in 1728, is an attractive little white structure with a fan window in the front, and a belfry and spire.

The PARSON LANCASTER HOUSE (*private*), **1.5 m.** on State 207, is a two-and-a-half-story unpainted dwelling with two huge elms in its front yard; it was built in 1766. Interesting architectural features include wide roof boards, single board wainscoting, white (pumpkin) pine paneling, HL hinges, hand-wrought latches, knobs, and locks, fireplaces with hand-carved woodwork, and a staircase with delicate balustrade. The floors, ceilings, and unpainted woodwork have the patina of age.

In the BLACK POINT CEMETERY, **1.7 m.** (L), the dark gray slate stones date back to 1739.

At **3 m.** is the junction with a road (L) that leads to the popular bathing resort, HIGGINS BEACH.

The private BLACK POINT GAME PRESERVE AND FARM, **3.7 m.** (R) on State 207, lies opposite the BLACK POINT FRUIT FARM, which has fine orchards. Small game such as partridge, pheasant, and rabbit roam unmolested in the small wooded preserve set aside by local residents.

MAINE

MASSACRE POND, visible (L) at **4.1 m.**, was so named because in 1713 Richard Hunnewell and 19 companions were set upon near here and slain by a band of 200 Indians.

Opposite the pond is the fairway of the PROUT'S NECK COUNTRY CLUB GOLF COURSE (*private*). At the seventh hole is a marker on the site of the first Anglican church in Maine, erected prior to 1658.

At GARRISON COVE, **4.8 m.**, the road emerges from the woods to a cliff from which is a splendid view of the bay with the white sands of Old Orchard Beach gleaming in the distance.

A marker at **5.2 m.** (R) indicates the spot where Chief Mogg Heigon, subject of Whittier's poem, *Mogg Megone*, was slain in 1677. This marker is at the eastern end of beautiful Garrison Cove on the site of Josselyn (or Scottow) Fort, a headquarters for defense in the first Indian war. Directly ahead is BLACK POINT, its rugged shore line sweeping westward toward Old Orchard Beach.

The PROUT'S NECK YACHT CLUBHOUSE, **5.1 m.** (R) on the ledges of the point, commands a wide view of the Atlantic.

Left of the highway is a path leading to the PROUT'S NECK BIRD SANCTUARY, given to Scarboro by Charles Homer in memory of his brother, Winslow Homer, the artist.

PROUT'S NECK, **5.5 m.** (40 alt., Scarboro Town), is a pretentious summer settlement. Left is the SITE OF A BLOCKHOUSE where in 1703 eight men under Capt. John Larrabee for several days withstood a siege by 500 French and Indian marauders.

In 1633 Thomas Cammock and his wife Margaret moved from Richmond's Island to Prout's Neck, then called Black Point. Here they were joined by Henry Josselyn and for a short time, in 1638, by his brother, John Josselyn. John's accounts of his visit, published as *New England Rarities* and elsewhere, repeat stories of sea serpents, witches' revels, and of a merman or triton that appeared in Casco Bay till Mr. Mitten chopped off its hand to prevent it from upsetting his canoe. Josselyn included a description of the native flora and of the Indians remarking, "There are many stranger things in the world than are to be seen between London and Stanes."

At **35 m.** (L) is the DANISH VILLAGE, a tourist camp with cabins patterned after the colorful little homes of a medieval Danish town, grouped about the *raadhus* (town hall). Architectural details have been faithfully copied in the hall, where meals are served, as well as in the individual cabins.

At **35.1 m.** is the junction with a dirt road.

Right on this road to SCOTTOW'S HILL. The first stagecoach road from Boston passed over this steep summit to avoid the marshes near the coast. At **0.6 m.** is the KING HOMESTEAD, a two-story gable-end house with a long shed at one end.

The highway crosses SCARBORO MARSHES, where underlying quicksands have caused great difficulties in road construction. Asphalt paving has been used because the surface invariably settles several inches within a few months after being repaired. In former days large crops of salt-marsh hay were gathered on the hundreds of acres of marshland bordering the shore S. of Portland. Seven-by-ten-inch oak slabs were fastened to the hoofs of the horses used in haying to keep them from sinking into the ground. Protected by game laws, plover, duck, and gulls feed uninterruptedly on the marshes where they were formerly hunted.

At DUNSTAN, **36.7 m.** (50 alt., Scarboro Town), is the ST. LOUIS SCHOOL FOR BOYS, conducted by the Sisters of Charity. Large residences in this vicinity have been converted into tourist homes and inns that advertise "New England shore dinners" — steamed and fried clams, lobster stew, and boiled and broiled lobster.

At SACO (*pron. So'ko*), **42.4 m.** (60 alt., 7,233 pop.), is the CYRUS KING HOUSE, 271 Main St., now the rectory of the Holy Trinity Roman Catholic Church. The house was built in 1807 by Cyrus King, member of the Scarboro family, which produced the first Governor of Maine. A later occupant of the house was Horace Woodman, the inventor, who in 1854 devised the self-stripping cotton card and many other textile manufacturing appliances.

Lyman Beecher Stowe, the author who is a grandson of Harriet Beecher Stowe, was born in Saco when his father was minister of the FIRST CONGREGATIONAL CHURCH, corner Beach and Main Sts.

YORK INSTITUTE, 375 Main St. (*open weekdays 1–4 p.m.*), a small brick building erected in 1928, contains a collection of Colonial costumes and furniture, paintings, statuary, Maine minerals, Indian relics, and historical documents.

THORNTON ACADEMY, 438 Main St., a coeducational school of high standing in general preparatory courses, was founded in 1811 and now has 200 students.

BIDDEFORD, **43.3 m.** (80 alt., 17,633 pop.), is united historically, industrially, and socially with its twin city, on the opposite bank of the Saco River. As a unit, the two cities rank second in industrial importance in Maine; Biddeford is the industrial part of the union, Saco being predominantly residential. The population, strongly Franco-American, is employed in the three large textile and textile-machinery mills and the several smaller manufactories.

As far as is known, Richard Vines was in charge of the first company of Englishmen to explore the site of Saco; he had been sent out from England in 1616 by Gorges, the most enthusiastic of the English

MAINE

promoters of settlement at the time, and others whom Gorges had interested in the enterprise. In 1629 Saco was granted to Thomas Lewis and Richard Bonython, and a permanent settlement was made shortly thereafter.

It is said that about 1675 some drunken sailors, rowing in the river and seeing an Indian woman and her infant in a canoe nearby, determined to test a legend they had heard to the effect that Indian offspring swam from birth by instinct. They overturned the canoe; while the woman reached shore safely, the child died a few days later as the result of the experience. Unfortunately for the settlers, the child was the son of Squando, an Indian leader, who executed terrible revenge on the whites.

The PEPPERELL MANUFACTURING CO. PLANT, 170 Main St. (*visited by permit*), an industry established in 1845, occupies an area of 56 acres and manufactures nationally advertised cotton products.

The SACO-LOWELL CO. PLANT, off Main on Smith St. (*visited by permit*), has built textile machinery for more than 100 years.

The YORK MANUFACTURING CO. PLANT, Main St. on Factory Island between Biddeford and Saco (*visited by permit*), also manufactures textiles.

The LAFAYETTE HOUSE, 20 Elm St., is a square, yellow, three-story house with a hip roof. It is on the property of the Diamond Match Co., which conducts many kinds of woodworking at this plant.

Between Biddeford and Kennebunk US 1 for a few miles follows the post road established for early mail carriers.

KENNEBUNK, **51.9 m.** (20 alt.; Kennebunk Town, 3,302 pop.), is notable for its fine elms. The town, settled about 1650, was for nearly a century in almost constant dread of attack by Indians. By 1730 shipbuilding had begun along the Mousam River. This industry and an active trade with the West Indies made Kennebunk a town of importance until the beginning of the Revolutionary War. Soon after the Revolution the Mousam River was again utilized in the development of industry. Small mills sprang up along its banks; shoes, twine, and lumber are still manufactured here. Kennebunk has one of the few municipally owned light and power plants in the State.

The FIRST PARISH UNITARIAN CHURCH, at the northern entrance to Kennebunk village, was built in 1774 and remodeled in 1803.

The fine steeple has a three-story tower with front windows and a top in three stages; the first stage is an open belfry, the second has a four-faced clock, and the third is an octagonal lantern cupola with elliptical openings. In 1803 a bell cast in the Paul Revere foundry was placed in the steeple.

The STORER HOUSE (*private*), on Storer St., was the home of Gen. Joseph Storer, Revolutionary soldier and friend of Lafayette. This large yet simple structure is representative of the excellent taste in home building that characterized the post-Revolutionary period.

Kenneth Roberts, author of *Northwest Passage* and other popular historical novels, was born in this house. Just beyond is the huge, spreading LAFAYETTE ELM, under which the French hero stood during the reception given in his honor in 1825 by the people of Kennebunk. The tree has grown so large that it has been necessary to prop up several of its massive limbs.

The BOURNE MANSION (1815), on Bourne St. (*private*), is a square three-story structure with four chimneys, two at each end of the building. The principal entrance, facing the garden, has a fanlight of thick leaded glass, a motif that is repeated above in the second-story window. Outstanding features of the interior are the curved staircase and the fine paneled fireplaces.

FIVE ELMS, on Main St. near Fletcher St., are believed to have been set out on the day of the Battle of Lexington. Directly back of the fourth elm is the NATHANIEL FROST HOUSE, one of many fine homes built by prosperous merchants and shipowners in the town's period of greatest affluence.

Left from Kennebunk on State 35 at **0.1 m.** is the ROBERT LORD HOUSE (1800–1803), similar in formality and dignity to the Sewell House, of the same period, in York. It is a massive, two-story, rectangular structure with a low hip roof and parapet rail. The symmetrical façade is finished with carefully matched siding simulating stone, and is broken by the lines of slender Doric pilasters, by a slightly projecting central pavilion with crowning gable pediment, and by a narrow belt course at the second-floor level. The elliptical fanlight of the entrance doorway and its dark louvred shutters are repeated in a large sentinel window in the pediment. In the second story is a triple rectangular window, its sections separated by slender paneled pilasters. The wall openings are framed with an unusually fine trim. The design of the parapet rail, though a trifle light in the absence of the usual corner posts, is notable for its delicately turned balusters. An older house (c.1767) forms a rear wing.

The TAYLOR HOUSE (1795–1797), adjoining the Lord House, is notable for its three exterior entrances. Of similar proportions and detail, these doorways are designed with flanking pilasters, semicircular fanlights, and crowning pediments. The interior is decorated with unusually fine putty-stucco ornament — a characteristic medium of the period used in simulating carved ornament on flat surfaces.

At **0.6 m.** is the junction with a tarred road.

Right here **1 m.** to a field road leading to a granite monument marking the SITE OF THE LARRABEE GARRISON HOUSE (1720), overlooking Mousam River. A bronze bas-relief on the monument depicts the garrison within whose walls were five houses.

On State 35 at **1.2 m.** is the yellow brick WEDDING CAKE HOUSE (*private*), one of the most extraordinary relics of the scroll-saw era extant. The house (*see illustration*), apparently built some time before the decorations were added, is a square, two-story structure of good proportions with a central doorway and, above, a graceful Palladian window. At the corners have been added series of slim, elaborately ornamented wooden pinnacles that rise several feet above the low roof; these are duplicated on each side of the entrance and, in miniature, in front of a trellised canopy over the steps that lead to the doorway. In between these pinnacles at the tops of the first and second stories, has been suspended an elaborate tracery, raised to Gothic peaks over the entrance canopy and the Palladian window; the effect is that of the paper lace mat on old-fashioned valentines. A long barn, touching the rear of the house on the right, also has pinnacles; its small high windows are outlined by large wooden arches. A local legend is that the decorations were added by a sea captain whose bride had been deprived of her large wedding cake when he was ordered hastily to sea in an emergency.

The LINDSEY TAVERN (1799), **56.7 m.** (L), now a tourist home, was a stagecoach stop on the old Post Road. Some of the original features of the interior, including stencilled wallpaper in the entrance hall, a Dutch oven in the dining room, and hand-made door hinges, have been retained.

WELLS, **56.9 m.** (50 alt.; Wells Town, 2,036 pop.), is a small settlement in one of Maine's oldest townships. Covering a large area that originally included Kennebunk, the town was often the center of hostilities during the Indian wars, which raged intermittently between 1650 and 1730. The names occurring most often in accounts of early Indian warfare are the names still most frequently heard in the town today. During a large part of the town's existence, farming has been the chief means of livelihood for the inhabitants. Increasing numbers of tourists and summer residents have afforded a large market for local garden produce.

At **57.9 m.** (L) is the JOSEPH STORER GARRISON HOUSE (*private*), where 15 soldiers withstood a two-day siege by 500 Frenchmen and

Indians in 1692. It is a weather-beaten two-and-a-half-story yellow structure with a foundation of granite.

At **58.1 m.** is the junction with an improved road.

Left on this road to WELLS BEACH, **1 m.** (20 alt., Wells Town), a popular resort with a good bathing beach.

The FIRST CONGREGATIONAL CHURCH, **58.3 m.** (R), stands on the site of the first church building in Wells, which was organized about 1643 by the Reverend John Wheelwright, who shared the beliefs of Anne Hutchinson, the English noncomformist. Wheelwright had been exiled from Massachusetts, had settled at Exeter and, when that was declared to be under the jurisdiction of Massachusetts, had migrated to this town with his family. About 1646 he made his peace with Massachusetts and returned to Boston. While a student at Oxford University he was apparently notable as an athlete, for Oliver Cromwell, his classmate there, said later in life that he had never felt as much fear before any army as before Wheelwright in competitive sports. The church Wheelwright built at Wells was burned by the Indians in 1692.

Between Wells and Ogunquit are (L) many glimpses of sand dunes, beaches, and the ocean. This section of US 1 is highly commercialized, appealing to the tourist trade with road stands, restaurants, and cabins.

OGUNQUIT, **62 m.** (60 alt., Wells Town), noted for many years only as a fishing village in a particularly beautiful setting, now has 16 hotels and is known for its colony of artists and actors (*see below*). Among the many recreations here is fishing for tuna, which has become popular along the southern Maine coast in recent years.

Left from Ogunquit on a winding road, which passes through heavily forested country broken by summer estates and affords splendid vistas of the ocean (L). The coast line is rocky.

At **0.9 m.** is the junction with a road (L) that leads **0.2 m.** to PERKINS COVE and an art colony. Grouped about the art school are small individualistically decorated cottages. The village abounds with art and antique shops and has several gaily decorated Chinese restaurants.

At **2.2 m.** is the entrance to the OGUNQUIT CLIFF COUNTRY CLUB.

At **2.7 m.** is the EPISCOPAL MEMORIAL STONE CHURCH with its bell in an arch of the roof over the door. It stands on a cliff overlooking the sea.

At **5.9 m.** the road rejoins US 1 at Cape Neddick.

MAINE   45

At **62.4 m.** is a junction with Agamenticus Road.

Right on this road is a camp site at the foot of MOUNT AGAMENTICUS (692 alt.), 5.7 m., where the Indian saint Aspinquid was buried. This, the highest of the hills in this relatively low area, long used as a point of navigation in the days of square-riggers, is still so used by coastal vessels. A 15-minute climb from the camp site along a bridle trail leads to the FIRE LOOKOUT STATION, from which is an extensive view of the sea in one direction, with BOON ISLAND LIGHT in the distance.

According to tradition, in April 1682 the *Increase*, a trader between Plymouth and Pemaquid, was wrecked on an offshore island, its only survivors, three white men and one Indian, existing as best they could on the rocky shores. They were nearly ready to give up hope of rescue when one day in May they saw smoke rising from the summit of Agamenticus. This smoke was that of the burnt offerings of hundreds of Indians from all over Maine, converts of Aspinquid, who was a disciple of John Eliot; they had brought deer, moose, fish, and even rattlesnakes to sacrifice in the flames to the memory of their departed leader. Heartened by the smoke that indicated the presence of people on the mainland, the castaways gathered driftwood and themselves built a huge fire, which attracted rescuers from the mainland. In gratitude for their salvation, it is said, the men named the island Boon. Boon Island Light was erected here in 1811.

At **62.8 m.** (L) is the new OGUNQUIT PLAYHOUSE. The Ogunquit summer theater group, one of the largest in Maine, has been under the direction of Walter Hartwig for several years, and has nationally known stage and screen stars as guest artists. During the season a new play is presented each week. The Workshop, an interesting development that attracts students of the theater from all sections of the country, makes several presentations during the summer.

In the vicinity of CAPE NEDDICK, **66.1 m.** (50 alt., York Town), are the well-built stone fences and rolling farmlands of southern Maine, with rock outcroppings typical of the New England glacial terrain.

At **70.2 m.** is a junction with a tarred road.

Right on this road is the MCINTIRE GARRISON HOUSE (*private*), **3.7 m.** (L), built between 1640–45 by Alexander Maxwell and restored in 1909 by John R. McIntire. As was customary in early garrisons, the second story overhangs the first so that beleaguered defenders could pour hot pitch and grease upon the enemy below. The building is constructed of heavy timbers interlocking at the corners and sheathed on the outside with weather-beaten shingles.

At the east end of the bridge (R) is a GRANITE MONUMENT with a bronze plaque bearing the following inscription:

"The Province of Maine. Originally extending from the Merrimac to the Kennebec Rivers, was granted Aug. 10th 1622 to Sir

Ferdinando Gorges and John Mason, by The Council for New England, established at Plymouth in 1635 when Gorges received the Eastern portion extending from the Piscataqua to the Kennebec, which thereafter retained the original name of the Province of Maine."

US 1 crosses the New Hampshire Line at **76.9 m.** in the center of the PORTSMOUTH-KITTERY MEMORIAL BRIDGE over the Piscataqua River.

NEW HAMPSHIRE

Maine Line — Portsmouth — Mass. Line, **15.1 m.** US 1.

Boston & Maine R.R. parallels route.
Well paved; all types of accommodations at short intervals.

Section 5. Maine Line to Massachusetts Line, *15.1 m.*

US 1 spans the restless Piscataqua River; the current of this turbulent stream is so swift that the water never freezes even when the temperature is far below zero.

From the earliest days the road between Portsmouth, N.H., and Newburyport, Mass., often followed or closely paralleled by the line of the modern highway, served to bind the sparse settlement together. Over this country road a lone horseman carried the mail between Portsmouth and Boston until the coming of the stagecoach. He forded rivers, crossed treacherous salt marshes, and, when necessary, fought off Indians and wolves in the discharge of his duties. Stavers Flying Stage Coach began a regular run between Portsmouth and Boston in 1761. This was a curricle, a two-wheeled, two-horse vehicle with room for three passengers. Over this route on December 13, 1774, Paul Revere rode to inform the Committee of Safety in Portsmouth of the British order that no more gunpowder should be exported to America. As a result the citizens were able to secrete what ammunition they had. Washington passed this way in 1775 after taking command in Cambridge, and again in 1789. James Monroe traveled it in 1817, and Lafayette in 1824, when he had become an almost legendary hero to the inhabitants, who lined the highway for a glimpse of him.

PORTSMOUTH, **0.5 m.** (30 alt., 14,495 pop.), ancient port (*see N.H. GUIDE*).

Points of Interest. Wentworth-Gardner House and many other points of historical and architectural interest.

US 1 in Portsmouth passes through narrow State Street, past the old EPISCOPAL CHAPEL, a wooden Doric structure (L), and the JOHN PAUL JONES HOUSE, built in 1738 (R), to Haymarket Square. Turning L. on Middle Street, it passes (R) the PIERCE HOUSE (*see illustration*), built in 1800; the BOARDMAN HOUSE, 1805 (R); the LARKIN HOUSE, 1815 (R); and the RUNDLET MAY HOUSE, 1806 (R).

The highway goes through pine woods and salt meadows, dipping into a hollow at **2.1 m.**, where Sagamore Creek, a tidal stream, winds along to Little Harbor and thence to the ocean.

At **5 m.** the northern outskirts of the beautiful old township of Rye are entered.

At **5.8 m.** is a junction with the paved and marked Greenland Road.

> Right on this road about 150 yds. to the SITE OF THE CAPTURE OF BREAKFAST HILL. A marker on top of a boulder (R) commemorates the capture of a number of Indians here in 1696. Eating a leisurely breakfast following the massacre on Portsmouth Plains the previous day, the Indians were surprised by Captain Shackford and a company of soldiers, who killed them and rescued the captives they had taken.

South of Rye Township US 1 runs through the prosperous village of NORTH HAMPTON, **6.1 m.** (99 alt., 695 pop.), around which are green acres that are either cultivated by farmers whose titles go back to the 17th century, or are beautiful estates of wealthy summer residents; the latter are between the highway and the sea. Probably settled first by Samuel and John Dearborn in 1690, North Hampton Town was the scene of many attacks by the Winnicummet Indians. To withstand their onslaughts its early houses were strongly built of wood backed with brick. Many of these are still standing. Formerly a part of Hampton Town, North Hampton was incorporated in 1742.

At **8.5 m.** is a junction with the paved and marked Atlantic Road.

> 1. Left on this road about 300 yds. is (L) the simple, white NORTH HAMPTON TOWN HALL, in the belfry of which hangs a bell made by the Paul Revere factory.

> 2. Right on Atlantic Road to NORTH HILL, on which stands NORTH HAMPTON CENTER. High above the sunny meadows, the white meeting house dominates the cluster of white farmhouses about the village green.
> Where the green is bordered on the W. by the Post Road, a MILEPOST is set in a stone wall. It reads:
>
> "P
> 10
> N
> 12"
>
> (Portsmouth 10 miles, Newburyport 12). This post was erected by Benjamin Franklin when he was Postmaster General under the Crown. South of this mile post on the Post Road is a tablet (R) at **0.25 m.**, marking the SITE OF THE HOME OF THE FIRST SETTLERS, Samuel and John Dearborn, and their descendant,

NEW HAMPSHIRE COAST

IRONWORKS HOUSE, SAUGUS, MASSACHUSETTS

PROVIDENCE HARBOR, RHODE ISLAND

HANNAH ROBINSON HOUSE, NARRAGANSETT, RHODE ISLAND

NEW HAMPSHIRE

Major General Henry Dearborn, who commanded the Army of the United States at the outbreak of the second war with England in 1812.

It was over this section of the road that, by order of Richard Waldron, constable of Dover, three Quaker women were dragged from Dover and flogged. The order, issued in 1662, stated: "You and every one of you are required in the King's Majesty's name to take these vagabond Quakers, Anne Colman, Mary Tompkins, and Alice Ambrose and make them fast to the cart's tail, and, driving the cart through your several towns, to whip them upon their naked backs not exceeding ten stripes apiece on each of them, in each town; and so to convey them from constable to constable till they are out of this jurisdiction, as you will answer it at your peril; and this is your Warrant." Whittier drew a vivid picture of this episode in his poem, *How the Women Went from Dover:*

> "Bared to the waist for the north wind's grip
> And keener sting of the constable's whip,
> The blood that followed each hissing blow
> Froze as it sprinkled the winter snow.

> "Priest and ruler, boy and maid
> Followed the dismal cavalcade
> And from door and window, open thrown,
> Looked and wondered gaffer and crone."

Fortunately, through the courage of Justice Robert Pike of Salisbury who trod the warrant underfoot, its provisions were carried out only at Hampton and Dover.

HAMPTON, **10.9 m.** (83 alt.; Hampton Town, 1,507 pop.), is a compact little village, its streets lined with lofty elms. Hampton was an outpost of the Massachusetts Bay Colony, which maintained a blockhouse here in 1635 as a protection against the numerous Indian attacks. The town was one of New Hampshire's four original towns and the mother of many of the surrounding little towns. A grant of the land was given to a group of Englishmen led by the Reverend Stephen Bachiler, who in 1638 sailed in shallops up the Winnicummet River "thru salt sea marshes to uplands brown." These pioneers, with thoughts turning homeward to England, promptly changed the lovely Indian name of Winnicummet (*beautiful place in the pines*) to Hampton at the incorporation of the town in 1639.

Although today this is a farming and shoe manufacturing community on a small scale, the tang of the sea is in the air and strange objects in the old houses are a heritage of the days when brigantines and clipper ships put out from Hampton Harbor to sail the distant seas.

Left on Winnicummet Road, which intersects US 1 in the village, is (R) the FIRST CONGREGATIONAL CHURCH, built in 1843; its pulpit is from the Fourth Meeting House, erected in 1797.

On this road in a quiet grove of pines lies the old BURYING GROUND, 0.5 m., with its ancient stones (1654–1800) almost hidden by fragrant pine needles.

At 11.4 m. on US 1 is a large square house (R) surrounded by an old-fashioned garden. This mansion is generally known as the home of Gen. Jonathan Moulton of Revolutionary War fame and locally as the HAUNTED HOUSE. A bit of the interior of the house, a fine specimen of Georgian architecture, has been pictured by Whittier in *The New Wife and the Old:*

> "From the oaken mantel glowing
> Faintest light the lamp is throwing
> On the mirror's antique mould
> High-backed chair, and wainscot old."

Reputedly a miserly man, General Moulton is said to have shown his thrift by removing the rings of his first wife at her death and presenting them to the second wife. In revenge the first wife is said to have returned and ever after haunted the place. The story goes, too, that the general agreed to sell his soul to the devil for as much gold as his boots would hold. The fireplace is pointed out as the place where the general placed his boots with the toes cut off, so that when the devil poured the money down the chimney it ran through the boots. Thus the fiend was outwitted.

About 300 yds. from US 1 on a road that runs E. from the Haunted House is the old MEETING HOUSE GREEN or Cow Commons, once the heart of the village. Nearby is a LOG CABIN (*open Wed. and Sat. aft.; free*), a reproduction of the first meeting house. The cabin's door was formerly the front door of the Garrison House, built by Col. Joshua Wingate on order of Governor Dudlye in 1703. Beside the cabin is the TUCK MEMORIAL HOUSE (*open. Wed. and Sat. aft.; free*) with a historical room containing many odd relics.

One of New England's most dreaded witches had her hut near the log cabin; here she was buried "in a grave by a ditch." Goody Cole was the fear of the countryside, for, it was charged, she had "made a league with the devil" and with his aid was able to render persons deformed, to torture, and even to drown with an invisible hand. Whittier speaks of her in *The Wreck of Rivermouth:*

> "'Fie on the witch!' cried a merry girl,
> As they rounded the point where Goody Cole
> Sat by her door with her wheel atwirl,
> A bent and blear-eyed, poor old soul.
> 'Oho!' she muttered, 'ye're brave to-day!
> But I hear the little waves laugh and say,
> The broth will be cold that waits at home;
> For it's one to go, but another to come!'"

Although none of the fantastic crimes attributed to witches could be laid directly at Goody Cole's door, she was persecuted and imprisoned by the town for years. In 1673 her plea for liberty was refused by Justice Jonas Clark of Salisbury Court in the following decision, "In ye case of Unis Cole now prisoner at ye Bar not Legally guilty according to Intitement butt just ground of vehement suspissyon of her haveing had famillyarrty with the deiull."

Opposite the log cabin (R) is the attractive MEETING HOUSE GREEN MEMORIAL PARK surrounded by a series of boulders marked with the names of the earliest settlers. The park was the joint gift of the towns that were once part of Hampton.

The salt marshes S. of Hampton figured rather prominently in the commercial history of this part of New Hampshire. Extensive commercial salt works were in operation on the edges of the marshes in Colonial days to extract the salt from the grass, which was set in cocks on the marsh to dry. A tide mill, of which there are no traces at the present time, was built here in 1681 for the purpose of grinding the town's corn in return for "a one-sixteenth part thereof," and was active until 1879.

At Taylor River, **12.5 m.,** was the shipyard where vessels, some of them of large tonnage, were built. At a bend in the stream known as the Mooring Turn, vessels were accustomed to ride at anchor. Beginning in 1682, many barques, brigantines, and sloops were built and launched to sail for distant ports.

HAMPTON FALLS, **13.2 m.** (62 alt.; Hampton Falls Town, 481 pop.), is a delightful village dignified by austere white churches. Originally a part of Hampton Town, Hampton Falls was incorporated as a separate township in 1726. In the early part of the 18th century this section was one of the busiest in all New England; sawmills, grist mills, shingle mills, woolen mills, cotton mills, and fertilizer plants kept many workmen busy.

In stagecoach days the village was a post station where changes of horses were made, from 100 to 125 horses being kept at one time for that purpose. WELLSWOOD INN (L), then known as Wells Tavern, was a stage house with 40 horses stabled across the road. So great was the local interest in horses that a horse show was held in Hampton Falls in 1726. Sunday travel was banned in those days and the tithing men of Hampton Falls were very active in promptly arresting and fining anyone so offending. The practice did not end until 1825.

On August 10, 1737, officials of New Hampshire and Massachusetts, forming an imposing cavalcade of stagecoaches, horseback riders, and carriages, met here to determine the boundary line between the two Colonies.

The MONUMENT in the square (R) was erected in memory of New Hampshire's first Governor, Mesheck Weare, President of New Hampshire from 1776–1784, who was born and lived here. Its inscription reads:

> "He was one of those good men
> Who dare to love their country and be poor."

The GOVERNOR WEARE HOUSE on Exeter Road near the square, built in 1748, is a splendid example of early Colonial architecture; in it, according to well authenticated tradition, both Washington and Lafayette were entertained.

ELMFIELD (L) is notable for its furnishings, which have been in the house since its early days. The old place is still owned by the Gove family, who built it in the early part of the 18th century. Edward Gove, grandfather of the present owner, was imprisoned for several years in the Tower of London for taking part in a conspiracy against Governor Crandon. He lived to spend his last years in this house, an invalid as the result, he said, of poison administered during his imprisonment.

Here John Greenleaf Whittier spent many summer vacations, and here in 1892 he died in the room overlooking the lovely old-fashioned rose garden. The log cabin and Colonial kitchen may be visited by permission of the owner.

All of this region is Whittier land. The poet took great pride in the fact that he was a lineal descendant of the Reverend Stephen

Bachiler, founder of Hampton, and showed a lively interest in the house of his ancestors.

1. Right from Hampton Falls on Exeter Road at **1.8 m.** is (R) APPLECREST FARM, which is most attractive in the spring when thousands of trees are in full blossom, and in the fall when crimson fruit is being picked and packed in a model packing house. Adjoining Applecrest Farm (R) the two-story unpainted house that was the BIRTHPLACE OF FRANKLIN B. SANBORN (1831–1917), journalist and author. He was one of the three founders of the Concord Summer School of Philosophy, and biographer of his friends Emerson, Thoreau, and Hawthorne. The gray two-story house (R) is the BIRTHPLACE OF RALPH ADAMS CRAM, distinguished American architect. At **3.6 m.** (L) is the old CRAM HOMESTEAD, an unpainted house of dignified lines, built in 1676.

2. Right from Hampton Falls on the Kensington Road to the FALLS OF FALLS RIVER, **5 m.**, where formerly were situated a fulling mill, a grist mill, and a sawmill run by water power. The mills have long since disappeared, but the charm of the falls remains. On the river's bank is (R) the DODGE HOMESTEAD. The original house, built in 1648, was in 1787 replaced by the present structure, which retains many of the original features and pieces of furniture of the Colonial structure.

A stone on the estate is by many local people considered proof that the Norsemen landed in or near Hampton in the early 11th century. Although covered with dry moss a series of marks can be found chiseled in the stone; at first glance these appear to be crosses such as the Indians used to guide their tribesmen through the woods, but closer examination makes it clear that they are not characteristic Indian symbols. They more nearly resemble the runic inscriptions of the Norsemen.

Behind the house on the river bank is an EPISCOPAL CHAPEL, said to be the smallest in the State; the little building of stone was fashioned from an old ice house. The chapel is privately owned but is always open to the wayfarer. Worshipers are called together every Sunday afternoon at four by an old brass bell taken from one of the ships built on the Hampton River in the early 18th century.

SEABROOK, **14.7 m.** (65 alt.; Seabrook Town, 1,666 pop.), a village with limited accommodations, is Old Worldish in appearance and atmosphere. Its landscape has been unchanged for three centuries; cocks of salt hay still dot the wide sand dunes beyond it as they did in Colonial days.

For 57 years a part of Hampton Town, the Seabrook section was settled in 1638 and did not become a separate township until 1768. Living was especially precarious here in early days because of frequent Indian attacks. The chief industry a century ago was the building of whaleboats, which set forth from Seabrook on fishing trips to the coast of Labrador. The names of some of the original settlers have come down for almost three hundred years, among them such names as Byrd, Peavear, Boynton, and Bachiler.

A part of the people of Seabrook speak a language reminiscent of rural England, and at times almost unintelligible to a visitor. Once these people were expert shoemakers, doing all their work by hand in ten-foot cabins; since the coming of machines the industry has been conducted in a factory. The employees work when they please and, if the mood suits them, sleep under a tree, in full view of the factory. Members of a long-lived race, active and hearty, many of them are working at the age of 90 years or more.

SEABROOK NURSERIES (L) in the season from May to September exhibit 20 acres of gladioli in every possible variety and color. YE COCK AND KETTLE INN (R) dates from the 18th century. The OLD MAN OF SEABROOK (L), an antique shop, is so named because of the curious figure of an old man hanging on its wall. The figure, originally a clothing store dummy in Newburyport, was brought to Seabrook about 40 years ago and placed in its present position.

At **15.1 m.** US 1 crosses the Massachusetts Line.

MASSACHUSETTS

N.H. Line — Newburyport — Boston — Dedham — R.I. Line, **77.9 m.** US 1.

Boston & Maine R.R. S. of Boston, and the New York, New Haven & Hartford R.R. parallel the route at intervals.
Good, hard-surfaced roadbed, mostly three and four lanes wide.
Usual accommodations at short intervals.

Section 6. New Hampshire Line to Rhode Island Line, 77.9 m.

US 1 is the most direct route, though not the most scenic, between Portsmouth, New Hampshire, and Pawtucket, Rhode Island. Even in the days of stagecoaches the section of highway between Newburyport and Boston, the Newburyport Turnpike, was known as the "airline route" because of its unwavering course. In its 35 miles it deviates only 83 ft. from a straight line; it runs through pleasant farm lands N. of Newburyport, then over the glacial hills of Topsfield and Danvers. At Lynnfield it runs through flat country as it passes Suntaug Lake between the red rock outcrops of Saugus, on the outskirts of Boston. There are no unnecessary hindrances to traffic in Boston on the through route, which follows a wooded parkway with overpasses and a staggered system of traffic lights. South of Boston the road, locally called the Providence Turnpike, is an express highway traversing only one center of size, North Attleboro, thence crossing rolling country, largely undeveloped.

At **2.4 m.** is SALISBURY (15 alt.; town pop. 2,245, incorp. 1640). In the tiny triangular green (L) is the QUAKER WHIPPING STONE, originally the stepping stone of the Friends' Meeting House, built in Salisbury in 1752; it marks the site of Maj. Robert Pike's championship of three Quaker women who had been ordered tied to the tail of an oxcart and whipped (*see Section 5*).

About 20 yds. N. of the square, on US 1, a marker (L) indicates the SITE OF THE BETSY GERRISH HOUSE, within whose narrow walls was held a session of the General Court. At that time the community was a "shire town" and the only settlement N. of the Merrimac River.

On State 110, 200 yds. R. of the square, is the green known as POTLID SQUARE. A boulder here marks the SITE OF THE FIRST LOG CHURCH OF SALISBURY (1640) and the SITE OF THE COURTHOUSE built in the same year. Settlers moved here in 1638 from Newbury, Mass., and Salisbury, England, and in attempting to develop the fishing, shipbuilding, and cooperage industries, incurred the hostility of the Indians, who resented the depletion of their food supply and of the forests.

Left from Salisbury on State 1A to the old BURYING GROUND, at the junction of State 1A and Beach Rd., laid out in 1639. This cemetery holds large flat stones known as "wolf slabs," which were placed on the ground to protect the graves of the early settlers from hungry wolves. Here are buried Maj. Robert Pike and the first five ministers of Salisbury.

At **2.1 m.** is SALISBURY BEACH (*salt-water swimming pool, recreation equipment*).

Along the three-lane concrete highway no vestiges remain of the dark forest that once menaced the dooryards of the early inhabitants.

At **4.2 m.** is the junction with First St.

Left on First St. are the remnants of the original settlement of Salisbury, the Ring's Island section. The sharply rising bank (L) and the tiny creek (R), **0.1 m.**, were the SITE OF THE FISH FLAKES AND SHIPYARDS of early days. Up the steep slope were once wheeled barrows of fish, brought from Labrador and Chaleur Bay, to be spread in the sun on drying racks or "flakes." The SITE OF THE OLD FERRY SLIP, **0.2 m.**, on the bank of the Merrimac River, is identified by rotting timbers at the water's edge. At **0.3 m.** (L) stands the NATHAN DOLE HOUSE (*open by arrangement*), built in 1680, and once occupied by the poet, Edna St. Vincent Millay. Nearby is MARCHES TAVERN, built in 1690 by John March, who ran the ferry connecting the settlement with Newbury and other nearby port towns. Seaward from the tavern are INDIAN SHELL HEAPS, now appearing as green mounds in the distance across the marshes. These accumulations of broken clam shells mark the spot where, in the summer months, the Indians gathered to fish in the Merrimac, before returning at the approach of winter to the protection of the inland woods.

At **4.5 m.** US 1 passes over the bridge that crosses the Merrimac River. The road affords glimpses of the waterfront, a short stretch of business section, and the white spires rising above the foliage of the residential parts of Newburyport.

At **5 m.** (L) is a glimpse of the rear wall and the squat stone frame of the old COUNTY JAIL (1744), its spiked metal fence imbedded in the rock base; during the Revolution, British privateersmen were shackled to its floor. Beyond are the ancient stones of the old HILL BURYING GROUND, holding the remains of soldiers of the French and Indian, Revolutionary, and Civil Wars. Here also is buried the self-styled "Lord" Timothy Dexter (1743–1806), eccentric Newburyport

MASSACHUSETTS 57

merchant who made a fortune by speculating in depreciated Colonial currency and in such trading deals as the sale of warming pans.

Along the highway are level stretches that were once the commons, where townsfolk pastured their flocks and herds; there is a shaded residential area (L).

NEWBURYPORT, **5 m.** (57 alt., pop. 14,815), historic port (*see MASS. GUIDE*).

Points of Interest. Caldwell Rum Distilleries, Old County Jail, Jackson-Dexter House, St. Paul's Church, Sumner House, Brown Park and Garrison Statue, Old South Church, and others.

From the western edge of Newburyport US 1 traverses the wooded and farming sections of N. Essex County.

At **7.4 m.** is the junction with a dirt road.

*Left on this road is a junction, **0.5 m.**, with a marked side road leading to* DEVIL'S BASIN, **1.6 m.** Geologists find in this abandoned quarry fine specimens of brittle dolomized rock, green- and yellow-veined serpentine, and masses of vesuvianite.

At **8.4 m.** US 1 crosses the PARKER RIVER, at this point a narrow stream in the midst of vivid green marshes. At **9.1 m.** (R), set back from the road, is the GOVERNOR DUMMER ACADEMY, a boarding school established in 1762. The original schoolhouse, standing among the clapboarded dormitories built at a later date, is a one-story building typical of the little district schoolhouses that were once the backbone of New England's school system. The finest building on the campus is the GOVERNOR DUMMER MANSION (1715), now occupied by the headmaster. Shaded by arching elms, this building is an outstanding example of early American-Georgian architecture. The carved detail of the doorway merits close inspection.

Several ghost stories center around the mansion. It is said that whenever August has two full moons, on the night of the first moon Governor Dummer rides his white horse up the broad staircase as he did on the night of the grand housewarming in 1715. Another story concerns the smiling ghost of a child who peeped through the kitchen doorway. Not until her bones were discovered in a moldering box in the cellar and given proper burial, did the little apparition vanish. It is also averred that the ghost of an English officer who was killed in a duel on the lawn occasionally reappears in full-dress uniform, with powdered wig embroidered cloak, and sword.

U. S. ONE

At **12.3 m.** is the intersection with State 133.

Right on this road is GEORGETOWN, **4.9 m.** (81 alt.; town pop. 2,009, incorp. 1838), offspring of the town of Rowley and one of the later settlements in Essex County. A local story is that land grants in the district were restricted by Ezekiel Rogers, head of the Rowley Company, so that Oliver Cromwell might find a refuge here in the eventuality that his political efforts to dethrone Charles I should be unsuccessful.

The BROCKLEBANK HOUSE (*adm. free*), about **0.4 m.** from the common on State 133, was built in 1670. This attractive gambrel-roofed dwelling was the home of Capt. Samuel Brocklebank, who was killed in King Philip's War. An old sign of the White Horse Tavern (1773) swings in front of it.

At **5.8 m.** on State 133 is the junction with a dirt road; L. here to the summit of BALDPATE HILL (312 alt.), a high point in Essex County, affording a view of green valleys and distant hills. This road passes two 18th century houses with steep-pitched roofs, and at **1 m.** (R) reaches BALDPATE INN (*still a hotel*). The inn has paneled walls and old-time fireplaces and furnishings.

At **17.3 m.** US 1 crosses State 97.

Right on State 97 is TOPSFIELD, **0.6 m.** (59 alt.; town pop. 1,113, incorp. 1648), which is built up around a lovely green and has the appearance of a town of old New England. Near the green are the CIVIL WAR MEMORIAL, representing a dying soldier handing the colors to a comrade, and the PEACE MEMORIAL dedicated to "Men and Women of Topsfield who helped to restore peace to a world at war, 1914–1918." Across from the memorials stands the PUBLIC LIBRARY containing murals of historic scenes, the work of Harold Kellogg, its architect, as well as collections of rare books and objects of historical interest. Nearby are the high school, the town hall, and the white-spired Congregational Church. Nothing remains to indicate that Topsfield was something of a boom town in Colonial times. In 1648 bog iron was dug and smelted at the Boxford Iron Works; excitement ran high when a copper vein was struck on the Endicott grant. Mining, however, proved unprofitable, and agriculture continued to be the mainstay of the town.

In the center of the village (R) is an old three-story, square, brick house with wooden ends. Near it, branching R. between the white church and the green, is an unmarked lane that passes through a pasture gate, meadows, and woods, to the PARSON CAPEN HOUSE (*open in summer; adm. 10¢*), which has been restored by the local historical society. A two-story structure (1683) of the type intended to withstand Indian attacks, it has an unusually deep second-story overhang, steeply pitched roof, central chimney, many-paned casement windows, and carved door brackets. On the corners of the overhang are pineapple drops. The Metropolitan Museum of Art in New York City has reproduced the kitchen in its American wing. Furnishings, of the period when the house was built, include a chair-table, a wooden bread-trough, wooden plates, and mugs. A brick oven is inside a fireplace 8½ ft. wide.

It is said that a maid servant of Parson Capen lost her soul by reading an improper book on the Sabbath; when Satan appeared to claim his booty the

MASSACHUSETTS

parson challenged him to a contest, with the terrified girl as the prize. Spilling half a bushel of flaxseed on the floor, the parson engaged to read a section of the Bible backwards before Satan could pick up the seed. The devil lost the contest and, in chagrin, vanished through a rat hole that has also been preserved.

The CHOATE HOUSE (*private*) is a two-story, hip-roofed, white frame building on a grassy terrace, above a shaded lawn surrounded by a fence with ball-topped posts. It has a parapet, four corner chimneys, a front doorway with an unusually fine fan light, and a Doric-columned portico.

State 97, N. of Topsfield, passes the PINE GROVE CEMETERY, 1 m. (L), containing stones dating back to 1663. Here are buried ancestors of Joseph Smith, founder of Mormonism. Next to the burial ground once stood a meeting house, built in 1663. In 1675, during King Philip's War, it was inside a palisade, with a watch house in the SE. corner.

At **3.2 m.** (R), with a large elm by the door, is the PERLEY-HALE-PERKINS HOUSE (*private*), built in 1760 by Maj. Asa Perkins. The fine old weatherbeaten house has a long roof and central chimney.

At **3.5 m.** is the junction with Depot St.

Left **0.5 m.** on Depot St. are (R) the extensive grounds of the KELSEY-HIGHLANDS NURSERY, equipped with a private airport. At **0.6 m.** (R) stands the picturesque CHAPLIN'S SAWMILL.

BOXFORD, **5.2 m.** on State 97 (95 alt.; town pop. 726, incorp. 1694), is a village in an unspoiled stretch of low rolling hills dotted with several large lakes. So salubrious was the air here in 1855 that the town physician remarked with regret that he might as well practice in heaven. The first settler, Abraham Reddington, arrived in 1645. The community has always been predominantly agricultural in its activities, though it has had various small industries to supply local needs and at one time had sawmills that prepared lumber for the shipyards along the coast. The single melodramatic episode in Boxford's peaceful history was the Ames murder trial of 1769. This trial was one of the few in New England at which the ordeal by touch was employed — a test based on the idea that the wounds of a corpse would bleed if the murderer touched the body.

Left of the green is the FIRST CONGREGATIONAL CHURCH, a white meeting house with a long row of horse stalls. On the opposite side of Depot Street is JOURNEY'S END (*open in summer by permission*), the residence of Frank A. Manny, author. This clapboarded, gambrel-roofed house contains an interesting historical collection. In the garden is a miniature sand village, *Boxford in the 80's*, which inspired Stanley Hall to write the *Story of a Sandpile*, a contribution to the modern playground movement.

On Elm St., a few hundred feet from Journey's End, is the PUBLIC LIBRARY (R), housing a small collection of historical exhibits.

At **17.1 m.** (L) is a view across far stretches of rolling hills and woodlands.

At **17.8 m.** (L) is the TOPSFIELD FAIR GROUNDS (*agricultural exhibits, races annually in mid-September*).

At **20.1 m.** (R) is an old MILESTONE, with *B* (Boston) and *P* (Portland) cut deep into the granite. Here US 1 twists through wooded and open land, passing at **21.6 m.** (R) the turreted red brick structure of the DANVERS STATE HOSPITAL FOR THE INSANE (*visiting 2–4 p.m.; special hours for groups interested in the work*), crowning the highest hill in the township.

US 1 passes pine groves, PURITAN LAWN MEMORIAL PARK (*a cemetery*), and SUNTAUG LAKE at **26 m.** (R).

At **26.7 m.** is SOUTH LYNNFIELD (77 alt.), a crossroads village at the junction with State 128.

> Right on State 128 **0.4 m.** is the junction with Summer St.; R. on Summer St. to PILLINGS POND (*boating, bathing, and fishing*), **1.8 m.** (R).
>
> LYNNFIELD, **3 m.** on Summer St. (136 alt., town pop. 1,896), is a little village on a plateau. It was settled in 1638 and known as Lynn End until the town was incorporated in 1782. Many of the residents of the town are employed in the nearby industrial centers.
>
> Grouped around the shaded green are small white houses of Colonial type. On the green is the WAR MEMORIAL BOULDER. At the base of the triangular plot the former FIRST CHURCH (1714), outwardly unchanged, houses the town's fire apparatus. Left of the green, on a tree-shaded hillock, are the lichen-covered stones of the old BURYING GROUND, containing the graves of the first three ministers of the old church and a number of Revolutionary War soldiers. One of the latter, Martin Herrick, was sent by the Committee of Safety to help spread the alarm on the eve of the Battle of Lexington. The epitaphs on some of the old grave stones are unconventional.

At **27.9 m.** (R) is the LYNN RESERVOIR; at **28.8 m.** US 1 skirts the 580-acre BREAKHEART RESERVATION in North Saugus, a State-owned tract with trails, picnic grounds, lookouts, and parking spaces.

At **29.1 m.** is the junction with Lynn Fells Parkway.

> Right on the parkway at **1.2 m.** is the junction with Howard St. At 7 Howard St. is the "SCOTCH" BOARDMAN HOUSE (*private*). Once the home of the Indian Queen Nanepashemet, this house (1651) later served as quarters for the Scottish prisoners captured by Cromwell at the Battle of Dunbar, who were sentenced to seven years' servitude in New England and indentured to the Saugus iron works. During frequent boundary changes, the dwelling has been in two counties and four towns. The original boundary between Lynn and Boston ran through the middle of the front door, which for many years bore the letters *B* and *L* on its two halves. The roof reaching almost to the ground, the broken line of the central chimney, and the second-story overhang are typical of the local architecture of the period in which the house was built.

At **30.3 m.** is a junction with Main St.

> Left on Main St. is SAUGUS CENTER, **0.7 m.** (20 alt.; town pop. 15,076, incorp. 1815). John Winthrop, son of Governor Winthrop, having learned of deposits here of bog-ore similar to that smelted in Sussex, England, went to

England in 1641 to organize a company to exploit the ore. Two years later he returned with capital and skilled ironworkers. In 1645, under the management of Richard Leader, the plant had an output of 8 to 10 tons a week, and in a few years had achieved a rate of production beyond the needs of the Colony. Among the articles made were the first fire engine (1654), kettles, anchors, bar iron and wrought iron for blacksmiths, and the first dies for coining money in America. These dies, used by the mint in Boston, were for cast-silver pieces with "the word Massachusetts with a pine tree on one side, and the letters N.E. ANNO 1652, and III, VI, or XII, denoting the number of pence, on the other." Difficulties with the ironworkers and financial backers brought the enterprise to ruin, however, and the indentured Scottish servants proved even less amenable than the paid workers. At the break-up of Hammersmith, as the mill was then called, the more skilled workers set up forges and blooming mills throughout New England.

Except for this venture, Saugus was largely agricultural through the first two centuries of its existence. Several factories that were opened in the 19th century turned out a variety of products — snuff, chocolate, nails, and shoes — but these industries declined and the town today is purely residential.

Clustered about the green are a GRAVEYARD, a CIVIL WAR MONUMENT, and the TOWN HALL. Close by, on Central St., is the restored old IRONWORKS HOUSE (*private*), built in 1643 by Farmer Thomas Dexter, founder of the ironworks. The house (*see illustration*) has diamond-paned casement windows, nail-studded doors, and an immense central chimney. Carved wooden ornaments, some of which are shaped like acorns, accent the acute angle of the roof line and hang from the second story. The beams of English oak in the center are exposed. It is said that the builder, little dreaming of the vast forests of the New World, brought timber with him from England for the framework. The fireplaces are at least 12 ft. wide, and contain pothooks and cranes supposed to have been made at the forge, the site of which is across the road.

Nearby are grass-covered cinder banks, relics of the early industrial venture.

At **32.5 m.** (R) is a granite milestone marking an old INDIAN TRAIL. According to tradition, William Richard and Ralph Sprague, the first white men to pass through this region, used this trail on their way from Salem (Naumkeag) to Charlestown (Mishawam) in 1629.

At **32.8 m.** is a junction with Salem St.

Right on this street is MALDEN, **1.5 m.** (12 alt., city pop. 37,277), an industrial city (*see MASS. GUIDE*).

Points of Interest. Gould-Webster Homestead, Waitt's Mount, City Hall, Parsonage House, Greene House, and others.

The SOLDIERS' MONUMENT, **34.9 m.**, on the corner of Broadway and Webster Sts., is an imposing bronze statue on a granite base erected to commemorate Everett men who served in the Spanish-

American War and with the American troops sent to China during the Boxer Rebellion.

EVERETT, 35.1 m. (12 alt., 47,228 pop.), an industrial center (*see MASS. GUIDE*).

Points of Interest. Parlin Library, Mystic Iron Works, Glendale Park, Immaculate Conception Church, and others.

At **36.7 m.** the Mystic River is crossed, and US 1 follows tne Northern Artery, one of the main routes for traffic to and from Boston.

At **38 m.** is the junction with Somerville Ave.

Right on Somerville Ave. is SOMERVILLE, **0.5 m.** (13 alt., town pop. 100,733), an industrial city (*see MASS. GUIDE*).

Points of Interest. Old Powder House, Samuel Tufts House, Ford Motor Co. Plant, Magoun House, and others.

Between Somerville and Cambridge, US 1 passes through a highly industrial area with a number of meat-packing plants.

At **39 m.** US 1 turns R. on Memorial Drive, which runs along the beautiful Charles River, and passes the buildings of Massachusetts Institute of Technology, **40.1 m.** (R), and (L) the Harvard Bridge and the boathouses used by the M.I.T. and Harvard crews. Here is a junction with Massachusetts Ave.

Right on this avenue to the center of CAMBRIDGE, **1 m.** (9 alt., town pop. 118,075), an educational center (*see MASS. GUIDE*).

Points of Interest. Harvard University, Massachusetts Institute of Technology, Radcliffe College, Sargent College, Christ Church, Fogg Art Museum, Longfellow House, and others.

At **41.2 m.** US 1 turns L. and crosses Cottage Farm Bridge to Commonwealth Ave., **41.3 m.**

Left on Commonwealth Ave. **2.5 m.** is the center of BOSTON (8 alt., city pop. 817,713), historical and industrial city (*see MASS. GUIDE*).

Railroad Stations. B. & M. R.R., North Station, 120 Causeway St.; Boston & Albany R.R., and N.Y., N.H., & H.R.R., South Station, Atlantic Ave. and Summer St.; Boston, Revere Beach & Lynn R.R., Rowe's Wharf, 350 Atlantic Ave. (ferry to East Boston); East Boston Terminal, Marginal St. near Jeffries.

Points of Interest. Boston Athenaeum, Public Library, Bunker Hill Monument, Charlestown Navy Yard and "Old Ironsides," Faneuil Hall, King's Chapel and Burying Ground, Museum of Fine Arts, Museum of Natural History, and many others.

MASSACHUSETTS 63

At **42.8 m.** US 1 follows the Jamaicaway, a boulevard running through an area where natural beauty has been conserved, and skirts JAMAICA POND.

At a traffic circle, **44.9 m.**, the route turns R. into a four-lane highway that passes the ARNOLD ARBORETUM, **45.8 m.**, and continues through a section of West Roxbury.

At **50.5 m.** US 1 passes over MOTHER BROOK, dug in 1639, the first canal in America. It connects the Charles and Neponset Rivers, thus making Boston an island.

The road skirts (R) the picturesque village of DEDHAM, **51.6 m.** (118 alt.; town pop. 15,371, incorp. 1636), historic town (*see MASS. GUIDE*).

Points of Interest. Thayer House, Norfolk County Courthouse, St. Paul's Episcopal Church, Fairbanks House, and others.

US 1 rises and dips through steep embankments, woodlands, and open fields.

At **58.3 m.** is the junction with Moose Hill Rd.

Left on this road to the entrance of the OBSERVATORY AND BIRD SANCTUARY at Moose Hill (540 alt.), **2 m.** The sanctuary, containing more than 2,000 acres, is in the charge of the Massachusetts Audubon Society.

At **62.5 m.**, adjoining the highway are the extensive farm lands (R) of the FOXBOROUGH STATE HOSPITAL FOR MENTAL DISEASES, a well-equipped institution.

At **62.4 m.** is the junction with Water St.

Right on this street is SOUTH WALPOLE, **0.2 m.** (200 alt.). On the corner of Neponset and Washington Sts. (L) stands FULLER'S TAVERN (*open*), a rambling, white building. Around it are great shade trees and a garden of lilacs, syringas, and perennials. This inn, built in 1807 and renovated in 1927, was a famous halfway house on the stagecoach route between Boston and Providence.

US 1 skirts the edge of TURNPIKE LAKE, **68.4 m.**, and reaches an elevation permitting a wide view of the countryside.

At **70.6 m.** is the junction with State 1A (N. Washington St.), an alternate to US 1 for a few miles.

Right on State 1A, at 362 N. Washington St. (R), is the WOODCOCK HOUSE, **0.1 m.** In 1669 John Woodcock made the first permanent settlement in the North Purchase — now North Attleboro — and established a tavern that, during its 170 years of service (1670–1840), was visited by many celebrities. In its earliest days the hostelry was one of a chain of garrisons reaching from Boston to Rhode

Island. Woodcock, wounded seven times in his encounters with Indians, killed many of them. In revenge they killed his son, Nathaniel, and placed his scalp on a stick in the old BURYING GROUND opposite the tavern.

NORTH ATTLEBORO, **1.4 m.** (183 alt.; town pop. 10,202, incorp. 1887), was formerly in Attleboro Town.

In 1780 a person who has survived in local history as "the Frenchman" established a jewelry business; this line of activity eventually became paramount in the town and declined only in recent years.

The NORTH ATTLEBORO HISTORICAL SOCIETY HEADQUARTERS (*open 3rd Tues. of each month, 2–5 p.m.*), 224 Washington St., is a two-and-a-half-story, clapboarded house with slate roof. The adjacent barn contains a number of historical relics.

At **1.8 m.** State 1A rejoins US 1.

At **73.9 m.** is the junction with Allen Rd.

Right on Allen Rd. **0.3 m.** to the junction with the Old Post Rd.; L. here to the FIRST CONGREGATIONAL CHURCH, **0.9 m.** (L), a clapboarded structure built in 1712.

Right from the Old Post Rd., opposite the church, **0.2 m.** on Mount Hope St., to a footpath (L) leading to the old POWDER HOUSE (1768), a circular brick building 12 ft. in diameter with a shingled conical roof. During the Revolutionary War and the War of 1812 ammunition was stored here.

In the BRICK SHOP, **1 m.** on the Old Post Rd., some of the first metal buttons in the United States were manufactured. The first die used in the jewelry business in this country was cut here by the Robinson-Jones Co. The two-and-a-half-story brick structure was built in 1812, and still contains some of the original equipment; it is used as a chemical laboratory by the sons of the present owner.

At **77.9 m.** US 1 traverses an old stone bridge and crosses the Rhode Island Line.

RHODE ISLAND

Mass. Line — Pawtucket — Providence — Narragansett — Conn. Line, **60 m.** US 1.

New York, New Haven & Hartford R.R. parallels this route.
Paved highway, some of it four-lane.
Accommodations of all kinds in Providence; limited accommodations elsewhere.

Section 7. Massachusetts Line to Connecticut Line, **60 m.**

The northern section of this route goes through the industrial and commercial area of the State, through Providence, the capital city, and its thickly populated environs of Pawtucket and Cranston. South of the latter city the route passes through a less densely settled section of the State, through the coastal townships of Warwick, East Greenwich, Narragansett, and the Kingstowns, which are rich in historic interest. The road in many places affords pleasant views of a prosperous farming country, and of the waters of Narragansett Bay and the Atlantic Ocean.

South of the Massachusetts Line US 1 runs for about three miles through the eastern section of Pawtucket.

PAWTUCKET, **1.5 m.** (25 alt., 77,149 pop.), industrial city (*see R.I. GUIDE*).

Points of Interest. Old Slater Mill, Old Pidge Tavern, Daggett House Museum, St. Mary's Church of the Immaculate Conception, New City Hall, Narragansett Park, and others.

US 1 bypasses many of the historic sites of this old city to run on Broadway past small stores and tenements.

At **1.7 m.** is the Division St. Bridge over the Pawtucket River, which once provided water power for the Slater cotton mill and other early textile factories. At the W. end of the bridge, the road turns (L) on Pawtucket Ave., on which is the PIDGE TAVERN, **3.1 m.** (L), said to be the oldest house in Rhode Island; the right end of this substantial two-and-a-half-story building faces the street.

At **3.2 m.** is the Pawtucket-Providence boundary line.

PROVIDENCE, **5.7 m.** (12 alt., 252,981 pop.), State capital (*see R.I. GUIDE*).

Points of Interest. Brown University, State House, Roger Williams Park, Rhode Island Historical Society, Rhode Island School of Design (arts and crafts), and numerous historic houses.

The city (*see illustration*), second largest in New England, is entered from the N. on Main St., once an Indian trail. Opposite the old JEREMIAH DEXTER HOUSE, 957 N. Main St., is the NORTH BURIAL GROUND, set aside in 1700 for a "training field, burying ground, and other public uses." Many famous Rhode Islanders are interred here.

Branching R. from N. Main St. at **4.3 m.**, the well-marked highway twists deviously through a number of side streets lying a short distance W. of the center of the city. From State St., beside the main line of the railroad (L), can be seen ST. PATRICK'S CHURCH (R), the STATE OFFICE BUILDING and the STATE HOUSE (R).

Turning R. on Fountain St., US 1 passes the rear of the PUBLIC LIBRARY and veers (L) into Franklin St.

At **6.9 m.** is a junction with Elmwood Ave., at which is GRACE CHURCH CEMETERY (L). US 1 turns (R) on Elmwood Ave.

At the junction with Reservoir Ave., **8 m.**, is a bronze STATUE OF COLUMBUS (R), modeled by Bartholdi, the sculptor of the Statue of Liberty in New York Harbor, and originally cast in silver for the 1893 World's Fair in Chicago.

At **8.8 m.** is an entrance to beautiful ROGER WILLIAMS PARK (L), a recreational area containing lakes, gardens, shady drives, tennis courts, the Benedict Memorial to Music, the Betsy Williams House (1773), a zoo, and a museum.

At **9.6 m.** is the Providence-Cranston boundary line. The highway runs through the eastern outskirts of the city of CRANSTON (*see R.I. GUIDE*), an industrial city.

In the southern part of the city US 1 traverses a fairly open countryside, dotted here and there with large factories manufacturing wire goods, textile machinery, and fire extinguishers.

At **10.6 m.** is the Cranston-Warwick boundary line. The 42-square-mile city of Warwick has no metropolitan center; within its limits are more than a dozen villages separated by large tracts of woodland and open fields. At the end of Elmwood Ave., **11.5 m.**, US 1 bears R. on the old Boston Post Road, the route between New York and Boston that has been heavily traveled since Colonial days. In this flat and sparsely wooded section is the STATE AIRPORT, **12.9 m.** (L), opened in the spring of 1936.

South of GREENWOOD BRIDGE, at **14.5 m.**, is the residential village of GREENWOOD (Warwick City, 50 alt.).

RHODE ISLAND

At **15.1 m.**, on the outskirts of Apponaug, GORTON POND (R) provides good fresh-water fishing and bathing.

Near Gorton Pond US 1 bears R. into Main St., village of APPONAUG (20 alt.), **15.7 m.**, the shopping district and the administrative center of the "city" of Warwick (*see R.I. GUIDE*).

The ARMORY OF THE KENTISH ARTILLERY, R. on Main St., is occupied by a company organized during the Revolution and chartered in 1797.

In Apponaug Four Corners the road turns L. and passes through the attractive residential village of COWESETT, **17 m.** (Warwick City, 20–200 alt.). The large estates on the ridge (R) command an extensive view of East Greenwich Bay (L).

At **18.3 m.** is the Warwick-East Greenwich boundary line.

EAST GREENWICH, **18.5 m.** (East Greenwich Town, 40 alt., 3,666 pop., incorp. 1677), is a village, the center of a town that was a part of Providence County until Kent County was formed in 1750. Many of the first settlers were veterans of King Philip's War. In pre-Revolutionary days the community produced pottery from coarse red clay dug from the vicinity of Quidnesset and fired in local kilns. The resulting product was of inferior grade, but pride in local industry gave it preference over English pottery. At the present time East Greenwich manufactures textiles and textile machinery, and ships tons of Rhode Island shellfish to other States. Though much of the township land is stony, truck gardens cover the more fertile acres.

In the village, which is built on the side of a long hill (R) facing Greenwich Bay, are many early American houses. On the SE. corner of Division and Pierce Sts. is the CAPT. JOHN CONGDON HOUSE (1711), a two-story frame structure with a gambrel roof. On the SW. corner of the same intersection is the ELDREDGE HOUSE, a large, white, frame house (about 1757). This building was bought in 1788 by Nathan Greene, who opened the first tannery in town. The SALTPETER LOT (L) is the place where Richard Mathewson and Earl Mowry manufactured gunpowder for the Continental Army.

WINDMILL COTTAGE, (L) at Division and West Sts., is so called because of the four-story hexagonal windmill attached to its W. side. This house (about 1818) was bought in 1866 by Henry Wadsworth Longfellow for his friend, George Washington Greene, diplomat, historian, and professor; Greene was a grandson of Gen. Nathanael Greene of Revolutionary fame.

Nearly opposite Windmill Cottage on Division St. (R) is the Gov. WILLIAM GREENE HOMESTEAD, or Samuel Gorton, Jr., House, the outstanding Colonial relic in this part of the State. It is a substantial white wooden structure, two and a half stories high, the main section rectangular in plan, with the long rear slope of the roof extending lower than does the front. An addition at the rear gives the house an L shape. The date of construction (1680) shown on the central stone chimney, pilastered and capped, probably the end chimney of the original house, applies to only the west end. The ell in the north end has a beautiful, pedimented doorway. Since 1718 this house has been in possession of the Greene family, and it was here that Gen. Nathanael Greene met and married Catherine Littlefield in 1774. The future general was very fond of dancing with his fiancée, notwithstanding his father's efforts to "whip him out of such idle propensities."

At the junction of Division St. and Howland Rd. a marker states that in September 1774 a Tory mob gathered to destroy the village of East Greenwich.

On Howland Rd. is the DANIEL HOWLAND HOUSE (1677), a typical early small New England farmhouse.

On Main St. (L) near the town boundary line is the VARNUM MEMORIAL ARMORY (1914), erected in honor of Gen. James Mitchell Varnum. This brick building with castellated roof holds interesting historical relics in its museum.

In this same closely built section (L) is the GREENE HOUSE, 86 Main St., a two-story frame building (1724). The addition on the northern end contained (1804) the first bank in East Greenwich. Albert C. Greene, United States Senator (1845–51), once lived here.

On Pierce St. near the FIRST BAPTIST CHURCH is the GENERAL VARNUM HOUSE (1733), a handsome, square, two-story frame house with low-pitched roof. The front door opens on a small porch with a roof supported by Ionic columns. The fine interior woodwork in the northeast parlor was copied by Stanford White for the Women's Building of the Jamestown Exposition. Varnum was the first colonel of the Kentish Guards, formed during the Revolution. Later he was a brigadier general in the Continental Army and judge for the Northwest Territory. Washington, Lafayette, and Thomas Paine were guests in this old mansion.

Nearby is the ARMORY OF THE KENTISH GUARDS, a small frame

structure with Doric pillars framing the central doorway. In the summer of 1774, 56 citizens of Kent County met to establish a military company. At the October session of the General Assembly they were granted the right to incorporate as an independent company under the name of the Kentish Guards. The company was, and still is, subject only to the orders of the Governor.

Opposite the armory is the EAST GREENWICH ACADEMY, a private coeducational school, founded in 1802 and first known as Kent Academy. In 1841 it was sold to the Providence Conference of the Methodist Episcopal Church. Dr. Eben Tourgee, who founded the New England Conservatory of Music in Boston, established the music department in this school. The original building was moved to Spring St. and is the headquarters of the EAST GREENWICH HISTORICAL SOCIETY.

Also on Pierce St. is the FRIENDS MEETING HOUSE (about 1804), where the many Quakers in this section, among them the prominent Greene family, gathered. Since the sect has nearly died out in this neighborhood, the old structure is seldom opened except on Quarterly Meeting Day, when members gather from all over the State to transact the business of the society.

Another historic building is the CAPT. THOMAS ARNOLD HOUSE (about 1735), 28 King St., where lived the first Federal Collector of Customs for the Port of East Greenwich. At the foot of this short street is the SECOND KENT COUNTY JAIL, built in 1804 and still in use, though much enlarged. Over the door of the old house formerly stood two painted wooden figures, chained together — one of a white man, the other of a Negro — signifying that justice implies impartiality to men of all races. These figures are now in possession of the Rhode Island Historical Society. On a hill at the end of Wine St., near King St., is the old BAPTIST BURIAL GROUND, dating back to 1729.

On the corner of Main and Court Sts. (R) is the KENT COUNTY COURTHOUSE (1750). This square, three-and-a-half-story frame structure with its clock tower is Georgian in character. Here the convention for the framing of the Rhode Island Constitution met in September 1842. The exterior of this beautiful building has remained unchanged, but the interior has been entirely remodeled. In the early days the courtyard had on one side of its walk a liberty pole and on the other side the pillory and whipping post. The ELDREDGE MEMORIAL FOUNTAIN now stands in the courtyard where once were the town pump and horse trough. At the end of Court St. is the DR. PETER TURNER HOUSE (about 1774), home of a Revolutionary Army surgeon.

Diagonally across Main St. from the courthouse is the Greenwich Inn (L) on the SITE OF THE COL. WILLIAM ARNOLD TAVERN (1770), later called the Updike Tavern. Abraham Lincoln stopped here overnight in 1860. The old tavern, scene of the organization of the Kentish Guards, was razed in 1896 to make way for the present hotel.

A few yards S. of the inn (L) is the METHODIST CHURCH (1833). In 1850 the old church, being too small for the growing congregation, was cut in two and the sections moved apart to make way for a new central section. In this meeting house, on November 5, 1842, the Constitution of the State of Rhode Island and Providence Plantations was adopted.

At 101 Marlborough St. stands an old three-story frame structure on a stone foundation, the FIRST KENT COUNTY JAIL (1780). It is now a dwelling house, but in the cellar are two of the original prison cells.

The EAST GREENWICH FIRE ENGINE COMPANY (L), a short distance S. on Main St., was chartered in 1797. Nearby is the old BRICK HOUSE (L), the first brick house to be built (1767) in East Greenwich.

At **19.4 m.** near the southern edge of the village of East Greenwich is the junction with Forge Rd., which leads to the peninsula of POTOWOMUT, a part of Warwick, though separated from the rest of that city by East Greenwich. The residents of Potowomut say they realize they belong to Warwick only when their annual tax bills arrive.

Left on Forge Rd., **0.2 m.** (L), is a spring on a trail frequently taken by Roger Williams, founder of the Colony. He named it ELIZABETH SPRING for the wife of his friend, John Winthrop, Jr. After Mrs. Winthrop's death, some time previous to 1675, Williams wrote to Winthrop of his stopping at this place on a trip to the Narragansett country, saying "Here is the spring, I say with a sigh, but where is Elizabeth? My charity answers, 'She is gone to the Eternal Spring and Fountain of Living Waters.'" A small marker at the bottom of a path descending from Forge Rd. bears the spring's name and the date 1645. At present the spring is dry.

On Ives St., which runs N. from Forge Rd., is GODDARD MEMORIAL PARK, a gift to the State in 1927 from Robert H. Ives Goddard of Providence, and his sister, the Marquise Madeleine D'Andigne of Paris. Planned by the original owners as a forest reservation, this 470-acre State park contains many rare species of trees. The park has facilities for swimming, baseball, tennis, golf, and riding. Picnic tables and fireplaces are in groves of white pine trees. In 1936, in connection with the State Tercentenary, several structures were erected to illustrate the village life of the Narragansett Indians. The reconstructions show a typical

RHODE ISLAND

round house, and a long house, with its imitation birch bark fastened to the roof poles by vines. A circular stockade was also built, with poles extending 9 ft. above ground, and tied together at the top by vines.

At the end of Forge Rd., about **1 m.**, are the SITE OF AN OLD FORGE and the NATHANAEL GREENE BIRTHPLACE. A granite monument near the shore of the Potowomut River marks the site of the old forge and blacksmith shop, which belonged to the Greene family. The birthplace of Nathanael Greene, brilliant Revolutionary general, is high on a hillside above the forge site. This large white frame house (1684) suffered from remodeling in several styles of architecture. Nine generations of the Greene family have lived here. Specimens of the massive anchors made at the Greene forge are in the yard. One anchor is held fast in a tree that has grown around it.

On US 1 at **20 m.** is the junction with the unpaved Pierce Rd.

On this road, and visible (R) from US 1, is the COGGESHALL HOUSE (about 1715), a two-and-a-half-story structure with a large pilastered stone chimney. It is now known as Spring Brook Farm.

HUNTS RIVER BRIDGE, **20.7 m.**, marks the East Greenwich-North Kingstown boundary line.

In the open, rolling country of this section of North Kingstown is the junction with the paved Frenchtown Rd.

Right **2.5 m.** on Frenchtown Rd. is the village of FRENCHTOWN, on the site of a 17th century Huguenot settlement that was broken up by boundary controversies between Rhode Islanders and the owners of the Atherton Purchase, who endeavored (1659-71) to keep this part of the Colony under the jurisdiction of Connecticut.

At about **21.5 m.** is the section known as Quidnesset, a flat but pleasant residential country dotted with groups of evergreen trees. It was here that clay was secured for the Colonial pottery works in East Greenwich.

At **22.7 m.** is the junction with the improved Newcombs Rd.

Left **2 m.** on this road is NORTH KINGSTOWN BEACH, a large summer colony with facilities for swimming, boating, and fishing. There are good accommodations in season.

Opposite the junction with Newcombs Rd. are the DANIEL FONES HOUSES (R), on land held in the Fones family since 1680; it was a part of the Atherton Purchase, bought from John Winthrop, Jr., about 1669. The Indians had sold it to Winthrop and others in 1659.

The well-preserved farmhouse near the road was the home of Daniel Fones, soldier and privateersman in the Revolutionary War. Extensively remodeled, its gambrel roof is the outstanding evidence of its construction in an early period, though not as early as the date on the chimney (1644) indicates.

The very plain two-and-a-half-story gable house, a few yards south, is the older of the two, although the date of its construction is unknown. Characteristic of the houses of that period are the windows with their small panes.

DEVIL'S FOOT ROCK, 22.9 m. (R), is a large flat rock with a curious depression that has traditionally been considered as an imprint of the devil's foot. The footprint, close to the road, according to legend marks the spot where the evil one stepped when he came over to the mainland from Conanicut Island.

At 23.3 m. is the junction with the improved Camp Ave.

Left 2.5 m. on the latter is QUONSET POINT, another summer colony with a good beach.

The RICHARD SMITH HOUSE, 24.3 m. (L), known also as the Updike House, and as Cocumcussoc, is scarcely visible from the highway because of surrounding trees. This two-and-a-half-story frame structure has a central brick chimney. The modern vine-covered piazza along the front and the sides disguises the old lines so that the house does not appear to be of late 17th century type. In 1639 Richard Smith built here his first trading post in the Narragansett Indian territory; its garrison served as headquarters of the Colonial troops during the campaign that ended in the Swamp Fight in 1675. A few rods in front of the house is a tablet marking the grave of 40 men who fell in this engagement. The house was burned in 1676 by Indians but a few of its beams are said to have been used in the present house, erected by Richard Smith, Jr., about 1680. The wife of Richard Smith, Sr., according to tradition, brought from England a recipe for cheese that became so popular that the local product was shipped to the southern Colonies and to the West Indies.

The PALMER NORTHUP HOUSE, 24.4 m. (R), an interesting old structure, is a two-and-a-half-story wooden house with a gable roof. A lean-to, adjoining the house on the rear and extending to the roof, gives the house something of a camel-back effect. A part of one side of this house consists of a stone wall that may have been a "chimney end" at one time. The uneven spacing of the windows, the small panes in the lower windows, and the "chimney end" are characteristic of American houses built about 1650; the date of construction of

RHODE ISLAND 73

this house is not known, but it is apparent that many improvements and additions have been made, as its mass and piazza are not at all characteristic of that early period.

In front of the Palmer Northup House, on the edge of the highway, is a stone marker stating that near here was situated the Roger Williams Trading Post, established in 1637. Williams spent much of his time here bartering with the Indians. In 1651 he sold his post to Richard Smith, whose trading house was only a few rods distant, in order to obtain money for his journey to England to seek the annulment of the patent (1651–52) under which William Coddington had established a separate government for Newport and Portsmouth.

At **25 m.** is the junction with Tower Hill Rd. or US 1B.

Right on this paved road at **0.6 m.** is the junction with State 102, part of which is still called the TEN ROD ROAD. It was originally laid out 165 ft. wide so that herds of cattle could easily be driven from western Rhode Island and from eastern Connecticut, to Wickford for shipment by sea.

The PHILLIPS HOUSE (R), **0.9 m.** on US 1B, in the small village of Belleville (North Kingstown Town), is sometimes called Mowbra Castle. The original house (about 1700) consisted of the ell and a part of the present main building. The chief architectural feature of the exterior is a stone pilastered chimney. During the Revolution Samuel Phillips, the owner, was a lieutenant in the Continental Navy. He commanded one of the five boats in the daring expedition that captured General Prescott in Portsmouth in July 1777 and brought him safely through the British fleet.

At **3.9 m.** is the junction with the dirt Shermantown Rd. Right **0.7 m.** on Shermantown Rd. is, on Congdon Hill, the Platform, the SITE OF ST. PAUL'S (the Old Narragansett) CHURCH, now in Wickford (*see below*). The church was founded through the efforts of the English Society for the Propagation of the Gospel in Foreign Parts. Dr. James MacSparran was appointed rector of this church in 1721, and served until 1757. The church was built in 1707, and was moved to Wickford in 1800. Dr. MacSparran is buried in the cemetery that adjoined the church.

At **4.9 m.** on US 1B is the HAZARD CARSON HOUSE (R), a two-story frame structure built about 1775. The living room in this house has a fine Colonial mantel and wainscoting.

At **5.5 m.** is the North Kingstown-South Kingstown boundary line. As the highway passes over the high rolling country in this vicinity distant views of the Pettaquamscutt River, or Narrow River, and Narragansett Bay (L) are unfolded.

In a field (L) at **5.6 m.** is an unmarked stone known as HANNAH ROBINSON'S ROCK. According to tradition Hannah Robinson, on her return to her father's house after having been deserted by her husband, asked the servants who were carrying her litter to stop that she might have a last look at her beloved Narragansett country (*see below*).

At **5.8 m.** is the junction with Bridgetown Rd. Left **0.6 m.** on Bridgetown Rd.

is the junction with the dirt Narrow River Rd. Left on the latter is the GLEBE, **1.1 m.**, a shingled two-and-a-half-story house with a gable roof. Here dwelt James MacSparran, rector of St. Paul's Church from 1721 to 1757, with his wife Hannah (Gardiner), whose family built the house about 1690. Notable are the hand-hewn and paneled walls. The house was known during the MacSparran occupancy as a center of lavish hospitality; here were often entertained Dean Berkeley and John Smibert, the artist. The only thing about South County that the famous Episcopal clergyman disliked was the climate, which he found "either frying or freezing."

At **7.45 m.** on US 1B are stone gateposts (L) through which can be reached, by a footpath that begins at the top of a hill **0.2 m.** inside the entrance, PETTAQUAMSCUTT ROCK, or Treaty Rock. On this spot was negotiated the Pettaquamscutt Purchase of 1658, by which a group of white settlers acquired from the Indians a large tract of land, the boundaries of which were not quite clear. The tract may have been 144 sq. m. in area. The rock is now on private land (*may be visited with consent of owners*).

At **7.7 m.** on US 1B is the junction with the dirt Middle Bridge Rd. At the junction is a tablet (L) inscribed "This Acre of Land was given by Samuel Sewall and Hannah His Wife, September 23, 1707, 'To build a public Meeting House on for the Solemn worship of God.' Dr. Joseph Torrey, minister of this church, 1732–1791, lies buried here."

Left **0.1 m.** on Middle Bridge Rd. is the HELME HOUSE (L), a plain two-and-one-half-story shingled house with a gambrel roof. Built before the Revolution, it is the last remaining house of what was known as Tower Hill, the capital of South Kingston. In Revolutionary days a small boy would be sent to the roof of this house to watch the movements of the fleet off Newport. Benjamin Franklin was frequently entertained in the house on his journeys between Boston and Philadelphia. The present owner is a descendant of Chief Justice Helme, whose name the house bears.

At **1.1 m.** on Middle Bridge Rd. is a market (R) near the SITE OF THE JIREH BULL GARRISON HOUSE, burned by the Indians December 15, 1675, during King Philip's War.

At **9 m.** on US 1B, in open rolling country, is the CARTER JACKSON MONUMENT (R), a low stone pillar, easily overlooked, which is completely covered by a lengthy inscription: "This pillar is erected to the memory of William Jackson of Virginia who was murdered upon this spot by ship captain Thomas Carter of Newport, Rhode Island, who having been shipwrecked and rendered penniless thereby, and being overtaken by Mr. Jackson, who also being on his way north, furnished him with money and use of a horse on the way. Having arrived at the point indicated by this pillar, Carter there robbed and murdered his kind and confiding benefactor with a dagger, about the hour of midnight, on January 1st, 1751. Was tried and convicted of his crime at the village of Tower Hill on April 4, 1751. And was hung in chains upon a gibbet May 10, 1751, at the eastern foot of Tower Hill, at the side of the public highway, where the shrieking — as it were — of its chains and during boisterous winds at night, were the terror of many persons who lived near there or passed nearby. One of these being the late Governor George Brown of Boston Neck. Who told this writer that such had been his own case when a youth, while on his way to the residence of College Tom

RHODE ISLAND

Hazard that he visited every week. It appears, that Carter threw Jackson in the Narrow River at the time he committed the murder, and that a negro found him therein, and near the above mentioned gibbet. A wayside innkeeper, Mrs. Nash, who lived about 10 miles westward from Tower Hill, happening to be at the village at the time that his body was found. She recognized it as being that of Jackson by means of a button she had sewn upon his vest only a few hours before he left her house, and that Captain Carter was with him. Carter was therefore arrested, tried, and condemned, and executed accordingly." Thomas R. Hazard wrote that as a boy he heard "ever and anon, one of Carter's bones fall cajunk to the ground."

As US 1B passes the brow of a hill near the Carter Jackson Monument, a panorama of the whole country to the S. comes into view. A little to the E. (L) is Narragansett Pier, to the S. is Point Judith, and slightly to the W. (R) is the village of Wakefield, in a valley.

At **10 m.** is the junction with US 1.

At **25.1 m.** on US 1 is the northern rim of the old village of WICK-FORD (North Kingstown Town, sea level), which takes pride in having more well-preserved 18th century houses than has any other village of its size in New England. Along West Main St., between this point and the village center, are eleven old buildings; but since only three date from before 1800 this may be considered one of the newer sections of Old Wickford. Much of the original village was laid out as a real estate development by Lodowick Updike, grandson of Richard Smith, the trader at Cocumcussoc (*see above*). Updike began selling lots in 1709. The first house in the village was probably erected in 1711, on the southern side of present Washington St.

On West Main St. at **25.2 m.** is the old TOWN HOUSE (R), a small one-story frame structure (1807). This plain building, reminiscent of countless New England schoolhouses, is now an American Legion hall.

Near the village center, a few yards W. of Bridge St., is the STEPHEN COOPER HOUSE (1728), probably the oldest house now standing in Wickford. It is a gambrel-roofed house, painted gray with brown trimmings.

In the center of the village, **25.4 m.**, US 1 turns R., but Main St., straight ahead, is a rich field for students of early American architecture. On this short street are no less than 20 houses built between 1728 and 1804. On adjoining or nearby streets are more than 40 other old houses, most of them dating from the 18th century.

The IMMANUEL CASE HOUSE, 64 Main St., probably built in 1786, is an outstanding example of a late 18th century home. It is a large two-and-a-half-story house, rectangular in plan, with two large brick chimneys rising from the ridge of its gable roof. The massive chimneys taper. Interesting features are the corniced windows and the paneled door; Ionic pilasters support the latter's entablature which had a decorated frieze; the entablature is topped by a pediment. The simple lines of the structure and the interesting details combine to give an impression of dignity and affluence. Immanuel Case was tavernkeeper in the old village of Tower Hill; he moved to Wickford in 1786.

Branching from Main St. E. of the Case House is Church Lane, which leads around a corner to the old NARRAGANSETT CHURCH (*open in summer; in winter on application to the Wickford House on Main St.*). This church was built on Congdon Hill and moved to Wickford in 1800. According to old records it was moved "between Tuesdays." It is an exceptionally fine example of an 18th century church. The building is severely plain in outline, without a tower or other external decoration, except a beautiful doorway surmounted by a large, curved, broken pediment, supported by two plain capped pilasters. A small dark tablet is in the pedimented field. The church is used for summer services; slave pews are still visible in the gallery.

YE OLD NARRAGANSETT BANK HOUSE (1768), on the SW. corner of Main and Fountain Sts., was once used by Deborah Whitford as a bakery. About 1805 it was remodeled by Benjamin Fowler, a merchant, landholder, and financier, to serve as a bank; since 1853 the building has been used for residential purposes. In appearance it is much like the Case House (*see above*).

On the E. side of Pleasant St., a few yards N. of Main St., is the JOHN UPDIKE HOUSE (1745), one of the largest and best-furnished homes of Old Wickford. The building is two and a half stories high, with a gable roof and central chimney. It was confiscated from a Tory owner during the Revolution.

At the E. end of Main St., **0.3 m.** from US 1, is a pleasant view of Wickford Harbor.

From Main St. a marked side road runs about **0.5 m.** to the STATE LOBSTER HATCHERY (*visitors welcome*), where lobsters are raised from eggs. The Wickford hatchery released about 1,500,000 lobsters in 1935.

At **25.9 m.** (R) is the SOUTH COUNTY BARN MUSEUM (*open Sat., Sun. aft. in summer; at other times by arrangement; adm. 25¢*), containing a

RHODE ISLAND

fine collection of the implements used in early times by farmers, mechanics, and housewives. The tools and products of the various craftsmen and artisans are gathered into small shop units to present an interesting and accurate picture of Colonial life. Here the visitor sees the tools with which the colonist tilled his fields; how he kept his livestock; how he spun yarn, wove cloth, and made clothing; what he used in caring for the sick; what he used when he hunted and fished, and traveled and traded by land and sea.

At **27.2 m.** is the small residential village of HAMILTON (North Kingstown Town, 20 alt.).

At **29.1 m.** is the junction with a paved side road. From the junction is clearly seen (L) CONANICUT ISLAND in the middle of Narragansett Bay, and in front of it smaller DUTCH ISLAND, site of Fort Greble. FORT GREBLE, constructed during the Civil War, is now garrisoned by a skeleton force. South of this point US 1 runs close to the bay, with many attractive views (L).

Left **0.5 m.** on the side road is PLUM BEACH, a small but excellent bathing beach. Here also at BARBOUR'S HEIGHTS the town maintained a coast guard and breastworks during the Revolution.

At **29.4 m.** is the junction with a dirt side road.

Right **1 m.** on the latter, in a little brook valley among low rolling hills, is (L) the GILBERT STUART HOUSE, built in 1751 (*open May to October; adm. 25¢*). Here in 1755 Gilbert Stuart, son of a snuff grinder, was born. He became a great portrait painter. For a hundred years after Gilbert Stuart's time a grist mill was operated here before the Gilbert Stuart Memorial, Inc., purchased and restored this old house. In the large barn-like structure, painted a dark red, snuff is once more being made.

The CASEY HOUSE, **30.1 m.** (R), built about 1725, was the scene of several Revolutionary skirmishes. The original floor of the dining room, which has been overlaid, is riddled with bullet holes, as are three of its doors. A closet at the right of the stairway served as a safe hiding place for the American minute-men. This house is to become the property of the Society for the Preservation of New England Antiquities, according to an agreement made by its present (1937) owner, Edward Casey. It is a two-and-a-half-story wooden structure, almost square in plan, with a large brick chimney rising from its gable-on-hip roof. Hip-roof dormers project on three sides of this roof. On the south side is a piazza topped by a paneled parapet rail and supported by six Doric columns.

At **30.8 m.** is the North Kingstown-Narragansett boundary line.
At **31.7 m.** is the junction with South Ferry Rd.

Left **0.5 m.** on the paved South Ferry Rd. is the FRANKLIN FERRY HOUSE (L), a rambling yellow farmhouse, used as joint dwelling and business office for the ferry, which began running shortly before 1700, and was for some time the only means of communication between Newport and the mainland.

In front of the Franklin House the paved section of South Ferry Rd. turns L.; and at **1 m.** (L) is the large, well-preserved HANNAH ROBINSON HOUSE (about 1710). This large two-and-a-half-story gambrel-roofed house (*see illustration*) was remodeled in 1755 by Rowland Robinson, a wealthy Narragansett planter, grandson of the builder, and father of Hannah. The house was once 105 ft. long, but the old kitchen and Negro quarters have been demolished, reducing the length to about 60 ft. The main part is rectangular in plan; joining it, and giving the entire structure an L-shape, is a large addition at the rear. The small window lights (panes) and the small clapboards indicate the early origin of the original structure. The house has a fine main doorway, surmounted by a broken pediment which rests on two fluted Doric pilasters; it probably does not belong to the original plan. The west bedroom, known as the Lafayette Chamber since it was occupied by the Marquis de Lafayette during the Revolutionary War, contains the names of French officers scratched on the windowpanes. In this house Hannah Robinson met the Frenchman with whom she later eloped. The story of her desertion, of her poverty and illness and her father's unrelenting anger, of the belated reunion of father and daughter, and of the return of the girl on a litter borne by slaves to this house to die, is well told by Alice Morse Earle in *Old Narragansett*.

On the unpaved section of South Ferry Rd., at **0.7 m.**, is the NARRAGANSETT BAPTIST CHURCH (L), a simple, white frame building visible for miles around because of its situation on a treeless hilltop. Regular services are no longer held here; the building is a social center.

At **0.8 m.** (R) on South Ferry Rd., on the slope of a hill overlooking the bay, is FORT PHILIP KEARNY, which was built on the site of the former village of South Ferry. During the Civil War the village consisted of eight or nine tenement houses, an inn, and a mill that manufactured jean. The mill engine room and dye house are still standing. In 1905 the Government bought 25 acres of this land from the Davis Pain Killer Manufacturing Company and built Fort Kearny. Two companies were stationed here during the World War. Mines were laid, and a net was strung across the bay to prevent the entrance of enemy submarines, should they try to move up the bay to Providence.

At **32.3 m.** is the junction with a paved side road marked "Bonnet Point." From this junction BEAVER TAIL LIGHT, at the southern end of Conanicut Island, is clearly visible.

Left on this road at **0.5 m.**, standing a little to the N., is the WILLIAM GARDINER HOUSE (L), a two-and-a-half-story dwelling erected in 1727. A large, capped, central brick chimney rises from the ridge of the gable roof, which slightly overhangs at the ends. The windows are topped by small cornices. This

RHODE ISLAND

was the home of a wealthy 18th century farmer, whose daughter Hannah married Mr. James MacSparran, rector of St. Paul's Church. She died in London during the plague.

On BONNET POINT, **1 m.**, which is now a summer colony, was a fort, erected in 1777 and twice rebuilt. During the Revolution it was used continuously, and again, during the War of 1812, a battery was stationed here. During the Civil War it was rumored that the Confederate cruiser *Alabama* was anchored in the bay and once again the fort was strengthened and a battery put on duty. The fortifications have since been demolished.

At **34.5 m.** is the junction with a paved side road.

Left **0.2 m.** on this road is the HAZARD HOUSE (L). It is a large, square, white, frame house (about 1740), with a front lawn sloping gently down toward the bay. From the front of the house is seen WHALE ROCK LIGHT, between the mainland and Conanicut Island. The lighthouse was completed in 1872.

The Hazard House is on the northern edge of the village of Narragansett, which is the administrative center for the township of the same name.

NARRAGANSETT, 36.1 m. (Narragansett Town, 100 alt.; 1,258 town pop.), is a village in a township that has been a separate political entity since 1901, though in 1888 it was set aside as a special district in the township of South Kingstown. Narragansett perpetuates the name of the tribe of Indians that at one time roamed over this territory. The Narragansett Indians were killed or driven away at the time of King Philip's War, 1675–76. The 19th century mansion of William Sprague, Governor of the State (1860–63), which burned in 1909, was built on the site of one of the camping grounds of Canonchet, last notable sachem of the tribe.

Narragansett Village is best known as a summer resort, though farming and fishing are carried on. Many years ago a long pier jutted out into the water just below the largest bathing beach, and here vessels of all descriptions landed passengers and cargoes. The heavy surf tore the pier away, but this part of the town is still known as Narrangansett Pier; its beaches are popular in summer.

One of the favorite stories of the town is that of a native who disciplined his son by beating him with an axe-helve. After one such beating he announced that the boy had run away to sea, but townspeople believed that the boy had been done to death and buried in the old man's cellar. When the father died, no one wished to stay with the body the night before burial; finally a volunteer watcher from Kingston appeared. He was awakened from a nap by the opening of the outer door, which unlatched itself and swung inward. He closed and latched it carefully. Again the door opened; this time he slammed it shut and whittled out a wooden plug to secure the latch as tightly as possible. He had hardly completed the task before the plug popped out, the door swung inward, and a heavy object was tossed into the room from the outer darkness. It was an axe-helve, worn and smooth from use. When the watcher found no one outside he shut the door a third time, and it remained closed.

Half a mile N. of the center of the village, and visible from US 1, is the private, well-equipped DUNES CLUB (L), named for its surroundings. The main clubhouse is a low, rambling, stucco structure 300 ft. long and two stories high, with an impressive clock tower. The club is near the northern end of the pier beach, a crescent-shaped strip of sand about half a mile in length.

Near the village center is SHERRY'S BATHING PAVILION (*open to the public*).

At **36.1 m.**, in the center of Narragansett, US 1 turns R. on Narragansett Ave.

Left (straight ahead) on the Point Judith Road. At **0.1 m.** on this road, L. on Beach St., past PETTAQUAMSCUTT PARK on the site of the former Hotel de la Plage, between the Casino Theater and the office of Narragansett Beach Corporation. The park serves as a convenient passageway to the beach walk and is a pleasant place to rest. Band concerts are held here during the summer months.

Just beyond the park the route swings R. on Ocean Rd. Near the turn are the TOWERS, formerly the old Narragansett Casino. Only a stone arch across the road, with two large towers at either end, is left of the old casino, which was destroyed by fire some time ago. Nearby is the COAST GUARD STATION (L), a two-story stone building with a slate roof (1887). At about **1 m.** the village of Narragansett gives way to the large estates of summer colonists, which line both sides of the highway

HAZARD CASTLE, **1.3 m.** (R), almost hidden from the road by trees, is a large building of rough stone, with two large granite towers. The house, an imitation of an English abbey, was begun in 1846 by Joseph Peach Hazard, but he abandoned it in an unfinished condition, and vegetation grew up in wild profusion. The house became known as the Haunted Castle. In 1883 a nephew of the original builder bought the place and completed it. A view from the top of the square tower — the other is hexagonal — 165 feet above sea level, includes every point from Newport to Block Island. In this building some years ago, Dwight W. Tryon, the New York artist, had a studio.

The entrance to the POINT JUDITH COUNTRY CLUB (*private*) is at **1.8 m.** (R). The club maintains a golf course, tennis courts, and polo grounds. The polo games (*adm. 55¢*) are held the last week in July and the first two weeks in August.

SCARBOROUGH BEACH, **3.5 m.** (L), is a State reservation with a fine beach. A large pavilion is now being constructed on the reservation.

RHODE ISLAND

At **4.7 m.** is the junction with a paved side road. Right **0.7 m.** on this road is SAND HILL COVE, another State reservation. The bathing beach is protected by the Point Judith Breakwater. GALILEE, **1.7 m.**, is an old-fashioned little fishing village.

Ocean Rd. ends at POINT JUDITH, **5.7 m.** Many stories are told about the origin of the name. Some say the point was named for the wife of John Hull, Boston goldsmith and mintmaster, while others say that it was named for Judith Stoddard, his mother-in-law. There is a legend that the name was given by some churchman from Boston, who took the name from the Bible. On some of the earliest maps the name is printed "Point Juda Neck." Another story is that a Nantucket captain was lost in fog and did not know in which direction to steer; his daughter, in the boat with him, presently cried out that she spied land; the old captain commanded anxiously, "Pint, Judy, pint!" Whatever the derivation of the name, Point Judith is a piece of land known to all mariners as one of the most dangerous spots along the Atlantic coast. The POINT JUDITH COAST GUARD STATION is on the point.

During the Revolution a coast guard and tower beacon were maintained here. In 1888 a Coast Guard station was built. The building burned down in 1933 and was replaced by a new station, completed in 1935. Near the station is POINT JUDITH LIGHTHOUSE. The first lighthouse was a wooden structure built in 1806. This was blown down in the great gale of September 1815. The present building is an octagonal stone building, built in 1816. The light is now operated by electricity. Though dangerous to seafarers, Point Judith appears tame on ordinary occasions. The land is flat, sandy, and nearly treeless. Only when high winds roll up great breakers does the point impress landlubbers with its threatening character. From the point there is an unbroken view of the Atlantic.

On Narragansett Ave., which US 1 follows, is the MANSION HOUSE, a four-story summer hotel containing the most beautiful corner-cupboard in South County; this cupboard may have been brought from an older house, the Thomas Mumford homestead, which stood near the Tower Hill Road and burned down many years ago. Thomas Mumford, one of the original Pettaquamscutt purchasers, owned large tracts of land in this part of Narragansett.

Near the western edge of the village is SPRAGUE MEMORIAL PARK (R). In the distance on a hilltop (R) is a tall brown structure, the TOWER HILL HOUSE (in South Kingstown), a home for underprivileged children conducted by Roman Catholic charities.

At **37.5 m.** is the Narragansett–South Kingstown boundary line.

At **38 m.** is the junction with US 1B (*see side tour above at* **25 m.**) and also the paved Kingston Rd.

Right **0.7 m.** on the latter road is the SCALLOP SHELL (R), the home of Miss Caroline Hazard. Miss Hazard, president of Wellesley College from 1899 to 1910, was the author of many books, including *Anchors of Tradition, Narragansett Ballads,* and *A Scallop Shell of Quiet.*

At **1.5 m.** is the village of PEACE DALE (South Kingstown Town, 40 alt.). This village is the home of the PEACE DALE MANUFACTURING CO., the chief industry of the place; its history dates from 1800. Isaac P. and Rowland G. Hazard here erected a mill for the making of fine woolens and in 1848 they procured a charter for the Peace Dale Manufacturing Company; the mill began to turn out shawls in 1849. In 1856 the works were greatly enlarged, and in 1872 a new mill was added for the manufacture of worsted goods.

In earlier times the farmers of Peace Dale raised large quantities of flax; the seeds were pressed into oil and the fiber of the flax was woven into linen. In 1751 the General Assembly passed an act to give bounties for the raising of flax. The stores all took flax in barter and each kept a machine for beating out the seed.

Near the center of the village, on Kingstown Rd., is the HAZARD MEMORIAL LIBRARY, a fine stone building erected by the Hazard family in memory of the late Rowland G. Hazard.

On the SE. corner of Kingstown Rd. and Columbia St. is the MUSEUM OF PRIMITIVE CULTURE (*open weekdays, 10 a.m.; free*). This collection, the work of Rowland G. Hazard, was inspired by his interest in primitive peoples. In the collection are several thousand specimens obtained from various parts of the United States and from many foreign countries. The bulk of the material is archeological, consisting of stone artifacts, such as arrows and spear heads; there are also baskets and costumes. A number of objects belong to the early history of Rhode Island.

At **38.6 m.** is the village of WAKEFIELD (South Kingstown Town, 40 alt.). The center of the village is crowded with small stores, but to the S. US 1 passes many large homes set amid beautiful tree-shaded lawns. The WAKEFIELD MANUFACTURING COMPANY, once known as the Narragansett Mills, was operating in Wakefield before 1800. After several changes in ownership and management, the company was sold (1866) to Robert Rodman, who for many years manufactured jeans and doeskins. The company is now managed by a New York concern that manufactures woolen cloth.

On High St. is the TOWN HALL, the administrative center of South Kingstown (sea level-333 alt., 6,010 pop.). South Kingstown was formerly a part of the township of Kingstown, incorporated in 1674, which was divided into North and South Kingstown in 1723. A settlement was made at Pettaquamscutt in 1657–58.

Before white settlers came the area was occupied by the Narragansett Indians. A few Indians remain in the township; most of them have some white or Negro blood.

On Old Kingston Rd. at Rocky Brook, **0.3 m.** W. of High St., is the WILLIAM RODMAN HOUSE, which some authorities believe to be the birthplace of Oliver Hazard Perry. The house more often referred

RHODE ISLAND 83

to as the Perry House is about two miles S. of Wakefield on US 1 (*see below*).

SUGAR LOAF HILL, which rises about 50 ft. above the highway at **39.2 m.** (R), is of disputed origin. Some have held it to be an artificial mound erected by the Indians, but geologists say that it is a natural hill. There is a good view from its summit.

At **39.25 m.** an older paved section of the Post Rd. branches R.

Right **0.1 m.** on this road is the WILLARD HAZARD HOUSE (R), better known as the Tavern. This long two-and-a-half-story shingled structure with a gable roof was built about 1740. Of unusual interest are its paneled corner pilasters. Here, according to Thomas Hazard's *Jonny-Cake Papers*, the widow Nash combed the hair of William Jackson, the unfortunate traveler from Virginia who was murdered by Thomas Carter (*see side tour at* **25 m.**). This house, with its tap-room and great ballroom on the second floor, was a favorite stage stop. It is still a hostelry, known as Ye Old Tavern.

At **0.2 m.** on the Old Post Rd. is the DOCKRAY HOUSE (R), one of the older houses of South County, and a famous landmark because of the chimney and oddly placed windows. John Dockray, a merchant from Newport, bought the land from Daniel Stedman, "with dwelling," on February 25, 1769. The ell, once used as a store, is believed to have been built in 1725.

At **40.8 m.** is the junction with a dirt lane.

Right **0.3 m.** on the latter is the OLIVER HAZARD PERRY HOUSE (*open May 30–Oct. 1; 11 a.m.–6 p.m.; adm. 25¢ each for members of large parties; otherwise adults 50¢, children 25¢*). It is a two-story, gambrel-roofed house, restored in 1929 by Mrs. Perry Tiffany, wife of the last descendant-owner. The land has been held by the Perry family since 1702, when Benjamin Perry came here from Sandwich, Mass. From here Oliver Hazard Perry went to take command of the American inland fleet on Lake Erie. The house contains many relics both of Commodore Oliver Hazard Perry and of his younger brother, Commodore Matthew C. Perry, who opened the ports of Japan to the world.

The SAMUEL G. POTTER HOUSE, **41.7 m.** (L), a one-and-a-half-story structure, was built about 1800 on a part of the John Potter estate by Samuel G. Potter, who was twice Lieutenant Governor. The house, surrounded by evergreens, stands back some distance from the highway.

At **41.9 m.** is the junction with an unpaved side road marked "Snug Harbor." Here is a good view of POTTER POND (L).

Left on this road **0.1 m.** is the JOHN POTTER HOUSE (R), a one-and-a-half-story shingled structure. Chronicles of this region describe John Potter as an 18th century squire, fond of fox hunting, the pleasures of the table, and good wine; as skillful in fishing for votes of Rhode Island freemen as for striped bass;

an acknowledged but not convicted counterfeiter — the legend being that when the King's runners were sighted, Potter threw his counterfeiting press into the deepest part of Potter Pond, from which it was never recovered.

At **42.7 m.** is the junction with a dirt road marked "Matunuck Point."

Left **1 m.** on this road is the HAZARD HOLLAND HOUSE (L). This house, situated some distance back from the road, was built about 1778 and once belonged to General Staunton, an 18th century soldier and politician. The house still has its original doors and windows, three of which have inside sliding shutters.

MATUNUCK BEACH, **1.6 m.**, is one of the oldest summer colonies on the Atlantic seaboard. There are many beautiful homes and hotels at this beach. To the W. of the beach are MATUNUCK POINT and the MATUNUCK THEATER-BY-THE-SEA, open during the summer months. It has a summer stock company with well-known players taking the leading roles.

The WAGER WEEDEN WATERING PLACE, **42.8 m.** (L), is marked by a tall stone slab, noting that water used to be brought to this spot from the pure waters of nearby Wash Pond by Wager Weeden (*see below*).

Opposite the Weeden tablet, on a hill back of several houses near the roadside, is the EDWARD EVERETT HALE HOUSE (R), with an "H" cut in its wooden window shutters. Here the author of *The Man Without a Country* spent his summers among the natural beauties he loved so much.

WILLOW DELL (1785), **42.85 m.** (L), a large house painted yellow, with red trimmings and green blinds, was the 19th century home of Judge Wager Weeden, grandfather of William Babcock Weeden, the historian.

At **44.1 m.** is the junction with the unpaved Moonstone Beach Rd.

Left **1.6 m.** on this road is the SAMUEL PERRY HOUSE (L). This structure must have been built between 1696, when Samuel Perry came to Kingstown and was made a freeman of the Colony, and 1716, when he willed the homestead, a mill, and 146 acres of land to his son James. With this house is connected the legend of the ring that returned from the sea. The wife of one of the Perrys, boasting of her riches, threw her golden wedding ring into the sea, remarking that it would be as impossible for her to become poor as for her ring to return. Some time later her husband cut her ring out of a fish that was being served at dinner, whereupon the lady grew pale with fear. Years later she died in poverty.

At the end of the road is MOONSTONE BEACH, **2 m.**, named for the yellow-white, or pearl-like, color of its sand.

The GREAT CHIMNEY HOUSE, **44.6 m.** (L), known also as the Browning House, built about 1750, now stands in a dilapidated condition in an auto scrap yard. Nearly opposite this weather-beaten,

RHODE ISLAND

shingled house is the QUAKER BURIAL GROUND, which is about 200 ft. R. of the highway and not visible from it. George Fox preached to the colonists in this vicinity in 1680, and soon after that his converts erected a meeting house near the present burial ground. James Perry, Sr., instrumental in its building, gave three acres of land for a free burial lot. The meeting house was torn down in 1888.

At **46.4 m.** is the South Kingstown-Charlestown boundary line. This part of Charlestown is flat and sandy. From the highway is visible (L) the ocean-front beach, which is separated from the mainland by Charlestown or Ninigret Pond. The evenly spaced summer cottages on the beach stand out sharply against the waters of the ocean like the teeth of a gigantic saw.

At **46.9 m.** is the CHARLESTOWN AIRPORT (L), a level field used only for emergency landings.

At **47 m.** is the junction with an unpaved road marked "Charlestown by the Sea."

Left **1 m.** on this road is CHARLESTOWN BEACH, offering surf bathing and camping places; the beach also has three good hotels, open in season. Here is the Charlestown Beachway where Charlestown Pond connects with the Atlantic Ocean.

GENERAL STANTON INN (*open in summer*), **47.5 m.** (R), is a three-story, gambrel-roofed, frame building, with shingled ends and a clapboard front, built about 1755. In the middle of the 19th century the inn was the real political headquarters of Rhode Island.

The cluster of houses and small stores at **48.1 m.** is the village of CHARLESTOWN, also called Cross' Mills (Charlestown Town, 20 alt.). In the village center, near the intersection with State 2, are two corn-meal mills. The larger and more modern of the two uses a Diesel engine for its power, but the meal is ground by stones that are over 200 years old. Across the street is the INDIAN MAID MILL, run by the old water power system.

Right from the village center on State 2; not far from the road at **2 m.** is the INDIAN BURIAL GROUND, a 20-acre plot of land owned by the Rhode Island Historical Society and maintained by the State. This was a burial plot for sachems of the Narragansett tribe. One of the graves was opened in 1869; the body had been buried in a log coffin in which were two kettles, one of brass and the other of iron.

The TOWN HALL is on State 2 at about **2.3 m.**

Charlestown Township (sea level–100 alt., 1,118 pop.) was taken from Westerly and incorporated in 1738. It was named for King Charles II, who gave Rhode Island its charter of 1663.

At **48.3 m.** is the junction with an unpaved road marked "Fort Ninigret."

Left **0.2 m.** on the latter is FORT NECK LOT, a three-quarter acre reservation owned by the Rhode Island Historical Society though maintained by the State as a park. It is at the head of a cove opening from Ninigret Pond. This fort was supposed for many years to have been the stronghold of the Niantic Indians, but it is now generally conceded that it was built by the early Dutch traders and used as a trading post. Bastions and other evidences of military engineering skill found in the fort, whose original outlines are now protected by an iron fence, seem to support this theory. Here Capt. John Mason of Connecticut and his little band of white men halted for one night on their long and dreary march into the Pequot country in 1637. Sitting around a council fire with the Niantic men, Mason persuaded Ninigret to join him in war against the long-time enemies, the Pequots.

At **49 m.** (L) is the KING TOM FARM (*open June to Sept. by permission of the owner*), once the property of the Niantic, Thomas Ninigret, better known as King Tom, who was born in 1736. He was sent to England for his education and brought back the plans for a fine home; he had the wainscoting and much of the other interior woodwork made in Newport. This structure was subsequently destroyed by fire but the outline of the house has been marked by a low wall; behind it a garden has been laid out and, on the foundation of the old chimney, is a bronze tablet bearing a picture of the original King Tom House.

On the farm still stands a two-and-a-half-story, gambrel-roofed house, painted yellow, which was built between 1746 and 1769. Also on the farm is CORONATION ROCK, on which the Narragansett Indians crowned their sachems; the date 1770 cut into it commemorates the year of the last coronation.

At **50 m.** is the junction with an unpaved road marked "Kimball Bird Sanctuary."

Right **1.3 m.** on this road is the KIMBALL BIRD SANCTUARY (*open at all times*), on the shore of Watchaug Pond. The grounds, beautifully landscaped with sumacs and red cedars, belong to the Audubon Society of Rhode Island. The sanctuary has been in existence for nearly 12 years. It is being improved by the addition of more facilities, such as bird houses and other equipment.

At **51.9 m.** is the junction with an unpaved road marked "Burlingame Reservation."

Right **1 m.** on this road into the BURLINGAME RESERVATION, a State park acquired in 1927. Its land area is 3,100 acres, about half of which is forested with broadleaf and pine. The reservation is a game preserve, containing partridge,

RHODE ISLAND

pheasant, quail, deer, rabbits, and squirrels. A water area of 500 acres provides swimming and skating in season.

At **52.5 m.** is the junction with an unpaved road.

Left **1.9 m.** on this road is QUONOCHONTAUG BEACH, where are several hotels with excellent accommodations for guests seeking summer diversion, swimming, boating, and fishing. The hotels and inns are comfortable, as well as moderate in their rates.

The GENERAL STANTON MONUMENT, **52.6 m.** (L), is a granite shaft about 20 ft. high, erected by the State in honor of Joseph Stanton, Jr., who was born in Charlestown in 1739. General Stanton was prominent as a soldier in the French and Indian War. He was a colonel in a Rhode Island regiment during the Revolution, and was also prominent in politics, being one of the first two United States Senators from Rhode Island.

Opposite the monument is the old WILCOX TAVERN (R), known also as the Monument House, built about 1730. It was here that General Stanton was born. Recently the house has been restored and refurnished in its original 18th century style.

At **53.7 m.** is the Charlestown-Westerly boundary line. Near this line, at **53.8 m.**, is the junction with a dirt road.

Left **1 m.** on this road is SHELTER HARBOR, at one time known as Music Colony, an exclusive summer resort not open to the general public. Many singers and artists have summer homes here.

At HAVERSHAM CORNER, **54.3 m.**, is the junction with the Watch Hill Shore Rd. (*see below*).

The countryside between **56.7 m.** and **57 m.** is hilly, and steep sand dunes are visible (L). The built-up section of Westerly begins at **58.8 m.**

US 1 passes the JOSHUA BABCOCK HOUSE, **59.1 m.** (R), a fine, well-preserved frame building erected about 1735. Joshua Babcock was a physician, military officer, and judge, and a friend of Benjamin Franklin, whom he frequently entertained in this house.

Near the Babcock House (R) is the SMITH GRANITE QUARRY (*visitors welcome*), established in 1847. Much fine monumental stone has been taken from this quarry, including a 50-ton block for the *Antietam Soldier* on the battlefield of Antietam.

WESTERLY, **59.7 m.** (sea level–240 alt., 10,997 pop.), a resort (*see R.I. GUIDE*).

Points of Interest. Lucy Carpenter House, Captain Card House, Westerly Memorial Bldg. and Library, Watch Hill, and others.

Left from the village center on Elm St., which becomes Watch Hill Rd. This route runs along the bank of the Pawcatuck River, past RIVER BEND CEMETERY, **1.4 m.**, and the old BABCOCK BURIAL GROUND, **2.5 m.** The summer resort of WATCH HILL, **5.5 m.**, has a fine beach and many little hills that afford charming cottage sites. Hotel accommodations are ample in season, and there are facilities for fishing and boating. About **1.5 m.** E. of the village are the cellar REMAINS OF FORT MANSFIELD, erected in 1898 and dismantled after the World War. The fort was on the elbow of NAPATREE POINT, the extreme southwestern tip of Rhode Island.

At **60 m.** on the PAWCATUCK BRIDGE, over the river of the same name, is the Connecticut State Line.

CONNECTICUT

R.I. Line — New London — New Haven — Greenwich — N.Y. Line, **119 m.** US 1.

New York, New Haven, & Hartford R.R. parallels the route.
Four-lane cement roadbed over major part of route. Excellent accommodations of all types at frequent intervals.

Section 8. Rhode Island Line to New Haven, **71.2 m.**

The first post rider on the American Continent was dispatched over this route, from New York to Boston, following the old Pequot Path, then only a blazed trail through the wilderness. Over this route in 1773 Paul Revere, spurring his foam-flecked horse, dashed on his way to Philadelphia with news of the Boston Tea Party. When the half-frozen horseman paused at Guilford to bait his horse, the astonished natives gaped wide-eyed at the streaks of war paint on his face. Today this highway, the Roaring Road, modern and efficiently policed, is the only direct route across southern Connecticut from border to border. A section of the chief vehicular highway through the North Atlantic States, it is the most heavily traveled road between New York and the cities of the New England seaboard. Although this route parallels the shore, it bypasses many of the picturesque coastal villages, and permits but occasional views of Long Island Sound.

US1 crosses the Pawcatuck River, **0 m.**, which separates Westerly, R.I., from the village of PAWCATUCK, in the Town of Stonington, Conn.

WEQUETEQUOCK (Ind., *head of a tidal river*), **2.5 m.** (Town of Stonington), is a village on the long flat inlet known as Wequetequock River.

Left from Wequetequock, at an irregular crossroad opposite the small 19th century meeting house, on a dirt road that leads across Wequetequock Cove and branches sharply R. past an old GRAVEYARD, 0.1 m., the earliest in the town of Stonington; here are "wolf stones," the heavy slabs of rude stone that were laid over graves in primitive settlements as protection against the bold and numerous wolves that then roamed the countryside. The oldest stone is dated 1690.

At **5.3 m.** (L) is STONINGTON (Stonington Town 11,025 pop.), a quiet old town of modest, shady streets on a narrow, rocky point. Off the Boston Post Road, quite by itself on a long point that juts out into the ocean and offers magnificent marine views, the community still has some of the atmosphere of old whaling days. Fishing gear and lobster traps are piled on the wharves at the end of the side streets, and during the summer there is much activity offshore.

Little remains of the shipbuilding that made Stonington a center of such importance in the colony of Connecticut that the village was popularly known as a "Nursery for Seamen." One of the first whaling franchises ever granted in America was issued to a Mr. Whiting for the waters between Stonington and Montauk Point in 1647.

The point of land on which the community stands was occupied by Narragansett Indians before the arrival of William Chesebrough and a group of colonists from Plymouth in 1649. Ownership of the territory was disputed for several years by Massachusetts and Connecticut. Massachusetts named the settlement "Souther Towne" in 1658. Connecticut renamed it Stonington in 1666, after the agreement of 1662 under which the town again came within the boundaries of the Nutmeg State.

During both the Revolutionary War and the War of 1812 the town was attacked by the British from the sea. Today there is little industry in the community. One factory produces fine silk-throwing machinery, one mill makes velvet, and another produces various forms of rubber molds.

The DUDLEY PALMER HOUSE (1700), 14 Elm St., a white clapboard, two-and-a-half-story peak-roofed house with a brick central chimney, has a delicately designed cornice with capped corner boards. A part of the home is used as a WHALING MUSEUM (*open weekdays, free*); its owner, Dr. J. H. Weeks, is an authority on local history and has collected many relics of whaling days.

In CANNON SQUARE, the southern center of the borough, stand two of the 18-pounders used in defense of Stonington during the British attack of 1814.

The old STONE LIGHTHOUSE, at the end of Water St., holds a tearoom and museum (*free*). It is a massive squat building of heavy granite blocks, once painted white, with an octagonal tower topped by a windowed hood from which the light shone. The diamond-paned casement windows, with exceptionally heavy window caps, evince a Tudor influence, strange to find in a New England lighthouse.

Among the historic maritime exhibits is the figurehead of the *Great*

CONNECTICUT

Republic, the largest ship of the mid-19th century, and one of the first to be rigged as a four-masted barque. Built in Boston by Donald McKay in 1853, her registered tonnage was 4,555. She caught fire and had to be scuttled while being loaded for her maiden voyage, and never went to sea as originally designed. Under modified rigging, she was a failure commercially but did good work as a troop ship in both the Crimean and the American Civil Wars.

The greater part of Stonington is on a peninsula close to the water. US 1 skirts the northern end of the village and turns abruptly R.

The route passes over an inlet of Stonington Harbor. For less than a mile it parallels the northern shore of the harbor, and then crosses a broad neck of land that terminates in LORD'S POINT, a summer colony on the sound. From the bridge crossing the long and narrow QUIAMBOG COVE, **8 m.**, is an excellent view (L) of FISHER'S ISLAND, three miles offshore — one of the numerous islands NE. of Long Island that are part of New York State.

At **9 m.** is the junction with a paved side road.

<small>Left on this road to MASON ISLAND, **0.8 m.**, which commands an impressive view of Fisher's Island. Mason Island, edged with rocky ledges and sandy beaches, was presented to Capt. John Mason of Windsor in appreciation of his victory over the Pequot Indians of Pequot Hill. It is now occupied by summer homes. Though the island is accessible by a private road over a causeway, sightseers are not welcome.</small>

MYSTIC, **9 m.** (Town of Stonington), is an old maritime community of trim white houses on green-fringed, irregular Mystic Harbor, the tidal outlet of the Mystic River. For generations Mystic was the home of daring mariners and fishermen, and was feared by the British during the Revolution as "a cursed little hornets' nest." It teemed with shipbuilding activity during the gold rush days, when the Mystic River echoed with pounding hammers "knocking away the shores and spurs," so that clipper ships might slide down the ways to make world records on their exciting runs around the Horn to California. Here was built in 1860 the *Andrew Jackson*, a modified clipper that combined cargo space with speed. It hung up a record of 89 days and 4 hrs., breaking by 9 hrs. the record of the famous *Flying Cloud* (1851). In succeeding passages the *Andrew Jackson* made the best average time of any ship sailing to San Francisco.

<small>Right from Mystic on State 159, a short distance, is (L) the MARINE HISTORICAL MUSEUM, housed in an old wooden mill building. Here is one of the finest</small>

collections of clipper ship models in America, in addition to old figureheads and paraphernalia of whaling and sailing days.

On the museum grounds is the hull of the sailboat *Annie*, which defeated all comers in the sandbagger class from 1870 to 1880. It was designed by D. O. Richmond, known as one of the most successful yacht builders of the era preceding ballast keel construction.

US 1 crosses the Mystic River to WEST MYSTIC, **9.7 m.** (Town of Groton), where the *Galena* (1862), one of the earliest ironclad warships, was built.

1. Right from West Mystic on Elm St. **0.9 m.** to PEQUOT HILL, on which is the MASON MONUMENT, marking the spot where Capt. John Mason with a force of 77 men captured and burned a Pequot Indian fort in 1637. More than 600 Indians were burned to death while they slept. "Seven escaped and seven died by the sword," said a report.

2. Left from West Mystic, State 125 runs along the shore of Mystic Harbor past numerous old houses and new summer homes to NOANK (Ind., *point of land*), **2.5 m.**, home of swordfishermen, lobstermen, and boatbuilders. Their wharves and craft fringe the waterfront; and their dwellings cluster on the hillside of the seagirt point, where the old lighthouse beacon has guided home generations of seafarers.

West of West Mystic, the road runs inland, crossing low hills which, several miles to the S., level into peninsulas, notably cottage-covered GROTON LONG POINT and EASTERN POINT with its exclusive summer colony.

At **11.7 m.** is FORT HILL (R), where Pequot reinforcements encamped when Mason burned their stronghold at Pequot Hill. The remnant of the tribe was pursued by Mason to Fairfield, and there perished in the Great Swamp Fight.

At the head of the salt inlet of Poquonock River the route runs through the hamlet of POQUONOCK BRIDGE (Ind., *cleared land*), **13.4 m.** (Town of Groton).

At **14.2 m.** is a dignified shaft in Avery Memorial Park (L), marking the SITE OF THE HIVE OF THE AVERYS, the homestead that from 1656 to 1894 was occupied by seven generations of the descendants of Capt. James Avery. The shaft, topped by a bust of the original settler in Puritan costume, was the gift of the late John D. Rockefeller, a descendant of the Averys, and was designed by the sculptor, Bela Lyon Pratt, another descendant.

North of the monument US 1 ascends to a hilltop from which, at **14.9 m.**, there is a wide view that embraces the countryside southward to Long Island Sound.

CONNECTICUT

At **16.4 m.** the road bypasses GROTON HEIGHTS, crowned by the granite obelisk of GROTON MONUMENT and the grass-grown breastworks of FORT GRISWOLD, scene of a disastrous Revolutionary battle in 1781.

At **16.5 m.** is GROTON (Groton Town 10,770 pop.), a summer resort whose main streets US 1 bypasses. The town spreads along the eastern bank of the Thames River opposite New London. From the water's edge to the hillcrest, the old shipbuilding village of narrow streets and small vine-grown houses slumbered for years, growing in its sleep and awakening just before the World War to be rediscovered by industry. Today, although submarines, engines, banjos, thread, and castings are produced here, Groton has remained a Yankee community.

Land in Groton was granted to New London settlers in 1648-9 and first occupied in 1649 by Jonathan Brewster, eldest son of Elder William Brewster of the Mayflower colony, who established a trading post at Brewster's Neck. Organized in 1705, the town was named for the county seat of the Winthrops in Suffolk, England. Agriculture was not profitable, but the fisheries were. From early times Groton men and boys have been engaged at sea; there have been many distinguished Groton skippers.

The MOTHER BAILEY HOUSE (1782), 108 Thames St., a two-and-a-half-story wooden building, owes its fame to an episode of the War of 1812. In June 1813 Commodore Stephen Decatur and his small fleet, pursued by a British squadron, had taken shelter in New London Harbor. Fearful of a repetition of the attack of 1781, terrified inhabitants bundled their household goods into carts and hastened inland. A messenger from the fort, sent through town to collect old rags for gun wadding, was therefore unsuccessful until he met Mother Bailey, who promptly removed her red flannel petticoat and remarked, "There are plenty more where that came from." After the war, President Andrew Jackson is reported to have visited Mrs. Bailey and presented the iron fence at the W. of the house as a token of appreciation.

The BILL MEMORIAL LIBRARY (*open Tues. and Thurs. 2-6 p.m.; Sat. 2-7 p.m.*), near the Groton Monument, has a fine collection of butterflies.

Near Groton is a U.S. SUBMARINE BASE (*visitors admitted*).

North of the village center, US 1 crosses the Thames River on a steel bridge sufficiently high to afford a view straight down New London Harbor (L), one of the deepest on the Atlantic coast, with more than three miles of navigable water frequented by seagoing vessels of many types.

The view (R) up the tidal course of the Thames River extends about two miles over part of the course of the annual Yale-Harvard crew races. On the western bank are the modern brick buildings of the U.S. COAST GUARD ACADEMY, and on the hilltop further N., the campus and native granite buildings of CONNECTICUT COLLEGE.

NEW LONDON, **18.6 m.** (29,640 pop.), a seaport (*see CONN. GUIDE*).

Points of Interest. Fort Trumbull, Old Town Mill, Huguenot House, Shaw Mansion Museum, Lyman Allyn Museum, Whaling Museum, Connecticut Arboretum, Connecticut College, and others.

West of New London, US 1 takes a somewhat winding course, keeping well inland but affording glimpses of the upper reaches of the estuary of the Niantic River.

West of the Niantic River is EAST LYME, **25.5 m.** (East Lyme Town 2,575 pop.), a rural village on whose side roads are many well-preserved homesteads of early settlers.

At the NE. corner of the junction with State 161, at the village center, stands the remodeled 18th century CALKINS TAVERN, where both Washington and Lafayette stopped. Further W. is the COLONIAL INN, built during the full flower of the Greek Revival; and at the rear of the small BAPTIST CHURCH is the JUSTIN BECKWITH HOUSE (1785), its elaborate façade exemplifying the beginning of the Greek Revival.

PATAGANSET LAKE, **26.3 m.** (R), has a number of different kinds of aquatic plants. The STONE RANCH MILITARY RESERVATION, **27.8 m.** (R), bordering US 1 intermittently for about two miles, was formerly the property of Fred Stone, the comedian, and was designed by him to imitate a typical western ranch. Now State-owned, it is maintained as a C.C.C. camp and public shooting ground.

West of the hamlet of LAYSVILLE (Town of Old Lyme), **32.1 m.**, which once supported a small woolen industry, US 1 traverses fertile valley farm lands.

Between **34 m.** and **35 m.** the highway passes the mile of roses (L) planted by Judge W. E. Noyes, along a stone wall of his estate. At **34.3 m.** (R) is the FLORENCE GRISWOLD HOUSE, with a two-story Ionic portico, rendezvous of many artists who have decorated the paneled walls of the interior with sketches. Notable among the many paintings of the exterior of this house is Metcalf's *May Night*, which won first prize in the Corcoran Gallery of Art (Washington, D.C.) exhibition in 1907, and is now owned by the Pittsburgh Art Gallery.

At a rotary at **34.5 m.**, US 1 turns abruptly W., avoiding the elm-shaded center of the ancient maritime village of Old Lyme, which is reached by continuing directly S.

OLD LYME (Old Lyme Town 1,313 pop.), which US 1 skirts at this point, is a resort and art colony. Here, the saying goes, "a sea captain once lived in every house." In dignified old dwellings their descendants treasure teak-wood chests, Paisley shawls, ivory images, and exquisite tapestries collected in the Orient. The variety of Old Lyme's landscape, combining shady streets with stretches of marshland and tranquil meadows with a rugged shore line, has attracted many eminent artists.

The town of Old Lyme, once known as Black Hall, was named for Lyme Regis in Dorsetshire, England, the port from which Matthew Griswold, the first settler, sailed for America. The town was set off from Saybrook in 1665 and incorporated as a separate town in 1855.

The GREEN has been the center of town life since the first settlement. Here stood the old whipping post and stocks, and here on March 16, 1774, Lyme had its own Tea Party when a traveling peddler was found to be carrying sacks of tea on the back of his donkey. While the unwary peddler paced the floor of a cell, the townsfolk gathered at the green and made a bonfire of his wares.

The CONGREGATIONAL CHURCH (*see illustration*), SW. corner Ferry Road and Lyme St., is a copy of a structure long recognized by artists as a fine expression of Colonial ecclesiastical architecture in New England. The original church, built in 1816–17 by Col. Samuel Belcher from plans of a Christopher Wren church in London, burned on the eve of July 4, 1907, was reproduced in the present building (1909). Above the Ionic portico, which has a rich and delicate cornice, the white steeple rises with a square clock tower, one closed stage and one octagonal stage to the slender spire. The small, square windows increase the effect of simplicity.

The old PECK TAVERN, Post Road and Sill Lane, now headquarters of the Old Lyme Guild (*annual exhibition of arts and crafts in late summer, adm. free*), is one of the town's earliest buildings. The porch is elaborately ornamented with carvings. Although many of its features are of later construction, the old taproom and a second-floor ballroom with a swinging partition belong to the early state.

The LYME ART GALLERY (*two annual exhibitions: water colors, etchings, drawings throughout June; paintings and sculpture from end of June to first week in Sept., adm. 50¢*), Boston Post Road, exhibits the canvasses of the many artists of distinction who have founded a large colony here.

At 35 m. US 1 crosses the Connecticut River. Good views of the broad stream unfold at this point. The FERRYHOUSE, on the site of the old landing that handled all cross-river traffic here from 1662 to 1911, stands below the eastern approach to the highway bridge.

At 37.3 m. is a junction (R) with US 1-Alt. US 1, following the Old Post Road, turns L. through the center of OLD SAYBROOK, 37.9 m. (Old Saybrook Town 1,643 pop.), at the mouth of the Connecticut River, one of the oldest towns in the State. This quiet elm-shaded village has changed little in the last century. Natives do a thriving business in renting small boats during the duck-hunting season. Along the waterfront lobstermen are busy with their traps and bait, and in the spring the teeming activity during the run of shad recalls the early importance of Saybrook's fisheries, when thousands of shad were caught daily, salted down, and shipped inland.

Saybrook Point was first occupied in 1623 by "two families and six men" sent by the Dutch of Manhattan Island to take possession of lands at the mouth of the river. Evidently they were soon frightened away by the unfriendly Indians, as there was no evidence of the settlement in 1633 when a party from a Dutch ship landed here, named the point "Kievet's Hook" because of the cries of the sandpipers, and affixed the coat of arms of the States General to a tree.

Wishing to eliminate the danger of Dutch occupation, the English granted a patent to Viscount Saye and Sele, and to Lord Brooke, who commissioned John Winthrop, Jr., as agent and governor of the "River Connecticut, the harbors and places adjoining these unto." Winthrop, arriving at Boston in October 1635 with Lion Gardiner, an engineer formerly in the employ of the Prince of Orange, immediately dispatched a party of men, who on November 9th reached this spot, which was later named for the two grantees. Winthrop and Gardiner arrived on November 24th. The Dutch shield was torn

CONGREGATIONAL CHURCH, OLD LYME, CONNECTICUT

NEW HAVEN GREEN, CONNECTICUT

down from the tree and in its place was carved a grinning face. The English had barely thrown up earthworks and mounted their guns when a Dutch fleet sailed into the harbor. The little fort brought out the Union Jack and manned its guns, and the Dutch withdrew without firing a shot.

In 1673 Governor Andros of New York attempted to take possession of Saybrook. Hoisting the King's flag over his ship he demanded the fort's surrender. Capt. Thomas Bull, then in command, promptly raised His Majesty's colors over the fort, and Andros, not daring to fire on a British flag, was persuaded to settle the matter at a conference with the General Court.

Saybrook was the original site of Yale College, which was established here as the Collegiate School in 1701. Although some of the early classes were held at the home of the Rev. Abraham Pierson, the first rector, in Killingworth (now Clinton), Saybrook was the official site of the college.

YE OLD SAYBROOK INN (1800), Main St. and the Old Boston Post Road, has a low hip roof surrounded by a simple balustrade over an elaborate cornice of Greek detail. The building was erected by Maj. Richard William Hart, a son of Gen. William Hart, who was one of the company that purchased lands of the Western Reserve from the State of Connecticut in 1795. In 1867–8, the house, while operated as a tavern by Captain Morgan, was visited by Charles Dickens, who depicted the old innkeeper as Captain Jorgen in *A Message from the Sea*.

The plain white CONGREGATIONAL CHURCH, Main St., of heavy construction, was built in 1839. Its small, square two-stage tower rises above a portico with four impressive Tuscan columns. On the church a plaque is inscribed, "This church was organized in the Great Hall of the Fort in the summer of 1646."

The BLACK HORSE TAVERN (1720), built for John Burrows, long enjoyed a profitable business when steamboat passengers landed at the wharf in its back yard to transfer to the Connecticut Valley Railway. Although the building has been remodeled, the old parlor still retains its two old summer beams and burnt oystershell plaster. The fireplace has some plain, though excellent, wide paneling.

Rejoined by US 1-Alt., which bypasses the old settlement, the highway passes numerous old houses that have been converted into antique shops.

At **42.1 m.** is the intersection with a dirt road.

Left on this dirt road, **0.4 m.**, to the shore of Long Island Sound; a short distance offshore is SALT ISLAND, affording anchorage for fishing schooners and other small craft. Accessible on foot only by sand flats at low tide, this islet was formerly the site of extensive salt and fish-oil works.

WESTBROOK, **42.3 m.** (Westbrook Town 1,087 pop.), is the birthplace of David Bushnell, inventor of the torpedo and of the first submarine used in actual warfare.

At **42.8 m.** (L) is the DAVID BUSHNELL HOUSE (*adm. 35¢*), the home of the inventor's uncle. The building (1720) has been restored and is now maintained as a museum. Among the exhibits are parts of Bushnell's original "turtle" submarine.

Crossing Patchogue and Menunketesuck Rivers just N. of their confluence at Menunketesuck Point, where sandbars across the marshy district made it possible to ford the streams before the building of bridges, US 1 passes a fine State-maintained PICNIC AREA, **44.1 m.** (R).

At **44.5 m.** is the junction with State 145.

Left on State 145 to the summer colony at KELSEY POINT, past GROVE BEACH, a mile-long stretch of sand that forms one of the finest bathing beaches in the State. This road rejoins US 1 at **2.6 m.**

CLINTON, **46.9 m.** (Clinton Town 1,574 pop.), a clean, quiet village, is one-half mile inland from the harbor once busy with shipping and ship-building, but now disturbed only by the unhurried pleasure boats and trawlers. The manufacture of Pond's Extract from native witch-hazel, cut in back-country brush lots and sometimes distilled in backwoods stills, is the town's chief industry. On the small triangular green (R) is a CANNON used by Gideon Kelsey in his single-handed defense of the local coast line against British invasion in 1812. Clinton township was once the more populous part of the old Town of Killingworth. It was incorporated as a separate town in 1838 and named for Governor De Witt Clinton of New York.

The STANTON HOUSE (L), built in 1789 and now a Colonial museum (*open weekdays 2–5 p.m.; free*), contains an excellent collection of old chinaware and furniture. The paneled dividing wall is hinged, and can be raised to hooks in the ceiling, making the front of the house one large room. The original wallpaper, a handsome French product, still covers two walls of the SW. room. The ADAMS STANTON

CONNECTICUT

STORE, in one room, has been restored to its early condition, with its original counter, shelves, and drawers still bearing the painted labels of their contents. The accountant's desk and ledgers occupy their place by a rear window. Behind this house is the old WELL used by the Reverend Abraham Pierson, first rector of the Collegiate School, later Yale College. The famed clergyman's homestead formerly stood on this site and the first Yale students attended classes there, until the college was moved to Saybrook. In the center of the green, opposite the church, is a MONUMENT commemorating the early years of the Collegiate School, 1701–07. Across the way is a MILESTONE (L), one of the many placed along the highways by Benjamin Franklin.

At 95 E. Main St. is the WRIGHT HOMESTEAD (1807), birthplace of Gen. Horatio G. Wright, commander at the Battle of Cedar Creek, whose skillful rallying of his panic-stricken troops made possible Sheridan's ride, the subject of the poem by that name. Fort Wright on Fisher's Island was named for him.

At **47.2 m.** is the intersection with Swaintown Road.

> Right on Swaintown Road; at its intersection with Cow Hill Road at **1.4 m.** is a LITTLE RED SCHOOLHOUSE, an example of the early New England country school. This one-room building, erected in 1800, has windows fitted with batten shutters.
>
> Left on Cow Hill Road, at **1.5 m.**, is the STEVENS FARM, cultivated since 1675 by nine generations of the Stevens family. The salt-box homestead, with exposed timbers in some of the rooms, was built in 1699. Among the many heirlooms preserved by the family is a copy of the original grant to the property received by John Stevens from King Charles II of England, as well as rifles used by members of the family in the Revolutionary and Civil Wars, and in hunting forays on Roast Meat Hill to the N.

At **47.9 m.** US 1 crosses the Hammonasset River and proceeds past many restaurants and hotels where shore dinners are a specialty. Water scenes and rural landscapes diversify the scenery. Long Island Sound is visible at frequent intervals with its pleasure craft spreading white sails, coastwise steamers plying between New York and New England ports, and tugs pulling strings of barges. Long Island, 25 miles distant, can be glimpsed.

At **48.6 m.** is the intersection with a hard dirt road.

> Left on this road into HAMMONASSET STATE PARK, a tract of 954 acres, with bathing, boating, and camping facilities for more than a million and a half visitors annually. The sandy beach, extending five miles along the shore, is the largest public beach in Connecticut.

MADISON, 51.2 m. (Town of Madison 1,918 pop.), contains many old landmarks grouped about a long, dignified central green. Here lived Cornelius Scranton Bushnell, builder of Civil War battlecraft and financial sponsor of Ericsson's *Monitor*. The GRAVES HOUSE (R), a salt-box structure E. of the green, dates from 1675, its weatherworn shingles bearing evidence of its age. Overlooking the green from the W. is the stately CONGREGATIONAL CHURCH (1838), whose gilded, cylindrical spire thrusting above the trees guided returning seamen straight to Madison Harbor. The Madison Historical Society occupies the NATHANIEL ALLIS HOUSE (*open weekdays in summer, 2–6 p.m.; adm. 25¢*) at the center; the structure contains a completely equipped Colonial kitchen, examples of early American clothing, furniture, embroidery, and pewter.

Right from the green on Scotland Road to DUCK HOLE, 1.5 m., at four corners near a bridge over the Hammonasset River; here an old mill dam in a sylvan setting offers a quiet resting place.

At **52.1 m.** is the junction with a dirt road.

Left on this dirt road to the shore where are stone wharves recalling the old shipping and shipbuilding trades that once flourished here.

At **52.9 m.** is the junction with a side road.

Left on this side road which follows Neck River to its mouth in Guilford Harbor, where the sandy beach of HOGSHEAD POINT looks out to FAULKNER'S ISLAND, the site of a Government LIGHTHOUSE four miles offshore.

A PICNIC AREA is just W. of an underpass at **53.4 m.** in the village of EAST RIVER, a rural hamlet E. of the stream of the same name.

The road now crosses the upper section of the village of Guilford, the center of which is reached by turning (L) on State St., which is at **56.3 m.**

GUILFORD (3,117 Town pop.) was named for the town in Surrey, England. Many old houses border the quiet streets, and the wide green, with its elms and Greek Revival church, has a tranquil simplicity characteristic of the town.

Founded in 1639 and originally named Menunkatucket, Guilford was settled by a body of Puritans from Kent and Surrey under the leadership of Henry Whitfield and Samuel Desborough.

Granite quarrying and oyster culture have flourished in the town throughout most of its existence. Quarries opened here in 1837 have

CONNECTICUT

provided stone for the Statue of Liberty foundation, breakwaters at Block Island, 13 bridges over the Harlem River, the foundation of the Brooklyn Bridge, the northern half of the Battery wall in New York, and the lighthouse at Lighthouse Point, New Haven.

A leading occupation is the cultivation of roses, carried on at the PINCHBECK GREENHOUSE on State St., one of the largest single hothouses in the United States. Covering more than 125,000 square feet in glass, the greenhouse is 1,200 feet long, and has produced a record output of 18,000 roses in one day; average production is about 7,000 daily.

Schoolroom furniture, canned goods, birch extract, toilet articles, iron, brass, and bronze castings are made here.

The CONGREGATIONAL CHURCH, framed by the trees on the green, was built in 1829 at the end of the decade in which the Greek Revival reached its fullest development. This church offers an interesting comparison with the Litchfield Congregational Church, built in the same year. Some of the details of the tall steeple in three diminishing stages with a conical spire, are purely Greek, as are the reeded and fluted Ionic columns of the portico, showing the advancing accuracy of the effort to return to original classical form.

The WHITFIELD HOUSE, one long block S. on Whitfield St. (*open daily 9–5; adm. free*), is probably the oldest house in Connecticut, but the present structure is largely a restoration. About a third of the heavy rear wall, the immense chimney that covers the whole north end of the house, and the line of the foundation are all that remain of the original stone house, which was built in 1639–40 by the Reverend Henry Whitfield, to serve not only as a home but as a meeting house, a fort, and for all public uses of the community, as the most important house in Connecticut towns often did.

In 1936, financed by W.P.A. funds, under the direction of J. Frederick Kelly, an authority on early Connecticut architecture, the house was restored as nearly as possible to its original appearance, even to the odd windows, which old prints show in the SW. corner. Now maintained by the State as a museum, the building houses a varied collection of old relics and curios.

The HYLAND HOUSE, Boston St. between Graves Ave. and Pearl St. (*open summer 9–5; small fee*), also known as the Fiske Wildman House, has been restored by the Dorothy Whitfield Historical Society, and is now a museum. Though many times reconstructed, the present Highland House is a fairly accurate representation of the original structure.

Guilford's beautiful, ledge-lined HARBOR is bordered by spacious country estates. On Rocky Island, reached by a foot bridge, is the Yacht Club. SACHEM'S HEAD, a rocky promontory, was the scene of a savage battle between two Indian tribes when the inlet, since called Bloody Cove, "ran red with blood." Here, according to tradition, the victorious chief Uncas overtook the Pequot sachem. Cutting off the head of the vanquished leader, Uncas fixed it in the crotch of a tree, where the skull remained for many years, a ghastly warning against further aggression.

On the NW. corner of US 1 and State St., at **56.1 m.**, is the COMFORT STARR HOUSE (1645), the only surviving wooden house built by the signers of the "stay together, work together" covenant drawn up by the original settlers.

Right from Guilford on State St. to the intersection with North St., **0.3 m.** Here at 1 North St. stands the HOME OF SAMUEL LEE, captain of the Coast Guard in Revolutionary days. During Captain Lee's absence Tories often raided the house in search of contraband articles that had been seized by the Coast Guard, but they were always outwitted by the captain's wife, Alice. It was she who fired a cannon in the yard to warn the colonists who were working in their northern fields, when the British landed at Leete's Island.

Further on State St., which becomes Nut Plains Road, is the delightful sequestered village of NUT PLAINS, **2.7 m.**, where hickory and walnut trees shade the quiet main street. Here lived General Andrew Ward, Revolutionary hero who covered Washington's retreat by keeping the camp fires at Trenton burning, thus successfully deceiving the British until the Continental Army had safely withdrawn. Among the ten grandchildren in General Ward's household was the studious Roxana, who tied her French textbook to the spinning wheel, so that she might study as she worked. She became Mrs. Lyman Beecher, mother of Henry Ward Beecher and Harriet Beecher Stowe.

At **3 m.** (L) stand two HALL HOUSES, the frames of which were raised on the same day in 1740. One, in dilapidated condition, boasts an ell-plan chimney. The other, built by a brother on adjoining property, is in excellent condition, although it has never been painted. Most of the interior woodwork is original, and since the timbering is exposed, offers a good example of early framing.

Passing a roadside picnic area, (L) at **58.6 m.**, US 1 swings N. around MOOSE HILL, affording a fine view of the Connecticut countryside. On a hillside (L), at **60.8 m.**, is the large red EDWARD FRISBIE HOMESTEAD, now known as the Hearthstone Tea Room. Although marked 1685, its architecture suggests that the present structure is mid-18th century — possibly built about the chimney of an earlier house. The interior is well-preserved and interesting, with an unusually large stone slab hearth.

At **63.1 m.** the road crosses the Branford River, which flows into Branford Harbor two miles S.

At **63.3 m.** is the intersection with US 1-Alt., a new four-lane highway bypassing the old and interesting village of Branford.

US 1, no longer than the cut-off, passes through the center of BRANFORD, **64.2 m.** (Branford Town 7,022 pop.), named for Brentford in the English county of Middlesex. It is a pleasant residential area, formerly a busy center of shipping. Here is the site of an important salt works, the product of which was used in the preservation of meat for the Revolutionary Army.

In this section are many fine old houses. One of the best is the SAMUEL FRISBIE HOUSE (L), on E. Main St. (US 1), a red two-story clapboard structure unaltered since it was built in 1792.

Grouped about the green, a large triangular plot (L), are the town's public buildings, churches, and monuments.

On the southern side of the green stands the small cupola-topped BRANFORD ACADEMY BUILDING (1870), now occupied by the local historical society. On the SE. corner is a small commemorative tablet calling attention to the SITE OF THE REVEREND SAMUEL RUSSELL HOUSE, where in 1701 ten clergymen met and donated books for the founding of the Collegiate School, later Yale College.

At **64.5 m.**, on a knoll overlooking a small green, is the JAMES BLACKSTONE MEMORIAL LIBRARY, a marble building of 1896, which, though having the pretentious architectural detail typical of that period, houses an uncommonly fine library for so small a town.

At **64.9 m.** is the junction with N. Harbor St.

Left on N. Harbor St. to BRANFORD POINT, **1.5 m.**, where are a large restaurant and a municipal bathing beach.

At **65.3 m.** the highway bears N. to rejoin the four-lane highway, US 1-Alt.

West of the village, US 1 ascends the Branford Hills, with good views ahead. At **66.9 m.** it passes LAKE SALTONSTALL. Here, on Beaver River (R), stands an old MILL with hewn timbering. It is on the site of the first iron mill in Connecticut, though undoubtedly it is not the original building. A clause in the deed making it mandatory for the owner to grind any corn or grain brought to him by a property owner of East Haven might prove embarrassing to the present owner, as only one millstone now remains.

EAST HAVEN, **67.5 m.** (East Haven Town, 7,812 pop.), includes comparatively level agricultural land devoted to truck gardening to the N., and residential colonies and summer resorts along the shore to the S. It is now receiving the overflow from many of New Haven's expanding activities.

At 57 Main St. stands a house (1694) so remodeled as to be scarcely recognizable as a Colonial structure; it is interesting, nevertheless, because the stone end walls and first story are parts of a structure that tradition says was the JOHN WINTHROP FORGE. This building was continuously in use as a blacksmith shop until 1920.

Near the center of East Haven is the junction (L) with Hemingway Avenue. On the SW. corner, facing the green, is the STEPHEN THOMPSON HOUSE (*private*), with stone end walls and overhanging eaves, dating from 1760.

Left on Hemingway Ave. four blocks is the ELNATHAN STREET HOUSE (1810), a splendidly preserved example of early 19th century construction, with an entrance porch in the Greek Revival style, said to have been built at the time of the original structure.

Left from East Haven village on Thompson St. to New Haven's MUNICIPAL AIRPORT, opened in 1931. It has a field capacity of 200 ships, a hangar, and modern equipment.

At **67.9 m.** is the intersection with State 142.

Left on State 142 are MOMAUGUIN POINT, **2.4 m.**, and other beaches, lined with summer cottages.

At **69.3 m.** is the intersection with Woodward Ave.

Left on Woodward Ave. to FORT HALE PARK, **1.8 m.**, with spacious, hilly, wooded grounds and a public bathing beach. MORRIS COVE, **2.4 m.**, is one of the less crowded shore resorts. LIGHTHOUSE POINT, **3.4 m.**, is a popular municipal park and resort for those who seek a safe, clean beach with ample parking space and the usual shore amusements.

At **70.2 m.** US 1 passes over the northern cove of New Haven Harbor, following Bridge St. and State St.

NEW HAVEN, **71.2 m.** (162,655 pop.), university community (*see CONN. GUIDE*).

Points of Interest. New Haven Green (*see illustration*), Center Church, New Haven Colony Historical Society Museum, Yale University, East Rock rose garden, Peabody Museum, and the Gallery of Fine Arts.

CONNECTICUT

Section 9. *New Haven to New York Line, 47.8 m.*

Westward from New Haven, **0 m.**, is the Allingtown section of West Haven Town. At the top of Allingtown Hill, **2 m.**, is the intersection with Prudden St.

Right on Prudden St. one block is a small triangular green (L), with a MONUMENT TO WILLIAM CAMPBELL, a British adjutant who, among other acts of mercy, saved the life of the local pastor, who had broken a leg in his flight from the Redcoats when they invaded the town on July 5, 1779. That same day the officer was mortally wounded.

The highway, here called the Milford Turnpike, cuts cross-country in a southwesterly direction to the Housatonic River.

At **6.6 m.** is the intersection with State 152.

Right along State 152 are the extensive FAIRLEA FARMS (R), where acidophilus milk was first developed; the road traverses fertile farming country to the center of ORANGE, **1.7 m.** (1,530 Town pop.), overshadowed by its white CONGREGATIONAL CHURCH (1810). The RACEBROOK COUNTRY CLUB, off Derby Rd., has one of the outstanding golf courses in Connecticut.

At **7.7 m.** US 1-Alt. branches R. to bypass Milford.

At **9.5 m.** on US 1 is MILFORD (Milford Town 14,870 pop.), a pleasant little residential community centered around the long elm-shaded village green. The little Wepawaug River flows through the center of the town and under numerous bridges, finally tumbling over a dam into a shallow bay so filled with silt and sand that it is navigable for only the smallest craft.

The town, an offshoot of the New Haven settlement, was founded in November 1640 for Milford in Pembroke, England. From the land of the original township, which extended 20 miles N., five separate towns have since been made.

Oysters and clams have been important Milford products since the earliest days of the settlement. The Connecticut Oyster Farms Company of Milford owns 7,400 acres of undersea oyster beds; there are many other large oyster firms in the town. Oyster farming is a typical Connecticut industry conducted on underseas acreage along the bottom of Long Island Sound. The shellfish are planted, cultivated, and harvested like any other crop. Pollution is a serious problem; efforts are made by the State authorities to eliminate this hazard through the gradual cleaning up of tributary streams that empty into the sound.

The CAPT. SAMUEL EELS HOUSE (*open weekdays, small fee*), 34 High St., owned by the Milford Historical Society, was built by Captain Eels about 1689, and is an authentic 17th century type. The sharply twisting "dog-legged" stairs are among its many unusual features. The wide, coved cornice at the front is one of the two of this once-common style now preserved in Connecticut. The position of the chimney, back of the ridge, is typical of the period of its erection. After 1754 this dwelling was the home of Capt. Stephen Stow, who served heroically as a volunteer nurse to 46 Revolutionary War prisoners, smallpox victims set ashore by a British prison ship on New Year's Eve, 1777; they were cared for at the homes of settlers until the next day, when the Town Hall was converted into a hospital. Stow and all the prisoners who died were buried in a common grave.

The old BURYING GROUND on Prospect St. is one of the oldest formal cemeteries in the State; in use since 1675, it contains the graves of Jonathan Law, Governor of Connecticut (1742–51); Robert Treat, Commander of the Connecticut troops during King Philip's War, Deputy Governor and Governor of the State for 32 years, and founder of Newark, N. J.; and the Reverend Samuel Andrew, rector of Yale College (1707–19). Here also stands a MONUMENT TO CAPT. STEPHEN STOW, marking the common grave where he and his patients are buried.

The charm of Milford centers about its two Congregational churches, West Main St., which stand on opposite banks of the Wepawaug and form a New England picture of unusual beauty. The FIRST CHURCH (1823), said to have been designed by David Hoadley, is of a type that became the flower of Connecticut's best period of church architecture. The design was copied in the Congregational Church in Cheshire, and by Levi Newell in the Southington and Litchfield Congregational Churches. It has a graceful Ionic portico, shielding three arched doors of approximately even height, and a belfry in two stages — one octagonal and one open and surmounted by a spire. The interior has a finely proportioned gallery and domed ceiling. PLYMOUTH CHURCH (1834), its neighbor, is in the heavier, more matter-of-fact Doric of the developed Greek Revival style. It serves the United Church as a parish house, and in summer as a playhouse.

The CLARK TAVERN, 46 West River St., is reputed to have been erected in 1660, but was so drastically remodeled between 1815 and

1875 that only an interior examination justifies an earlier date. Washington stopped here for supper in 1799, when the building was kept as a tavern by Andrew Clark. According to the story of his visit as originally told by Grandmother Clark and handed down by her descendants, when Washington was served with the milk and bread he had ordered for his supper, he objected to the pewter spoon and asked for a silver one. When told that the tavern did not afford silver spoons, he handed a shilling to an attendant and directed that he "go to the minister's and borrow one."

The Milford bypass merges with US 1 (L) W. of Milford center at **8.6 m.**; the route continues to the village of DEVON, **12.1 m.** (Town of Milford), a residential community with beaches and cottages on the shore to the S.

The WASHINGTON BRIDGE, **12.4 m.**, carries US 1 over the Housatonic River into Fairfield County. Here is the SITE OF A FERRY that started operations in 1650 under Moses Wheeler, said to have been the first white centenarian in the country. South of the bridge was the scene of the cross-river swim (1649) of a Milford man who thus evaded a public lashing to be administered for breaking the blue laws. His offense had been to kiss his wife on the Sabbath. He was later joined by his family in Stratford, where he subsequently became a leading citizen.

At **13 m.** US 1 turns L. to pass through Stratford, US 1-Alt. bypassing the business section of the village.

STRATFORD, **14 m.** (Stratford Town 19,212 pop.), a village with many well-preserved old houses, is now principally a residential suburb of Bridgeport, though it also has some factories. Early activities were confined to shipbuilding and oyster fishing.

On Main St. (US 1) is (L) the oldest EPISCOPAL BURYING GROUND in the State, laid out in 1723 at the rear of CHRIST CHURCH.

In Stratford the Reverend Samuel Johnson organized a congregation and built the first Episcopal church in Connecticut (1723–43). Atop the present building is a weathercock from the spire of the original structure, still bearing the bullet holes of British marksmen under Colonel Frazier, who, when quartered here in 1757–58, amused themselves by using the vane as a target.

The conspicuous DAVID JUDSON HOUSE (*open daily, adm. 25¢*), on Main St. (L), now owned by the Stratford Historical Society, has in its doorway the earliest bull's eye glass in the State. In the cellar of the house (1723) is a great fireplace with two Dutch ovens; the oak beam forming the cellar lintel is 18 inches square. There is a notable example of the early use of fluted pilasters in the upstairs paneling.

A block L. of the Post Road and paralleling it is Elm St., on which are many well-preserved old houses dating from the early 18th century.

US 1 turns R. from Main St. into Stratford Ave.

Left from the corner of Main St. and Stratford Ave.; Main St. passes the Sikorsky airplane plant (L), where amphibian "clipper" ships are made, and the BRIDGEPORT AIRPORT (R), formerly the Mollison Airport, so named for the British fliers who crashed here in 1933 after their successful flight over the Atlantic. Across the most extensive salt meadows in Connecticut is the solitary old LIGHTHOUSE (1822) at STRATFORD POINT, **3.3 m.** In Long Island Sound, 6.5 miles due S., is the STRATFORD SHOAL LIGHTHOUSE.

US 1 crosses the newest of the many bridges that gave the city its name.

BRIDGEPORT, **17.3 m.** (146,716 city pop.), industrial center (*see CONN. GUIDE*).

Points of Interest. Burroughs Library Historical Collections, Seaside Park, Beardsley Park, Anne Hathaway Cottage, Barnum House Museum, Stratfield Cemetery, and others.

At **22 m.** is FAIRFIELD (17,218 Town pop.), an old Colonial town. At the business center on the modern highway are small neat shops, a motion picture theater, a modern brick bank building of Colonial design, and a library. In sharp contrast is the old town center, a block S. There, beneath the shade of towering elms, 18th and 19th century mansions, standing back from the road on wide lawns, border the winding streets about the old white Town House.

Around the edges of the township, especially on the eastern boundary, industry has made use of lands not suited to residential purposes.

The Fairfield land was twice purchased from the Pequonnock Indians — on May 11, 1639, and on June 24, 1649; a quit claim deed was obtained from the Sasco Indians, February 11, 1661. Named possibly in a descriptive sense, or for Fairfield in Kent, the settlement soon received a patent. Anticipating the confiscatory methods of Sir Edmund Andros, who claimed all unoccupied lands for the Crown, the territory was divided into lots that ran from the shore inland for about ten miles.

During the Revolution the village was burned by British raiders under General Tryon. Driving the militiamen back to the hills, the British looted and fired the village during a severe thunderstorm. About 200 houses were destroyed and the resulting bitterness aided recruiting of the Continental Line. Whaleboat crews conducted reprisals upon the Tories of Long Island and many Fairfield sailors sought vengeance upon British shipping.

The FAIRFIELD MEMORIAL LIBRARY (*open 9–8:30*), SE. corner Unquowa Rd. and New Post Rd., a two-story brick building with limestone trim, belongs to a society organized and incorporated in 1876. Memorial Hall, on the second floor, is notable for its panels commemorating early settlers. One wing of the building is devoted to the exhibits of the Fairfield Historical Society, which include many rare old books, early town documents, and maps.

The TOWN HOUSE, corner Old Post Rd. and Beach Rd., on the green, was originally built in 1794. The central part, a dignified, hip-roofed, white clapboard structure surmounted by a white belfry, has been restored to the original lines. Restoration in 1937 included the addition of wings to provide office space. At the western end of the green was formerly a pond in which suspected witches were given "trial by water." If they floated they were believed to be guilty, but if they sank they were adjudged innocent. Here Mercy Disbrow and Elizabeth Clawson were bound and thrown into the water. According to records of the time, "they buoyed up like a cork." At the edge of the green stands the old TOWN SIGN POST, still in use.

The THADDEUS BURR HOUSE (*private*), built in 1790 on the Old Post Rd. between Beach and Penfield Rds., and now surrounded by lofty elms, is a house whose present appearance belies its age. Built to replace the original Burr Homestead, destroyed during the British invasion, it was a copy of the Hancock House in Boston, and all of the glass for the windows was the gift of John Hancock. The colonnade of heavy Tuscan pillars, the front doorway, and the third story were added about 1840. In the garden is a hedge of very old arbor vitae. In the original homestead, John Hancock and Dorothy Quincy were married August 8, 1775. Dorothy had been a visitor here during the siege of Boston and carried on a gay flirtation with Col. Aaron Burr, much to the discomfort of her fiance.

The old MILESTONE, on Mill Plain Rd., about 1,500 ft. N. of the Post Road, is one of the stones erected along the old coach routes by

Benjamin Franklin in 1753, and is inscribed "F XX M N H" (Fairfield. 20 miles to New Haven).

At **23.1 m.** is a junction with Bronson Rd., where US 1 crosses the railroad on a concrete overpass.

> Right on Bronson Rd., which turns N. by way of an overpass and goes up to the Colonial settlement of GREENFIELD HILL (Town of Fairfield), **3.3 m.**, site of the academy conducted by the Reverend Timothy Dwight from 1786 until 1795, when he became president of Yale College. Grouped about the green are numerous old houses and taverns, and nearby (west side of Hillside Rd.) is the HUBBELL HOUSE (1751), where Dr. Dwight held his first classes before the erection of the academy building, now gone. In spring the village streets are beautiful with pink and white dogwood; there are excellent views of the sound from several points.

At **24.1 m.** (L) among some willows is a granite monument marking the SITE OF THE GREAT SWAMP FIGHT, which ended the Pequot War in July 1637, when the survivors of that hostile tribe were either killed or sold into slavery. Subsequently, this fertile territory was settled in comparative peace.

WESTPORT, **27.9 m.** (Westport Town 6,073 pop.), is a village in a town that is chiefly residential; many artists and literary folk have established studios and permanent homes along the shore and about the countryside.

Among the residents are Van Wyck Brooks, author of *The Flowering of New England;* Lillian Wald, founder of the Henry Street Settlement; John S. Curry, the artist; Rollin Kirby, the cartoonist; and William McFee, the author of sea stories.

On the hill that US 1 descends to reach the center of Westport is the well-proportioned CONGREGATIONAL CHURCH (L), shining-white behind tall spruces.

On the brow of the hill in the western end of the village stands (L) the BEDFORD HIGH SCHOOL, gift of a native son. In the school auditorium are murals painted by John Steuart Curry, a prize winner in the Carnegie International Exhibit of 1933, whose work is also represented at the Metropolitan Museum of Art in New York. The Curry murals here depict *Tragedy* and *Comedy,* and include such recognizable figures as Little Eva, Uncle Tom, Charlie Chaplin, Sherwood Anderson, Theodore Dreiser, Eugene O'Neill, Mickey Mouse, Will Rogers, Hamlet, a Kewpie doll, and Mr. and Mrs. Curry. Friends and neighbors served as models for some of the figures.

CONNECTICUT

Right from Westport on State 57 through rough hill country to WESTON, 5 m. (Weston Town 670 pop.). From this high ground are fine views of the surrounding countryside, especially from the lawn of the CONGREGATIONAL CHURCH (1830), a simple, well-proportioned structure, whose small windowpanes are now turning violet through age. At the entrance to a residence across the way are old gas lampposts that once lighted New York City street corners. The street names can still be discerned.

At **31.1 m.** a right-angle turn (L) leads past the Norwalk Green. NORWALK, **31.5 m.** (Norwalk Town 36,019 pop.), industrial center (*see CONN. GUIDE*).

Points of Interest. Town House with D.A.R. collection, Roger Ludlow Memorial, Theater-in-the-Woods, and numerous old houses.

Left from Norwalk at the traffic rotary is SOUTH NORWALK, **1.2 m.** (Town of Norwalk), where the manufacturing plants of the town are concentrated.

US 1 now passes a succession of hot-dog stands, gasoline stations, and billboards.

DARIEN, **35.6 m.** (Darien Town 6,951 pop.), is a residential village largely peopled with commuters to New York. To the S. winding lanes go down to Long Island Sound; N. of the main road the wooded countryside is dotted with homes.

Right from Darien on State 29 to NEW CANAAN, **5.1 m.** (New Canaan Town 5,456 pop.), which has carefully tended country estates and polo fields. This town is exclusively a residential community, situated on high ridges, which in many places afford views of the sound.

On Mead St., close to the center, is the NEW CANAAN BIRD SANCTUARY in MEAD MEMORIAL PARK, one of the first established in the United States.

Left from New Canaan on Railroad Ave., R. on Weed St., L. on Wahackme Road to its termination at Ponus Road, and R. on that highway, to the PONUS MONUMENT, **1.3 m.**, erected in honor of Chief Ponus, to mark the old Indian trail that led to the Hudson River.

In the western part of the Town of Darien US 1 passes the village of NOROTON, **37.2 m.**, named for Chief Rooaton, whose name is also preserved in the place names of nearby Rowayton and Roton Point.

Left from Noroton on Ring's End Rd. to Swift's Lane (L), **0.3 m.**, where a miniature COLONIAL VILLAGE (*private*), a collection of small old buildings moved from various New England towns, is visible from the roadway.

At the end of Ring's End Road, **0.5 m.**, on the waterfront is the old MILL AND CUSTOMHOUSE, erected in 1737.

STAMFORD, **40.2 m.** (56,765 pop.), manufacturing and residential city (*see CONN. GUIDE*).

Points of Interest. Old houses, Stamford Museum.

Right from Stamford on State 104, **8.3 m.**, to the junction with a cross-country path that runs **0.2 m.** to the precipitous gorge of the Mianus River on the New York Line. Within the shade of primeval hemlocks, the narrow river swirls through dark pools and tumbles over shoals strewn with boulders of pink quartz, forming one of the wildest spots near New York City.

At **41.4 m.**, midway between the railroad and the Post Road along the Stamford-Greenwich town line, is LADDIN'S ROCK (L), on a private estate. According to local legend, Indians attacked the home of an old Dutch settler, Cornelius Labden, who was forced to see his family scalped. But Labden escaped; he leaped upon his horse and galloped through the hemlocks toward the brink of a cliff crying, "Come on ye foul fiends; I go to join your victims." In the rush of pursuit, the Indians blindly rode their horses over the cliff, and all went crashing to their deaths at the jagged base.

The CONDE NAST PRESS, at **41.5 m.**, is a modern industrial plant in landscaped surroundings. Here are published *House Beautiful* and *Vogue*.

At **43 m.** the highway runs through MIANUS, named for Chief Mayannos, and then crosses the river below a dam that impounds the waters of old DUMPLING POND (R). When the British raided this section in 1779 some of the soldiers tarried at the gristmill, then a century old, about 1.5 miles upstream from the present bridge. They invited themselves to a meal of dumplings that the miller's wife chanced to be making; she told them to wait a few minutes until the food was cooked. Taking advantage of a lapse in their attention, she irately threw the dumplings into the millpond, an act commemorated in the name.

COS COB, **43.8 m.** (Town of Greenwich), is a village bearing the name of an Indian chief.

On the plains N. of the millpond immediately L. of US 1, are a large BURIAL MOUND and the SITE OF THE INDIAN VILLAGE OF PETUQUAPAEN. Here the Dutch and English united to annihilate the Siwanoy tribe, which had been resisting the encroachments of white settlers upon the Indians' best hunting ground. According to a contemporary account, "the Lord having endued the colonists with extraordinary strength," not a man, woman, or child of the several

UTCHINSON RIVER PARKWAY, SAXON WOODS, NEW YORK

BUSH HOMESTEAD, PORT CHESTER, NEW YORK

GEORGE WASHINGTON BRIDGE, NEW YORK CITY

US 1, STRETCH OF NEW JERSEY

hundred inhabitants escaped the fire set to their wigwams on a bitter February night in 1644, "nor was any outcry whatsoever heard." Public thanksgiving and general rejoicing were the order of the day when this news reached New Amsterdam.

Conspicuously situated (L) on the western shore of Cos Cob Harbor is the POWER HOUSE of the main line of the New Haven Railroad.

At **45.4 m.** US 1 climbs PUT'S HILL. Here in 1779 General Israel Putnam made his escape by horse from the British. Although the Tories abandoned their chase at the brink of the precipice down which the daring Putnam plunged, they succeeded in firing a bullet through his hat. At this, he turned around in his saddle and is supposed to have shouted his favorite oath, "God cuss ye, I'll hang ye to the next tree when I catch ye."

At the top of the hill is the stone CONGREGATIONAL CHURCH (L), for years a guide to fishermen far out in the sound, and visible for many miles in all directions.

GREENWICH, **45.8 m.** (33,112 pop.), residential city (*see CONN. GUIDE*).

Points of Interest. Bruce Mansion Museum, Putnam Cottage with D.A.R. collection, Indian Burial Ground, Little Captain's Island (public bathing beach), many beautiful estates, and fine old houses.

Left from Greenwich on Greenwich Ave.; then on Steamboat Rd. to the dock, **0.9 m.**, for boats plying to LITTLE CAPTAIN'S ISLAND, 2.5 miles offshore (*round trip 25¢*). Here is a public picnic ground and bathing beach (Island Beach). A mile distant is the old stone lighthouse on the rockbound tip of GREAT CAPTAIN'S ISLAND, southernmost extremity of New England. These islands — named for Captain Patrick, the earliest settler in Greenwich — and BYRAM POINT, on the mainland, are the only points in New England lying below the forty-first parallel. From Great Captain's Island the skyscrapers of New York City, 20 miles distant, seem a mirage rising over the water.

US 1, here lined with roadside stands catering to every conceivable demand of a motoring public, continues to the New York Line at the Byram River, **47.8 m.** On the Connecticut bank of the stream (L) is the weathered LYON HOUSE (1670), a modest outpost bordering the current of the heaviest traffic along the Atlantic seaboard.

NEW YORK

Conn. Line — Port Chester — New Rochelle — New York — N.J. Line, **22.2 m.** US 1.

New York, New Haven & Hartford R.R. and New York, Westchester & Boston R.R. parallel this route.
Four-lane concrete roadbed except for macadam stretches through business centers. Complex network of roads in Westchester County makes it necessary to follow directions carefully.
Accommodations limited because of proximity to New York City.

Section 10. Connecticut Line to New Jersey Line, **22.2 m.**

This section of the through route, known as the Boston Post Road, follows the shore of Long Island Sound across Westchester County, a county of suburban homes, large estates, and wealthy clubs, of natural beauty in proximity to carefully landscaped parkways.

At the Connecticut-New York Line US 1 crosses the Byram River, which runs along the northwestern border of PORT CHESTER, **0 m.** (34 alt., 22,622 pop.), first known as Saw Pit, which was settled about 1650. The Byram River, now the State Line, in Colonial days flowed through the center of the village. Unlike other communities on the route, Port Chester is partly dependent on its manufacturing plants. The principal products are candy, ammonia, nuts and bolts, furnaces, coal and gas ranges, soft drinks, and commercial cartons.

At **0.5 m.** (R) is the five-story PLANT OF LIFE SAVERS, INC. (*guide service free*), national headquarters of the confectionery firm.

The PORT CHESTER LIBRARY AND MUSEUM, Westchester Ave. and Haseco St., contains a collection of Currier and Ives prints, Japanese and Chinese furniture imported by local sea captains, amusing collection of political campaign buttons of recent years, and several Indian implements found in the vicinity.

The SAMUEL BROWN HOME, Browndale Pl., was built in 1660. The house has been altered several times and a wing was added to the original structure 70 years ago; but interior walls, doors, and floors are unchanged. The Dutch oven and the fireplaces have been sealed.

The BROWN GRAVEYARD, Indian Rd., a huddle of fallen tombstones in an overgrowth of brambles and trees, was the private

NEW YORK

burial ground of descendants of the Brown family from 1660 to 1900. Forgotten today, it lies at the rear of a vacant lot between modern bungalows.

The BUSH HOMESTEAD (1750), Lyon Park overlooking King St. (*open Tues., Thurs., Sat., 9–4:30; apply to caretaker*), a well-preserved house (*see illustration*) in the Colonial style, built shortly before the Revolution by Abraham Bush, a sea captain, was the headquarters in 1777–78 of Gen. Israel Putnam. The original furniture has been preserved, including the bed and desk used by "Old Put." Aaron Burr, as a colonel under Putnam, visited the house frequently.

US 1 winds through the narrow streets of the business district and beneath railroad crossings to the southern edge of the village.

Right from the State Line on Putnam Ave.; at **0.7 m.** L. on N. Regent St. (State 120 B); at **1.5 m.** R. on Westchester Ave. (State 119, 120); at **4.2 m.** R. on the Hutchinson River Parkway (*see illustration*); at **4.3 m.** L. on Parkway. This parkway, a four-lane road, cuts through terraced and forested countryside of Westchester County and provides an alternate route between the Connecticut Line and New York City. While somewhat longer than the main route, it is more scenic and is free from busses and trucks, traffic lights, and cross traffic (*speed limit of 35 m.p.h. strictly enforced*). Traffic from side entrances and exits is regulated by a system of islands separating north- and south-bound traffic.

For the first eight miles the parkway is bordered by public and private golf courses and large estates. At **7.1 m.** is SAXON WOODS PARK, the county's 749-acre recreational development, containing bridle paths, trails, picnic grounds, and a public 18-hole golf course (*nominal fees*).

At **12.5 m.** a traffic circle gives entrance to the Cross County Parkway (R).

At **15.8 m.** the parkway swings L. to join US 1, **0.2 m.** E. of the New York City Line (*see below*).

At **1.6 m.** on US 1 is RYE (49 alt., 37, 495 pop.), settled in 1660 by people from Greenwich, Conn. The Post Road here roughly follows the line of an Indian trail from Manhattan Island to a "wading place" across the Byram River. The first country road was laid out in 1672. In size a city, but an incorporated village by preference, Rye is visible from the highway only as a series of landscaped apartment houses and mansions.

The JAY MANSION (*not open*), Locust Ave. and Post Rd. (R), a two-story structure, Greek Revival in style, was built in the second quarter of the 19th century on the site of the home of John Jay. It was Jay who was largely responsible for the draft of the first New York State Constitution and who helped negotiate the treaty of peace with Great Britain at the end of the Revolutionary War. From

1790 to 1794, as first Chief Justice of the U.S. Supreme Court, he handed down important decisions interpreting the new Federal Constitution. After serving two terms as Governor of New York, he retired to this 800-acre estate in 1801 and became a gentleman farmer, writing conservative political advice to newspaper editors for 28 years. His body lies in the family plot in the rear of this house.

The HAVILAND INN (*open*), on Purchase St. (R), was built in 1730 and is now the village hall. The original windows are intact; the beams are wooden-pegged; hand-hewn shingles cover three-quarters of the structure; several of the doors have Colonial "HL" hinges. Dame Tamar Haviland, a war widow, was here hostess to Washington on several occasions. John Adams and General Lafayette danced Virginia reels in the ballroom on the second floor.

At **3.4 m.** is a junction with Cross County Parkway.

Left on the parkway to PLAYLAND, **0.9 m.** (*open all year; free parking*), the largest recreational center in Westchester Co. The 273 acres include a salt-water bathing beach with accommodations for 10,000, a boardwalk, a fresh-water swimming pool, a dance hall, a skating and hockey rink, a picnic grove, and an amusement park (*open summer*).

The RYE COUNTRY CLUB (*not open to public*), **4.1 m.** (L), is an exclusive social center.

MAMARONECK (Ind., *he assembles the people*), **5.2 m.** (47 alt., 11,766 pop.), was settled by English farmers about 1650. Woolen cloth, food, perfume oil, and motor oil factories provide local employment for some of the residents, but the majority are commuters to New York City. Seven yacht clubs have private basins along the jagged shore line of the village harbor. Swinging between private estates, the Post Road swings to Long Island Sound, but presents only a dismal view of marshland, fishing huts, and boat docks. The estates of Ethel Barrymore, James Montgomery Flagg, and Robert ("Believe It or Not") Ripley are near the village.

Inns and taverns, decorated with chromium in the modern manner, are numerous S. of the village.

At **6.2 m.** is the junction with State 126 (Mamaroneck Ave.).

Right on State 126 just beyond the junction is CLOSET HALL (R), now a gas station and restaurant. James Fenimore Cooper, the novelist, lived in this house after his marriage with Susan DeLancey of Mamaroneck. The building formerly stood on Heathcote Hill, overlooking the sound.

NEW YORK

At **6.6 m.** is a junction with Orienta Ave.

Left on Orienta Ave. to beach and yacht clubs on the sound, **1.3 m.** On this street stood the early movie studios of D. W. Griffith, screen pioneer. The productions *Way Down East*, *Orphans of the Storm*, and *Valley Forge* were filmed with local backgrounds.

LARCHMONT, 7.7 m. (100 alt., 5,282 pop.), is a residential community with no industries. More than half the population commutes daily to New York City.

NEW ROCHELLE, 8.9 m. (72 alt., 54,000 pop.), suburban city (*see N.Y. GUIDE*).

Railroad Stations. N.Y., N.H., & H. R.R., R.R. Place between North Ave. and Mechanic St.; N.Y., Westchester & Boston R.R., Port Chester Ave. and Quaker Ridge. Trains at 15-min. intervals during rush hours.

Points of Interest. Jacob Leisler Monument, Thomas Paine Memorial and Museum, Salesian College, Hudson Park, the College of the City of New Rochelle, Fort Slocum Ferry, Glen Island, the Casino, and others.

Left from New Rochelle on Echo Ave., R. on Pelham Rd. to State 1B, the Shore Rd., which closely follows the shore of Long Island Sound to the New York City Line. Views of the sound are almost continuous.

At **2.1 m.** (R) is BOLTON PRIORY (*not open*), built in 1838 by the Reverend Robert Bolton. Washington Irving, a friend of the Bolton family, gave yellow bricks from the old Dutch Church at Sleepy Hollow for the lettering of the construction date above the door.

CEDAR KNOLL (L) was for many years believed to be haunted on moonlight nights by decapitated Siwanoy warriors holding their heads in their hands.

At **2.4 m.** (L) is the NEW YORK ATHLETIC CLUB (*private*), one of New York City's wealthiest sport clubs. The clubhouse, visible beyond wide landscaped lawns, is Italian Renaissance in style.

PELHAM MANOR, **11.4 m.** (100 alt., 11,851 pop.), a purely suburban community, was named for Thomas Pell, who in 1664 purchased lands along the sound from the Siwanoys. The title was later confirmed by James II of England and the territory formed into the Manor of Pelham.

At **11.7 m.**, on Pelhamdale Ave., is the former route of a tiny trolley that is said to have given Fontaine Fox, the cartoonist, the inspiration for his *Toonerville Trolley* sketches. The line followed the street from Pelham Rd. (State 1B) to the Pelham railroad station.

At **12.2 m.** is the junction with Split Rock Road.

Left on this road, which runs to the New York City Line, **0.5 m.**, then SE. through Pelham Bay Park to Pelham Bridge Rd. (State 1B). Split Rock Rd. was once the private driveway from the manor house of Thomas Pell to the Boston Post Road. Washington's army retreated along this route after the Battle of Pell's Point, October 18, 1776, took place in the vicinity of the cleft 10-ft. boulder that stands (R) near the New York Line.

At **12.4 m.** (R) is a junction with the **Hutchinson River Parkway,** alternate route from the Connecticut Line (*see above*).

At **12.5 m.** is the junction with S. Fulton Ave.

Right on S. Fulton Ave. to S. Columbus Ave., **1.1 m.**; L. on S. Columbus Ave. to St. Paul's Church and Eastchester Common, **1.2 m.** (L). Situated on the marshy land beside the Hutchinson River, named for Anne Hutchinson, this old church stands surrounded by giant gas and oil tanks and concrete factories that here sprawl over the New York City-Mount Vernon Line.

The rectangular church, built in 1761, has stone walls now weathered with age; it is of a simple style, with a square tower above the front entrance. The bell, presented long before the Revolution, and cast by Lester and Pack, who also cast the Liberty Bell, was buried in 1775 to prevent its being made into cannon. It is still rung at services.

After the Battle of Pell's Point, Hessian troops seized the church and used it as a barracks and hospital. Ninety Hessians who died the first night were buried in a sandpit at the foot of the cemetery; the grave is now marked. The cemetery also contains an Indian grave marker dated 1687, another stone dated 1704, the graves of many Revolutionary soldiers, and the vault in which was buried George Washington Adams, the son of President John Quincy Adams who was drowned nearby in 1829.

The pewholders and vestrymen of St. Paul's at the end of the Revolution included members of the Van Cortlandt, Rhinelander, Pinckney, Morgan, Drake, and Roosevelt families.

Aaron Burr pleaded cases in the church after the Revolution, when it was used as a courthouse.

A part of the old village green lies between the church and the sunken highway. Colonial troops drilled here for both the French and Indian and the Revolutionary Wars. Coaches rolled by on the 14-day trip to Boston (today planes pass over the church on the 85-minute Boston run). In 1733 John Peter Zenger, New York newspaper editor, was arrested for his account of an election for assemblyman held here; his release several months later helped to establish the American principle of freedom of the press.

At Guion's Tavern, situated at the western end of the village green, Washington paid off his troops after the Battle of White Plains, October 28, 1776. The desk he used is owned by a member of the church.

At **12.6 m.** is the New York City Line. This back door of the metropolis offers no breath-taking vista; it is but a flat stretch of Hutchinson River marshes, bridges, and gas stations, with the brick blocks and old wooden houses of the northernmost Bronx in the background.

NEW YORK

NEW YORK CITY (51 alt., 6,930,450 pop.), most populous city in the world (*see N.Y. CITY GUIDE*).

Railroad Stations. Baltimore & Ohio bus terminal, 42nd St. opposite Grand Central Terminal, W. 23rd St. and Liberty St. ferries; Central R.R. of New Jersey, W. 23rd St. and Liberty St. ferries; Delaware, Lackawanna & Western, Barclay St., Christopher St., and W. 23rd St. ferries; Erie, Chambers St. and W. 23rd St. ferries; Lehigh Valley, Pa. Station, Cortlandt St. ferry; Long Island, Pa. Station; New York Central, Grand Central Terminal, 42nd St. and Park Ave.; New York, New Haven & Hartford, Grand Central Terminal and Pa. Station; New York, Ontario & Western, Cortlandt St. & W. 42nd St. ferries; Pennsylvania, Pa. Station, 7th to 8th Aves., 31st to 33rd Sts., Cortlandt St. ferry; West Shore, Cortlandt St. and W. 42nd St. ferries.

Points of Interest. The Battery, Central Park, the Empire State Building, Metropolitan Museum of Art, Museum of Natural History, Museum of the City of New York, New York Public Library, Radio City, Wall St., and many others.

US 1 cuts through the Bronx and across northern Manhattan; it crosses the Hudson River on the George Washington Memorial Bridge (*see illustration*) to New Jersey. These parts of the city are essentially residential, with neighborhood shopping centers somewhat resembling the Main Streets of second-class cities. The elevated railway structures, the subway kiosks, and occasional views of the towers of Columbus Circle and beyond, are reminders, however, that this is part of America's greatest metropolis.

The Bronx, one of the five boroughs of the city, was named for Jonas Bronck or Brounck, who in 1638 built the first manor house N. of the Harlem River. When in 1639 the Dutch West India Co. sold land here the area was called Broncksland, of which the present borough name is a corruption.

At **12.9 m.** the broad macadam highway crosses the HUTCHINSON RIVER, named for Anne Hutchinson, Boston nonconformist who was banished by Massachusetts Puritans after violent controversies; she left Rhode Island after the death of her husband and settled in this area; in 1643 she was slain by Indians at Throgg's Neck. The river has been developed as a barge canal, giving access to Long Island Sound through East Chester Bay.

The banks of the river were one of the sources of the clam and periwinkle shells that the Indians and the Dutch settlers used as money. White shells were known as "wampum," black and purple as "suckauhock."

This approach to New York City is dismal and uninteresting. Gas stations, auto junk yards, diners, and third-rate roadhouses line the highway. Weedy lots sprawl to the backdoors of private homes and apartment houses.

At **14.5 m.** the road crosses a hill in the Williamsbridge section and gives a view of a jagged mass of apartment houses and modern stores, with the dim outline of lower Manhattan skyscrapers on the southern horizon. On the E. are the towers of the Tri-Borough Bridge, opened in the summer of 1936; spans from 125th St., Manhattan, and Southern Blvd., the Bronx, converge on Randalls Island in the East River; and from there the bridge continues across Wards Island to end at Astoria Boulevard in Queens.

At **16.3 m.**, at the edge of Bronx Park, is the junction with Fordham Rd. US 1 turns R. on Fordham Rd.

In the next half mile Fordham Rd. bisects BRONX PARK, 719 acres, a forested tract along the Bronx River, famous for its zoo (L) and its botanical gardens (R).

The NEW YORK ZOOLOGICAL PARK (*free except Mon. and Thurs.; free on all holidays*), founded in 1897 and locally called "the Bronx Zoo," has one of the largest collections of wild animals, birds, and reptiles in the world. The 160 acres of exhibits, near Lake Agassiz and Bronx Lake, formed by Bronx River, include, besides bear dens, houses for elephants, lions, primates, zebras, land and aquatic birds, reptiles, large and small mammals, ostriches, antelopes, kangaroos, and wild swine. There are restaurants and administration buildings on the grounds.

The buildings are of neo-classical design with brown Tiffany brick walls and limestone trim. The stone cornices and pediments have elaborately carved figures of animals.

The NEW YORK BOTANICAL MUSEUM, together with the gardens, is one of the largest in the world. The gardens date back to the time of Pierre Lorillard, nature lover and snuff maker, who built a mill on the river in 1840, later constructed a stone mansion, and set out large, old-fashioned gardens that are still visible.

After cutting through the park Fordham Road becomes a business street with department stores, offices, theaters, banks, trolleys, and busses.

At **16.9 m.** is a junction with Southern Blvd. (State 1A).

State 1A, alternate route through the city to Jersey City, follows Southern Blvd. across the Bronx, and 1st and 2nd Aves. down Manhattan to Houston St., and across to the HOLLAND TUNNEL under the Hudson River to New Jersey.

NEW YORK

The route offers views of East River shipping and bridges, the Cornell-New York Medical Center, the Rockefeller Institute of Medical Research, Tudor City, Bellevue Hospital, sections of New York's East Side, the Bowery, and Greenwich Village.

On Fordham Rd. (R) at **17.4 m.** is FORDHAM UNIVERSITY, largest Roman Catholic college in the United States. In 1841 when, as St. John's College, it opened its doors to its first student body of six, its president was the Reverend John McCloskey, later first American cardinal. Only part of the courses are offered in the 20 English Gothic field-stone buildings on the main campus; several branches are maintained in downtown Manhattan.

At **18 m.** is a junction with Grand Concourse (State 22 and 100), one of the main thoroughfares of the Bronx, running S. to Madison and Fifth Aves. in Manhattan.

Right on Grand Concourse is (R) POE PARK, **0.1 m.** (*adm. free; open weekdays except Mon., 10–1, 2–4:30; Sun., 1–4:30*), containing the white cottage built before 1816, in which Edgar Allen Poe lived from 1845 to 1849. The furniture is in keeping with the period when Poe lived here, but was not used by him. The poet's young wife, Virginia, died in this house in January 1847.

At **18.4 m.** US 1 turns L. on University Ave.

At **18.6 m.** is the campus of NEW YORK UNIVERSITY (R), chartered in 1831, now with a student body of 34,000 and a faculty of 1,800. The buildings on University Heights house only the colleges of arts, pure sciences, and engineering, the Guggenheim School of Aeronautics, various administrative units, and extracurricular activities. Other divisions are in downtown Manhattan, the most important on Washington Square, and on Long Island. The HALL OF FAME (*see illustration*), dominating the campus at the edge of the Harlem River, is a one-story open arcade with granite base. Bronze busts of the great men of American history stand in openings between limestone piers. The arches offer framed views of the Palisades on the New Jersey shore, and of Manhattan Island.

At **20.1 m.** the route turns R. on 181st St. and crosses Harlem River on a broad concrete bridge with sweeping views of Manhattan L. and R. The river, really a strait, separates Manhattan from the mainland. Barge, tug, and steamer traffic splashes busily through the channel. Below, at the water's edge on the Bronx shore, runs the main line of the New York Central R.R. Left are the towers of the midtown district, with the spiked summit of the Chrysler Building and the mooring mast of the Empire State Building standing out clearly from the others.

At **20.9 m.** the route crosses BROADWAY, New York's "Main Street" since the 17th century, first known as Heere Straat.

At **21.1 m.** the route turns L. on Fort Washington Ave.

At **21.2 m.** the route turns R. on W. 179th St. to the entrance of the GEORGE WASHINGTON BRIDGE (*50¢ for pleasure vehicles pd. at N.J. end; 5¢ for pedestrians*), spanning the Hudson River and forming a dramatic gateway to New Jersey. Construction was begun in 1927; the cost was $57,000,000. The bridge is of the suspension type with a graceful 3,500-ft. main span joining the severe steel towers, 630 ft. high, on the New Jersey and New York shores. These towers are twice the height of the Palisades at this point, though this fact is not apparent to those crossing the structure. The roadway in the center of the bridge is 250 ft. above the water. Four cables, each 36 inches in diameter and each containing 26,474 wires, provide strength sufficient to support the present deck and an additional deck that can be added if necessary to meet future traffic demands. Franklin D. Roosevelt, then Governor of New York, delivered one of the dedication speeches at the opening of the bridge on October 24, 1931. The bridge is owned and operated by the Port of New York Authority.

Immediately below the bridge is the SITE OF FORT WASHINGTON (R), key American fortification on Manhattan Island during the first year of the Revolution. It occupied the highest part of the island between the present 181st and 186th Sts. Three thousand Americans, considered among the best of Washington's troops, surrendered the fort to General Howe on November 16, 1776, completing the abandonment of New York.

From the roadway of the bridge the view southward includes the tallest buildings of Manhattan, the tower of Riverside Church at 120th St., the unbroken line of apartment houses along Riverside Drive, the North River berths of the largest ocean liners, and the busy ferry traffic between the New York and New Jersey terminals. Northward in the Hudson is the path of summer excursion boats to Bear Mountain, and of freight and passenger vessels to Albany. On the New Jersey side, partly hidden by foliage in summer, is the sheer face of the Palisades, now disfigured in places by factories at the foot of the cliff. Excavations for the New Jersey Bridge approach revealed the tracks of dinosaurs in the Triassic rock of the Palisades. This barricade of rock, once a molten mass, was given the form of columns when the substance cooled, shrank, and cracked beneath the earth's surface. It was covered for ages by a layer of sediment several thousand feet deep that was subsequently worn away.

At **22.2 m.** is the New Jersey end of the bridge.

NEW JERSEY

N. Y. Line — Fort Lee — Jersey City — Trenton — Pa. Line, **68.6 m.**
US 1.

Erie R.R. parallels the route N. of Jersey City and Pennsylvania R.R. and Baltimore & Ohio R.R. between Jersey City and the Pa. Line.
Superhighway of four to six lanes throughout, paved almost entirely with concrete. Accommodations in cities along route.

Section 11. New York Line to Pennsylvania Line, **68.6 m.**

US 1 in this State, designed to speed the heavy traffic flow between New York and Philadelphia, avoids most urban congestion and cross traffic. It bypasses the center of every city. Because the road (*see illustration*) runs for miles without a turn and carries more traffic than any other State highway, many New Jersey residents avoid it. Those who prefer scenery to speed, and historic landmarks to traffic circles, turn off at Elizabeth to State 27, an alternate route to Trenton; but the motorist who likes to test his skill on a modern highway, and is cautious enough to avoid trouble with the State police, should follow US 1. The route is carefully patrolled and traffic regulations are enforced.

From George Washington Bridge, where the New York Line is crossed, US 1 twists through a breath-taking series of underpasses and overpasses until it straightens out for a gradual descent along the western slope of the Palisades on the Bergen Turnpike. Metropolitan residential and industrial development has claimed all of the land here, except for the marshy lowlands of Overpeck Creek. Westward are the clusters of commuters' towns, and in the distance the hazy outline of the Ramapo Mountains. From Jersey City the road sweeps upward to Pulaski Skyway, giving the last panorama of the New York City hinterland, a region of smokestacks and marshes, of a few skyscrapers and many tenements, of patterns in steel rails and confusion in garbage dumps. Between Newark and Linden the industrial area thins out; southward the highway traverses New Jersey countryside, with farms, woodland, nurseries, and only an occasional factory until the outlying part of Trenton is reached. Hills are rare, and there is little in the landscape to divert the driver's attention from the long, straight path of concrete lying ahead.

FORT LEE, **1.1 m.** (280 alt., 8,759 pop.), appears chiefly as an

NEW JERSEY

assortment of roadhouses, oil stations, and small eating places. The residential and business district is off the highway (R). Little of the community is seen, however, because of the series of highway underpasses and overpasses designed for automatic sorting of the bridge traffic. The driver needs to watch carefully for US 1 markers.

During the Revolution this plateau at the crest of the Palisades was selected by Washington as the site of the fort for which the town is named. His plan was to prevent the British fleet from sailing up the Hudson River to West Point. From the rocky bluff, Washington watched the attack and surrender of his garrison at Fort Washington, directly across the river, in November 1776. A few days later he was forced to abandon Fort Lee. The approximate site of the old fort is marked by a monument, the work of Carl E. Tifft, in MONUMENT PARK, Palisade Ave. Early in the 20th century Fort Lee became one of the cradles of the motion picture industry. Serial thrillers are no longer made here, but a printing studio that normally employs several hundred persons still operates. Some of the barn-like buildings used by the old studios are near the highway (L). A red dome and gilded cross (L) are on the CONVENT OF HOLY ANGELS.

Swinging S. after its separation from the other bridge exits and approaches, US 1 crosses Main St., Fort Lee, down which Washington marched after evacuating the fort. For a short distance the highway runs on the western crest of the Palisades ridge. Here there is no rock wall, but elevation is sufficient to permit a broad view of Overpeck Creek in the valley below and, beyond the next ridge, the slender line of the Hackensack River. On clear days the Ramapo Mountains are visible still further NW.

The road begins its descent to the valley on a long, straight enbankment. Below (R) lies the community of PALISADES, with a cluster of apartment houses, smaller dwellings, and schools.

The recent real estate development of MORSEMERE, **3.6 m.**, has a modern business district in the English cottage style. Another through highway is in the center of the main street at a lower level; US 1 is at street level and turns (L) on an overpass.

In the residential section of Ridgefield, the highway is no longer concrete paved. A WORLD WAR MONUMENT stands in a small plot (L); just S. of it is the old SAMUEL WRIGHT HOUSE (R), hugging the slope. Built in 1790, it is an excellent example of Dutch Colonial architecture. Dormer windows and other alterations have not spoiled the original charm. Other old houses are still standing along this part of the road.

RIDGEFIELD, 4.5 m. (30 alt., 4,671 pop.), has an unpretentious shopping center on the highway. The most noticeable building is the two-story RIDGEFIELD NATIONAL BANK of red brick (R).

South of Ridgefield the highway is almost at the floor of the valley. Tracks of the Erie R.R. run parallel in the meadowland (R). On either side of the road are drab homes and factories.

Approach to FAIRVIEW, 5.5 m. (20 alt., 9,067 pop.), is announced by the acrid smell from a bleachery (R). A few hundred yards from the highway (R) is a scattered group of 54 small gray buildings, the plant of the INTERNATIONAL FIREWORKS COMPANY, one of the largest manufacturers of display fireworks. Here were made the elaborate fireworks for the inaugurals of Presidents Wilson, Hoover, and Roosevelt; routine business is the making of "True Lovers' Knots" and "Fountains of Youth" for conventions of fraternal orders and for civic celebrations.

Between Fairview and North Bergen the route passes a CEMETERY (L) and an adjacent MONUMENT WORKS that sells bird baths and bridge prizes as a side line. The tracks of the West Shore R.R. are bridged near the entrance to the railroad's tunnel under the Palisades ridge. The highway, of recent concrete construction, climbs over a rocky hump. Factory buildings of the NORTH JERSEY INDUSTRIAL TERMINAL are R. Three miles westward are the twin towers of radio station WINS at Carlstadt.

On the upward slope (L) are rocky outcroppings of the underlying Palisades, upon which small houses barely find a foothold. Below, on the valley's edge (R), are railroad yards and a roundhouse of the N.Y. Central — a scene painted in grays and blacks.

NORTH BERGEN, 8.3 m. (25 alt., 40,714 township pop.), has churches, stores, a second-hand lumberyard, and two large gas tanks on or near the highway. The business section gives no indication of the large number of people living in this residential township.

Entering the outlying northern section of Jersey City, US 1 becomes Tonnelle Ave. The highway overpasses the main line tracks of the Pennsylvania R.R. just W. of the only trunk line tunnel from New Jersey into Manhattan. The streamlined electric locomotives operated between New York City and Washington use these tracks.

To the SW. is the irregular hump of SNAKE HILL, lone break in the

NEW JERSEY

uniform flatness of the marshlands. Geologists say that it is probably the eroded stump of an ancient volcano that once cast up enough molten rock to form the Watchung Mountains, 10 miles westward. A peculiarity of residential planning along the road here is the practice of putting tiny huts on stilts. This may be for protection against dampness in the lowlands (R), but on the hillside it perhaps merely indicates conformity with the local *mores*.

The meadowlands have their own skyline. On the banks of the Hackensack River (R) stand the six great chimneys of a public service electric and gas plant, adjacent to a gas and coke plant. Beyond are small hills of coke, several times the height of a freight car. The towers of railroad and highway drawbridges are grouped nearby at the river.

At **11.9 m.** the highway crosses the main line tracks of the Erie R.R. and the Lackawanna R.R., and there is a view of Jersey City's skyline. No towering office buildings dominate here, but rather the broad bulk of the American Can Co., which is now (1937) working three shifts a day, in part because of the use of cans for beer. The gray stone clock tower of ST. JOHN'S ROMAN CATHOLIC CHURCH, near Journal Square in the heart of Jersey City, stands out.

At **12 m.** is a traffic circle at the entrance to Pulaski Skyway.

Left from US 1 (straight ahead from the circle) on a concrete highway to the center of JERSEY CITY, **0.5 m.** (80 alt., 316,715 pop.), industrial city (*see N.J. GUIDE*).

Railroad Stations. Pa. R.R., Exchange Place; Erie R.R., foot of Pavonia Ave.; Central R.R. of N.J., Phila. & Reading Ry., and Baltimore & Ohio R.R., foot of Johnston Ave.; Hudson & Manhattan R.R., Journal Sq., Exchange Pl., and Erie Stations.

Points of Interest. Site of Paulus Hook Fort, Peter Stuyvesant Statue, Old Bergen Church, Medical Center, Colgate Clock, St. Peter's College, and others.

Swinging R. from the traffic circle, US 1 enters PULASKI SKYWAY. This steel and concrete viaduct, named for the Polish nobleman who lost his life in the American Revolution, is 3.4 miles long, rises 145 ft. above two rivers, and cost $21,000,000. An average of more than 30,000 vehicles used it daily in 1935. This was a pioneer achievement in the solution of the problem of handling through-traffic in one of the most congested traffic areas in the world; the situation here was aggravated by the marshy terrain, which lessened the possible number of highways and bridges.

Climbing an easy grade, the road crosses the Hudson and Manhattan R.R. ("the Tubes") and approaches the cantilever span across Hackensack River. Were it not for the heavy I-beam railing, an excellent view of the waterways adjacent to New York Harbor and of the Newark industrial area could be obtained. As it is, however, the area is in full view only when the two high points of the skyway are crossed; from those points are seen the tall office buildings of Newark and the gas tanks of Harrison. Seen by a glance through the railing is (L) one of the great garbage dumps for which the Newark meadows are known. Next is seen the large plant of the WESTERN ELECTRIC Co., at the head of Newark Bay where the Hackensack and Passaic Rivers unite. The sun glints sharply from the roofs of hundreds of employees' cars, parked in neat formation next to the factory. To the rear (L) are the towers of midtown and then downtown Manhattan, then the slight elevation that is Brooklyn, the gap of the Narrows (entrance to New York Harbor), and finally the hilly outline of Staten Island, 8 miles S. The usual haze from factory smoke often obliterates part of the view, and the no-parking rule makes use of field glasses impracticable.

Two more large public service plants of the dominant power and local transportation company of the State are R. of the skyway. One of these is unusual because it boils mercury instead of water to operate its turbine for generating electricity.

The view further (R) is up the valleys of Hackensack and Passaic Rivers. The best picture of Newark, straight ahead, is from the cantilever span across Passaic River. At the western end of the skyway the highway enters the Newark city limits. Elevated on a fill, the road takes a straight course through a concentrated industrial area, with freight tracks of the Pennsylvania R.R. running parallel (R). Next along the route is one of Newark's less prosperous residential districts.

Once more the highway climbs, bridging the main freight line of the Lehigh Valley R.R. It descends on a broad embankment, curving in a wide arc. On both sides are home-made huts and garden patches, occupying what was once a dumping ground. Built of materials salvaged from dumps, the huts have served for several years as daytime shelters for men, women, and even children from needy families in Newark, who come here to raise vegetables for immediate consumption and for canning. The gardeners take almost belligerent

BAYONNE BRIDGE, NEW JERSEY

STATE HOUSE, TRENTON, NEW JERSEY

NEW JERSEY

pride in their work, competing for prizes for the best yields. In summer the huts are brightly decorated with flowers, flags, and latticework.

At **18.1 m.** is a traffic circle.

Left from the traffic circle is a paved road leading past the NEWARK AIRPORT, with a public parking space next to the flying field, **0.2 m.** Here the motorist may watch take-offs and landings at the busiest airport of the Nation, mail and passenger terminal for New York City as well as Newark and Jersey City. Each day there are 122 arrivals and departures of scheduled airliners; the rush hours are from 4:30 to 6:30 p.m. For a view of night-flying, with the large field illuminated by floodlights, the best time is about 8:30. The airport, established in 1928, was reclaimed from marshlands by the city of Newark; it represents an investment of $9,500,000.

At **19.1 m.** is the junction with State 21 and State 29, overpassed by westbound traffic on US 1.

Right on State 21 is the business center of NEWARK, **1.8 m.** (115 alt., 442,337 pop.), industrial city (*see N.J. GUIDE*).

Railroad Stations. Pa. R.R., Lehigh Valley R.R., and Hudson & Manhattan Tubes, Raymond Plaza, West; Erie R.R., Broadway (N. Newark) and foot of 4th St.; Delaware, Lackawanna & Western, Broad St. at Lackawanna Pl.; Central R.R. of N.J., Broad St. near Edison Pl.

Points of Interest. Four Corners, Port Newark, Newark Museum, Newark University, Old Stone Schoolhouse, Military Park, Washington Park, and others.

Between this junction and Elizabeth the road is a broad belt of asphalt with some curves and so crowded with trucks and pleasure cars that it is of more than usual danger. Concrete paving has not yet been laid because the earth fill is still settling into the marsh. On either side of the low embankment the flats are covered with tall meadow grass and cat-tails, brightened with sunflowers in the summer months. The meadow (L) is being filled and graded over a large area for an extension of Newark Airport.

Visible (L) several miles to the S. is the beautiful sweeping arch of the BAYONNE BRIDGE (*see illustration*), extending across Kill van Kull between Bayonne, N.J., and Staten Island, N.Y.; opened to traffic in 1932, this is the longest steel-arch bridge in the world, with a span of 1,675 ft., and the top of its arch is higher than the towers of Brooklyn Bridge. Almost straight ahead from this point on the roadway is the cantilever span of the GOETHALS BRIDGE, which has carried traffic between Elizabeth, N.J., and Staten Island, N.Y., since its completion in 1928. These bridges, distinguished engineering achievements, compare favorably in design with outstanding architectural monuments.

Some of the large industrial plants of Newark (R) are next to the main line tracks of the Pennsylvania R.R. ELIZABETH AIRWAY RADIO (L) is a station maintained by the U.S. Department of Commerce to guide planes within a radius of 100 miles, by means of the radio beam, to Newark Airport.

The city limits of Elizabeth at North Ave. are marked by the first traffic light W. of Jersey City. The highway is safer here, with a grass strip dividing the street. Frame houses and some industrial and business establishments are on both sides of the road. After dipping under a highway crossing and the main line tracks of the Central R.R. of N.J., the route leads R. at **22.6 m.** on E. Jersey St.

ELIZABETH (43 alt., 114,589), industrial and residential city (*see N.J. GUIDE*).

Railroad Stations. Pa. R.R., Central R.R. of N.J., Baltimore & Ohio R.R., and Reading Ry., Broad St. at the Arch.

Points of Interest. Governor Williamson House, First Presbyterian Church, Union Square, Nathaniel Bonnell House, Gov. Jonathan Belcher Mansion, Elias Boudinot House, Liberty Hall, and others.

South of E. Jersey St. the highway passes for a short distance over a concrete and steel viaduct, bridging cross streets near the center of Elizabeth. The elevation is enough to give a fine view of the city, with the needle-like spire of old FIRST PRESBYTERIAN CHURCH and the tall, white tower of UNION COUNTY COURTHOUSE (R). The narrow channel of ELIZABETH RIVER, crossed by the viaduct, seems unbelievably small to have been an important waterway during Colonial days and early years of the republic.

US 1 passes through the fringe of an extensive oil refining district. Storage tanks of the Standard Oil Company are illuminated nightly with colored lights. A familiar sight is the Standard Oil herd of goats that keeps the grass around the tanks closely cropped; they are used instead of mechanical lawnmowers because of the risk of sparks. The road here enters the first open country W. of George Washington Bridge.

LINDEN, **25.9 m.** (25 alt., 21,206 pop.), has a business district to serve local people and the endless chain of motor traffic. A large portion of the population works at local industrial plants. On the highway (R) is WHEELER PARK, an attractive recreational area maintained by the county. Just beyond the park (R) are two of Linden's newest and most important industries, the neatly landscaped plant of the Gordon Gin Co. and a plant of General Motors. The Bayway refinery of Standard Oil is within the municipality. Several miles from US 1 (L) are the twin masts of radio station WOR's transmitter at Carteret, each 485 ft. high.

RAHWAY, 27.6 m. (20 alt., 16,011 pop.), is another community of two-story frame houses, with the main business section off the highway (R). There are some attractive homes in this suburb.

West of Rahway US 1 swings R., ascends an embankment, and crosses RAHWAY RIVER. The big dome of the NEW JERSEY REFORMATORY, with its buttressed concrete wall and surrounding farm, is close by the highway (L). A school for juvenile offenders is conducted here, giving industrial training in several crafts.

The route enters farming country in this section; red barns and an occasional dairy herd are reminders of the rural setting that was unbroken until the construction of the speed highway several years ago, with its attendant lunch rooms and filling stations.

At **30.7 m.** is the Rahway Clover Leaf, first highway intersection of this type built in the country, and a model for later highway-crossing eliminations. Adjoining the road (R) is a new cemetery development, one of several modern burial grounds or memorial parks along the route. Absence of residential neighborhoods on US 1 from this point S. to Trenton should not tempt the driver to excessive speed, since State police in passenger cars as well as on motorcycles are frequently encountered. Their uniforms of French gray coats and dark blue trousers with a broad gold stripe are noteworthy.

At **33.7 m.** is ROOSEVELT PARK (R), a tract of 192 acres that is the first unit of the Middlesex County park system. Unemployed men under the Emergency Relief Administration and the Works Progress Administration set to work on a small wilderness of marsh and underbrush and made a park, well-landscaped and equipped with all facilities for picnickers. Over the hill is an artificial lake, and within the park area are the new MIDDLESEX COUNTY TUBERCULOSIS HOSPITAL, a handsomely designed building erected with the aid of Federal funds, and the KIDDIE KEEP-WELL CAMP, where undernourished children are given summer vacations.

A ravine, through which runs a single-track freight line of the Lehigh Valley R.R., is bridged as the highway rolls with scarcely a curve through somewhat undulating country. The landscape here has few distinctive features. For 5 miles the road is paralleled (L) by the rusty rails of what was once a high-speed electric line between Elizabeth and New Brunswick. Electric cars are no longer operated but every Tuesday a small motorbus, equipped with steel flanges on the tires, makes one trip as far as Bonhamtown Junction, now the end of the line. At this point the flanges are removed, the bus is driven off the rails and turned around, and the flanges replaced. Weeks pass without any passengers being carried; the sole purpose of the run is to hold the franchise.

At **35.5 m.** is the junction with a concrete and asphalt road. This point was known as Bonhamtown Junction in the days of trolley operation.

Left on this road is BONHAMTOWN, **0.8 m.** (80 alt., 800 pop.), a country village with two small churches, a school, and a general store on a winding main street. The settlement dates far back into the Colonial period, and was the scene of skirmishes during the Revolutionary War. It is the site of the United States Army's RARITAN ARSENAL, a large depot for the storage and distribution of ordnance material (*not open to the public*). In the magazine area enough ammunition to supply a field army for more than 30 days can be stored. The cost of plant and equipment on this 2,200-acre area was $14,000,000; the value of material in storage is about $240,000,000.

PISCATAWAY, **3.5 m.** (120 alt., 2,011 pop.), has a few modern business buildings scattered along its main thoroughfare. By far the most interesting and attractive structure in the community is ST. JAMES EPISCOPAL CHURCH (L), a glistening white building, almost square, with four large pillars and a tiny steeple. This edifice, the third built by a parish organized in 1714, was consecrated in 1837. It is a reproduction of the church destroyed by the tornado of 1835, which tossed the pulpit into Raritan River. (The pulpit was found on the shore of Staten Island, 15 miles away.) The original bell, brought from England in 1702, still hangs in the belfry.

Curious inscriptions are found on the stones in the adjoining graveyard. One, dated 1693, tells of twin boys who skipped Sunday service to gather mushrooms in the woods. The mushrooms were, as the epitaph has it, "poyseond." Another tombstone is that of Harper, reputedly an atheist, who had obtained the deed to his new brick house on the day of the 1835 tornado. Celebrating his acquisition at the village tavern, he ran out into the road when the windstorm struck the town and defied God to kill him. Hardly had the blasphemous words left his lips, so the story goes, when the church roof blew off and a flying timber crushed him to death. Piscataway was the scene of a bitter dispute among its Baptist residents, beginning in 1705 and lasting for a century. The township became known as Quibbletown and was so recorded in official documents during the Revolution. American soldiers bestowed their own nickname: Squabbletown.

At **3.7 m.** this side road rejoins US 1.

NEW JERSEY

At **36.6 m.** US 1 crosses Raritan River on COLLEGE BRIDGE, a handsome structure of reinforced concrete arches. Part of the campus of NEW JERSEY COLLEGE FOR WOMEN is visible (R), spread out upon the bluff above the river. The spire is that of COLONIAL CHAPEL, on the campus. Beyond are some of the buildings of New Brunswick; and the view upstreet is not unlike that of Stratford-on-Avon. The road passes the NEW BRUNSWICK WAR MEMORIAL (L).

At **37.1 m.** is the junction with State S-28, at a traffic circle.

Right on State S-28 is NEW BRUNSWICK, **2.5 m.** (50 alt., 34,555 pop.), university town (*see N.J. GUIDE*).

Points of Interest. Rutgers University, Joyce Kilmer Memorial, Buccleuch Mansion, Guest House Museum, Red Lion Tavern, White Hall Hotel, factories, and old houses.

South of New Brunswick are the grounds of the NEW JERSEY STATE COLLEGE OF AGRICULTURE (R). The main line tracks of the Pennsylvania R.R. are crossed on a high embankment and bridge.

The highway closely follows the original route of stagecoach days, when it was an important land link between the water highways of the Raritan and Delaware Rivers. For almost 25 miles there is no curve perceptible to the eye, although there are two or three slight deviations from a straight line. To prevent collisions, the 6-mile stretch S. of the railroad overpass has been divided by a center strip, and the work is being continued toward Trenton. The concrete was forced apart by compressed air to make room for the strip and curbs; a new subgrade was prepared at the side, and as much as a 500-foot length was moved into position at one time.

Nurseries and well-kept farms are on both sides of the road. From a low-lying ridge at **51.1 m.** is a view (R) of PRINCETON UNIVERSITY across the meadowland of an intervening valley. The university buildings, largely hidden by oaks and elms, are dwarfed by the massive Tudor tower of the chapel. In the foreground is the bulk of Palmer Stadium, while through the trees an occasional glimpse of Carnegie Lake is caught.

At **51.4 m.** is the ROCKEFELLER INSTITUTE FOR MEDICAL RESEARCH (L). In the laboratories here a staff of scientists carries on experimental work in plant and animal pathology. One of the major problems of the institute has been the control of the Japanese beetle.

At **52.7 m.** is the junction with a dirt road, marked by a gatehouse.

Left on this road and visible from the highway is the WALKER-GORDON FARM (*open*). Operated by the Borden Milk Company, the plant is known for its rotolactor, a revolving platform that combines the method of an automobile assembly line with the mechanical features of a carousel, for the purpose of milking cows efficiently. The cows step on and off the platform, milked and stripped in 12½ minutes, after one complete revolution of the wheel. The 1,400 cows are milked by the rotolactor in less than 6 hours.

PENN'S NECK, **54.9 m.** (100 alt.), is one of the most attractive hamlets on US 1. Here the road underpasses the Princeton Branch of the Pennsylvania R.R. Beyond the cut of the hill are two Colonial mansions; a nursery rose-field (L) provides several acres of color during the season.

Crossing the abandoned DELAWARE AND RARITAN CANAL on a drawbridge at one of the few places where water still remains, the highway runs on to Trenton. At **58 m.** (L) is an artificial lake on Shabakunk Creek, a branch of historic Assunpink Creek. Herons often alight here, close by the highway.

At **65.9 m.** is the junction with US 206, at a traffic circle.

Left on US 206 is the center of TRENTON, **2.2 m.** (60 alt., 123,356 pop.), State capital (*see N.J. GUIDE*).

Railroad Stations. Pa. R.R., Clinton St. near Greenwood Ave.; Phila. & Reading Ry., N. Warren and Tucker Sts.

Points of Interest. Battle Monument, State Capitol (*see illustration*), Masonic Lodge House Museum, Douglas House, State Museum, Lenox Pottery Works, and various churches and houses.

Swinging R. from the traffic circle, US 1 runs along the edge of the city of Trenton, past rows of typical brick houses built close to the sidewalk as in Philadelphia. The road drops gradually on Calhoun St. toward the Delaware River, crossing branch lines of the Reading and Pennsylvania Railroads and the old Delaware and Raritan Canal feeder. Sanhican Creek, in MAHLON STACY PARK, is bridged just before the road ascends a short embankment to the Calhoun St. Bridge, which crosses the Delaware River. Slow driving is required on this old structure, which has withstood many floods and ice jams.

At **68.6 m.**, on the bridge, the Pennsylvania Line is crossed.

PENNSYLVANIA

N.J. Line — Morrisville — Philadelphia — Swarthmore — Kennett Square — Md. Line, **83.5 m.** US 1.

Reading R.R. parallels the route between Morrisville and Philadelphia; Pennsylvania R.R. parallels the entire route.
Well-paved, all-weather route. Accommodations at short intervals; hotels in cities.

Section 12. New Jersey Line to Maryland Line, *83.5 m.*

Between the western bank of the Delaware River and the Maryland Line, US 1 pursues a southwesterly course across the undulating terrain of Bucks County, through the city of Philadelphia, and over the section of the highway known as the Baltimore Pike.

The highway crosses the Delaware River on the TRENTON-MORRISVILLE BRIDGE at a point where in 1804 the first bridge across the Delaware was built.

Bucks County was established in 1682 by William Penn as one of the three original counties. The rolling surface and fertile soil of the county are adapted to agriculture, the chief occupation of the inhabitants; small farms predominate.

MORRISVILLE, **0.6 m.** (21 alt., 5,368 pop.), incorporated in 1804, was named in honor of Robert Morris, "financier of the American Revolution" and a signer of the Declaration of Independence. Prior to this time it had been known as the Falls of the Delaware. Morris maintained an imposing mansion and stables, patterned after the English stables of the period, on a 2,800-acre tract here. Jean Victor Maria Moreau, one of Napoleon's marshals, who fell into disfavor, lived in the mansion during his exile. In 1915 the tract was subdivided and modern dwellings were built upon it.

The first European settlement in the county was made by the Dutch West India Company on a small island near the western bank of the Delaware, below the falls. Three or four families lived around the company's trading post there from 1624 to 1627. Nothing remains of the island except a large sand bar, nearly opposite Morrisville. A ferry operated here more than 50 years before Penn's arrival in America.

Morrisville was seriously considered by Congress as a site for the permanent capital of the United States, when, on October 7, 1783, a resolution was presented ". . . that the Federal Town should be erected on the banks of the Delaware at the Falls near Trenton on the New Jersey side, or in Pennsylvania on the opposite." Southern interests sought to have Annapolis chosen as the National Capital; Washington advised against Morrisville, and Alexander Hamilton, in a historic instance of logrolling, favored the present site on the Potomac River. Despite the formidable opposition the Morrisville plan was defeated by only two votes.

The route passes through narrow streets, with thin sidewalks flanked by rows of brick houses. At **1.1 m.** (R) is a three-story dwelling in the American-Georgian style, built by Thomas Barkley in 1750 and restored in 1921, which served as General Washington's headquarters prior to the surprise attack on Trenton that caught the Hessians in the midst of a Christmas celebration. Barkley's estate was the site selected for the proposed Federal buildings.

The highway continues through Penn Valley, which is dotted with old brownstone and limestone houses. The homes of early Quaker settlers are identified by dormer windows and wide English chimneys.

At **6.1 m.** is OXFORD VALLEY (80 alt., 283 pop.). The Watsons, owners of a large tract of land on the south side of Edge Hill, were the original settlers. Old brownstone houses, surrounded by huge trees, are scattered along a hillside that slopes gently downward to Queen Anne Creek.

According to a possibly erroneous local legend, Oxford was so named because of the likeness of an ox on the village tavern sign, and the bad ford over the creek. Valley was added to the name in 1844, when a post office was opened.

The LANGHORNE SPEEDWAY at **8 m.** (R) has attracted many of the country's best-known automobile race drivers since it was built in 1925. The national motorcycle championship races have been held here on several occasions.

SOUTH LANGHORNE, **9 m.** (120 alt., 789 pop.), is a suburban development that has grown up around the old Eden post office and the Langhorne station on the Reading R.R.

Right from South Langhorne on State 113 is LANGHORNE, **0.6 m.** (103 alt., 4,333 pop.), formerly called Four Lanes End. This is an attractive residential town with homes set in well-kept lawns. There are several mansions far back in spacious grounds. Lafayette stopped at the RICHARDSON HOUSE, 115 E. Maple Ave., to have his wounds dressed when he was being carried by boat from the

Battlefield of Brandywine to be placed in the care of the Moravian Sisters at Bethlehem. It is now the Community House.

Opposite the Community House is the HICKS HOUSE, a brick dwelling built in 1763 by Gilbert Hicks, an officer of the British Crown. Hicks' life was threatened by the townspeople after he had read from the courthouse steps the Amnesty Proclamation of General Howe and his brother, Admiral Howe, dated November 30, 1776. He fled the town and joined the British Army in New Jersey. The New Jersey Legislature held sessions in the Hicks House after being driven across the Delaware in advance of Washington's retreat in December 1776.

ST. MARY'S MANOR, on Manor Ave., is a school conducted by the Fathers of the Society of Mary for the education of foreign missionaries.

On State 113 is WRIGHTSTOWN, 7.3 m. (320 alt., 64 pop.). The LENAPE MONUMENT near a huge chestnut tree in this village marks the starting point of the Indian Walk. The land involved in the "Walking Purchase" was part of the tract deeded to William Penn by the Lenni-Lenapes more than half a century earlier. This tract was to be bounded by the Delaware River and the Neshaminy Creek, and was to extend as far N. as a man could walk in three days. Penn "walked out" one and a half days in a leisurely manner and, at a point near what is now Wrightstown, decided he had as much land as he would need.

When settlements began to infringe on Indian domain the almost-forgotten treaty was resurrected. After a tribal council the Lenapes agreed to allow the remaining day and a half to be walked out.

The Penns offered 500 acres of the new tract and five pounds sterling to the person who walked the greatest distance in the given time. Richard Marshall, James Yeates, and Solomon Jennings, supposedly fast walkers, were selected. Three Indians were to accompany them.

Late in September 1735 (some authorities set 1737 as the year), the walkers started at sunrise from an old tree below the Wrightstown meeting house. The strenuous pace forced Jennings and two of the Indians to drop out in two and a half hours. The remaining Indian stopped at Easton. By sundown the north side of the Blue Mountains had been reached. When the Indians realized the walk was to continue for another half day, they declared they were being cheated out of all their good land. An eyewitness said the last part of the first day's journey was covered by twilight. At sunrise the walk was resumed. Yeates lasted only a short time. Marshall, continuing alone, by noon reached a spur of the Second or Broad Mountain, approximately 65 miles from the starting point.

In order to include the rich Minisink lands, the Pennsylvania proprietaries ordered the surveyors to draw the boundary line at an angle instead of straight. The Minisink was the ancestral homeland of the Lenapes and, since they felt the proprietaries had taken advantage of them, they refused to vacate. When, however, they were ordered to move by the Six Nations Confederation, which claimed ownership of all Lenape lands by right of conquest, they acceded. Some of them migrated to Ohio and others to the Wyoming Valley.

The highway traverses beautiful farm country dotted with wooded sections, and roughly parallels Neshaminy (Ind., *two streams* or *double stream*) Creek (L).

138 U. S. ONE

OAKFORD, 11.5 m. (88 alt., 500 pop.), is the gateway to one of Philadelphia's summer bungalow colonies on Neshaminy Creek. Small frame bungalows are scattered through a wooded ravine formed by the stream.

At **13.2 m.** (R), at the foot of a gradual descent, is a fine example of an early Colonial farmhouse. Poquessing (Ind., *the place of mice*) Creek, **13.6 m.**, is the dividing line between Bucks and Philadelphia Counties.

Within the city limits open fields, truck gardens, and small farms line the highway, and wooded valleys and rolling hills slope away to meet the sky.

At **15.3 m.** is the junction with Red Lion Road.

Right on this narrow macadam road, which passes a commercial airport and numerous old stone farmhouses, is BRYN ATHYN (Welsh, *hill of cohesiveness*), **4.1 m.** (280 alt., 736 pop.). The BRYN ATHYN CATHEDRAL (*open weekdays 3–5 p.m.; Sat. 10–12 a.m. and 3–5 p.m.*) is a center of the General Church of the New Jerusalem (Swedenborgian). The cathedral (*see illustration*) is being built in 14th century English Gothic style with later additions in 12th century Romanesque.

A frame chapel was erected here in 1895 by followers of Emanuel Swedenborg (1688–1772), a Swedish scientist and philosopher who, about 1747, began to promulgate a new system of theology. In 1908 John Pitcairn donated $30,000 to the Swedenborgians, and shortly afterward plans were drawn up for a building program that would take 50 years to complete. The cornerstone of the cathedral was laid in 1914 and the edifice was dedicated in 1919 — the year in which the society received $2,000,000 under Pitcairn's will.

Raymond Pitcairn, son of John, is (1937) resident architect of the cathedral. Customs and practices of the building crafts guilds of the Middle Ages have been adopted; materials are finished by hand, granite is quarried nearby, and all timber except the teakwood used in the floors and doors is taken from neighboring woods.

The characteristic cruciform plan of the English parish churches has been followed, and a handsome square pinnacled tower, rising to a height of 150 feet above the crossing, dominates the group. Metamorphosed granite of yellow, red, green, and gray tints gives the buildings a warm tone.

The main façade, on the W., consists of a porch of three bays between buttresses, surmounted by a stone-carved and pinnacled parapet, with a lofty, five-light window above. The movement of this façade to a point 50 feet W. of its present location is contemplated, to allow the addition of three bays to the nave of the church.

Within the west door, which is of temporary material but fitted with exquisite monel metal hinges, is the narthex, also three bays in width.

The chancel is in three sections, each rising three steps above the preceding one. The Great Altar is similarly elevated three steps above the sanctuary floor and is 12 steps above the nave. The three sections of the chancel are symbolic of the

PENNSYLVANIA

three degrees of the internal mind and of the three heavens defined in the Swedenborgian faith.

The stained glass windows of the church, depicting the story of the Scriptures, are exceptionally fine. They are warm in color, except in the sanctuary, where blue predominates.

From the south transept, there is an entrance into the council building, which is of simple 12th century Norman design. The hall in this building is notable for its variety of stone carving. The corbels supporting the roof trusses are carved to represent the heads of leading characters in the history of the New Church.

The choir hall, entered from the north transept, has a broad white plastered wall, heavy stone trim, and huge oak beams.

US 1, here Roosevelt Boulevard, leads to Broad St.

Right (straight ahead) from the corner of Roosevelt Boulevard and Broad St., on Hunting Park Ave., for US 1-Alt., which avoids the heavy traffic of the city. Hunting Park Ave. runs down to Schuylkill River; R. here on East River Drive, a pleasant parkway that crosses City Line Ave.; L. on this broad avenue to Lansdowne Ave.; L. on Lansdowne Ave. to LANSDOWNE, **12.2 m.**, at the junction with US 1 (*see below*).

US 1 turns (L) from Roosevelt Boulevard on Broad St. to the CITY HALL (*see illustration*).

PHILADELPHIA, **30 m.** (408 alt., 1,950,961 pop.), largest city in the State (*see PA. GUIDE*).

Railroad Stations. Baltimore & Ohio, 24th and Chestnut Sts.; Pennsylvania, Broad and Market Sts. and 30th and Market Sts.; Pennsylvania and Reading Seashore Lines, foot of Market St.; Reading System, North Broad St.; Reading Terminal, 12th and Market Sts.

Points of Interest. Independence Square Group, Christ Church, Franklin Institute, Free Library, Art Museum, Rodin Museum, United States Mint, University of Pennsylvania, Fairmount Park, and others.

Right, around City Hall and two squares on Broad St., to Walnut St.; R. on Walnut to 34th St. where Woodland Ave. intersects; L. into Woodland Ave. to 39th St. where Baltimore Ave. intersects; R. into Baltimore Ave. (US 1), which crosses Cobbs Creek.

This creek, the dividing line between Philadelphia and Delaware Counties, was named for William Cobb, who purchased an old Swedish mill and a sizable tract of land on the banks of the stream. The Indians called the creek Karakung (*place of the wild geese*), and the Swedes, Amosland. At its mouth on Tinicum Island, Johann Printz, Governor of New Sweden, in 1643 established a fort and built a home for himself; not long afterward he started a Swedish settlement at Upland, nearby, on the site of the present Chester.

This was the first permanent European settlement in what is now Pennsylvania.

YEADON (L), **35.5 m.** (100 alt., 5,430 pop.), a thickly settled suburban community, with stone and box-like brick houses, was named for William Bullock's estate, Yeadon Manor. Yeadon is in Delaware County, which took its name from the river; the river was named for Thomas West, Lord de la Warr, Governor and Captain-General of the Colony of Virginia, who explored near its mouth in 1610. The highway cuts through a corner of the borough, passing FERNWOOD CEMETERY (R).

LANSDOWNE, **36.8 m.** (120 alt., 7,782 pop.), was named for Lord Lansdowne, a consistent friend of the American Colonies, both before and after the Revolution. It is a fine residential community with wide, well-shaded streets and large homes set on broad lawns. Many of the houses, built during the late 19th century, bristle with turrets and towers and have elaborate decorations. There are also many half-timbered houses, in modern adaptations of the Elizabethan style.

A 200-year-old SYCAMORE TREE, with a spread of more than 100 ft., stands in front of 47 E. Lacrosse Ave.

CLIFTON HEIGHTS, **38 m.** (160 alt., 5,055 pop.), named for Clifton Hall, residence of Henry Lewis, a Welsh Quaker, became a borough in 1895. Several large textile mills operate here.

At Springfield Inn is the junction with Saxer Ave.

Right on Saxer Ave. **1.5 m.** to the junction with Springfield Rd.; L. of the junction is SPRINGFIELD MEETING HOUSE. The first meeting house on this site, built about 1700 by members of the Society of Friends, was made of logs. This structure, destroyed by fire, was replaced by a stone building in 1738. Eventually it became inadequate, and in 1851 the present stone edifice was constructed. It was in the earlier structure that, in 1754, a group of Friends entered into a weighty discussion concerning the future of young Benjamin West. West wanted to study art, contrary to his father's wishes. Although the Quakers considered such a calling frivolous, one of the speakers pleaded the youth's cause so convincingly that the meeting was constrained to give him its blessing (*see below*).

The highway continues through a beautiful wooded region checkered with fine farms and estates. At **39.4 m.** (R) is the TEMPLE LUTHERAN CHURCH RECREATION CENTER.

At **40.2 m.** the highway runs to the N. of MORTON (205 alt., 1,340 pop.), established as a village about 1866. It was named for

PENNSYLVANIA

John Morton, the Pennsylvania delegate to the Continental Congress in 1776 and a signer of the Declaration of Independence.

The highway descends, passing a large swimming pool (R) and crossing Stony Creek, a branch of Darby Creek. A typical old Delaware County homestead is passed at **40.6 m.**

At **41.2 m.** (L) the highway skirts SWARTHMORE (115 alt., 3,405 pop.), an attractive residential suburb and college town. The homes here show the American Colonial influence with a simplification of detail. Limestone is generally used in construction, and a few of the houses have double chimneys. The town has almost no business section.

The community grew around SWARTHMORE COLLEGE, founded by the Society of Friends in 1884, to give Quaker youths opportunity for advanced educational training under the supervision of members of their own faith. The charter was revised in 1911 to make the institution non-sectarian. The enrollment is limited to 250 men and 250 women, and a high scholastic standard is maintained.

Thirty-four buildings are scattered over this 237-acre campus, which includes a large wooded tract and the beautiful rocky valley through which Crum Creek flows. PARRISH HALL is the main college building. The LIBRARY contains 90,000 volumes. The Friends' Historical Library, housed in a wing of the Library Building, contains books on Quaker history, religion, and attempts at social reform, and a special collection of manuscript records of Friends' Meetings. The SPROUL ASTRONOMICAL OBSERVATORY is well equipped for advanced research.

The BIRTHPLACE OF BENJAMIN WEST (1738–1820), Quaker portrait painter (*see above*), is on the campus. The distinctive feature of the simple gray stone structure is the "Germantown hood," a shingle-covered cornice projecting from the walls between the first and second story. The purpose of the hood is to protect the lower walls from driving rain. West studied abroad and was one of the first American artists to receive European recognition; one of his pictures, *Penn's Treaty with the Indians*, is in Independence Hall in Philadelphia.

The highway at this point descends, passing a factory (L) and, at **41.7 m.**, crossing the DELAWARE COUNTY MEMORIAL BRIDGE, which honors local veterans of the World War, over Crum Creek (cor. of Swed. *cromkill* or *crumkill*, *crooked creek*). The Indian name for the stream was Okehocking, for a tribe of that name. A number of mills were early established along its course. Valuable mineral deposits and quarries fringe its banks; feldspar and Wissahickon gneiss are found.

PINE RIDGE, 42.2 m. (160 alt., 40 pop.), is one of the newer suburban communities. Its attractive frame and brick houses are scattered over a hill heavily grown with pine trees, which conceal them from view.

At **43 m.** is the junction with State 252 (Providence Road).

1. Left on this road to Yale Ave., **1.8 m.**; L. here to LAPIDEA MANOR, **2 m.** (R). This fine old residence was the home of the late Gov. William Cameron Sproul. The grounds extend northward half a mile to Crum Creek and constitute part of the extensive tract at one time owned by Thomas Leiper. Leiper's home, STRATHAVEN, built here in 1785, is now occupied by his descendants. Leiper is generally credited with having constructed the State's first railway, which was horse-drawn. He built the rail road in 1805 to haul stone from his quarries to the banks of Crum Creek. The tracks were of white oak, the wheels of iron. Leiper's son later built a canal along Crum Creek and abandoned the rail road.

2. Right on State 252 to ROSE TREE HUNT CLUB, **1.6 m.**, one of the oldest hunt clubs in the country. The club owns more than 100 acres and has hunting privileges on more than 8,000 acres. Its meets, held semi-annually, in the spring and during Thanksgiving week, attract thousands from all over the East.

At **43.4 m.** is a junction with Winchester Road.

Left on this paved highway at **1.3 m.** to the HEDGEROW THEATER, one of America's first summer playhouses. It is housed in a 125-year-old mill. A group of actors who took over the building in the early 1890's and produced a series of plays, became a self-sustaining permanent repertory company. This group became known throughout the United States as a result of the fine work of Jasper Deeter, the director, a former Harrisburg newspaperman. He took over the direction with a company of six actors and actresses in April 1923.

Misfortune dogged the company's footsteps in many of its early ventures. Much credit for its continued existence belonged to Harriet Moore, the 83-year-old cook, who was adept at holding off bill collectors. Financial difficulties continued to distract the group until Ferd Nofer took over the business management. There are now 22 members of the Hedgerow Company living in the community. They cultivate a truck garden and raise sheep, thus obtaining vegetables and wool for their own needs. A printing press has been added to the permanent equipment. Members construct all the stage property.

The theater seats 168 persons, and frequently plays to a house of 220. Performances are now given the year around. In the winter of 1934–35 a troupe of 17 made a profitable tour of the South and Southwest. Ann Harding, stage and motion picture star, was one of the members of this colony. Among other prominent figures of the screen and legitimate stage who started their careers at Hedgerow are: Dorothy Peterson and John Beal of the movies, Max Morris Carnovsky of the Group Theater, Allyn Joslyn, and Harry Bellever.

PENNSYLVANIA

MEDIA, 43.5 m. (160 alt., 40 pop.), is the center of the Rose Tree Valley section and seat of Delaware County. It was so named because of its central position in the county. The majority of Media's homes were built during the post-Civil War period. Strongly constructed and set back from the streets on shady lawns, they present a gloomy appearance.

When Media was founded in 1683 by members of the Society of Friends, a controversy arose over the liquor question. The problem was settled by a clause in the charter, making it unlawful "for any person or persons to vend or sell vinous, spirituous, or other intoxicating liquors within the limits of the said borough, except for medical purposes or for use in the arts." Media thus became the first Pennsylvania town for which direct legislation forbidding the sale of spirituous liquor was enacted. The Pennsylvania Liquor Law, enacted following repeal of the prohibition amendment to the United States Constitution, abrogated the former act of the legislature, and the sale of liquor in Media is now legal.

At 44.1 m. the highway crosses Ridley Creek, whose banks are a favorite haunt of hikers, picnickers, and vacationists. In the early days of colonization it was the home of a wandering tribe of Indians known as the Okehocking.

This section of the State was settled by Quakers and Scotch-Irish Presbyterians; the latter erected the first church, probably about 1720.

The highway ascends a steep hill and winds through a stand of fine hardwood trees. The PENNSYLVANIA TRAINING SCHOOL, known locally as the Elwyn School for Feeble-Minded Children, is at 44.8 m. (L).

At 45.3 m. (R), on a wooded slope, stands the BLACK HORSE INN, opened in 1739; it is built of stone, with low doorways. Once an important stop on the Baltimore-Philadelphia stage route, it is now a station of the Pennsylvania Highway Patrol.

The highway leads downhill and crosses a branch of Chrome Run. The COMBS CONSERVATORY OF MUSIC is (R) at 45.6 m. and a LIMESTONE QUARRY (R) at 45.7 m. The road crosses Chrome Run at 45.8 m., after which it climbs uphill past wooded picnic grounds (R). At 46.1 m. (R) is a fine vista down Dismal Run Glen. The road passes over a steep knob and to the L. is an excellent view of the Chester Creek Valley. At 46.9 m. are the WAWA DAIRY FARMS, typical of the many fine modern dairy establishments in the county. The road then makes an S-curve downgrade through a wooded glen.

At **47.6 m.** the highway crosses Chester Creek, the second largest creek in Delaware County. The Swedes, who settled near its mouth at Upland, named it Upland Kill. Both branches of the stream furnish water power for numerous small mills. The creek was once navigable by large boats for a distance of two miles, but today is much diminished in size because several communities, particularly West Chester, take from it their water supply.

Old homes, some built more than 200 years ago, are along the creek and highway. These are in marked contrast with the fine modern estates a few hundred yards farther on, after the highway makes an S-curve upgrade. At **48 m.** is a glen (R), affording a view over the Chester Creek Valley. Conifers and hardwood trees, planted in a reforestation program, line the road here.

IVY MILLS, **48.8 m.** (330 alt., 65 pop.), was named for the IVY PAPER MILL, erected in 1729 by Thomas Willcox. Hand methods were used in this mill long after machines were being employed elsewhere in paper mills. The village consists of a few houses. There are several large orchards in the vicinity.

At **49 m.** is a fine view across the northern part of Aston Township. At **49.1 m.** the route passes (R) the PYLE BLACKSMITH SHOP, reminder of the days when the great stage route connected the States of the Atlantic seaboard.

MARKHAM, **50.1 m.** (240 alt., 134 pop.), former site of the Concord flour mills, was once an important milling, shipping, and post office center for the surrounding rural area. Its long street lined with frame houses follows the course of a sycamore-shaded stream.

US 1 ascends a steep hill, at its summit passing the DANTE ORPHANAGE OF THE SONS OF ITALY (L).

CONCORDVILLE, **51.1 m.** (240 alt., 134 pop.), a village with old stone houses, lies deep in a wood on a high ridge. The CONCORD MEETING HOUSE, in a group of old trees, dominates the scene; its outmoded carriage shed still stands. Overlooking Brandywine Valley, the meeting house commands one of the finest views in Delaware County. The meeting was established prior to 1686. The land for the meeting house, which was built in 1694, was leased to the trustees by John Mendenhall for "one pepper corn yearly forever." The British used the building as a base hospital after the Battle of Brandywine.

PENNSYLVANIA

The village took its name from Concord Township, largest in the county. Established in 1683, this township was named by the Quaker settlers in token of the harmonious relations existing among them. The feeling of concord was not, however, extended to their Indian neighbors, for in 1685 they petitioned the Penn government against the Indians "for ye Rapine and Destructions of Hoggs."

South of the crossroad the road descends through rugged, rolling country, Brandywine Summit and other ridges rising L. After crossing a branch of Harvey Run, the road follows a ravine worn by the stream. The BRANDYWINE BAPTIST CHURCH (*see illustration*), built in 1715 and remodeled in 1770, is (R) at **53.8 m.** It was the third Baptist church erected in the State. The churchyard contains a number of old tombstones, including some marking graves of Revolutionary soldiers.

CHADD'S FORD, **54.9 m.** (168 alt., 200 pop.), scene of the Battle of Brandywine, lies at the bottom of a gentle slope on the eastern bank of the sparkling creek. The present-day stream carries but a small volume of water, but in the days of early settlement floods and ice made the ford so hazardous that it became necessary to provide ferry service. The service, begun in 1737, was abandoned after a bridge was built.

The Continentals suffered a major defeat here on September 11, 1777, when Washington, in an effort to prevent the British from reaching Philadelphia, hurled his army of about 12,000 men at a force of 18,000 British and Hessian soldiers under General Howe, who was marching N. from Wilmington. Maneuvering by both sides for possession of the bridge over Brandywine Creek resulted in a military chess game lasting many hours. Finally, late in the afternoon, the British gained the bridge by crossing the creek above it and executing a flank attack on the American forces. The victors moved on to Philadelphia, while Washington and his troops sought refuge NW. of the city. This battle, nevertheless, taught Howe to respect his foes. Lafayette, attempting to rally the harassed center, late in the battle was severely wounded in the leg.

Right are battle memorials, among them a beautiful MARBLE ARCH. Beyond them are farmhouses that were used as headquarters during the day's struggle.

Brandywine Creek forms part of the eastern boundary of Chester County, one of the three original counties laid out by Penn in 1682.

The county was named for Chester, England, home of Robert Pearson, close friend of Penn. Comfortable stone and brick homesteads with the usual big, gray barns, dot this rich agricultural district.

Originally, the Great Valley, or the Chester Valley as it is sometimes called, was shared by English and Welsh Friends; the latter had settled to the E. in Tredyffrin and Westtown Townships. German settlers came later into the northern section, and the southwestern section was colonized by Scotch-Irish Presbyterians.

CHADD'S FORD JUNCTION, 55.3 m. (168 alt., 60 pop.), consists of a few old houses and deserted mills.

South of Chadd's Ford the highway curves L. and parallels Ring Run, picturesque tributary of the Brandywine.

Kennett Township, through which US 1 passes, was the scene of Bayard Taylor's *Story of Kennett*, a tale of the Revolution based on historic incidents of the region. One of the old buildings in the township is the MEETING HOUSE (R) at **58.1 m.**, built in 1707. This stone structure commands a fine view of the valley and the distant hills (L). The old carriage sheds and the grove of trees, typical of most Friends' meeting houses, are present.

US 1 runs through East Marlboro Township, which also served as the locale of Bayard Taylor's novels. Prior to and during the Civil War, East Marlboro was a hotbed of abolition sentiment. Many of the Quaker homesteads were utilized as stations of the "underground railroad," by which fugitive slaves were protected and aided in their flight northward.

At **59.1 m.** is the ANVIL TAVERN (R), around which General Knyphausen's Hessian division bivouacked the day before the Battle of Brandywine.

At **59.2 m.** (R) is the gateway to LONGWOOD GARDENS (*open weekdays and first Sun. of month; 11 a.m.–5 p.m.; free except Sat. and Sun., when fee is 25¢*), a 1,000-acre estate, most of which is devoted to the growing of farm produce. A nine-hole golf course covers 50 acres, and the remainder is given over to flower gardens, lawns, ponds, and woods.

The land, now owned by Pierre S. DuPont, was conveyed to George Pierce by William Penn in 1701. Two grandsons of George Pierce assembled the trees and plants for the first gardens, even carrying specimens of cypresses all the way from the Dismal Swamp in Virginia to Longwood in their saddlebags. Once known as Pierce's Park, the estate received its present name shortly before the Civil

PENNSYLVANIA

War. It was then known as Long Woods and was used as an "underground station" by Wilmington, Kennett Square, and Hamorton Friends.

Near the entrance is a group of FOUNTAINS that play promptly at two o'clock each day in good weather. Beyond them are a lake, a circular CLOCKTOWER (R) with a fine set of chimes, and a rocky eminence (L).

The CONSERVATORY (L) covers an area of 107,825 sq. ft. In it, among other plants are vines that produce peaches, azaleas from Belgium, chrysanthemums from the Orient, and exceptional specimens of orchids and acacias. On the first Sunday in each month, an organ recital is given in this building.

Beyond the conservatory is the OPEN AIR THEATER. A vine-covered stone wall is the backdrop; neatly trimmed boxwoods form the wings, and water spouted from fountains and colored by light is used for a curtain. Pine and hemlock trees clothe a ridge that looms behind the stage. The seating capacity is 2,200.

Further on (L) is a natural lake. Left of this lake is a formal WATER GARDEN, copied from the one in the gardens of the Villa Gamberaia, near Florence, Italy. The garden contains six pools, each centered with a fountain, in a rectangular plot of close-cropped lawn, bordered by rows of smaller fountains along the longer sides of the rectangle, interspersed with boxwood, and with a backdrop of trees. The four larger pools are rectangular, cut out on the inner corners to follow the curve of a circular fountain in the center. The sixth pool lies at the end of the garden opposite an observation platform, which stands in the position occupied by the villa in the original garden in Italy.

At **59.3 m.** is LONGWOOD VILLAGE. The old LONGWOOD MEETING HOUSE (R) was the scene of many anti-slavery speeches. A cylindrical stone monument in the burial ground marks the GRAVE OF BAYARD TAYLOR (1825–75), who died in Berlin (*see below*).

The road runs through a mushroom-producing area, with many nurseries visible from the highway. This industry is quite profitable.

KENNETT SQUARE, **62.1 m.** (380 alt., 3,091 pop.), founded in 1705 on a ridge and named for a village in Wiltshire, England, is a town of red brick and stone houses standing along narrow winding streets.

The SITE OF THE BIRTHPLACE OF BAYARD TAYLOR, novelist, journalist, poet, and diplomat, is at Station and Union Sts. Taylor was one of the first of America's adventurous but penniless youths to seek knowledge and experience in the old cities of Europe. His *Views Afoot or Europe Seen with a Knapsack and Staff* was a best-seller in 1846. At the age of 21 he was publishing a newspaper in Phoenixville, and in 1847 he became a member of the staff of the New York *Tribune*. He was one of the first white men to penetrate Africa, and he accompanied Perry to Japan. He died soon after he became American Minister to Germany.

The BAYARD TAYLOR MEMORIAL LIBRARY, S. Broad St., contains first editions of his books, and some of his paintings and drawings.

South of Kennett Square US 1 dips down through excellent farming country. Fine Colonial farmhouses dot the landscape at close intervals. At **63.5 m.** (R) lies the GREEN BANK FARM, an outstanding example of an old farm that has been modernized without destroying its original charm.

TOUGHKENAMON, **64.6 m.** (320 alt., 450 pop.), is named for Toughkenamon Ridge (R), N. of the hamlet. The Indians called this elevation Doch-can-a-mon (*firebrand hill*).

In addition to mushroom nurseries, there are numerous greenhouses devoted to the cultivation of roses and carnations in this area. Most of the buildings along the route are of brick or stone interspersed with occasional white and yellow frame dwellings built in the style common to the late 19th century.

AVONDALE, **66.5 m.** (272 alt., 763 pop.), is a busy marketing center for mushroom growers, with banks, stores, and low office buildings jammed together in the center of the town. Most of the brick buildings are gleaming red, the result of several coats of paint. The highway twists and turns in the village to avoid a maze of creeks and railroad tracks.

The highway describes several sharp curves while climbing a wooded slope. Old brownstone homesteads, many built by the first settlers, are scattered along the highway.

The AVONGROVE CONSOLIDATED SCHOOL is (R) at **67.8 m.** S. of this point the road bears L. to traverse a charming countryside. At **68.1 m.** (R) are nurseries, among the leading producers of roses and carnations for eastern city markets. Several hundred square feet of glass cover extensive plantings, and beds of red, white, and yellow roses are close to the road, a delightful roadside decoration. Signs invite passersby to visit the gardens.

PENNSYLVANIA 149

Still in the mushroom and flower-growing area is WEST GROVE, **68.1 m.** (320 alt., 1,375 pop.), long the scene of annual Methodist camp meetings. The town is clean and modern. Long rows of brick houses with porches flank the street.

JENNERSVILLE, **71.5 m.** (578 alt., 250 pop.), a rural hamlet, was named for Dr. Edward Jenner, who introduced and developed vaccination. Dr. Josiah Ankrim, a resident, chose the name because of his admiration for the English physician.

At **74.6 m.** (L) is the LINCOLN UNIVERSITY CAMPUS extending over 450 acres. A stone archway stands at the entrance. This institution is maintained by the Presbyterian Church for the education of young Negro men and women. It was founded in 1854 as Ashmun Institute, and in 1866 received its present name in memory of the "Great Emancipator." It has preparatory, college, and theological courses. Brick dormitories, a chapel, and the administration building with classrooms and laboratories compose the university group. The enrollment is 450.

At **76 m.** red soil begins to supplant the limestone. The road crosses a more rugged country, dipping and rising with the slopes and bridging several small streams.

OXFORD, **78.1 m.** (535 alt., 2,606 pop.), is a bustling distributing center, with well-kept streets and houses. It was named for the college town in England. Great quantities of milk are shipped daily from this point to the Philadelphia market.

At **78.4 m.** the pike passes the OXFORD FRIENDS' MEETING HOUSE (R), constructed of brick in 1879 and standing among trees. Left at this point is a fringe of mills and sheds, paralleling a railroad.

Jack pines, scrub oaks, and other stunted growths appear in greater numbers as the highway nears the Maryland State Line.

At **81.5 m.** (L) is NOTTINGHAM (500 alt., 30 pop.), in which is the SITE OF THE NOTTINGHAM FRIENDS' MEETING HOUSE (c. 1719). The PRESBYTERIAN CHURCH (R) was built in 1802. The houses are of stone and well built.

The highway now traverses West Nottingham Township, laid out in 1702 as part of the "Nottingham Lots," consisting of a tract of 18,000 acres. The area was supposed to be in Pennsylvania, but the Mason-Dixon Line placed the larger part of it in Maryland. Two manors of 5,000 acres each, which had been set aside for Letitia

Aubrey, Penn's daughter, and for William Penn, Jr., were in the northwestern part of the area.

SYLMAR, **83.2 m.**, is a border hamlet with a name made by combining syllables from the words Pennsylvania and Maryland.

At **83.5 m.** is the Pennsylvania-Maryland State Line. This, the MASON-DIXON LINE, was surveyed and marked by Charles Mason and Jeremiah Dixon, English astronomers, in 1763–67. These men had been commissioned by the Penns and the Calverts to determine the boundary in order to settle disputes among claimants of land under various grants dating back to 1682. George Calvert, Lord Baltimore, founder of Maryland, under his grant claimed a part of Pennsylvania that would have included the site of Philadelphia as far N. as the Holmesburg section. This dispute was adjusted in 1738 and a boundary line was established 15 miles below Philadelphia. Later the present line was run, Mason and Dixon placing stone markers at 5-mile intervals along a stretch of 132 miles. On the side facing Pennsylvania the letter *P* and the arms of the Penn family were carved; on the Maryland side, the letter *M* and the crest of the Calverts. The Mason-Dixon Line was generally accepted as the dividing line between the free and the slave States — the North and the South.

MARYLAND

Pa. Line — Rising Sun — Bel Air — Baltimore — Washington, D.C., **89 m.** US 1.

Baltimore & Ohio R.R. roughly parallels the route between Baltimore and Washington; Greyhound, Pan-American, and Safeway-Trailways busses follow the route throughout.

Well-paved roadbed throughout; some steep grades and sharp curves; traffic heavy, particularly between Baltimore and Washington. Tourist homes and tourist camps along route; hotels in cities.

Section 13. *Pennsylvania Line to Baltimore,* 49.8 m.

US 1 is one of two main routes between Philadelphia and Baltimore. The other, US 13-40 (*see MD. GUIDE*), is less scenic and has heavier truck traffic, though somewhat greater historic interest.

US 1 traverses rolling country, skirting streams in deep valleys, wending along high tablelands, and overlooking fertile and well-cultivated fields. Dairying is a means of livelihood.

The highway crosses the Maryland Line at the village of SYLMAR, **0 m.** (470 alt., 37 pop.).

At **1.9 m.** (R) is a marker inscribed NOTTINGHAM LOTS (*see Section 12*).

RISING SUN, **2.8 m.** (387 alt., 565 pop.), is an important banking and trading center for the area, making considerable sales of farm supplies and building materials. A large and well-equipped plant here handles and ships milk.

The community, which is on the brow of a hill, was founded by Henry Reynolds and known as Summer Hill until 1816, when the present name was adopted. This name was taken from that of an old tavern whose sign bore a picture of a sun on the horizon. This old hostelry stood on the spot now occupied by the bank; the present RISING SUN HOTEL, formerly the Maryland House, is on the opposite corner. The original structure on this site was the Odd Fellows' Hall, which was burned, rebuilt on a larger scale, and subsequently turned into a tavern.

In Rising Sun, at **3.4 m.**, is the junction with a paved road.

Left on this road to the junction with another road at **1.5 m.**; R. here and L. at **2.2 m.** to WEST NOTTINGHAM ACADEMY, **2.6 m.**, the oldest surviving Presbyterian educational institution in the New World. At the entrance to the academy grounds (L) stands the WEST NOTTINGHAM PRESBYTERIAN CHURCH, a large stone building set in a beautiful grove of trees. Among the early settlers in the Nottingham section were many Scotch-Irish Presbyterians; in 1724 they organized a congregation known as Lower Octoraro, under the presbytery of New Castle. The site of the earliest meeting house is uncertain; four or five years later a new meeting house was erected on a site of the old cemetery near the high school campus in the present village of Rising Sun. The congregation then became known as the Nottingham. The Whitefield revival caused a split in 1741, and the New Light faction built a meeting house of its own near the older place of worship.

The Reverend Samuel Finley (1715–66), a native of Ireland who was ordained in America in 1744 and took active part as a revivalist in the Great Awakening in Pennsylvania, was a pastor of the new congregation from 1744 to 1761, when he became president of Princeton College. The two congregations were reunited in 1784 and the present church was completed in 1804.

The date of the founding of the academy is usually given as 1741 but it was probably opened after Finley became the pastor. Under the capable direction of Finley it gained high prestige, drawing students from long distances. After Finley's departure from the academy and especially later in the troublous times of the Revolution and the period following, the school lost ground and by the end of the century had suspended operation.

In 1812, however, a charter and an annual grant of $800 (later reduced to $500) were obtained from the legislature and the school was revived, the leader and headmaster for many years being the Reverend James Magraw, pastor of the West Nottingham Church. The practice of having the local pastor serve as headmaster was followed for the greater part of the century. For many years most of the pupils of the revived school came from the neighborhood; those from outside the neighborhood were boarded in private homes. In 1906, to accommodate the boarders and with a view to expansion, the Magraw homestead was acquired. To gain additional support for the old Presbyterian school it was placed under control of the synod of Baltimore.

The academy is situated on a beautiful 340-acre tract of rolling land. At the entrance, opposite the church, is the ADMINISTRATION BUILDING, a former residence. The entrance road swings R.; on the far side of the turn is a MEMORIAL ARCH commemorating two signers of the Declaration of Independence who were former students at the school. A path runs under this arch to what is called the OLD ACADEMY, erected in 1865 to replace what is believed to have been the third academy building. Farther back on the grounds is MAGRAW HALL, a large stone building erected a few years ago after the burning of the old Magraw house. This is the main dormitory and school building. The school has dormitory facilities for 52 boys, and an enrollment of 70 to 80, including day students.

RICHARD'S OAK, **6.1 m.** (R), close to the road, is sometimes called the Lafayette Oak. A tablet on the tree says that it has a circumference of 21 ft. 8 in., a height of 70 ft., and a spread of 105 ft., and that it is thought to be over 500 years old. Lafayette and the 1,200 New England soldiers he was leading to Virginia to operate against

MARYLAND

Benedict Arnold are said to have camped near the tree on April 12, 1781.

The road now descends to OCTORARO CREEK (Ind., *rushing waters*), **6.8 m.**, crossing on a new bridge. The old road swings a little to the L., crossing on the old Porter's Bridge. Formerly a number of grist and paper mills lined the banks of this stream, which has always been good for bass fishing.

At **7.2 m.** (R) is the junction with a paved road, the former Conowingo Road, the main route prior to the building of the new road over the Conowingo Dam.

At **8.9 m.** is the junction with US 222 (R) and with an unnumbered road (L).

1. Right on US 222 at **0.2 m.** (L) is the entrance to the estate, SUCCESS (*open*), with a shabby house reputed to date from about 1734 occupying an elevated site. The one-and-a-half-story main structure, which was apparently built in two parts, has a gambrel roof and dormer windows, and was constructed of squared logs, now covered by weather-boarding. About 1849 the original log kitchen was replaced by one of stone that contains the great fireplace of the former structure; this fireplace has a crane for hanging pots and takes logs eight ft. long, which, it is said, were in former times hauled by a horse. In the main house is what is known as the Betsy Ross room; local tradition has it that this Philadelphia upholsterer was a frequent visitor, and that she conceived the idea of the five-pointed star for the flag she was asked to make, from this five-cornered room. The room is not star-shaped, however, but five-walled, the fifth wall being a chimney that cuts across one corner of the square room.

2. Left from the junction of US 1 on the unnumbered paved road is the entrance lane, **0.4 m.** (L), to OCTORARA. This beautiful estate is the residence of Mr. and Mrs. Jotham Johnson (*open upon written request addressed to Rowlandsville, Md.*). The house, approached by a tree-bordered lane about a quarter of a mile long, stands on a beautiful, tree-covered lawn and amid landscaped gardens; a double row of boxwood 200 ft. long ends in a circle. The house commands a fine view with glimpses of Conowingo Lake and the river. The tract, originally part of the estates of the Hall family of Mount Welcome (*see below*), was also known as Mount Independence. The house, said to have been built in the late 17th century, was originally a small stone structure; it is the center of the present building. In time a frame wing was added. In 1807 the place was bought by Henry White Physick of Philadelphia, who built the stone kitchen wing and the stone barn. His brother, Dr. Philip Syng Physick, who acquired the place in 1823, tore down the frame part, which was in bad condition, and in 1824 built the present large brick wing, which is now the main house. The front piazza was subsequently added.

Continuing S., the road shortly descends to Octoraro Creek, **1.3 m.**, the last part of the way on a steep grade, with a sign warning: "*Descend in second gear.*" The scenery here is arresting, the stream rushing in a deep gorge, on the far side of which is the village of ROWLANDSVILLE (170 pop.). The paved road ends at the foot of the hill, but a crushed-stone road continues along the stream, passing the bridge to the village, and twice crossing railroad tracks; at **2.2 m.** the route meets US 222 (*see below*).

At **9.1 m.** (R) on US 1 is an old house known as MOUNT WELCOME (*open*). The tract Mount Welcome, originally 1,000 acres, was one of the earliest grants in this section, and was for many years in the possession of the Hall family, who played a prominent part in the history of Cecil County. The original house, of which a few ruins remain, stood nearer the river.

The main part of the present two-and-a-half-story house is of brick, now covered with plaster, and the gable roof contains a central dormer window. The second-story floorboards are a foot wide and the doors, some of them only three-fourths of an inch thick, hang true. Behind the main structure is a smaller one of stone containing the ancient fireplace with its pot-cranes.

At **9.4 m.** is the present village of CONOWINGO (Ind., *at the falls*), principally made up of filling stations and roadside restaurants. The road now descends to the Conowingo Dam. At the east end of the dam, **9.9 m.**, is the junction with US 222.

Left on US 222, which descends immediately and runs almost at river level, though for the first two or three miles at some distance from the stream. At **0.8 m.** is the junction with the Rowlandsville road (*see above*).

A marker at **0.9 m.** indicates the SITE OF A SUSQUEHANNOCK INDIAN FORT that in 1682 was involved in the Maryland-Pennsylvania boundary controversy. An Indian fort had been named during the negotiations as being on the 40th parallel of latitude; the fort in question was several miles up the river. George Talbot, grantee of Susquehanna Manor, by mistake drew his line from this lower fort.

At **2.2 m.** (L) are a few houses and a sign reading "Sportsmen's Haven," and at **3.5 m.** (L) is a large old stone building with a sign offering accommodations to fishermen. The road here runs fairly close to the river. On an island reached from this point is a fishermen's club. In the spring fishing is good for rock and wall-eyed pike, and in the fall for bass. Between the first rapids in the river and the Conowingo Dam, trolling is popular; below the rapids rod fishing prevails. The bed of the old canal, which can be discerned along much of the way, here is distinctly visible (R). A short distance beyond and now used as a baseball field is the bed of an old mill pond, into which logs floating down the canal were turned off to a nearby sawmill.

At **3.7 m.** (R) are the RUINS OF AN OLD STONE MILL that stood by the canal. The river here comes into full view. Nearby is another inn catering to fishermen.

At **4 m.** is a marker indicating SMITH'S FALLS, or, as it was marked on Capt. John Smith's map, "Smyth's Fales." In 1608 Captain Smith ascended the river

MARYLAND

to this point, marking it on the map he made with a cross that he explained meant "to the crosses hath bin discovered what beyond is by relation." The PORT DEPOSIT QUARRIES (L) have been operated since 1808. They cut into the face of the cliff and extend to a height of 150 to 200 ft. The stone, called Everlasting Granite, has been used in many buildings in this region, notably in Mount Royal Station in Baltimore.

At **4.6 m.** the road passes under the railroad viaduct and reaches the north end of PORT DEPOSIT (20 alt., 963 pop.). Here the river is flanked by steep cliffs that for the most part rise almost sheer to heights of over 200 ft., broken at only three places, called "hollows." (*Boats and guides are available.*) Main Street, a mile long, lies between the railroad tracks and the cliffs. A few houses are in the hollows on the cliffside. The town is for the most part not attractive, though some of the old buildings are of interest. In 1729 Thomas Cresap was operating a ferry near here, known as the Upper Ferry, to distinguish it from the Lower Ferry near the mouth of the river, which had been established in 1695. Since the Upper Ferry was at the head of navigation, residents of the vicinity petitioned for a road on which tobacco casks could be rolled and other produce brought to the landing and to the nearby "merchants' mill." The road was made, and also one running toward Philadelphia. At the time the Maryland Canal was completed in 1810 the place was known as Creswell's Ferry, for Col. John Creswell, the ferry owner. The canal brought such a boom that the town was laid out in 1812; in the following year it received its present name because of the fact that it served as a storage place for goods to be shipped by water. In May 1813 the settlement still had no great importance and the British, entering the Susquehanna, did not bother to attack it.

Unsuccessful efforts to build a bridge across the river were made in 1808 and 1813, but in 1819 a mile-long bridge, consisting of several spans that extended from island to island, was completed. This was burned in 1823, the fire being caused, it is said, by friction from the iron runners of a sleigh passing rapidly over it. The bridge was rebuilt a few years later and served until 1854, when one of the spans broke under the weight of a drove of cattle; it was not rebuilt and ferry service was resumed and continued by county subsidy until a few years ago. The arks and rafts operating on the Maryland Canal brought increasing trade to the town; in 1822, $1,337,925 worth of goods, mainly lumber but including large quantities of wheat, flour, whiskey, and iron, were handled by the little port. The development of railroads and other factors gradually lessened this trade.

At **5.2 m.** (L), next to the Roman Catholic Church, is a long double house with a first story half brick and half stone, and two frame upper stories; this is an old INN, dating from the early days. Farther on (R) is a house with a porch enclosed by beautiful ORNAMENTAL IRONWORK. At the northeast corner of Main St. and Woodlawn Road is the ANGLERS' INN, occupying a stone house a century old. A few doors below the southeast corner of the junction is a STONE HOUSE, reputed to be one of the oldest in the town, with iron railings on the second- and third-story porches.

On Main Street is a large brick building, the day school of the JACOB TOME INSTITUTE. On the opposite side of the street is the TOME MANSION, formerly the residence of Jacob Tome, the institute's founder, who was born in Pennsylvania

U. S. ONE

in 1810 of German Lutheran parents. In the spring of 1833, practically penniless, he arrived at Port Deposit on a raft. In time he made a fortune in the lumber business, which was then booming at Port Deposit. His subsequent business interests were varied. During the Civil War Tome served as a member of the finance committee of the Maryland Senate, and was an adviser to President Lincoln.

Left on the Woodlawn Road at **0.7 m.** is (L) the dirt lane leading to ANCHOR AND HOPE FARM (*open*), originally consisting of two old tracts, Anchor and Hope and Raycroft's Choice. The house is reputed to be over 200 years old — a long stone structure, substantially but rather crudely built. It was the first inn in this area, and was called the Ferry House. The living room, the former taproom of the inn, contains two stone fireplaces, one at each end, and in a corner a cubicle with a sliding panel — the ticket office, where ferry and stagecoach tickets were sold.

Along the SUSQUEHANNA RIVER, on which is CONOWINGO DAM (*power station open daily 9 a.m. – 4 p.m.*), are high ridges with steep wooded bluffs bordering a flat river valley that is a mile wide; the river in low water flows over a shallow rocky bed, and in flood swells broadly and rushes with great force. Conowingo Lake, extending 14.5 miles up the river, has lessened the ruggedness of the banks, but on the whole has greatly enhanced the scenic beauty. Downstream from the dam the river retains its natural aspect.

US 1 crosses the Susquehanna River on the crest of the dam, which is provided with spillways under the roadbed. Before the building of the dam in 1928, the highway crossed on the old Conowingo Bridge, two miles N. The Conowingo power plant was built by the Philadelphia Electric Co., and completed in 1928. It has seven units of 54,000 horsepower each, with provision for ultimate installation of four additional units. The transmission lines carry the current at 220,000 volts, delivering at Philadelphia each year many million kilowatt hours. The dam is 4,648 ft. long and is based on solid rock at a depth of 96.5 ft. The turbines are spaced along the dam, the large power station being at the western end.

From the bed of the river, the height of which has been raised by the dam, were removed rocks bearing inscriptions that are attributed to a lost race of higher culture than that of the Indians of the period when the white men arrived in America. The rocks are now in the collection of the Maryland Academy of Sciences in Baltimore (*see MD. GUIDE*).

The former centers of the shad fishing for which Chesapeake Bay is famous were the upper waters of the bay and the Susquehanna River. Herring, also, were plentiful. The shad formerly had a free run to their spawning grounds up the river, but now the power dams block the way. This situation is being overcome to some extent by artificial propagation and stocking. Conowingo Lake is also stocked with large-mouth bass and blue-gill sunfish.

The Susquehanna River, though one of the long rivers in eastern United States, winding 420 miles, has rapids and shoals in its lower course, so that it is navigable for only about five miles from its mouth in Chesapeake Bay. In the past, however, during the spring freshets, log rafts and flat-bottomed arks were floated down stream, though such trips were always hazardous. Navigation was greatly helped by the completion in 1797 of a canal a mile long, around the Conewago Falls above Wrightsville. The movement of products down the river attained a large volume, reaching a peak in the second quarter of the 19th century, when as many as 2,000 to 3,000 rafts made the trip each season.

This method of shipment, of course, did not serve well for more perishable products. The city of Baltimore early took an interest in the improvement of navigation on the Susquehanna as a means of developing the trade of the great region tapped by that river. In 1783 a group of leading citizens incorporated themselves as the Proprietors of the Susquehanna Canal, to promote this development. They had ambitious dreams of a major waterway to extend as far as Buffalo. The immediate project, along the east bank of the river from the Maryland-Pennsylvania Line to the head of navigation near Rock Run at the north end of the present town of Port Deposit, was completed in 1805; but the canal was too narrow and had to be widened in 1810 or 1812. This canal, known as the Maryland or Susquehanna Canal, was one of the earliest in the country. Although it brought prosperity to Port Deposit, it was not a paying venture.

When the Susquehanna and Tidewater Canal was projected on the west side of the river, the conflicting interests were settled by acquisition of the Maryland Canal in 1837 through an exchange of stock. The business of the Maryland Canal declined, especially after the railroad paralleled it, and it finally ceased operation.

The building of the Union Canal to connect Philadelphia with the Susquehanna, the Chesapeake and Ohio Canal project, and other plans of eastern cities for securing the trade of the western territory caused growing concern in Baltimore. In 1823 a survey was made for a canal from the Conewago Falls along the western bank of the

Susquehanna to a point near Havre de Grace, thence across the lowlands to Baltimore. This project was not carried out at the time, but in 1835 the legislatures of Pennsylvania and of Maryland authorized canals, respectively, from Wrightsville to the State Line and from the State Line to Havre de Grace, subsequently united as the Susquehanna and Tidewater Canal. Excavation started in 1836, and the canal was completed in 1840. Owing to high prices in the boom period of the 1830's, the total cost was $3,500,000, the third greatest for an ante-bellum waterway. The canal was 45 miles long, with a width of 50 ft., a depth of 5 to 6 ft., and locks 170 ft. long and 17 ft. wide, permitting it in later years to accommodate boats of 150 tons capacity. The enormous capitalization and indebtedness prevented its being profitable, but it enjoyed a large volume of business over a period of years. A large part of the traffic went to Baltimore, but for fully 20 years, from 1840 to 1860, more than one-fourth of it consisted of trade with Philadelphia that passed through the Chesapeake and Delaware Canal, owing to the fact that the Union Canal was too small. After the 1860's railroad transportation caused a rapid decline in the traffic on the Susquehanna and Tidewater Canal, and in 1870 the canal company leased the property for 999 years to the Philadelphia & Reading Railroad Co. Inadequate maintenance resulted in a still further decline in business. In 1894 a freshet greatly damaged the banks of the canal, which were never repaired, and in 1895 the lock gates were permanently closed.

In 1866 a branch railroad from Perryville to Port Deposit was completed, following which the Columbia & Port Deposit R.R. was built (1866–77).

At **10.8 m.**, the western end of the dam, the highway begins a rapid ascent.

At **11.1 m.** (R) is STATE POLICE SUBSTATION F, with a wide parking space offering a fine view of Conowingo Lake.

At **12.5 m.** is the junction with an unnumbered State road.

Left on this road; at **0.1 m.** (R) is the old DEER CREEK FRIENDS' MEETING HOUSE, a small stone building, rectangular in shape and of plain design. Behind it is the burying ground. Over the doorway of the building is the inscription: "Founded 1737. Rebuilt 1784. Restored by Hugh J. Jewett in 1888." The original meeting house of logs, established for a branch of the Bush River Meeting, is supposed to have been in a grove on the opposite side of the road. After the Hicksite movement split the Society of Friends, a group from the Deer Creek Meeting in 1829 built a separate meeting house. Rebuilt in 1877, it is at the south

end of Darlington. A few years ago the two groups reunited. During the summer services are held regularly on Sunday mornings in the old meeting house.
DARLINGTON, 0.5 m. (324 alt., 500 pop.), is strung along the highway for a mile. At 1 m. a dirt road (L) leads 200 yds. to the FRIENDS' MEETING HOUSE (R), where services of the united meeting (*see above*) are held during the winter.

The State road continues S., passing several fine estates. This rural section, including the broad Deer Creek Valley, is beautiful. At 2.3 m. the highway crosses DEER CREEK. On the near side of the creek is (R) the ESTATE OF FRANCIS STOKES (*private*) of Philadelphia. The stone building on the bank of the stream, just inside the entrance, is WILSON'S MILL, believed to have been built in the 18th century; it has not operated for many years, but the millrace is still running. A few hundred feet back, near the stream, is the miller's house, also of stone, now occupied by the overseer of the estate. The stone mansion, on an elevation (R) just beyond the old mill, dates from shortly after the Civil War. The lovely garden along the millrace is only occasionally open to the public; the estate, however, is visible from the road.

At 13.1 m. (R) is the junction with a paved road marked by a sign, "Hopkins Corner." This is the old Conowingo Road, which crossed the river about two miles above the Conowingo Dam. The bridge site was submerged by the lake, and the road now comes to a dead end at that point.

Right on the old Conowingo Road to BERKELEY, 0.9 m. (150 pop.); R. on a side road (macadamized for short distance, then graveled) to a lane, 1.1 m. (L). A marker, on the opposite side of the road but with an arrow pointing to the lane, reads: "Lafayette at Col. Rigbie's House." Left on this lane, at the top of a hill commanding a fine view, is COLONEL RIGBIE'S HOUSE (*open*), 1.4 m., where Lafayette and his officers were entertained on April 13, 1781. At this point in the march, rumblings of disaffection were heard among the troops, who were poorly clad and without shelter, but Lafayette promptly arrested the ringleader, who was convicted as a spy and executed, and the troops went on toward Virginia.

Col. Nathan Rigbie in 1708 acquired Phillips' Purchase, a tract of 2,000 acres bordering the Susquehanna River. The present homestead comprises but 100 acres around the old house. Col. James Rigbie inherited it from his father, Col. Nathan Rigbie, and lived here until his death in 1790. He was high sheriff of Baltimore County, an important office at that time, and was captain and later colonel of a company of militia. The original one-story stone house, now to the rear of the main house and partly covered by weatherboards, was built in 1732; it still contains the great fireplace with its cranes and pothooks. The main house, built of wood in 1750, is one and a half stories high, with dormer windows; it has beautiful paneled walls and a staircase with low risers and carved walnut balusters and handrail. The present owner has endeavored to preserve the Colonial aspect of the house.

At 16.3 m. is the junction with two unnumbered roads.

1. Left from this point on the Churchville road, which runs S. through the beautiful Deer Creek Valley with its fine estates; the valley is wide, sloping down

gently from high ridges. At **2.7 m.** the highway crosses Deer Creek. On a knoll (R) beyond the stream is PRIEST NEALE'S MASS HOUSE (*open*). The entrance lane is at **2.9 m.**, and the house stands back about 250 yards from the highway. Deer Creek Chapel had been established in this neighborhood by the Jesuits as early as 1747. In 1764 Thomas Shea deeded the tract of land known as Paradise, sometimes spelled Paradice, to Father Bennett Neale.

It is believed that the present structure was built by Father Neale, though it may have been that a house already standing was remodeled by him for purposes of worship. In order to conform to the law at that time, which banned Roman Catholic churches, it was in the form of a dwelling, a hall being used as a chapel. Although named St. Joseph's Chapel, it was known as Priest Neale's Mass House. The original house, not of large size, is one-story, almost square, with thick stone walls that have been plastered over. In the rear is a frame addition. The place was sold by the Jesuits about 1800, and thereafter used exclusively as a dwelling. The old chapel hall is now divided into rooms.

2. Right from US 1 on the Whiteford road is DUBLIN, **1 m.** (455 alt.), an attractive crossroads village. The highway traverses tableland for the most part; just before reaching Whiteford it descends from the ridge that flanks a broad valley.

At **7.2 m.** is the junction with State 165 in the village of WHITEFORD (536 alt., 268 pop.), which is strung for some distance along this highway. The area is noted for its slate, particularly that from the Peach Bottom Quarry in Whiteford. The deposits are in the adjacent ridge, which State 165 skirts. The quarries have not been worked actively for the last decade or two, though the mining of deposits beyond the Pennsylvania Line to the N. has recently been resumed. The former quarry workers are now employed in a mill that grinds the stone for use as roofing material.

a. Right from Whiteford **0.8 m.** on State 165 is CARDIFF (398 pop.). Whiteford, Cardiff, and Delta across the Pennsylvania Line form practically a continuous community along the highway.

Cardiff, settled about 1860 and called South Delta, was subsequently named for Cardiff, Wales. This Welsh community retains to some extent the Welsh customs and speech. The male inhabitants are almost all employed in the nearby quarries and in the plant of the Cardiff Marble Co., established about 1917. This section is famous for its verd-antique marble used for tiling throughout the United States.

b. Left from Whiteford **2.2 m.** on State 165 is PYLESVILLE (358 alt., 50 pop.). Near the village is an asbestos quarry, the only one in the country producing the type of asbestos needed for making acid filter paper. Maryland is one of the half-dozen important producers of asbestos in the United States.

At **4.7 m.** on the main side road is the junction with State 24; R. on a road marked "Bush's Corner" **1.5 m.** to ST. MARY'S ROMAN CATHOLIC CHURCH, where an annual tilting tournament is held in August. Tournaments have long been popular gatherings in the rural sections of the States S. of Pennsylvania; in most other States they have nearly disappeared, or exist only as fashionable revivals.

CITY HALL, PHILADELPHIA, PENNSYLVANIA

BRANDYWINE BAPTIST CHURCH, PENNSYLVANIA

MARYLAND

There are several places in Maryland where they have been continued without artificial stimulation. For weeks before the event the countrymen practice riding a course of traditional length, attempting to catch on their lances a series of small rings suspended from arches; this feat requires considerable skill. Until about 1917 the contestants wore medieval costumes but at present they wear whatever they choose. They are entered under titles they select — the Black Knight, the Knight of Hard Bargain, the Knight of Love's Adventure, and so on, the name usually being taken from that of an estate or village where they live. The contest is opened with a speech by the local politician or orator, who gives the charge to the knights, reminding them that they are carrying on a traditional "defense of Christianity and womanhood"; a band usually sounds a fanfare and the marshal announces: "Knight of Hard Bargain, prepare to charge." The man named rides his cavorting steed to the head of the course; the marshal continues: "Charge, Sir Knight," and the rider, with lance set, dashes forward. The contestants are eliminated by decreasing the size of the rings, the smallest ring in some cases being little larger than a finger-ring. Each knight has a lady of his choice, the winner of the contest crowning the Queen of Love and Beauty. The tilting is a gala event for the countryside, some of the contestants traveling long distances to participate. After the riding there are usually a chicken-supper and dance.

Beyond the junction with the unnumbered roads, US 1 begins gradually to descend, crossing Deer Creek at **18.5 m.**, then rising again on an easy grade. The scenery along the creek is picturesque, and for several miles along the highway are sweeping views, especially over the valley (R).

At **23.1 m.** is the junction with State 23. On the far corner at this junction is St. Ignatius Roman Catholic Church, a large stone structure that has stood for a hundred years. Services in this section were started by itinerant priests who traveled on horseback.

Right **2 m.** on State 23 is FOREST HILL (544 alt., 365 pop.), the trading and banking center of a rich dairying section that provides a large part of the milk supply for Baltimore. In the vicinity are several canneries and a plant nursery.

Right from Forest Hill on State 24, which at **1 m.** enters the valley of Deer Creek; the road gradually descends and skirts Stirrup Run and Deer Creek. Above the confluence of these streams, Deer Creek runs through a gorge with steep, wooded sides; the highway parallels the creek for two or three miles. This picturesque section reaches its climax in the Rocks of Deer Creek, **5 m.** Here, at a narrow point, rock cliffs rise on both sides to a height of 250 ft. above the stream. There are picnic tables here and a path that ascends the cliff. The large frame building by the railroad was formerly a hotel.

Beyond Forest Hill on State 23 is JARRETTSVILLE, **8.2 m.** (265 pop.). The mining of chrome was formerly an important industry in this section, but the deposits have long since been exhausted.

Left from Jarrettsville **2.6 m.** on State 165 to old Harford Baptist Church (R) near Winters Run. This church, dating from 1754, is the second oldest of the denomination in Maryland. It was founded by a group that withdrew from the Chestnut Ridge (or Sater's) Church to form a Particular (Calvinistic) Church, the Chestnut Ridge Church being General Baptist (Arminian). Over the door of the old Harford Church is inscribed "1787," indicating the year of its erection. It is believed, however, that the original structure was largely retained in the rebuilding. The church is a plain brick building, rectangular in shape. The present membership is small, services being held only once a month by itinerant ministers.

At **12 m.** (R) on State 23 is the BETHEL PRESBYTERIAN CHURCH. The present building, erected in 1802, is the third built here, the original structure dating back at least to 1769, when the first regular minister was called.

BEL AIR, **26.1 m.** (396 alt., 1,650 pop.), is a busy and thriving town, the seat of Harford County, and the trading and banking center for a rich farming section. It has three inns and a number of boarding houses. Three weekly newspapers are published — the *Bel Air Times* and the *Aegis* for Bel Air, and the *Harford Democrat-Enterprise* for Bel Air and Aberdeen.

Harford County was until 1773 a part of Baltimore County, old Harford Town on Bush River being first designated as the former's county seat. In 1782 an election held to decide the county seat was won by Aquila Scott's Old Field, the site of the present Bel Air. A strong movement in favor of Havre de Grace developed, but a second election in 1787 again resulted in favor of Belle Air, as the name was originally spelled. The town was incorporated in 1901.

Bel Air does not present a modern or planned appearance; it is a charming place, however, with tree-bordered streets and comfortable houses. The population is composed largely of families with distinguished Maryland lineage; there is, accordingly, a pride in local history.

Entering Bel Air from the N. US 1 makes a sharp turn (R) into Broadway, which is lined with rows of large maple trees, arching overhead.

At a traffic light US 1 turns L. into Main St. A short distance beyond this turn, Bond St. branches R. from Main St. The US 1 markers follow Bond St., which affords a slight cut-off.

On Bond Street is (R) the COUNTRY CLUB INN, a long wooden, two-story structure with the lower walls now stuccoed; it stands in attractive grounds. The original log building, no longer in evidence, is incorporated in the southeast end. In cutting a window some years ago, a workman found between the logs a shingle bearing the date 1718, which is believed to have been the date of erection. The main addition was built in 1790; since that time there have been alterations and additions. Formerly the old Eagle Hotel, the inn has entertained many distinguished guests. It contains old furnishings of interest.

The ARMORY (L), on Main Street, is the home of the local company of the Maryland National Guard, and also serves as a community hall. Directly opposite is the HARFORD COUNTY PUBLIC LIBRARY, occupying a small house believed to be very old. On Pennsylvania Avenue is the former BEL AIR ACADEMY, a substantial structure built of stone, now plastered over; it is now a private residence. The school was chartered by the legislature in 1811, and opened in 1816 as the Harford County Academy, with the Reverend Reuben Davis as principal. He was a noted educator in his day; a large portrait of him hangs in the office of the Board of Education in the courthouse. Some years after the academy was opened, it was raised to the rank of a college, renamed Maryland College, and empowered to grant degrees. It is believed that no degrees were granted, however, as the school shortly reverted to the status of an academy, this time being called Bel Air Academy. In 1888 a consolidation was effected with the town's public elementary school, and some of the elementary grades were housed in the academy building until about 1907, when its use was discontinued; the united institution was called the Bel Air Academy and Graded School until 1907, when the name Bel Air High School was officially adopted for the higher grades.

The COURTHOUSE is a large brick building, built in 1858 and enlarged in 1904; the original courthouse, built in 1791, was burned. The courthouse is a local "hall of fame," housing the portraits of many Harford County celebrities, including that of the actor, Edwin Booth, who was born near Bel Air.

Kenmore Inn is on the SITE OF THE WILLIAM PINKNEY HOUSE. Pinkney, born in Annapolis on March 17, 1764, was a statesman, diplomat, and lawyer. He served as Attorney General of the United States from 1811 to 1814, and later as U.S. Senator from Maryland.

On the southern outskirts of Bel Air, at **27 m.** (R), are the HARFORD COUNTY FAIR GROUNDS, where the annual fair is held in October. The Harford County Pony Show is held here in June.

US 1 between Bel Air and Baltimore, known locally as the Bel Air Road, has an excellent new three-lane roadbed. At **29 m.** is the junction with State 147, the Harford Road, an alternate route between here and Baltimore, only slightly longer than the main route. STATE POLICE SUBSTATION D is at the fork between the roads.

On US 1 at **29.3 m.** (L) is the junction with a dirt road, marked by a sign reading "Fresh Air Farm."

Left on this dirt road **1 m.** to the FRESH AIR FARM, containing 38 acres, with suitable buildings and playground facilities, including a swimming pool. It is maintained by the Children's Fresh Air Society of Baltimore, for the benefit of neglected and destitute boys and girls between 5 and 12 years of age. Since its establishment in 1891, it has cared for nearly a quarter of a million children. During school vacation it has a new set of 350 children every 10 days. The main dining hall is in a great stone barn reputed to have been built in 1819. Milk and vegetables for the table are produced on the farm.

At **30.3 m.** is the junction, marked "Lynch's Corner," with a macadam road.

Left on this road **1.4 m.** is (L) an old STONE BARN, now in dilapidated condition, that was originally part of a stagecoach station. After the Battle of Monocacy, on July 9, 1864, the Confederates had a free hand for a time in Maryland. Gen. B. T. Johnson was detached with a cavalry force to destroy the lines of communication with Baltimore. From Cockeysville Johnson sent Maj. Harry Gilmor with a detachment of the Second Maryland Cavalry, C.S.A., to burn the railroad bridges over the Gunpowder and Bush Rivers. Gilmor's raiders moved along the Joppa Road to Magnolia Station, where they captured the morning express from Baltimore, set fire to it, and backed it onto the Gunpowder Bridge. On their way to Gunpowder, Gilmor and his men camped in and around this building.

Left from this point **1.6 m.** on a dirt road is (R) the entrance to OLNEY (*open on request*), home of J. Alexis Shriver, former secretary of the Maryland Historical Society. Between the road and the house is woodland, and behind it is a delightful garden enhanced by evergreens and boxwood. The tract, originally called Prospect, was acquired by John Norris in the 1700's but the main part of the present house, typically Southern in appearance, was built in 1810. The place has always been in careful hands, and when the present owner in 1927 undertook its restoration to former beauty and its embellishment, he had a structure basically sound to work with; he was aided by an architect who had done much work on old houses and who later reconstructed Wakefield, the birthplace of George Washington. The chief addition to the exterior was a portico salvaged when the old Atheneum Club building in Baltimore was razed; this structure had been built in 1830 as a residence. The four marble columns of the portico, weighing 18 tons each, had been cut at the Beaver Dam quarries and their transportation to Baltimore was an even greater problem than was their later conveyance to Olney. On the marble door-lintel are cherubs, representing Art and Literature, carved by Jardella for the mansion Robert Morris was building when his land speculations brought him to bankruptcy; the lintel was acquired and used by one of his creditors in a house that, because of the ornament, became known as Angel House. The interior of the Olney house has beautiful woodwork and contains fine old family furniture and many articles of historic interest.

US 1 descends and at **31.5 m.** crosses LITTLE GUNPOWDER FALLS, the dividing line between Harford and Baltimore Counties; the narrow wooded valley presents an attractive view.

At **33 m.** (L) is the HOODOO MARKER, so called because of the inscription: "Cursed be he who removeth his neighbor's landmark, and all the people shall say amen. Deuteronomy, Chap. 27, Verse 17." Above this is the boundary inscription: "This stone is in place of a double poplar tree, a boundary of expectation francis freedom alias young's escape and the second boundary of onion's prospect hill, the latter now owned by Edward Day." This ancient marker, much used by surveyors, is a rough shaft about nine feet high; only the side bearing the inscriptions is smooth. The dark stone, hard as flint, and now painted white on its face, is close to the road, though owing to a fill the top of the stone is now at the road level. The stone, thought to be at least 150 yrs. old, is probably a relic of a lifetime of quarreling between brothers, John and Edward Day. The only near reconciliation of the men occurred when Edward was supposed to be on his deathbed and his pastor, shocked by the idea of one of the brothers going to death with the breach unhealed, persuaded John to enter the sick man's bedroom. He thought his efforts had been successful until John was about to leave. Edward called him back for a last word, "John, if I die this is a go; if I get well it's all off." He recovered and the brothers died enemies.

At **33.5 m.** (L), on the outskirts of Kingsville, is ST. JOHN'S P.E. CHURCH, situated on the strip of ground lying between US 1 and the Jerusalem Road. Copley Parish Church, originally named for Governor Copley and later named St. John's, was erected in 1692 at Elk Neck on the northern side of Gunpowder River. Joppa Town, founded in 1712, became the county seat and the congregation of St. John's two years later built a new church there, this time of brick; by 1750 the population of the area had increased to the point that a "chapel of ease" was built at the forks of the Gunpowder; 18 years later, however, when Baltimore became the county seat, a steady decrease in population began. When a new building was needed in 1815, Edward Day is said to have given three acres of ground and with his own funds built a church at this fork of the roads. Later a chancel, belfry, and vestry-room were added to the original plain structure; in 1896 a new building was erected beside the old. The parish's old communion service, one of the many presented in the name of Queen Anne, is kept in the Diocesan Library in Baltimore.

The St. John's Church lot is bounded at the south end by a road forming a short cut between US 1 and Jerusalem Road. On US 1, at the far corner of this junction, is a sign with an arrow pointing across the road to a paved road that branches (R) from US 1.

> Right on this road at **1.1 m.** (R) is the SITE OF ISHMAEL DAY'S HOUSE. A small farmhouse now stands on the old foundations. When on July 11, 1864, one of Gilmor's Confederate cavalrymen pulled down the Union flag, Day, the owner of the house, shot him and escaped into the woods. The Confederates burned the house and barn.

KINGSVILLE, **33.6 m.** (271 alt., 50 pop.), is a banking and trading center.

KINGSVILLE INN (R) is a long two-and-a-half-story building with a central gable and six dormer windows. The earliest part, now the south end, was a dwelling built by the Reverend Mr. Deans, rector of St. John's Church, then in Joppa Town. The date of erection, 1753, is inscribed on a fireback recently removed from the fireplace in the living room; this lovely piece of ironwork was cast at the Piney Grove furnace just above Joppa. In the living room are the original paneling and window seats, and the stairway and the mantel on the second floor are worth attention. On the front door is the original knocker. It is not definitely known when the building was enlarged and converted into an inn, but it was probably early in the 1800's. Except that the stone walls have been plastered over, the front of the structure retains much of its early appearance; it has been enlarged by wooden additions in the rear.

The house has the usual tradition that Washington and Lafayette were guests, though the story cannot be substantiated. John Paul, a son-in-law of the Reverend Mr. Deans, operated a gristmill on the Little Gunpowder Falls stream at the Philadelphia Road. Accused of selling flour to the British, he was arrested and sentenced to death, but escaped and hid in a cave that is below Vinegar Hill near Franklinville, on the Little Gunpowder Falls stream about three miles SE. of Kingsville. According to one account, Paul eventually managed to board a ship bound for England.

> Left from Kingsville on a macadam road is JERUSALEM, **2 m.** (20 pop.), on the far side of the stream called Little Gunpowder Falls. Just E. of the bridge is (R) JERUSALEM MILLS (*see illustration*), established in 1772 by David Lee, a

MARYLAND 167

Quaker from Bucks County, Pennsylvania. A number of the oldest mills in the State were founded by Quakers from Pennsylvania, who appreciated the value of Maryland's streams as sources of power. During the Revolution, David Lee, though a Friend, operated a gun factory in a two-story stone building still standing behind the mill and now used as a dwelling. The mill has stone walls in the first story, but the upper two stories are of wooden construction. The present basement and first story are parts of the original building. The ceilings are supported by two-foot-thick, hand-hewn beams of white oak that show no signs of decay. It is believed that the original building had a second story with sloping roof, but that the present upper structure was erected later; it has two tiers of dormer windows, an unusual feature for a mill. The mill is still active, using a ponderous stone grinder. During the Civil War, the grandson of the founder did a flourishing business and built himself a mansion of 20 rooms that is still standing a short distance from the mill.

At **35.6 m.** the highway dips to cross the main GUNPOWDER FALLS. At **36.4 m.** is a junction with a marked dirt road.

Right on this dirt road **0.6 m.** is (R) the entrance lane to PERRY HALL MANSION (*open*), situated on an elevation that commands a wide view. The former house on the site, built about 1750 for Harry Dorsey Gough, was one of the largest in Maryland; after a fire in 1824 half the structure was rebuilt.

The first definite record of the place is in an advertisement of April 19, 1783, for a gardener. Gough, one of the wealthiest landowners in the State, spent lavishly both on his home and for the improvement and beautification of his grounds. In Gough's time the estate contained several thousand acres, but it now has only about 200.

The thick walls are of brick, now plastered over, and the foundation is massive. The main part of the house (*see illustration*) is three-storied with dormer windows, and the wing is two-storied; there was formerly a similar wing on the other side and pavilions beyond the wings. In one end was the chapel and in the other an elaborate Roman bath, an unusual feature in houses of the period in America. A painting of the house, made in 1800 and now in the museum of the Washington Monument in Baltimore, shows the house in the days of its glory. At present it is merely a large substantial house without special distinction; the paneling and other interior woodwork have been taken away. The flooring is fire-proofed with a layer of plaster. The wide center hall and fireplaces in each room remain.

Perry Hall holds a high place in Methodist annals. Through his wife's influence, Gough was converted to Methodism, and erected a chapel. His home was a center of hospitality for itinerant Methodist preachers, notably Asbury and Thomas Coke. Here in December 1784 assembled a group that then rode to Baltimore for the Christmas Conference at Lovely Lane Meeting House, where the Methodist Episcopal Church in America was organized and Francis Asbury was elected superintendent.

PERRY HALL, **36.7 m.** (256 alt., 263 pop.), extends thinly along US 1. Between here and Baltimore the roadside is more closely built up, though there are long gaps of open country.

At **38.5 m.** (L) is the junction with the Joppa Road, originally an Indian trail that was used in 1695 by a troop of rangers from the Garrison Fort.

Between this point and Baltimore the highway is four lanes wide.

FULLERTON, **40.5 m.** (220 alt., 1,813 pop.), is an old village that has developed with Baltimore. The name of the village is now loosely applied to the settlement along the highway from this point practically to the city line.

At **45.5 m.** is HERRING RUN PARK, extending along the stream valley, and at **46 m.** (R) is CLIFTON PARK. At **46.7 m.** is the junction with North Ave.

US 1 bypasses downtown Baltimore; R. on North Ave.; L. at **50 m.** on Monroe St., which at the lower end swings L. along Carroll Park; R. at **52.5 m.** on what is known as the Washington Pike. There is no fast boulevard route through or around Baltimore; traffic moves slowly on North Ave. because of the many streetcars and traffic lights. Those unfamiliar with the city are advised against attempting short cuts because of the ravine that bisects the city, and the narrow, sometimes cobblestoned streets in the downtown area.

To downtown Baltimore: Right on North Ave. to St. Paul St., a boulevard, at **48.2 m.**; L. on Fayette St. at **49.6 m.** to City Hall, **49.8 m.**

BALTIMORE, **49.8 m.** (80 alt., 804,874 pop.), historic and industrial city (*see MD. GUIDE*).

Railroad Stations. Pennsylvania R.R. and Western Maryland Ry., Pennsylvania Station, Charles St. S. of North Ave.; Baltimore & Ohio R.R., Mount Royal Station, Mount Royal Ave. two blocks W. of Charles St.; Baltimore & Ohio R.R. and Baltimore & Annapolis R.R. (electric), Camden Station (downtown), Howard and Camden Sts.; Maryland & Pennsylvania R.R., North Station, two blocks W. of Charles St.

Points of Interest. Washington Monument, Johns Hopkins University, Walters Art Gallery, Baltimore Museum of Art, Fort McHenry, Goucher College, Peabody Institute and Conservatory of Music, and others.

Section 14. *Baltimore to Washington, D. C., 39.2 m.*

From City Hall, Baltimore, **0 m.**, W. on Fayette St. to Monroe St.; L. to the foot of Monroe St.; then R. on the Washington Blvd. Here the route for a time follows a route that is congested during rush hours and on holidays.

The route between Baltimore and Washington is through a gently rolling country, with few steep hills. It is generally lacking in scenic

MARYLAND 169

interest, though occasionally affording pleasant views. Truck farming is predominant, especially in the vicinity of the cities. There are no large towns.

At approximately **4.7 m.** is the boundary line between the city of Baltimore and Baltimore Co.

HALETHORPE, **6.7 m.** (180 alt., 1,831 pop.), is a suburb the majority of whose inhabitants are employed in Baltimore.

Between September 24 and October 15, 1929, there was held in a large field (L) in Halethorpe the Fair of the Iron Horse, commemorating the centennial of the introduction of the steam engine in rail transportation. The fair was arranged under the auspices of the Baltimore & Ohio Railroad Co., the first to run steam trains out of Baltimore.

On this same field in 1910 was held what its sponsors claimed to be the first major airplane meet in the United States. A group of business and professional men financed the exhibition. Among the flyers taking part were Hubert Latham, Count de Lesseps, Ely Willard, James Radley, Tony Drexel, and Arch Hoxey. It was during the meet that Latham in a 50-horsepower monoplane flew over Baltimore, in the first successful flight made over a large American city. He won a prize of $5,000 and an extra $500 donated by Ross Winans, who watched the flight from his home. Virtually every resident of Baltimore paused to gape at the marvel of a man-made machine piloted by a human being, flying over a city. Thousands of visitors came from other cities to witness the breath-taking feats of the daring pioneer fliers at Halethorpe Field. Today mail and passenger planes fly over Baltimore daily without even a passing notice from most of the citizens.

South of Halethorpe US 1 traverses rolling country, with fine farm lands on each side. Truck farming is now carried on almost exclusively, though long ago the section produced much tobacco.

RELAY, **7.7 m.** (200 alt., 2,016 pop.), on the eastern bank of the Patapsco River, derives its name from the fact that when the Baltimore & Ohio R.R. used horses to draw passenger coaches and freight cars over the rails from Baltimore to Ellicott Mills, it was at this point that a relay of horses was attached to the train and the journey up the Patapsco Valley was resumed.

THOMAS VIADUCT, the oldest railroad viaduct of its type in the world, spans the river at this point. It cannot be seen from US 1, but is reached by a side road from either end of the highway bridge. Over this viaduct, which today echoes to the thunderous passage of modern giant locomotives, steel passenger cars, and ponderous freight trains, a century ago puffed diminutive locomotives drawing tiny wooden passenger and freight cars. According to engineers the structure, despite its age, is in as good condition today as it was in 1835 when it was built. It is constructed of native granite from a design by Benjamin H. Latrobe, son of the Benjamin Latrobe who designed the Roman Catholic Cathedral in Baltimore. The span is 612 ft. long, with eight elliptical arches. More than 24,000 cubic yards of masonry went into its construction and its cost was approximately $150,000. Today it would be impossible, experts say, to duplicate the bridge for a sum anywhere near the original cost. It would also be difficult, it is said, to procure skilled labor, particularly stone masons, able to do this kind of work. The bridge is built in an arc but easily accommodates the largest modern passenger and freight cars.

Beneath the structure is one of the best gudgeon fishing spots in the State. Anglers of all ages and both sexes come by the hundreds to cast their lines for the tiny fish that make such a succulent meal. Few bother to pick the small bones from this fish when it is properly cooked; there are those who prefer gudgeon to lobster, shad, trout, bass, or any other kind of sea food.

Right from Relay along the stream into the lowest section of the PATAPSCO STATE PARK, which lies between Relay and Ellicott City. (*Permits for camping may be obtained from State Department of Forestry, Fidelity Building, Baltimore, Md.; permission for a single night's camping obtained from the park superintendent at Ilchester.*) The RIVER ROAD through the park is a scenic drive of exceptional beauty. For almost the entire length of the area, the Patapsco River flows through a deep broad gorge, the wooded hills on either side rising to an elevation of 250 ft. above the stream.

From the plateau above flow numerous streams, which produce cascades and miniature waterfalls as they tumble over rocky ledges. Foot trails and bridle paths have been laid out. The most picturesque is the CASCADE TRAIL along Cascade Branch at Orange Grove, halfway between Relay and Ellicott City.

ELKRIDGE, **8.7 m.** (1,556 pop.), is skirted by US 1. The land rising from the Patapsco River is hilly and picturesque, and in recent times has had considerable development as a residential suburb of Baltimore. Elkridge, still important as a trading center for the surrounding farm area, was in Colonial days, when it was known as Elk Ridge Landing, one of the principal shipping points in Maryland for tobacco, grain, and timber. The creek has now silted up. From 1750

MARYLAND

until the Revolutionary War it was a port of entry for Anne Arundel Co., which at one time included parts of what is now Howard Co. Special excise and customs agents were stationed at the port by the British for the purpose of assessing the tobacco shipped from there, mainly to foreign countries. The tobacco was rolled by Negro slaves from the plantations in huge hogsheads, and the route from the N. to the landing to this day retains the name of Rolling Road. During the Revolutionary War the tobacco trade languished considerably, but local forges and furnaces were kept busy turning out arms for the Continental Army.

At Elk Ridge Landing in 1765 Zachariah Hood, British Stamp Act agent in Maryland, was hanged in effigy. Lafayette and his troops camped here April 17 and 18, 1781, on their way to engage the forces of Cornwallis in Virginia.

At **9.8 m.** is the junction with an unnumbered road.

Right on this road **1 m.** to the second paved road R.; then L. at the first fork to BELMONT (*private*), **2 m.**, a notable place of the past. The brick house, now covered with yellow plaster, was built in 1783 by Caleb Dorsey, who had become wealthy through trading in iron ore mined near Elk Ridge Landing. He developed the place for his bride, born Priscilla Hill, of West River. The low, rambling structure has much charm and is surrounded by gardens that were the pride of the owner and his wife, who planted the beautiful box hedge that is now 15 ft. high in some places. On each door of the house is a huge iron "witch cross" and on the main door an iron plate with the inscription "C&P 1783."

Belmont was until his death in 1829 the home of Alexander Contee Hanson, an editor and a Congressman from Maryland, who was the grandson of John Hanson, President of the Continental Congress in 1781.

WATERLOO, **13.7 m.**, is a crossroads community where once stood a famous inn of its day, Spurrier's Tavern, which burned many years ago. A small modern house stands on part of the foundations of the old structure. The tall cedars that once shaded the tavern and an ancient stone smokehouse are still here. Spurrier's Tavern was for many years a stopping place for travelers between Washington and Baltimore and between Annapolis and Frederick. Here the roads to these places crossed, and many famous men came to the tavern for food, refreshments, and rest. On June 18, 1795, George Washington wrote in his diary "dined and lodged at Spurrier's where my horse died (overcome by heat)."

LAUREL RACE TRACK, **19.2 m.** (L), on the northern outskirts of the town of Laurel, is one of the best patronized tracks in the United

States. The grandstand, seating about 10,000, is usually well filled each day of the fall racing season, which lasts a full month. The track was opened in 1912, and is the only one of the four one-mile tracks in Maryland that takes its full quota of racing days consecutively. The other tracks divide their quotas into spring and fall meets of two weeks each. The feature races and prizes here are: Laurel Handicap, Maryland Handicap, and Selima Stakes, each for $30,000; Washington Handicap, $25,000; Richard Johnson Stakes, Spalding Lowe Jenkins Handicap, Governor Ogle Handicap, and Chevy Chase Steeplechase Handicap, $10,000 each; and Capital Handicap, $5,000.

LAUREL, 19.7 m. (156 alt., 2,532 pop.), is on land once owned by Richard Snowden, an officer in Cromwell's army, who came to Maryland late in the 17th century. The Snowdens had extensive holdings and played an important part in the development of this entire section of country. The town apparently derives its name from the fact that mountain laurel in profusion covers the hill back of the town. In its early history, the town was known as Laurel Factory.

High-grade iron ore was discovered on the Snowden tract, and the Patuxent Iron Ore Co. was formed in 1736 to exploit the find. In 1811 Nicholas Snowden erected a flour mill; previously, grain grown in the section was shipped by water to mills in nearby towns. The mill ceased operations in 1824. A brick house standing beside the old millrace is pointed out as NICHOLAS SNOWDEN'S MANSION.

In 1887 David Weems conceived the idea of connecting the larger centers of the country with fast electric rail service. His original plans were for an electric line between Boston and Washington, passing through New York, Philadelphia, and Baltimore. Leading scientists in the field of electricity became interested in the idea, and at Laurel was constructed a circular track several miles in circumference, the superstructure of which carried an inverted overhead T-rail to serve as a trolley as well as a guide. The locomotive weighed three tons and had three axles, each serving as a shaft for a powerful motor. The drivers, 40 in. in diameter, were set to a 28-in. gage track, and were connected directly with the motors, no gears being used. Built exclusively for speed, it was more or less streamlined; the locomotive actually attained a speed of 120 miles per hour at the trials. The locomotive maintained this speed for 22 minutes, when the superstructure collapsed under the terrific strain; the huge steel bulk hurtled through the air for a distance of more than a hundred feet and was demolished. Proponents of the electrification scheme dropped the project because funds to continue the experiments were not available.

At the eastern edge of Laurel, along the Patuxent River, have been found TRACES OF AN EARLY INDIAN SETTLEMENT (L). Here are abandoned quarries that were worked long before the coming of the white man to this section. The quarries, from which was obtained stone especially adapted to the fashioning of cooking utensils and ornamental jugs, have yielded many fine products of Indian workmanship. In pits and in fields nearby have been found bits of pottery, arrowheads, and grooved axes. The fondness of these Indians for oysters is also plainly manifested by the presence of huge piles of oyster shells, uncovered in the course of digging operations. That the Indians who once inhabited this site knew how to extract copper from ore and work it is evidenced by the many pieces of crude plates, shields, and ornamental bangles found in the vicinity.

At **20 m.** is the junction with a paved road.

Left on this road to (R) the entrance lane of MONTPELIER (*private*), **2 m.**, which stands about a quarter of a mile from the highway. Construction of this large brick house, whose walls are laid in Flemish bond, was begun some time before 1751 by Thomas Snowden and completed by his son, Maj. Thomas Snowden; the son himself is said to have done some of the carving in the drawing room.

The house stands on a little knoll, from which ground falls away so abruptly that the floors of the wings, which have octagonal ends, are considerably lower than is that of the main section. Near the house are several hundred feet of fine old boxwood in double rows, part of it trained to form a cool alley between the house and a little gazebo with a charming view.

The rich garden entrance leads into the center hall, from which open rooms ornamented with elaborate carvings.

At **9 m.** is the BOWIE RACE TRACK, constructed by the Southern Maryland Agricultural and Breeding Association. The track was completed in 1914 and has been in operation ever since, the pari-mutuel betting system being used. Bowie, one of the State's most popular and solvent tracks, is a regulation mile in length, with a chute running into the home stretch, making it possible to run events of more than a mile if desired. The home stretch is 90 ft. wide, permitting the line-up of large fields. The back stretch is 75 ft. wide. The grandstand seats 14,500 persons.

The eastern racing season is ushered in at Bowie the first Monday in April. Thirteen-day meets are run in the spring and in the fall. Among stake events and handicaps on the program are Bryan and O'Hara Memorials, Rowe Inaugural, Bowie Memorial, Kindergarten Stakes, Southern Maryland Handicap, Endurance Handicap, and Thanksgiving Day Handicap. Because of its proximity to

174   U. S. ONE

Washington, the Capital's social set, members of the diplomatic corps, and many Government officials are frequently in attendance during the meets.

At 21.7 m. on US 1 is the junction with a dirt road.

Left on this road **0.3 m.** is the entrance lane to OAKLAND (*private*). The mansion, on an elevated site, can be seen from US 1. It stands on an estate that originally contained 2,000 acres and was built in 1798 by Richard Snowden, son of Maj. Thomas Snowden of Montpelier. The house is a sturdy brick structure distinguished by fine front and rear doorways and by the excellence of the brickwork, the customary monotony being varied by heavy, glazed headers. In the rear is a charming terraced garden from which the rolling country can be viewed for many miles. A wing contains the kitchen, pantry, and servants' quarters. In each room of the house is a fireplace across the corner farthest from the entrance door. The ceilings are high and the wainscoting and paneling especially attractive. An unusually wide staircase, with a Fairfax clock on the landing, ascends from the first floor hall. The remnants of a secret stairway that led from the sitting room to the master's bedroom can still be seen.

This sitting room was a favorite gathering place for notables who liked to play cards for high stakes. A favorite legend associated with the place is that one evening, during a boisterous game in which the stakes were unusually high, one of the players was suddenly called away by an urgent message. As the guest hurriedly left to answer the summons, the host, annoyed at the interruption, is said to have remarked, "I will play with the devil if he takes your place"; whereupon a tall slim man is said to have entered the room and asked that he be allowed to enter the game. "Be seated," the host invited, "though we do not know your name." The stranger, without deigning a reply, sat down and began to play and soon had won all the money in sight. The other players afterward said they had noticed a forked tail beneath the visitor's cloak but many to whom they told the story were sceptical, remembering the host's possession of a fine wine supply.

MUIRKIRK, **23.2 m.** (109 pop.), was once the center of a large iron manufacturing industry, the ore being mined in the nearby hills. It is believed that the place was named for a Scot named Muir, whose interest in the activities being carried on there was so great that he even spent Sundays in the mines or at the furnaces. His home later became known as Muir Kirk, or Muir Church.

The original furnaces were built in 1747. Still standing are SIX CHARCOAL OVENS of brick, in the shape of beehives, after the manner of those in England at that time. Iron produced at Muirkirk mills had a remarkable degree of tensile strength, and for that reason was much in demand and commanded a high price. The mills outlasted practically all other iron forges in Maryland operating during and after the Revolutionary War. In Civil War days, the Muirkirk forges supplied the Federal Government with a considerable number of

MARYLAND 175

cannon and cannon balls. Later, with the advent of modern armament, the plant manufactured gun carriages, and even engaged in the peaceful business of manufacturing car wheels. In 1880 an explosion razed the entire plant, but it was immediately rebuilt.

At about the time of the World War, the plant began manufacturing a high grade ochre from ores obtained in the vicinity. In 1924 a firm that made coloring matter took over the business, and now, instead of Maryland ores, high grade ores from Spain, Germany, Sardinia, France, India, South Africa, and Chile are used in the manufacture of pigments sold all over the world. At one time hundreds of men were employed at the mills and in the nearby mines. The population dwindled to slightly more than a hundred, though a gradual increase has come in recent years.

Left from the bridge and across the railroad tracks, opposite the railroad station, is the BIG HOUSE (*private*). A driveway bordered by linden trees leads to the dwelling, a three-story and basement structure. Built by William E. Coffin for his son about 1847, it is a double dwelling with a central hall and 17 rooms. In the cellar is an artesian well that supplies water to the household. There is a private gas plant used to light the place before there was electric service. The dining room, which runs the entire width of the house, is paneled with walnut and chestnut boards two inches thick. On the first floor is a ballroom with a raised platform that was sometimes used as a stage. Legend has it that the Coffin family was exceptionally hospitable and diplomatic and that at times during the Civil War Confederates were being entertained in one section of the double house, while Union leaders were enjoying a feast in another.

At **23.4 m.** (L) is a marker commemorating the first official telegram. It recites that this telegram, reading "What hath God wrought," passed over the wires on a line of poles along the B. & O. R.R. from Washington to Baltimore on May 24, 1844.

At **24.2 m.** (R), on a large estate, is the AMMEMDALE NORMAL INSTITUTE. The buildings are visible from the highway, though set back several hundred yards. This is the Provincial House and Novitiate of the Brothers of the Christian Schools for the District of Baltimore. The institute prepares young men for the teaching brotherhood and also serves as a retreat for members of the order who are physically unable to carry on their work. The members of the brotherhood cultivate the extensive farm on the estate. The organization was first established in America at Baltimore by two members who came from Canada in 1845.

At **25.1 m.,** by the Beltsville Station, is a junction with a paved road.

Left on this paved road, which crosses the railroad tracks; there L. on a dirt road **0.5 m.** to the former VAN HORN'S TAVERN (L), now a run-down private dwelling.

On the paved road at **0.5 m.** from US 1 is the entrance to the NATIONAL AGRICULTURAL RESEARCH CENTER (*best visiting hours 9–4 weekdays, 9–1 Sat.*), largest farm demonstration unit in the world; a 14,000-acre testing ground equipped with barns, laboratories, and research facilities to accommodate the work of 20 subdivisions of the Department of Agriculture Bureaus of Soil Conservation, Forest Service, Dairy Industry, Animal Industry, Chemistry and Soils, Food and Drug Administration, Biological Survey, and Plant Industry.

The center coordinates the work of local agencies and undertakes basic investigations. Here scientists are developing new strains of plants and livestock, inventing new farm machines, fighting animal parasites and diseases, improving marketing methods, studying nutrition problems, and finding new uses for farm products.

Although more than 500 trained people are employed here, and the annual cost of their experiments averages approximately a million dollars, the center is proving a good investment. One investigation in the storing of sweet potatoes, for example, has resulted in an annual saving to potato growers sufficient to pay the operating cost of the center for ten years.

A paved road, East-West Highway, runs through the grounds.

At **0.8 m.** is a DAIRY LABORATORY (R), with nearby homes for maintenance.

At **0.9 m.** is the ADMINISTRATION BUILDING, a two-story light-colored stucco building with a red roof. On the first floor are offices; in the basement laboratory innumerable white mice used in a nutrition experiment are confined in cages, each of which bears the pedigree, health record, and diet of the occupants. Even to the untrained observer the difference made in the animals' health and energy by the various diets is apparent.

In back of, and beside, the administration building are the DAIRY INDUSTRY BARNS and SILOS, where experiments are proving that sperm cells taken from a prize bull can be kept at low temperature and shipped to a distant farm for artificial insemination. The last barn in this group contains the bulls, and beside it, visible from the highway, is a BULL EXERCISER resembling a huge, rimless wheel placed in a horizontal position. For two hours each morning the bulls are harnessed to the spokes and a man sitting on the hub, forces them, by means of a long whip, to plod in a circle. This forced exercise not only improves the bulls' dispositions but also increases the number of years that they can be used for breeding.

At **1 m.** is a hard-surfaced drive curving L. in front of an old red-roofed house built of brick painted a creamy white. This is BIRMINGHAM MANOR (*not open*), built in 1785 and now the general superintendent's residence. The drive continues past two large red brick buildings, the NUTRITION LABORATORIES of the

MARYLAND

Bureau of Animal Industry. Diets are worked out here to increase the fertility of cows, to produce hogs with firm flesh, and to prevent perosis or slip tendon in chickens.

At **1.3 m.** on East-West Highway is a junction with a dirt road; L. **0.2 m.** to a junction with a second dirt road; R. a few feet to the SHEEP BARN (L), a two-story red brick building with one-story white stucco wings on each side. Here are bred sheep superior in wool production and grade karakuls, the offspring of Black-faced Corriedale or Highland ewes and Karakul rams.

At **1.5 m.** on East-West Highway is the junction with a hard-surfaced road; L. on this **0.1 m.** to a dirt road (R) leading to the HOG BARNS. At **0.5 m.** are the POULTRY LABORATORIES, four large cream-colored stucco and brick buildings. Here incubator eggs, just before hatching, are placed in "pedigree bags" to help identify the new-born chicks; flocks are tested for tuberculosis; trap nests identify good laying hens; and short-legged small-boned early maturing turkeys are being bred.

At **1.9 m.** on East-West Highway is (R) a LOG RECREATION BUILDING (*kitchen facilities, dance hall*). Here is a junction with a dirt road; L. on the road a few feet are the DOGS' RUNWAYS and HOUSE. Hungarian Pulis are being cross-bred in an attempt to produce a superior type of sheep dog.

At **2.4 m.** is the MACHINE SHOP (R); here is a dirt road (R) leading to the HORSE BARN built with an unusually high first story and wide center aisle so horses can be exercised in bad weather. Insulated ventilation shafts in the loft carry off the exhausted air from the stalls below.

At the end of East-West Highway, **2.5 m.**, is the junction with a dirt road; R. on this **0.2 m.** is the center's GOAT BARN. In the goat herd high-grade milk does are produced by selective breeding from the Toggenberg and Saanen strains. The kids are all bottle fed so that an accurate record can be kept of their mothers' milk production.

At **26.2 m.** on US 1 is a junction with a hard-surfaced road.

Right here to the Bureau of Plant Industry's HORTICULTURAL STATION, **0.2 m.**, a part of the National Agricultural Research Center (*see above*). Behind the two large white-trimmed red-brick laboratories are a series of greenhouses in which seedlings are nourished in "manufactured" soil containing carefully measured chemicals; experiments are hastened by budding and new varieties achieved by crossing. The station has rendered fruit and vegetable growers valuable service by developing a lettuce immune to brown blight and mildew, a mildew-resistant melon, and the Marglobe tomato that not only resists Fusarium wilt and nailhead rust but produces a fruit so solid it brings a fancy price to the grower.

At **26.5 m.** (R) is RHODES TAVERN, one of the few inns remaining from Colonial days. A marker here recites: "Lieutenant General George Washington dined at Rhodes Tavern on his last journey from Philadelphia to Mt. Vernon December 18, 1798." During the stagecoach era, this was the first stopping place for feeding and watering horses on the trip from Washington to Baltimore. The tavern, now operated as a tourist inn, is a three-story structure containing 17 rooms and 11 fireplaces. The beams are of 14-in. square oak timbers and some of the mantels are of unusual design. In the kitchen the huge brick fireplace, with built-in oven, occupies the entire space across one end; the three-cornered cupboard, the hand-wrought meat hooks, the original locks which were brought from England, and the doorknobs remain. The building stands in a 10-acre lot; among the old trees remaining are two English elms, supposed to have been imported, and some cedar and walnut trees. There are six springs on the property, from one of which water is piped into the house.

BERWYN, **28.4 m.** (1,000 pop.), is largely a suburb of Washington.

Left from Berwyn on a paved road **3.5 m.** is GREENBELT, officially known as the Berwyn Resettlement Project, a model village projected by the Resettlement Administration. In addition to providing low-priced housing for persons with moderate incomes, construction of this model settlement gave work to thousands of mechanics and laborers who were previously unemployed. The project, begun in October 1935, is scheduled to be completed by the end of 1938 at a total cost of approximately $9,000,000. It is estimated that eventually a thousand family units will be available, of which about 300 will be apartments. Each group or row of houses accommodates six family units. There are a few one-story dwellings, though the majority are two-story structures (*see illustration*).

The village stands on a gently rolling, wooded tract of 3,800 acres. A small stream wending its way through the village to empty into a lake on the outskirts has been taken into account in the landscaping of the area and the arrangement of the buildings, which have been planned with care to relieve the monotony inherent in a development where all houses are being built from two basic plans to keep costs low. In the planning of the village the most modern standards of construction, ventilation, heating, sanitation, and arrangement have been observed. A central plant will supply heat to the individual units; the village will have all the usual community facilities, including a community hall and library. Furniture has been especially planned for the houses, to fit the spaces properly, specifications for the several types being based on sound design, solid construction, and low cost.

Underpasses have been built at the highway crossings for the protection of pedestrians, and on the fringe of the village is garden space where householders may raise their own vegetables; small farms are also available for those who want to supply part of the community need for foodstuffs.

The property is being managed by a non-profit organization, supervised by the Federal Government to prevent profiteering and speculation. The community as a whole will pay taxes to the State. No family is permitted to live in the village that has more than a certain income, determined by the organization.

MARYLAND

At **28.7 m.** is the junction with a paved road.

Left on this side road is LAKELAND, **0.5 m.** (300 pop.), a Negro suburban community. The place received its name from the large number of artificial lakes, in which goldfish are propagated. The site was surveyed and developed into a subdivision by Edwin Newman, who built several residences and a large hall, the latter for many years serving as a meeting place for fraternal organizations. This subdivision was developed in 1890 by white residents, but by 1900 the influx of Negro residents had grown to such proportions that the few remaining whites moved out.

At COLLEGE PARK, **29.2 m.** (316 pop.), is the seat of the UNIVERSITY OF MARYLAND, a coeducational institution. Chartered in 1856 as the Maryland Agricultural College, it was the second agricultural college in the Western Hemisphere, having its inception principally through the efforts of a group of enterprising southern Maryland farmers, interested in stimulating agricultural research. For three years after its charter was granted, it was privately operated, but in 1862, under the Land Grant Act passed by the National Congress and accepted by the State General Assembly, it became in part a State institution. In 1914 it was taken over entirely by the State, and in 1916, under a new charter granted by the General Assembly, it became Maryland State College. In 1920, by an act of the legislature, the professional schools of the University of Maryland in Baltimore were merged with the college under the new name, the University of Maryland.

The university grounds comprise 286 acres. A broad, rolling campus is surmounted by a hill overlooking a wide area of surrounding country. On this hill are most of the 26 buildings.

The LIBRARY BUILDING is situated in the center of the campus on a slope commanding a view of the surrounding countryside. Tall trees form a setting for the red brick and limestone building. The main stairway enters the delivery hall on the second floor, from which there is access, through an arched entrance, to the reading room, which occupies the entire front of the second floor and seats 250; the room is attractively decorated with walnut woodwork and furnished with pedestal tables and Bank of England chairs. The library has about 58,000 volumes.

In the Student Center are offices of the student publications, the Religious Work Council, and the Maryland Christian Association. Three student publications are conducted under the supervision of a faculty committee: the *Diamond Back*, a weekly six- to eight-page newspaper published by the students; the *Terrapin*, the student annual, published by the junior class; and the *Old Time*, a comic magazine issued quarterly.

Many of the original forest trees still stand on the grounds, which are attractively laid out in lawns and terraces, with ornamental shrubbery and flower beds. Below the brow of the hill, on each side of the Washington-Baltimore Boulevard, are the drill grounds and athletic fields.

The buildings of the MARYLAND AGRICULTURAL EXPERIMENT STATION adjoin the boulevard. About 100 acres are used by the College of Agriculture for experimental purposes, and for orchards, vineyards, and poultry yards. Recently an additional 200 acres were purchased about two miles N. of the university campus, to be devoted exclusively to research in horticulture. The station has done noteworthy work in the field of tree and plant culture. Experiments begun in the apple orchards of western Maryland in 1933 developed a great amount of valuable information concerning the nutritional changes in fruit trees resulting from the addition of chemicals and sugar to the soil. Tobacco yields have been increased and made more uniform as the result of a series of experiments lasting over a period of 21 years. One of the present problems is the eradication of the oriental fruit moth, which is causing Maryland fruit growers heavy losses.

On the university grounds (R), opposite Ritchie Stadium, is ROSSBURG INN, now used by the Agricultural Experiment Station, a three-story structure of brick that may have come from England, for the clay used in their manufacture is different from any found in this part of the country. The building had a gabled roof, which was changed to a mansard in 1888 when the large front porch was built; the upstairs floors, the stairway, the railing, and the archway on the first floor are all old. In the days when the house was used as an inn, the front room on the left, now a laboratory, was the main reception room, with a private stair leading down to the wine cellar.

The keystone over the door of Rossburg Inn has on it the name T. Coad, the date 1798, and a figure that represents Silenus, eldest of the satyrs and teacher of Bacchus. General Lafayette, on his last visit to America, stopped overnight at Rossburg Inn, and his name has been given to a room on the second floor. The inn is said to have been the scene of several murders.

MARYLAND 181

RIVERDALE, **30.7 m.** (37 alt., 1,533 pop.), is a community many of whose inhabitants are employed in Washington. On Arthur Ave. is CALVERT MANSION (*private*), built about the middle of the 18th century by Baron Von Stein, a refugee nobleman, for his daughter, who married Charles Benedict Calvert, grandson of the sixth Lord Baltimore. The stuccoed Georgian building is of brick. The boxwood hedges on the terrace have been removed, but an old cannon, said to have been one of the four brought over by Maryland pilgrims in the *Ark*, still stands in the rear garden. The mansion has been the scene of many distinguished social gatherings, and it is said that Henry Clay wrote the Missouri Compromise while a visitor here.

HYATTSVILLE, **31.4 m.** (46 alt., 4,264 pop.), is the home of many Federal employees and business and professional people employed in Washington, and is a banking and commercial center for the surrounding area. The town, incorporated in 1880, was named for Hyatt, who was its first postmaster. Hyatt's home, known as HYATT MANOR, Rhode Island and Hyatt Aves., was built in 1850. It is a large, square-built brick structure, painted yellow, with porches across the front of both the first and second stories.

The FIRST PRESBYTERIAN CHURCH, Wine and Johnson Aves., has a silver communion set said to have been sent as a gift by Queen Anne in 1707.

At Hyattsville there are alternate routes into Washington, both marked US 1.

Right on an extension of Rhode Island Ave. which runs to the center of the city; Rhode Island Ave. intersects 16th St. NW. eight blocks N. of the White House, **38.1 m.**

The older route of US 1 (L) crosses the viaduct and enters the District of Columbia on the Bladensburg Road.

At **32 m.** on the Bladensburg Road, just N. of the bridge over the Anacostia River, is the junction with a dirt road marked Locust St.

Right on Locust St. **0.2 m.** (L) is an EIGHT-SIDED HOUSE, an odd-looking three-story frame structure to which a brick kitchen has been added. A number of such houses were built in this area years ago, but most have disappeared.

BLADENSBURG, **32.4 m.** (10 alt., 816 pop.), chartered in 1742, was formerly one of the busiest ports in Maryland. Now only a little stream at this point, the Anacostia River was once navigable to

Garrison's Landing, the name by which the town site was then known. At the height of its prosperity, it enjoyed a considerable export trade in tobacco and flour. There were a number of flour mills, wholesale merchandise stores, tobacco warehouses, several firms of shipping agents, inns, and other establishments incident to a busy port.

Here is the SITE OF THE BATTLE OF BLADENSBURG. Here, in the War of 1812, an army of untried militiamen made an unsuccessful attempt to save the city of Washington from capture by the British forces under General Ross. In August 1814 an enemy fleet commanded by Admiral Cockburn, with several thousand veterans of the Napoleonic campaigns aboard, arrived in Chesapeake Bay. Commander Barney with a small American flotilla had been virtually bottled up in the Patuxent River since late in 1813 by another squadron. The British plan was to dispose of Barney, land troops, and march overland to Washington, which spies had told them was poorly defended. Realizing the hopelessness of his position, Barney burned his ships to prevent their capture by the enemy, first, however, removing the cannon which later was used with some effect against the foe.

Barney marched his men, about 400 in number, to join the defense of the Capital, where, in response to a call from President Madison, militia from Maryland, Pennsylvania, and Virginia had been concentrated for nearly a year. When news reached the military authorities at Washington that the British had landed and were on the march to take the Capital, this force, numbering about 7,500, was sent out under orders to halt the advancing enemy. The raw, untrained men had been denied the necessary preparation and proper equipment for their task because of the bickerings and petty jealousies. Interposed between the oncoming British and the country's Capital, under leaders of whom they knew little and whom they trusted less, the militia met Ross' column of experienced soldiers, numbering between five and six thousand officers and men, at this place on August 24, 1814. Inefficiency of organization, lack of coordination between units resulting in conflicting orders, and the consequent loss of morale among the rank and file had the inevitable result; in spite of the efforts of their commander, General Winder of Maryland, to rally them, the American ranks, after a brief and ineffective resistance, broke and fled. What has been called an ordered retreat was in reality a rout and Ross continued to the Capital

MARYLAND 183

unopposed. He entered the city, from which the Government had already fled, and burned various parts of the city in retaliation, it was said, for the earlier burning of York, Ontario, by American troops. The Nation's Capitol was partly destroyed, as were a number of other public structures.

Near Bladensburg was at one time a secluded field to which gentlemen frequently resorted to settle their disputes by duels. Among the 50 or more encounters that are said to have taken place on this spot, known as the BLADENSBURG DUELING GROUND, was the one in which on March 22, 1820, Capt. Stephen Decatur lost his life at the hands of Commodore James Barron.

At **33.7 m.** is the District of Columbia Line. A marker reads: "Maryland. At this point George Washington first entered Prince Georges County as it was then constituted, August 1751, and made his last exit therefrom December 18, 1798. *Ave, Ave, atque Vale: Hail, Hail and Farewell.*"

A short distance S. of the District Line US 1 follows the recently extended New York Ave.; New York Ave. joins Pennsylvania Ave. at 15th St. NW.

On Pennsylvania Ave. at the foot of 16th St. NW. is the WHITE HOUSE, **39.2 m.**

DISTRICT OF COLUMBIA

WASHINGTON (40 alt., 486,869 pop.), the National Capital (*see WASHINGTON: CITY AND CAPITAL*).

Railroad Stations. Baltimore & Ohio R.R., Chesapeake & Ohio Ry., Pennsylvania R.R., Richmond, Fredericksburg & Potomac R.R., and Southern Ry., Union Station, Massachusetts and Delaware Aves.

Points of Interest. National Capitol (*see illustration*), White House, Library of Congress, Lincoln Memorial, Washington Monument, Washington Cathedral, Folger Shakespeare Library, Supreme Court Building, and many others.

VIRGINIA

Washington, D.C. — Fredericksburg — Richmond — Petersburg — N.C. Line, **205.9 m.** Mount Vernon Memorial Highway and US 1.

Richmond, Fredericksburg & Potomac R.R. parallels this route between Washington and Richmond; Seaboard Air Line and Atlantic Coast Line between Richmond and Petersburg; and Seaboard Air Line between Petersburg and the N.C. Line.

Well-paved roadbed but in many places too narrow for the heavy traffic; drivers should be particularly watchful for trucks at night because they often stop on the highway, and the rolling nature of the country frequently prevents a clear view of the road for any considerable distance.

Accommodations of various kinds at frequent intervals; better hotels principally in cities.

Section 15. Washington, D.C., to Richmond, Va., *113.4 m.*

There are two routes for US 1 between the White House in Washington and US 1 S. of the Potomac River:

By the 14th St. Highway Bridge: E. from White House on Pennsylvania Ave. to 15th St. NW.; R. on 15th St. to Pennsylvania Ave.; L. on Pennsylvania Ave. to 14th St. NW.; R. on 14th St. to bridge, **2 m.** At the south end of the bridge, straight ahead for US 1 or R. in a loop to reach Mount Vernon Memorial Highway (US 1-Alt.), which runs under south end of bridge. This route has many traffic lights and is apt to be congested between 7 and 9 a.m. and 4 and 6 p.m.

Between the south end of the 14th St. Highway Bridge and Alexandria, Va., and between Alexandria and a point 8 miles S. of that town, two routes are available: the Memorial Highway and US 1. The former is a boulevard close to the river, passing Mount Vernon; the latter a narrow heavily traveled highway with many busses and trucks and few points of interest.

By Arlington Memorial Bridge: W. on Pennsylvania Ave. to 17th St. NW.; L. on 17th St. to Constitution Ave.; R. on Constitution Ave. to 23rd St. NW.; L. on 23rd St. and around Lincoln Memorial to bridge, **1.5 m.**; L. on Mount Vernon Memorial Highway.

From the Arlington Memorial Bridge, ARLINGTON (*open daily Apr.–Aug. 9–6; March and Sept. 9–5; Oct.–Feb. 9–4:30; adm. free*) is plainly visible on the bluff ahead. The house was built by Robert E. Lee's father-in-law, George Washington Parke Custis. Its stately portico affords a superb view of the Potomac and overlooks Arlington National Cemetery (*see WASHINGTON: CITY AND CAPITAL and VA. GUIDE*), on its one-time lawn. It was occupied for many years after Lee left it to head the armies of the Confederacy, but it is now maintained as a memorial to him. It is one of the earliest examples of the Greek Revival style of architecture. The front of the mansion is supposed to have been modeled on the Temple of Theseus at Athens; the design of the pediment resembles that of the Temple of Athene at Aegina. The stones for its foundation came from the land nearby, and the bricks of clay were burned upon the place, under the supervision of Custis. The eight large white columns of the portico were built of brick and cemented over to give perfectly rounded circumferences.

Construction on the north wing was begun in 1802, but the mansion was not entirely completed until shortly before the Civil War, thus accounting for the asymmetrical arrangement of the interior.

Mary Ann Randolph Custis, daughter and sole heir of the master of the estate, lived at Arlington from the time of her marriage to Lt. Robert E. Lee in 1831 until 1861, when the mansion was taken over by the Union forces. In 1864 title to the property passed to the United States in lieu of unpaid taxes illegally levied. In 1874, one year after the death of Mary Ann Custis Lee, the house was returned to its rightful heir, George Washington Custis Lee, son of Robert E. Lee, who later sold Arlington to the U. S. Government for $150,000.

After the death of Martha Washington many of the heirlooms at Mount Vernon — portraits, silver, china, and furniture, including the bed upon which George Washington died, the camp tent he used throughout the Revolutionary War, and Martha Washington's money chest — were brought to this house, but many of them have since been returned to Mount Vernon. The furnishings of Arlington are of the period in which the house was built; some were formerly used here.

The interior, with its high ceilings, large paneled doors with wide molded trim, and graceful archways, is in keeping with the simple character and scale of the great portico. Its arrangement is typical of the Virginia mansions of the era in which it was built; that is, it has a broad central hall dividing the rooms. Near the west entrance are the family dining room and parlor (L). There is an exceptionally long drawing room (R).

In the south wing of the mansion is the formal dining room, beyond which is the study. Along the west wall is the small conservatory, the Camellia House.

From the Memorial Highway, which swings L. at the end of the

VIRGINIA

bridge, there are excellent views of the city of Washington; the WASHINGTON MONUMENT and the CAPITOL are outstanding landmarks, particularly striking at night when they are illuminated.

At **3.2 m.** the boulevard passes under the south end of the 14th St. Highway Bridge (*see above*), whose roadway runs straight ahead to US 1 past the WASHINGTON AIRPORT (R). The boulevard, the alternate to US 1, is broad and well landscaped, running close to the Potomac River for many miles. Just S. of the Highway Bridge it passes one of several lagoons along the route, the ROACHES RUN SANCTUARY for waterfowl, under the protection of the Federal Government. Parking places at intervals offer vistas of the city and the river. The road swings in broad curves and the conspicuous GEORGE WASHINGTON NATIONAL MASONIC MEMORIAL (R) in Alexandria is seen for some distance before the city is reached. At a traffic circle on the northern edge of the city the boulevard is joined by US 1 (R).

ALEXANDRIA, **10 m.** (52 alt., 24,140 pop.), historic city (*see WASHINGTON: CITY AND CAPITAL and VA. GUIDE*).

Points of Interest. Christ Church, Gadsby's Tavern, Carlyle House, and many others.

At the southern end of the small city US 1 turns R. on Franklin St.; the boulevard runs straight ahead, crossing HUNTING CREEK on a long, low bridge. In 1676 Governor Berkeley built a fort near the creek for defense against the Susquehannock Indians who did not accept the European invasion of their lands with complacence. South of the creek the boulevard enters 8 miles of wooded parkway that is particularly delightful in the spring when the purple blossoms of the Judas-tree mingle with the pink and white dogwood blossoms and the ground is almost solidly covered with flowering bluets and spring beauty.

COLLINGWOOD, **15.3 m.** (L), a remodeled Colonial house that is now a tearoom, is on the Old River Farm of the Mount Vernon estate. From Johnson Spring, which supplies the restaurant, pre-Revolutionary vessels plying out of Alexandria took water for their voyages. A secluded corner of the grounds was frequently used for duels in Colonial times.

The entrance to MOUNT VERNON (*open daily March–Oct. 9–4:30, Nov.–Feb. 9–4; adm. 25¢*), **18.8 m.**, for many years the home of George

Washington, now a museum (*see WASHINGTON: CITY AND CAPITAL and VA. GUIDE*), is flanked by a modern building that houses a restaurant.

The boulevard swings R., passing the probable site of one of the King's Houses noted on Capt. John Smith's map made a few years after the founding of the Colony of Virginia; Thomas Jefferson found Indian artifacts in his rambles on the grounds of Mount Vernon and made some attempts at exploration of the site but no one has yet continued his work, though recent explorations of other sites indicated on the Smith map have produced many relics of the pre-settlement period.

At **19.3 m.** (R) is the restored MOUNT VERNON GRIST MILL (*open on application to caretaker, next door*); here grain was ground for market, as well as for the estate.

At **21.2 m.** the boulevard again joins US 1; L. on US 1.

High on a hill opposite the junction is WOODLAWN (*open only during April Garden Week*). The land, formerly part of the Mount Vernon estate, was left by Washington to Lawrence Lewis, his nephew, who became the husband of Nellie Custis, granddaughter of Martha Washington. The house (*see illustration*), in Federal Georgian style, was designed by William Thornton, architect of the National Capitol, but has a likeness to Kenmore in Fredericksburg, the home of Lawrence Lewis' mother, though Woodlawn was built on a much grander scale. The square two-story brick building has the usual central hall of the period; it has story-and-a-half wings with story-and-a-half connecting pavilions. A high brick wall joins the kitchen and library wings with outbuildings. Particularly noteworthy are the arched mullioned windows of the pavilions and the hipped floor. The broad brick terraces on the river front have beautiful gardens and much old boxwood.

US 1 between Fredericksburg and Washington more or less follows an Indian trail established long before the Europeans penetrated the country. Because it provided the shortest route along the Virginia bank of the Potomac River, colonists persisted in using it despite the mire, difficult fords, and other obstacles that drew their curses. Prior to 1700 a public highway was established here by law and landowners whose side fences crossed it were compelled to maintain gates for the convenience of travelers. Several ferries to the Maryland shore were operated along the Potomac for the use of

VIRGINIA 189

those who wanted short-cuts to Baltimore and Philadelphia. Almost every diary and travel book written by people who used the trail in the days when it was known as the Potomac Path, and later as the King's Highway, recorded some near-disastrous adventure on it. Dr. Coke, an English tourist of the late 18th century, nearly perished in fording Accotink Creek during a freshet; John Marshall spoke feelingly of miring his horse; and Thomas Jefferson bemoaned the fact that the best speed he could make was three miles an hour. Testy John Randolph of Roanoke likened the Chopowamsic Swamp to the Serbonian bog that swallowed the unwary forever. As late as 1820 the mail had to leave Alexandria before sunup in order to reach Fredericksburg before sundown the same day. The earliest travelers went afoot, later ones on horseback. As the colonists prospered, some used private coaches and buggies, though the majority still rode horseback.

At **21.6 m.** US 1 crosses the boundary of a military reservation through which it runs for about a mile. At **21.9 m.** is an entrance to FORT BELVOIR, formerly Fort Humphreys.

> Left on this road **1.5 m.** is the neat parade ground surrounded by administrative offices and the quarters for officers and men. The reservation occupies a large peninsula, part of a huge grant made by Charles II to Lord Culpeper that came into the hands of the fifth Lord Fairfax when he married Culpeper's daughter. The son of this marriage cleared the title and sent his cousin, Col. William Fairfax, to America as his agent, granting him 2,500 acres called Belvoir and including the peninsula. In 1741 Colonel Fairfax built a house that Washington described as having "nine rooms and suitable outhouses." In 1743 Colonel Fairfax's daughter married Lawrence Washington, who built Mount Vernon as his home. George Washington was a frequent visitor at Belvoir and there practiced surveying. The house, which stood on a bluff above the river, was demolished by gunfire as the British fleet came up the river during the War of 1812; the daffodils that bloom profusely around the ruins in the spring are thought to be descendants of those planted in the Colonial garden. On the northern shore of the peninsula are an EXPERIMENT STATION and a FISH HATCHERY of the U. S. Bureau of Fisheries.

ACCOTINK, **23.3 m.**, a collection of filling stations and lunchrooms, took its name from Accotink Creek (Ind., *boat* or *canoe*).

POHICK CHURCH of Truro Parish, **24.2 m.** (*open daily in summer, 10 a.m.–4 p.m.; in winter on Sat. and Sun.; free*), was constructed in 1769–74 under the supervision of George Washington, George Mason, and George William Fairfax, leading landowners of the parish. Washington owned two pews here for his family and guests, dividing his attendance between Pohick Church and Christ Church,

Alexandria. The well-proportioned building, of brick laid in Flemish bond and of Aquia sandstone, went through such a long period of neglect and vandalism that the interior is largely a restoration. During the Civil War Union soldiers tore out the pews, used the baptismal font for a watering trough, and set up a target against one wall; the font, found many years later in a neighboring farmyard, is almost the only original piece of furnishing. The restored pews are unlike the earlier ones, which were high-backed to give privacy to the occupants.

At **24.5 m.** is the junction with a paved road, locally called the Back Road.

Right on this road, which follows the old Indian trail used in fording Occoquan Creek; the settlers early established a ferry near the river to avoid this detour. LORTON, 0.5 m., is the seat of the DISTRICT OF COLUMBIA WORKHOUSE.

OCCOQUAN (Ind., *hooked inlet*), **2.5 m.** (221 pop.), a small trading center, was founded in 1804. On December 27, 1862, Occoquan was raided by Wade Hampton. Right from Occoquan an unpaved road leads **5 m.** to MINNIEVILLE near which is BEL AIR, the home, during his married life, of Parson Mason Locke Weems, George Washington's first and most imaginative biographer. This house was built in pre-Revolutionary days by Col. James Ewell, a classmate of Jefferson's at William and Mary College, and a prosperous citizen of Dumfries, before nature and war combined to ruin the tobacco trade at this point. His widow would have lost her home had not her daughter Fannie married the energetic author and bookseller. Weems' wife and children lived in the family house, and he visited them briefly at intervals as he journeyed N. and S. The square brick house is rather small and, as in other Colonial houses, the visitor is moved to wonder how it was possible to find sleeping places for the large family and their many guests. The house has not suffered from ill-advised restorations and, except for the lack of outbuildings, is about as it was in the days when it was Weems' legal residence. It is undistinguished in architecture, but the paneled drawing-room is attractive; a basement kitchen has a fireplace in which a large hog could be roasted. The view from the house is exceptional; on clear days Washington landmarks are visible.

The Back Road returns to the main road at Woodbridge, **4.5 m.** (*see below*).

At **25.5 m.** on US 1 is the junction with a dirt road.

Left on this road is GUNSTON HALL, **4 m.** (*house never open to public; gardens only during annual April Garden Week*). The house stands on land patented in 1651 by Richard Turney, who was hanged for his part in Bacon's Rebellion of 1676, and was built by the fourth George Mason, author of the Virginia Bill of Rights. The plans were made by William Buckland, probably with the assistance of Thomas Mason, brother of the owner, who brought Buckland from England for the work. The building is of rectangular story-and-a-half type characteristic of 18th century Virginia architecture, but its details are highly individual. Both front and rear porches are noteworthy, the former closely following the lines of the Temple of Tyche at Eumeneia in Asia Minor, and the latter being eight-sided, with pointed arches, one of the rare examples of Colonial Gothic. The enrichment of ornament in the interior is not surpassed in any other house of its day in America; the Chinese Chippendale drawing-room represented the most fashionable mode in England at the time of the building. Another unusual feature is the staircase, with risers so low that it gives almost the effect of a ramp. The gardens are beautiful and the boxwood is famous. The tenant-owner has deeded the place to the State of Virginia for future preservation.

At WOODBRIDGE, **29.8 m.** is the junction with a side road (*see above*).

On US 1 at **32.3 m.** (L) are two gateposts marking the entrance to RIPPON LODGE (*private*). The house, recently much remodeled, was designed in 1725 by Richard Blackburn, the British architect, who later designed Mount Vernon for Lawrence Washington. During the Revolutionary War it was a center of military activities for the region.

DUMFRIES, **36.8 m.** (157 pop.), is hardly a shadow of the port that successfully rivaled Alexandria in pre-Revolutionary days. Even before the Revolution, Quantico Creek began to fill with silt, so that ships were unable to reach the warehouses and wharves where tobacco was loaded and the finery and staples of England unloaded. English merchants, long envious of the local monopoly attained by the Scottish merchants, watched the decline with satisfaction, but it spelled ruin to some of the nearby Colonial planters. In the days of prosperity, however, many of the planters had resented the Scots' practice of meeting twice a year at Dumfries to decide on the rate of exchange and the price to be paid for tobacco. There are many records of the gay social life of Dumfries in its prime — of the tea drinkings, balls, and parties. The town even supported drama; Washington in his diary noted that he stopped here to see *The Recruiting Officer*.

At **41.2 m.** (R) is one of the entrances to CHOPOWAMSIC PARK, which comprises 11,000 acres of submarginal land being developed by the National Park Service into a camping center.

TRIANGLE, **38.6 m.**, is at one of the entrances to the QUANTICO MARINE BASE, where several thousand marines are stationed. The Government reservation is a plot of 2,000 acres on the Potomac. After the World War, hundreds of wooden transport ships were towed to anchor off the peninsula; some have been burned, while others remain rotting in the water.

CHOPOWAMSIC CREEK, **39.4 m.**, was long a difficult problem for the early road builders, and one of the causes of the near-disappearance of the road for a time. After the railroad was extended from Richmond to Fredericksburg travelers found it more comfortable to go between Fredericksburg and Washington by steamboat than to endure the hazards of the Potomac Path. The advent of the automobile stimulated engineers to efforts that eventually brought the road back to utility.

At **43.2 m.** is AQUIA CREEK (Ind., *bush nut*), near which Giles Brent and his sisters, Margaret and Mary, built homes after disputes with Lord Baltimore caused them to move from Maryland. The Brents arrived in Maryland in 1638 and for many years were prominently identified with affairs there. In 1650 Giles Brent first patented land in Virginia. His other patents and those of his sisters followed in quick succession.

Mistress Margaret Brent, who appears in Maryland records as "Margaret Brent, Gentleman," was one of the most remarkable women in Colonial history. She appears frequently in the records of her two States, negotiating transactions of her own and acting as attorney for her brother, her sister, and neighbors who needed her help. She was the first woman in America to ask for "voyce & vote allso." Because Leonard Calvert, Governor of Maryland, made her his sole executrix in an oral will that tersely instructed her "to take all and pay all," and because the Maryland Council made her administratrix of Lord Baltimore's revenues, she argued before the Assembly that she should be given full rights of citizenship. When the request was denied by Governor Greene, she declared that she would protest all action taken by the Assembly if she were not present and granted "as aforesaid voyce & vote allso." Her brother's difficulties with Lord Baltimore, arising from Giles Brent's claims to land he considered due him because of his marriage to the daughter of the Piscataway chief, and Margaret Brent's indignation that Lord Baltimore should resent her having paid hired soldiers out of his revenues were responsible for the Brents' moving to Virginia and for the speedy colonization of the vast territory known then as Northumberland County.

The Brents, however, were not the first settlers on Aquia Creek. Much earlier eight Spaniards of the Society of Jesus came from Mexico and attempted to found a mission at Aquia. They were killed by

JERUSALEM MILLS, MARYLAND

HOUSE AT GREENBELT, MARYLAND

the Indians a few months later. A monument in memory of the priests and the early Brents has recently been unveiled beside the highway. It is near the site of Brenton, which was planned as a sanctuary for peoples of all religious faiths and which was made possible by the Charter of Religious Liberty granted in 1686 by James II of England.

Aquia Creek was for ten years after the Indian war of 1676 the northern frontier of Virginia. On it was the supply base of the Army of the Potomac for the Fredericksburg campaign (1862) and the Chancellorsville campaign (1863).

At **44.2 m.** (L) is AQUIA CHURCH on the site of an earlier structure. Over the south door of the present building is inscribed: "Built A.D. 1751, destroyed by fire 1754, and rebuilt in 1757 by Mourning Richards, undertaker (contractor); William Copein, Mason." The two-story building is in the form of a Greek cross. It has two tiers of windows set deep in thick brick walls; the lower windows are square, containing 18 panes each, while the upper windows are oval-topped. There are three double-door entrances at angles of the cross. Unlike most old Virginia churches, it has a bell and clock tower. The communion service given to the parish in 1739 was buried for safekeeping during three wars — those of 1776, 1812, and 1861. The construction cost of the church was paid in tobacco, the current medium of exchange.

At **45.4 m.** stood PEYTON'S ORDINARY, a country tavern at which Washington sometimes stopped for meals when journeying to Fredericksburg to visit his mother. The place was something of a social center for the poorer landowners of the countryside. Rochambeau's army camped near it during the Revolution.

STAFFORD COURTHOUSE, **47.5 m.**, seat of Stafford Co., was occupied by the Army of the Potomac from November 1862 until June 1863. The courthouse contains only a few early records. Most of them were destroyed or carried off during the Civil War. Some early records taken away during the war were found in the New York State Library and returned to Stafford within recent years.

Left of the highway in the section near the mouth of Potomac Creek Capt. John Smith in 1608 saw the Indian village Patawomeck, which contained the King's House of Powhatan. From this village Pocahontas, daughter of Powhatan, was kidnaped in 1613 by Captain Argall, who planned to hold her as hostage until her father returned

U. S. ONE

rifles and other articles he and his followers had stolen. It was during this period of captivity that Pocahontas met and married John Rolfe; she never returned to the village.

Travelers landed from steamers near this point to take the stagecoach to Fredericksburg, an early railroad terminus. Charles Dickens landed here on his way to Richmond, and returned by the same route in March 1842.

On the creek, land was laid off in 1691 for a port and the seat of Stafford Co., called Marlborough. Houses were built and the county court was held here for several years. The town did not grow, and in 1747 John Mercer bought the county's rights in it.

FALMOUTH, 55.4 m., now only a small village, was founded in 1727 as a trading post for the Northern Neck and became a milling center to which ocean ships came to load foodstuffs for England. Here were flour mills, tobacco warehouses, and stores. In return for foodstuffs sent overseas came English goods to satisfy the needs and fancies of a prosperous community. For a brief period Falmouth was the rival of Fredericksburg across the Rappahannock River; a bridge subsequently built across the river gave Northern Neck territory the advantage of greater tonnage that docked a mile downstream, diverting commercial importance to Fredericksburg and the south bank and leading to the gradual decline of this early port. In Falmouth Basil Gordon became one of America's first millionaires. George Washington lived near the town as a boy.

Right 1 m. from Falmouth and visible from US 1 is the HOME OF THE LATE GARI MELCHERS, American artist. Trained at Dusseldorf, Melchers achieved a reputation in Europe for his paintings of Dutch peasant life. In Virginia his favorite subjects were mountaineer types, such as those in *The Pot Boils*.

US 1 crosses the Rappahannock River near the spot where a fort was built in 1676 to protect the settlers from the Indians.

FREDERICKSBURG, 56.5 m. (50 alt., 6,819 pop.), Colonial port (*see VA. GUIDE*).

Points of Interest. Kenmore, home of Washington's sister; Rising Sun Tavern; law office of James Monroe; apothecary shop of Dr. Hugh Mercer; and others.

1. Right on Canal St. in Fredericksburg; R. at Prince Edward St.; thence on the old River Road to power canal; on a bold eminence here (R) is SNOWDEN, 1.5 m., originally known as Smith's Hill. Snowden was built in 1808 by Yeaman Smith, son-in-law of the Reverend James Mayre, Sr., Huguenot, rector of old St. George's Church, Fredericksburg, and tutor of George Washington and his brothers.

VIRGINIA

Shortly before the Battle of Fredericksburg, a hurried conference was held in the parlor of this rectangular brick building with white-pillared portico. Not long after the Federal advance reached Stafford Heights, Gen. E. V. Sumner, commanding the Right Grand Division of the Army of the Potomac, dispatched a note to Mayor Slaughter, of Fredericksburg, advising that he would bombard the town at daybreak the following morning in retaliation for the firing on Union troops from Fredericksburg. Mayor Slaughter communicated with General Lee, who could not go to Fredericksburg and arranged to meet the city's chief executive here, outside the town limits; Lee was unable to offer protection to the town.

2. Left from Fredericksburg on State 218 **4 m.** to WHITE OAK PRIMITIVE CHURCH, built in 1789. It is a low building of frame construction, and rests on a foundation of rough-hewn stones. A wing for Negroes was added to the original building. The interior is plain, the woodwork of pine, and the original wooden benches are still in place.

In Fredericksburg at **56.9 m.** US 1 swings (R) into Lafayette Blvd., which comes to a dead end at the SUNKEN ROAD, **57.6 m.,** the western city limits.

Straight ahead is the entrance to the NATIONAL MILITARY CEMETERY on MARYE'S HEIGHTS, where are buried 15,296 victims of the Civil War, only 3,000 of them identified.

Fredericksburg and Petersburg, N. and S. of Richmond, received the brunt of the four-year drive of the Federal armies to capture the Confederate capital. The 100-mile stretch of US 1 S. of Fredericksburg runs through the heart of an area that has seen more bloodshed than has any other on the continent of North America; here were fought some of the battles that helped to decide whether the land between Canada and Mexico should remain under one powerful government or should be broken up into two or more governments. Had the Federal Government not prevailed, it is possible that America would have become another constantly embattled Europe.

The first major drive for the capture of Richmond came in the early winter of 1862 when Federal troops moved S. under Gen. Ambrose E. Burnside; General Lee had come rapidly E. to block the advance, and a delay in the arrival of pontoon bridges needed by the Federal forces for crossing the Rappahannock River at Fredericksburg enabled him to concentrate two corps on the heights to the S. and W. of the town. On December 12 the Federal troops had crossed the river. The following day two attacks were ordered, one at Hamilton's Crossing, 3 miles S. of Fredericksburg, and one on Marye's Heights. The Hamilton Crossing attack was repulsed and the Federal troops retired. Behind the Sunken Road at the foot of Marye's

U. S. ONE

Heights ran a stone wall forming a parapet behind which the Confederate troops successfully repulsed seven major attacks. Two days later the Federal troops withdrew across the river. The Federal force numbered 142,551 and the Confederate 91,760 in this battle; the Federal loss was 12,653 and the Confederate 5,309.

Right from the end of Lafayette Blvd. in Fredericksburg on Sunken Road; there are no scars here as reminders of the desperate attacks in which thousands fell under heavy fire, their bodies freezing in the bitter north wind.

At **0.2 m.** (L) is the entrance lane to BROMPTON, a two-story brick building with one-story wings; its high gabled roof extends forward to form a pedimented portico that is supported by four slender Ionic columns. The unusually delicate detail of the portico cornice, repeated under the eaves of the wings, and the lunette in the pediment are noteworthy. Brompton was built about 1837 by John L. Marye and had a peaceful existence prior to the day when its porch was used as a Confederate observation post on the progress of Federal troops across the city below.

US 1 turns L. at the end of Lafayette Blvd., **57.6 m.**, and follows Sunken Road.

At **59.2 m.** (L) is an entrance to the FREDERICKSBURG NATIONAL MILITARY PARK (*see VA. GUIDE*).

Left along this winding road, which follows the line of the Confederate earthworks of December 1862; on the heights is HAMILTON'S CROSSING, **5 m.**, where an unsuccessful attack by Federal forces was made on December 13.

At **61.9 m.** is the junction with State 51.

Right along State 51, a paved road running through thinly settled farming country. Here and there, close to the road, are old log cabins, still capable of giving shelter. At **5.7 m.** (R) is an entrance to the SPOTSYLVANIA NATIONAL MILITARY PARK (*see VA. GUIDE*) leading to the Bloody Angle, where on May 12, 1864, occurred the severest fighting of the Battle of Spotsylvania Court House. Over 160,000 men, the Federals outnumbering the Confederates two to one, fought in this area from May 7 to May 20, 1864. The Federals left behind 17,555 dead; the Confederate loss is unknown. The battle was notorious for the bitterness and hand-to-hand nature of the fighting; survivors reported that the little brooks actually ran red with blood. It was from this battlefield that Grant wrote, "I intend to fight it out on this line if it takes all summer."

SPOTSYLVANIA, **6.6 m.**, is little but a green with a courthouse and jail, and an old hotel. Spotsylvania Co. was formed by an act of the Virginia Assembly of 1720 which recited that "the frontiers toward the high mountains are exposed to danger from the Indians and the late settlement of the French to the westward" and that it was necessary to organize the territory; it provided that "fifteen hundred pounds current money of Virginia shall be paid by treasurer to the governor for these uses to wit: £ 500 to be expended in a Church, Court House, Prison, Pillory and Stocks, in said county; £ 1000 to be laid in arms, am-

VIRGINIA

munition, etc., of which each Christian Tyetheable is to have one firelock musket, one socket, bayonet fixed thereto, one cartouche box, eight pounds bullets and two pounds powder." The county was later divided; the seat at first was Germanna, but it was moved to Fredericksburg in 1732 because Germanna did not have accommodations for the justices and others coming to the court. In 1778 the seat was moved to Andrew's Tavern near the center of the county, and in 1839 to its present site.

The two-story yellow COURTHOUSE with a porticoed front was built in 1870 to replace one that was half destroyed during the battle of 1864; the little jail (R) was built in 1854.

SPOTSYLVANIA TAVERN, opposite a corner of the green, is at the head of State 51 and forces the highway to turn sharply (L). It is a long rambling two-and-a-half-story building; the roof slopes forward to form a portico supported by four large pillars that spread out into square bases. The little stoop rises to the front door under the portico. This inn, which was also damaged in the battle, sheltered Confederate leaders when Lee occupied the hamlet on the night of May 9, 1864.

It was in Spotsylvania not far from the courthouse that in 1816 death finally stopped the incessant and restless travels of Francis Asbury, first bishop of the Methodist Episcopal Church in America.

Between Fredericksburg and Petersburg US 1 follows the Telegraph Road, laid out in 1847 along the line of the Washington-New Orleans Telegraph Co. The earlier and somewhat longer road between Fredericksburg and Richmond passing through Hanover is now State 2. In the infancy of telegraph lines every additional mile was a worry; consequently, when this line was laid out, the shortest route between the two cities was used and, the wires being fragile, a road was cut along the right-of-way to facilitate repairs.

THORNBURG, **70.6 m.,** is a crossroads formerly known as Mud Tavern.

Left from Thornburg on a winding asphalt road to a fork at **3.6 m.**; L. at the fork and R. when the road reaches a dead end at a country road that runs through fields and crosses a railroad track, just beyond which at **5.4 m.** is the short lane (L) leading to the little white house that was the DEATH PLACE OF "STONEWALL" JACKSON (*open; free*). Lee and Jackson, splendid tacticians and hard fighters, had held back forces twice the size of those they commanded for a year and a half without permitting a single major victory by their opponents. After Jackson's surprise attack on the Federal troops at Chancellorsville, in which the Federals were completely defeated, he went scouting along the front alone, as was his unwise custom; in the twilight he was shot by his own men. His arm had to be amputated and an attempt was made to send him to Richmond for hospital care. By the time he reached the railroad he was too ill to travel farther. His death on May 22, 1863, at the age of 39, was a serious loss to the Confederacy.

The house, the only remaining building of the former Fairfield Plantation at Guinea Station, is a memorial to Jackson; in the rear room is the bed in which

Jackson died and on the walls are various pictures and mementos. For some years the house was kept up by the railroad company owning the property but it has been given to the Federal Government.

Every few miles along US 1 in this area are Virginia highway markers indicating the sites of various episodes in the movements of troops back and forth through the area in the different campaigns. At the southern end of Thornburg is a marker at the place where Sheridan, attempting a raid on Richmond, was, on May 9, 1864, attacked by Wickham's cavalry.

MT. CARMEL CHURCH, **85.1 m.** (R), was organized in 1773. The red brick building has a gabled roof extending forward to form a pediment as high as are the pillars supporting it. The hamlet now called Carmel was formerly called Polecat, because of its proximity to Polecat Creek.

US 1 crosses the SOUTH ANNA RIVER at **86 m.** on a double bridge at the point where Lee crossed on May 27, 1864, on his way to head off Grant at Cold Harbor. Heavy concrete paving now covers the slick red mud and mire through which the armies of the Civil War plodded and stumbled, requiring days to go distances that modern motorized armies would traverse in a few hours. The old battle areas, like the nearby Colonial homes, are relics of an outmoded past; motor cars, airplanes, and long-range guns have changed the conditions and technique of warfare as much as they have those of civilian life. A lone ace in an airplane can today do as much reconnaissance in an hour as did hundreds of scouts working for weeks 75 years ago; the fighting forces have become machines and there is little place for the individual exploits of the past.

At **88.4 m.** (R) stands a pillared white brick house where, according to tradition, Lee stopped to drink buttermilk that made him ill for several days. Because of this illness, it is said, he did not attack Grant here as had been his intention. The rippled old glass in the many-paned windows shows that the house has suffered neither attack nor neglect, as have many of its contemporaries.

DOSWELL, **89.8 m.**, is a crossroads in an area that was a well-known ante-bellum horse-training center, where Negro jockeys achieved considerable reputations.

GUM TAVERN, **92.8 m.**, is a crossroads hamlet.

Right from Gum Tavern along State 51, a paved road passing scattered log cabins and farmhouses. OLD FORK CHURCH, **6.2 m.** (R), was built in 1735. Parish records show additions were made to the original building in Colonial times, but the brick walls, laid in Flemish bond, show little evidence of the patching. There are small porches on the front and one side supported by stone pillars that widen considerably toward the base.

Inside at the rear is a slave gallery, but little else remains to indicate age, pews and walls having been renovated at intervals throughout the years. Extending along the rear outer wall of the church (R) is a long, narrow brick-walled enclosure containing a single row of gravestones. This church was attended by the Nelsons and the Pages, and these names appear frequently on the gravestones scattered around the building. At the eastern end of the church is buried the wife of Thomas Nelson, commander of the Virginia Militia, 1777-81, and a signer of the Declaration of Independence. Mrs. Nelson was long custodian of the communion silver of the church in her nearby home, Airwell, which, like many Old Dominion homes, has been destroyed by fire.

ASHLAND, **97.2 m.** (221 alt., 1,297 pop.), owes its existence chiefly to RANDOLPH-MACON COLLEGE for men, which has 250 students. It was the first college in the United States to be founded by the Methodist Episcopal Church. The charter was granted at the 1829-30 session of the Virginia Legislature, and the college was opened at Boydton in Mecklenberg Co. in 1832. John Randolph of Roanoke, Va., and Nathan Macon of North Carolina were honored in the name. In 1868, when the Virginia Conference of the Methodist Episcopal Church joined with the Baltimore Conference, the school was moved to its present site to please the Maryland group. In 1890 the Randolph-Macon system was organized; it now includes preparatory schools for boys at Front Royal and Bedford City, one for girls at Danville, and the Randolph-Macon Women's College at Lynchburg.

The rambling buildings are hidden by tall trees, and the campus is particularly delightful in the spring when thousands of yellow daffodils cover the lawns.

1. Right from Ashland on State 54, an asphalt-paved road, is NEGRO FOOT, **8.7 m.**, a crossroads with a name that is a grim reminder of former days, when the members of certain types of offenders were cut off and hung by the wayside as a warning to their fellows.

Right **0.2 m.** from this settlement on a dirt road to a fork; R. at the fork to the entrance of SCOTCHTOWN, **2.4 m.** (L), a house of obscure history but peculiar charm. Tradition is that it was built about 1698 or shortly thereafter; when William Byrd made his *Progress to the Mines* in 1732 he stopped here to ask for information and advice from Charles Chiswell, whose father had built the house. The land is not particularly fertile and has changed hands frequently; Patrick Henry held it from 1771 until 1777, and is said to have bought the place as a speculation. The next owner was John Payne, the Quaker, one of whose many children, a daughter Dolly, then a young girl, later became the wife of James

Madison. John Payne sold the place in 1783 because his conscience would no longer permit him to own the slaves then necessary to operate a plantation. In later years Dolly Madison told many stories of her happy life at Scotchtown and of the beauty of the grounds and gardens. Now only the tall ragged remnants of a box hedge along the lane leading to the front door give evidence of former landscaping. The house is occupied by tenants.

Scotchtown, standing on a high brick foundation, is unusually large for the time in which it was built — 100 by 50 ft.; it has four big rooms on each side of a wide entrance hall, each room with a fireplace. Above this main floor is an attic with 5,000 sq. ft. of floor space receiving light only from small windows in the ends. The high roof, pierced only by four chimneys, would give a barren appearance if the ends of the ridge were not hipped; at the top of the unpainted clapboard walls, now silvery with age, are carefully spaced corbels that give a surprising touch of elegance to the otherwise severe-looking building.

Scotchtown has even more legends than the average old house; the usual story is told of Cornwallis' having ridden up the steps and through the halls; there are hints of a murder committed here and of an Indian raid — said to be responsible for the faint brown mark on the hall floor pointed out as a bloodstain. The trapdoor in the hall is said to have provided Patrick Henry with a hiding place when British soldiers appeared to arrest the fiery radical who was inflaming the colonists.

2. Left from Ashland on State 54 at **1.4 m.** is the junction with a gravel road; L. on this gravel road is the entrance to HICKORY HILL (*gardens open during annual April Garden Week*), **2.8 m.**, an old estate whose house, built in 1734, was rebuilt after destruction by fire in 1875. The present house is a tall irregular structure characteristic of the 1870's. The gardens are particularly worth attention, the outstanding attraction being the ancient BOX WALK, 307 ft. long and arched 30 ft. above the broad path. During the Civil War the house was used as a hospital; one of Lee's sons, "Rooney," while here recovering from a wound, was captured by Federals. It was owned by Gen. W. C. Wickham, Brigadier General of Cavalry in the Confederate Army, and is still in the hands of his family.

East of the junction with the road leading to Hickory Hill, State 54 winds into HANOVER, **6.6 m.**, a settlement that, like other Virginia county seats, exists chiefly as court center. Hanover Co. was formed in 1720 and named in honor of George I, Elector of Hanover.

The little T-shaped brick COURTHOUSE, standing on a slight hill, has great charm. From the front it appears to be much smaller than it really is, because the shallow cross bar is made shallower by a loggia and is pierced on either side of the entrance door by windows that are duplicated in the rear wall. The brick walls of the cross bar and of part of the stem of the T, which holds the courtroom, are beautifully laid in Flemish bond; the pattern was not repeated when the courtroom was enlarged at the rear.

The interior lacks distinction and is in no way reminiscent of the day in 1763 when Patrick Henry established his reputation by his oratory on the side of the vestry in the Parsons' Cause. From the early days of the Colony the clergy had received salaries in tobacco, in addition to the use of glebe lands and homesteads; in 1748 the Provincial Assembly had set this annual salary at 16,000 pounds of tobacco. The salary fluctuated in value as the tobacco market rose and fell. The planters of Virginia were growing somewhat restive under the exactions of the Established Church and in 1758, a year when the price of tobacco went particularly high, passed an act, similar to one they had passed in 1755, providing that the clergy should be paid that year in currency, at the rate of two pence a pound, a price below the market rate for tobacco. The clergy promptly carried their complaints to the King and the act was disallowed; various clergymen then brought suit against the vestries for the remainder of the salaries legally due them in 1758. The Reverend James Maury brought such a suit before the court in Hanover Co. and the vestry, after trying to get various able lawyers for their defense, selected young Patrick Henry to represent them.

Henry was a young man of poor local reputation — a restless fellow who had failed at one business after the other. He was living at the time in the tavern across the street from the courthouse. Having married the tavernkeeper's daughter, he helped his father-in-law at the tavern bar while he waited for the legal practice that rarely came. Henry's father was in court when his son rose to speak, and it is said that he blushed uncomfortably over his son's stammering introduction. But Patrick Henry was a born orator and, as soon as he forgot his neighbors' opinion of him, made such an impassioned speech that, though the court supported the Crown in disallowing the act of 1758, the fascinated jury awarded the suing clergyman only one penny damage. According to contemporary report, Henry argued that the King had no right to disallow such an act and by so doing "from being a father to his people, degenerates into a tyrant and forfeits all rights to his subjects' obedience." The conservatives of the Colony were shocked by this radicalism but those who were smarting under the exactions of English businessmen made Henry a popular hero.

The COURTHOUSE TAVERN, where Henry lived and worked at times, is a long L-shaped building with a veranda filling in the angle of the L. Entrance is now through a basement door in the toe of the L, which holds a square room that was the bar; it looks now as it probably looked when the justices arrived for court sessions 170 years ago. The long dining room (R) is of good proportions, low-ceiled, with fireplaces at the ends. The room above was formerly used for assemblies but has been divided into bedrooms.

Not far from the courthouse is the little COUNTY JAIL where, as is the custom in rural Virginia counties, no jailer is in constant attendance and the prisoners talk sociably through barred windows to any friends who care to visit them.

YELLOW TAVERN, **105.6 m.**, is a hamlet that took its name from a former stage house. A short distance N. along US 1 is the SITE OF THE BATTLE OF YELLOW TAVERN, in which the brilliant 19-year-old cavalry leader, Gen. J. E. B. Stuart, was fatally wounded May 11, 1864, in a brush with Sheridan's troops in their attempted raid on Richmond. His death was a great blow to Lee and to the Confederate cause.

ST. JOSEPH'S VILLA, **105.9 m.** (R), is a Roman Catholic orphanage founded by Mrs. James H. Dooley of Richmond.

The HERMITAGE GOLF CLUB, 107 m. (*not open to the public*), at the head of a long green slope (R), has an entrance on a side road. It is a smart private club with members chiefly from Richmond.

BROOK HILL, 107.6 m. (L), a Victorian house nearly hidden by trees, stands back from the highway in beautiful grounds.

This section of US 1 is known locally as Brook Road; Lafayette followed it with his troops on April 27, 1781, when he was hurrying to oppose the British invasion of Richmond. A month later he followed it in retreating to the N. before Lord Cornwallis' troops.

At **108.1 m.**, within the city of Richmond, is the junction (R) with BELT BOULEVARD, an alternate route of US 1 that bypasses the center of the city and crosses the James River on BOULEVARD BRIDGE (*toll, 10¢*).

At the junction with the Belt Boulevard US 1 swings L. and then R. to Capitol Square.

RICHMOND, 113.4 m. (15-206 alt., 182,929 pop.), State capital (*see VA. GUIDE*).

Railroad Stations. Richmond, Fredericksburg & Potomac R.R., Seaboard Air Line Ry., and Chesapeake & Ohio Ry., Broad St.; Atlantic Coast Line R.R., Main St.; and Southern Ry., Hull St.

Points of Interest. State Capitol, Confederate and Valentine Museums, St. John's Church, St. Paul's Church, and others.

Section 16. Richmond to North Carolina Line, *92.5 m.*

Four lanes wide between Richmond and Petersburg; S. of latter two lanes wide with soft shoulders. Because of heavy traffic, including many busses and trucks, great care must be exercised in driving; passing other cars is dangerous because of the unbanked edges of the pavement.

US 1 S. of the State capitol in Richmond runs through a smoky, hilly, industrial section of the city.

At 21st and Broad Sts. is the junction with State 5 (*see Side Route 3*), which follows the north bank of the James River.

Between the two lanes of US 1 and below their level at **7.3 m.** is an old bridge spanning Falling Creek, near which the first iron furnace in America was built in 1619. This bridge was the work of Col. Claude Crozet, a French military engineer who had crossed the Alps with Napoleon and later came to America to follow his profession. He was a professor of mathematics at West Point and became first president of the board of the Virginia Military Institute; twice he served the State as a highway engineer.

VIRGINIA

At **8.4 m.** is an entrance to the RICHMOND NATIONAL BATTLEFIELD PARK.

Left on the park road **1 m.** is the river bluff on the James River where Capt. A. H. Drewry of the Confederate forces built fortifications that enabled him, on May 15, 1862, to drive back the Union fleet, which was attempting to reach Richmond. Among the Union boats was the ironclad *Monitor*, which had engaged the *Merrimac* at the mouth of the James River two months earlier. The crew of the *Merrimac* were among those manning the guns that greeted the Union fleet. The earthworks are well preserved and the view of the river is particularly fine.

Here along US 1 is a mile-long double row of sodium vapor highway lamps; these were installed in February 1936 by the Virginia Electric Power Co. as a demonstration of this type of highway lighting.

Visible at the side of the highway (L) at **10.9 m.** are parts of the earthworks thrown up for the Battle of Drewry's Bluff of May 14–16, 1864. At this point the Confederate Army under General Beauregard met the Union lines advancing on Richmond from the S. under General Butler and drove them (L) into the "Bottle" created by a bend of the James River.

HALF-WAY HOUSE, **11.2 m.**, is an old-time stagehouse that took its name from its position between Richmond and Petersburg. The side that now faces the road was originally the rear, the road having formerly run a hundred feet or more farther E. During the Battle of Drewry's Bluff the place served as Union headquarters, and the taproom was used by the staff doctors as an office. The house, erected in 1740, has recently been restored to some semblance of its earlier appearance and is again an inn; the log cabin and nearby wellhouse are recent additions, though the well itself has served many generations of travelers. In the early days of the inn notices on the walls announced that the charge for a meal was 15 lbs. of tobacco, while the charge for lodging for both master and servant was 10 lbs. of tobacco. Local tradition is that the mint julep originated in this place. Today modern murals in the dining room depict early traffic on the pike.

At **12.4 m.** is DUTCH GAP.

Left from Dutch Gap on a dirt road **2 m.** is the SITE OF HENRICOPOLIS, a city the colonists in 1613 planned to establish inland as a seat of government and a college. Since the marriage of John Rolfe to Pocahontas the settlers had been at peace with the Indians and felt safe in moving up the river. The town was laid out and construction started on the buildings.

Ralph Hamor, the Colonial secretary, described the town: "There is in this town three streets of well-framed houses, a handsome church and the foundation of a more stately one laid of brick, in length an hundred foote, and fifty foot wide, beside store houses, watch houses, and such like; there are also, as ornaments belonging to this town, upon the verge of this river, five faire blockhouses, or commanders wherein live the honestes sort of people, as in farmes in England, and there keep continuall centinell for the townes security . . ."

Suddenly in 1622 came a concerted and well-planned attack on the white settlements, intended to wipe them out completely. For four years the crafty old emperor, Opechancanough, had planned the attack, all the time professing great friendship for the English. Only a few months before the massacre, however, he sent word to Governor Wyatt that, so dear to him was the peace existing between the English and his people, "the sky should fall" before he broke it. On the morning of the massacre the Indians visited several plantations, bearing gifts of game, and breakfasted with the English in a friendly manner. So skillfully was the affair planned that towns and plantations in the region were attacked simultaneously. The attack on Jamestown failed, but that on Henricopolis resulted in the wiping out of the infant city.

At **13.4 m.** is the junction with State 10.

Left on this well-paved road, which runs through rolling wooded country and fertile fields and crosses the Appomattox River, is HOPEWELL, **8.3 m.** (10 alt., 11,327 pop.), a modern industrial city that has grown up on the site of one of the earliest settlements in the Virginia Colony. This settlement was, with Henricopolis, one of the planned cities of 1613. By 1619 the town had a primary preparatory school for the college being organized at Henricopolis. The massacre of 1622 almost obliterated all signs of habitation. In 1635 the land on which the city now stands was given by royal grant to Capt. Francis Epps, who built a home and named his estate Appomattox Manor. After a time, because the place was at the head of deep water on the James River, a settlement grew up on the Epps land on what became known as City Point; ships from all over the world came to load wheat, cotton, and tobacco and to unload coffee and other foreign products. The development of railroads diverted trade to other places and the town gradually lost importance; it had a temporary revival during the Civil War when General Grant used it as a headquarters and base of supplies in the siege of Petersburg and Richmond. In 1912 descendants of Captain Epps, still in possession of the manor, sold several thousand acres of their land to the E. I. du Pont de Nemours interests as a site for a dynamite plant. The plant, completed in 1914, was used for the manufacture of gun-cotton at the outbreak of the World War, and 29,000 people were working there by 1918. After the war the population dropped back to 1,300, but since that time there has been a steady peace-time growth as one industry after another has reopened the wartime factories or built new ones. Among these are manufacturers of cellulose products, paper products, and china.

At the northern end of the city, on Cedar Lane not far from Broadway, is APPOMATTOX MANOR, containing part of the original house built by the Epps family; the present two-story structure has fretwork trimmings of the kind associated with the General Grant period, a fitting decoration since the house was used by Grant as his headquarters. It was here that he received President Abraham Lincoln and members of his Cabinet in the anxious week that preceded the surrender at Appomattox. The view of the river from the house is pleasantly rural in spite of the nearness of the bustling city.

Right from Hopewell on State 36 **6.1 m.** is the junction with a dirt road; R. on this road **6.6 m.** to MERCHANT'S HOPE CHURCH, built about 1657, in the parish of Martins Brandon. This little brick building, undistinguished architecturally, is peculiarly forlorn in appearance in spite of the efforts that have been made to keep it in repair.

South of Dutch Gap the highway markers commemorating events of the Civil War increase in number because Petersburg was the center of the area in which Lee made his last desperate stand, contending against starvation and discouragement that were causing many desertions from his army, as well as against the superior numbers of Grant's army. From May 1864 until April 1, 1865, the taking of Petersburg, the key supply city, was a main Union objective. Butler had been defeated at the Battle of Drewry's Bluff in May 1864 and bottled up between the James and the Appomattox Rivers. In the following month 1,300 Union cavalrymen made an unsuccessful surprise raid on the city. Beauregard was holding off Grant's army with a small force when Lee arrived with reinforcements. Grant settled down to a siege that lasted nine months; both armies threw up extensive earthworks to the E. and S. of Petersburg, and Grant succeeded but slowly in his attempt to encircle the city. The dead, wounded, and missing on the Union side at the end of these operations numbered 42,000 and on the Confederate 25,000.

At **20.7 m.** is a junction with County 626.

Right on this road **1.5 m.** near Swift Creek is (L) COBBS HALL, ancestral home of Thomas Bolling, where was established, in 1815, one of the first schools for deaf mutes in America. John Bolling, a descendant of Pocahontas, was the first pupil to be educated at this school.

COLONIAL HEIGHTS, **21.1 m.** (2,331 pop.), is a residential suburb of Petersburg.

Along the bluff of the Appomattox River at **22 m.** (R) is OAK HILL, Archer's or Hecter's or Dunn's Hill. A stone marker on the lawn at the end of the block indicates the spot near which Lafayette's artillery is said to have been placed, overlooking Petersburg and the Appomattox River bottom. The gaps in the large boxwood hedge, tradition says, mark the holes through which the guns were trained on the British forces occupying Petersburg.

US 1 crosses the Appomattox River just N. of Petersburg.

PETERSBURG, **22.2 m.** (14-85 alt., 28,564 pop.), an industrial city (*see VA. GUIDE*).

Points of Interest. Old Blandford Church, Seward Mansion, Folly Castle, and others connected with the Civil War.

CENTRAL STATE HOSPITAL, **24.8 m.** (L), was the first hospital in the country established solely for the treatment of mental diseases in Negroes. It was founded in 1869 in temporary quarters near Richmond and moved to its present site in 1885, the land having been purchased and given to the State by the city of Petersburg. Patients work on the farm that provides the institution with part of its food.

At **27.3 m.** is a marker (L) indicating where the Confederate Gen. A. P. Hill was killed on April 2, 1865, at the age of 40. Hill did not know that Lee's line had been broken at last in the siege of Petersburg and rode into a party of Union troops advancing on the city. He had been one of Lee's most reliable young lieutenants and had taken a prominent part in most of the major engagements of the Army of Northern Virginia. His is said to have been the last name on the lips of both Lee and Jackson, on each occasion being mentioned in delirium preceding death.

This section of US 1 follows what was the BOYDTON PLANK ROAD of stagecoach days, a route between Petersburg and an area with springs that were very popular in the days when the fashionable world spent its summers at mineral water resorts in the hills. The sound of the coachman's horn was as familiar to the countryside as was later the whistle of the locomotives, though the sounds had different purposes. The locomotives' whistle was chiefly a warning, but the coachman's horn was advance notice to would-be passengers and to the landlords who were preparing meals; the number of toots indicated the number of passengers who planned to eat at the long tables of the inns. Then, as now, Virginia ham was served at every meal, with corn and other hot breads. In addition chicken, sometimes venison, crackling bread, black bean soup, and many other foods associated with Virginia hospitality were offered.

The junction with White Oak Road is at **31.1 m.**

Right along this dirt road, which was entrenched in the early spring of 1865 when Lee's right rested here. The Union General Warren, attacking Lee's works on March 31, was driven back, but returned with reinforcements, forcing the Confederates to retreat. At FIVE FORKS, **6 m.**, the two forces met on April 1, with overwhelming defeat for the Confederates. The surrender at Appomattox took place eight days later.

DINWIDDIE, **37.4 m.** (237 alt., 200 pop.), is the seat of Dinwiddie Co., formed in 1752 and named for Robert Dinwiddie, at that time Royal Governor of the Colony. The white COURTHOUSE with porticoed front stands on a slight rise facing the highway. In it are preserved a part of the county records that escaped burning and pillage during the Civil War. Diagonally across the highway is a little frame house in which Winfield Scott, later hero of the War of 1812 and of the Mexican War, and General in Chief of the U. S. Army at the outbreak of the Civil War, practiced law before entering the Army.

DEWITT, **41.6 m.**, is a crossroads.

Left from Dewitt on a rough dirt road to SAPONEY CHURCH, 5 m., a small wooden structure in a grove of trees far from any house. It was built in 1726 and is still in use. "Mr. Banister," the minister at Saponey Church, accompanied William Byrd, a leading planter of Colonial times (*see Side Route 3*) on a trip to North Carolina in 1733. At every halt he christened and performed the marriage ceremony for wilderness settlers, sometimes having to marry the parents of the children he was christening. Byrd reported that the settlers were unconcerned over the lack of clergy in their region.

US 1 crosses NOTTOWAY RIVER at **50.4 m.** at the place where Byrd crossed it in 1733 when on his way to inspect his North Carolina holdings; this trip he described in *A Journey to the Land of Eden*. South of the river the party stopped at a plantation where Byrd indulged a penchant by prescribing for the ills of the owner. Lack of physicians in the Colony turned many planters into amateur doctors; Byrd's large library contained copies of most of the current medical books, including some full of quackery. At this stop Byrd called in an old Indian, Shacco-Will, who said he knew the location of a silver mine. Byrd listened without belief, adding in his diary, "To comfort his Heart I gave him a Bottle of Rum, with which he made himself happy, and all the Familey very miserable by the horrible Noise he made all Night."

WARFIELD, **56.1 m.**, is a hamlet that holds the SITE OF BISHOP ASBURY'S EBENEZER ACADEMY, founded in 1793. The school passed out of existence long ago, but was widely known for several years.

At **62.7 m.** is the junction with State 34, an improved road.

Left on this road is LAWRENCEVILLE, 7 m. At 9 m. is the SITE OF FORT CHRISTANNA, founded in 1714 by Gov. Alexander Spotswood as a protection to the settlers against the Indians, though it served other than military purposes. An officer and 12 men were placed at the fort. Their duties were to patrol the district between the Roanoke and Appomattox Rivers and to give warning of any encroachment or hostile movement on the part of unfriendly Indians. All trade with the Indians of southside Virginia was carried on through Fort Christanna. The London Company, which founded the colony, had in its charter as one of the purposes of colonization the propagation of the faith among the natives of the area. This purpose was never entirely neglected and at intervals attempts were made to educate the more friendly Indians with the idea of making them helpful to the colonists. Fort Christanna had a chapel and a school in the shadow of its five cannon. When the fort was abandoned as the frontier moved westward, the school was moved to Williamsburg and became part of William and Mary College.

At 72.3 m. (L) is the SITE OF SALEM CHAPEL, one of the pioneer Methodist churches of the State; it was destroyed by fire about 1870. Francis Asbury described it as "the best house we have in the country part of Virginia." He held four sessions of the Virginia Annual Conference here — in November 1795, April 1798, March 1802, and April 1804.

This section of US 1 runs through sparsely settled, eroded red hills where the woods are young growth and the farms are small. The chief crop is tobacco, but as the highway nears the Roanoke River fields of cotton become more frequent.

SOUTH HILL, 77.4 m. (439 alt., 1,405 pop.), is the third largest bright-leaf tobacco market in the State. Auctions are held almost daily during the selling season, from October 1 to March 1, in four large warehouses, each with its own distinctive name and something of an individual atmosphere. There are also several large drying and rehandling plants, a large stemmery, and modern facilities for handling tobacco of this and other sections.

Before the coming of the railroad, farmers had to haul their tobacco to the Petersburg market in wagons, often taking a week to make the round trip, camping out at night and undergoing many hardships. Now early in the morning scores of springless wagons and automobile trucks, piled high with the golden leaves, come in from the rural districts of southside Virginia and North Carolina. Throughout the day buyers, growers, auctioneers, and others thread their way through the lanes of tobacco "in the loose" on the warehouse floors. The process of auctioning the "weed" is an interesting sight. The lingo used by the auctioneers is understood only by the buyers, who represent the leading tobacco manufacturers. To the

VIRGINIA

uninitiated, it is meaningless jargon. So mysteriously is the auctioning process conducted, a price fixed, and a sale made, that only a few know the quantity of tobacco sold or the price paid. A sign language is used by the auctioneers. The leaves are arranged in rows in large flat baskets, the size of the piles varying according to type. So rapid are the transactions that sales run about three a minute. The buyers are not of the fly-by-night type; they have established their homes here and are well known to the operators of the warehouses.

South Hill is also one of the leading cotton markets in Virginia. A lumberyard on its outskirts is one of the town's chief all-year industries.

Although nearly all business done here during the tobacco selling season is on a credit basis, the growers pay cash for their purchases after they have disposed of their crops. With the opening of the selling season, the town takes on new life; business booms and an air of prosperity prevails.

US 1 crosses the ROANOKE RIVER at 88.1 m. The Roanoke was the first waterway used for transportation to the western part of the State; as early as 1825 there was a well-organized stream of flatboats operating on it between Albemarle Sound and Danville.

The NORTH CAROLINA BOUNDARY is crossed at 92.5 m. The trip of the Commissioners of North Carolina and Virginia to settle this line is commemorated in Col. William Byrd's *History of the Dividing Line*, a lively account of a prosaic undertaking.

Byrd had a poor opinion of the North Carolina Commissioners, reporting that they stayed with the party only until provisions brought from civilization had been eaten up. At the point where US 1 crosses the Virginia-North Carolina Line he reported poor stony soil and weak vegetation. The party was living on wild animals when they could be found, and Byrd reported that "the Paw (of a bear) which when stript of the hair, looks like a Human Foot, is accounted a delicious Morsel by all who are not Shockt at the ungracious Resemblance it bears to a Human Foot."

An Indian "whose Hunting Name was Bearskin," a member of the Saponey tribe who had been sent from Fort Christanna to help the party, was a constant source of interest to Byrd, who questioned him in detail on the life and habits of his fellow tribesmen. It was this Indian who supplied the Commissioners with Indian names for the various creeks and rivers they crossed, some of which have survived.

NORTH CAROLINA

Va. Line — Henderson — Raleigh — Southern Pines — Rockingham — S.C. Line, **180 m.** US 1.

Seaboard Air Line Ry. parallels route between Norlina and Rockingham; Greyhound Line busses follow route throughout.

Paved highway. Hotels in cities and towns; tourist homes, inns, and camps along route.

Section 17. Virginia Line to Raleigh, 66 m.

Between the Virginia Line, **0 m.**, and Raleigh US 1 runs through rolling farm lands and occasional pine and oak forests; here and there is thick undergrowth from which rise such trees as poplar, ash, gum, juniper, and linden.

Bordering the highway are fields of cotton, corn, and tobacco, cultivated by white and Negro tenant farmers. In spring wild flowers bloom in profusion by the roadside, the white blossoms of dogwood contrasting with the tightly closed lavender-to-purple buds of the Judas-tree, while the ground beneath is carpeted with a tangle of honeysuckle vines. During the autumn goldenrod, asters, and gentians flower against a background of brilliant red and tawny golden leaves. The wintry scene is characterized by leafless boughs against a changing sky, except where evergreens break the monotony of grays and browns.

WISE, **4 m.** (389 alt., 265 pop.), named in 1887 for John S. Wise, Governor of Virginia, is a farm village of modest houses, a few stores, and a small hotel, on top of a low hill.

NORLINA, **8 m.** (437 alt., 761 pop.), the second largest town in agricultural Warren Co., was for many years a convenient lunching spot for train passengers. Houses are scattered and the town extends into the fields surrounding the center.

Prior to the Civil War this section of northern Warren Co. produced wheat in large quantities, though few cereals other than corn are planted today. The section is a part of the State's "black belt," populated by descendants of slaves numerous in a region of antebellum plantations. Three families living in this neighborhood are said to have owned a thousand Negroes each.

A predominance of Negroes, except in villages, is immediately noticeable. Their tumbling shacks of split logs and pine slabs are

NORTH CAROLINA

scattered over the countryside; hundreds of them work in the fields.

Operating in this section and throughout the slave States prior to the Civil War were unofficial groups of men known among the Negroes as paddyrollers, who conceived it their duty to check Negroes on the roads at night to catch those without passes, to punish the freed Negroes who became obnoxious or unruly, and to return fugitive Negroes to their owners. This complement to the system of slavery was naturally inimical to abolitionist societies.

The name may have been derived from the fact that paddles were used in administering punishment, the Negroes being bent over barrels for the process. The barrels would roll under impact from the blows; hence, paddle-roller, shortened in southern euphony, became paddyroller.

Another explanation of the derivation is from the word "patroller," a southern colloquialism of "patrol," slurred in Negro patois to paddyroller.

The social status of Negro slaves and ex-slaves, here and elsewhere in the South, depended upon the social and economic status of their white masters. A gentleman planter who owned a thousand slaves imparted to his Negroes considerably more social prestige than that enjoyed by the slaves of a planter whose wealth permitted only a dozen or so. An only slave owned by a poor master was social trash among his own color. Impecunious whites are still referred to as "po' white trash."

Some Negroes continue to bear the names of the families owning their forbears, but many more have assumed surnames that happened to appeal to them. There are white families today that take pride in the number of Negroes bearing their names, regarding it an indication of the families' former wealth.

RIDGEWAY, **10 m.** (415 alt., 250 pop.), is a village of a few small homes in the center of a settlement of prosperous colonists of German descent who intensively farm small plots and raise fine vegetables, berries, fruits, and a variety of cantaloup that takes its name from the community. The Ridgeway cantaloup, developed here by W. L. Baxter and Charles Peter from England, and the Scott brothers from Pennsylvania, has become widely known for its flavor.

These people came to this area under the leadership of a Lutheran minister named Newman. Most of them came from Bavaria, Alsace,

Wurttemberg, or Hesse, by way of New York and Pennsylvania. In the vicinity of Ridgeway they purchased parts of POPLAR MOUNT, a 3,000-acre estate owned by Weldon Nathaniel Edwards and inherited at Edwards' death in 1873 by Marmaduke Hawkins, an adopted son. In 1880 Hawkins negotiated with Newman for the sale of a part of the plantation W. of Ridgeway, and during 1883–85 about 24 families settled there.

"They told us all the good points of the land, and the country, and the climate, and left out the bad," the colonists declared; but by industry and perseverance they were able to reclaim the worn, overworked soil. Knowing nothing of tobacco or cotton culture, and disgusted with the slipshod, unintensive methods of cultivation in the area, the Germans turned to truck gardening and fruit culture, planting vineyards and berry patches. Vine blight injured their plants and prohibition ruined the grape market, but dewberries and later cantaloups became money crops. Since the beginning of the settlement, when most of the colonists spoke no English, the Lutheran Church has been the center of social life in the community. During the early days the pastor acted as interpreter. The church also served as a schoolhouse, and until the children began attending State schools, both English and German were taught. Today church services are in German, except on the second and fourth Sunday mornings of each month, when the pastor uses English. The first generation born in the colony understands the German language but uses it little; members of the second generation are little different from other young North Carolinians.

The colonists have won the respect of their neighbors by reason of their thrift, cooperative spirit, and hard work.

Right from Ridgeway on an unpaved road to POPLAR HOUSE, 4 m., home of Weldon Nathaniel Edwards (1788–1875), member of the U. S. House of Representatives from North Carolina (1815–27). The antebellum house is not noteworthy but the surrounding grounds have hundreds of trees imported from foreign lands prior to the Civil War.

MANSON, 12 m. (428 alt., 70 pop.), is a community of farm houses clustered near a flag station. About 1850 the Roanoke Ry. Co. built a line running from here to Clarksville, Va. During the Civil War General Longstreet sent soldiers who took up the entire railroad and laid it between Greensboro and Danville, Va., in order to transport supplies from western North Carolina to Richmond. Part of the

NORTH CAROLINA 213

road near Manson was rebuilt about 1890 but was not a financial success. Manson was originally called Clarksville Junction. Following a train wreck caused by misread orders, the name was changed to Manson to avoid confusion with Clarksville, Va.

MIDDLEBURG, 17 m. (461 alt., 138 pop.), another farming community, incorporated in 1781, derived its name from the fact that it was midway between terminals of the Raleigh and Gaston Ry. The crossing was formerly known to railroad employees as Mrs. Polly Hawkins' Crossing, this sister-in-law of Governor Hawkins being the largest landowner in the vicinity when the railroad was built in 1840. Another member of the family, Dr. Joseph Hawkins, established a medical school at his home here in 1808. When the house burned in 1923 the skeletons used by the school were still in the closet.

Several granite quarries are operated near Middleburg.

At **18 m.** is the junction with a dirt road.

Left on this road to the ROBIN CARROLL PLACE, 0.5 m., formerly called Pleasant Hill, once the home of Philemon Hawkins, Jr., and the birthplace in 1777 of William Hawkins, Governor of North Carolina (1811–1814). At 6.5 m. is ASHLAND, built in 1746 by Samuel Henderson. At 7.5 m. is the grave of Richard Henderson, Judge of the Crown (1735–85).

At **19 m.** US 1 passes the edge of GRAYSTONE (L), whose name is taken from the color of the granite found nearby. Population fluctuates with mining operations in the quarries, which provide the chief means of livelihood for inhabitants of the village, though much of the work is performed by State convict labor. The stone is used in road construction and to some extent in building.

US 1 passes the PLANT OF THE AMERICAN AGRICULTURAL CHEMICAL CO. (L).

HENDERSON, 23 m. (490 alt., 6,345 pop.), an industrial town in the bright-leaf tobacco belt, is the seat of Vance Co. The business district is small and cluttered but is traversed by a main street of more than average width. Residential streets are shaded and lined with attractive houses in marked contrast with dwellings in most small cotton-mill towns.

Huge warehouses lie dark and still in spring and summer, but in September bustle with activity. Then lunchrooms and cafes, rooming houses and hotels are crowded to capacity as hundreds of farmers arrive, some of them several days before the market opens. By automobile, truck, wagon, and even by cart and buggy, they pour into town. Auctions are held daily except Saturdays, and all markets remain open until Christmas. The larger ones may be open until January or February.

The sale of tobacco at these auctions, as at others, is accompanied by bewildering scenes and jargon intelligible only to warehouses habitués. An expert at judging tobacco tells how it is done: "You pick out a bunch of tobacco from one of the piles and hold it up to your nose, so you can smell it. Then you take one of the leaves and smooth it out nicely so you can see how it is formed. You also feel its texture. Then you shake your head and say, 'It ought to have brought more than that.'" Actually the marketing of the tobacco is a highly organized system. The majority of warehousemen in tobacco-growing sections have been in the business practically all their lives. They have invested large sums in the erection of warehouses and other properties, and since everything they own is tied up in the business they are eager for the farmers to be satisfied.

Henderson was laid out in 1840, when Lewis Reavis gave several acres of land to the old Raleigh and Gaston Ry. At his request, the town was named for his friend, Chief Justice Leonard Henderson. The town grew about the railroad station instead of at Chalk Level to the N., where the Raleigh-Richmond and Salisbury-Hillsboro stagecoach roads crossed.

The city was chartered by the legislature in 1841; the bill as enacted provided that the town should be built upon land within a radius of 1,200 miles, which would have included Maine, Florida, part of Texas, and a considerable section of the Atlantic Ocean. A clerk changed the description to read 1,200 yards, as had been intended.

Vance Co. was formed in 1881 from Granville and parts of Warren and Franklin Cos. It was named for Zebulon Baird Vance, three times Governor of North Carolina (1863–65, 1876–79, and 1879), becoming U.S. Senator (1879–94) early in his third term.

Industries include cotton mills, a fertilizer plant, an automobile factory, and tobacco warehouses.

There is a golf course at the West End Country Club.

In this community John Chavis (1763–38), Negro slave, school teacher, and preacher, lived and taught both whites and Negroes.

Chavis was owned by the Bullock family. Demonstrating early in life his aptitude to learn, he was sent to Princeton University to be educated under Dr. Witherspoon. The story is related that Chavis went to the university as the result of a wager to determine whether a Negro was capable of receiving higher education. His long and useful career attested his unusual qualifications. For many years he served as a Presbyterian minister. Following the Nat Turner rebellion in Virginia, the North Carolina Legislature passed an act making it unlawful to teach a Negro, or any person of African descent, to read or write. Upon the advice of friends, Chavis discontinued his work and was thereafter compensated by the Presbyterian Church. His activities as a teacher and preacher extended, however, over the first 30 years of the 19th century. Children of many prominent North Carolinians attended his school, among them the two sons of Chief Justice Henderson. As a child, U.S. Senator Willie P. Mangum (1831–36, 1840–47, President pro tem. 1842–45, 1848–53), who was also a member of the U.S. House of Representatives (1823–26), was one of Chavis' pupils; another was Charles Manly, later Governor of North Carolina (1849–51). Chavis often preached in white churches. One of these, the Nutbush Presbyterian Church, is still standing at Townsville.

Henderson is the home of the Castello family, former circus riders and show people, whose real name is Loughlin. Three brothers are in business here, but they still give their professional name to their children, since it is enough to guarantee holders a job, or at least a meal, on any circus lot in America. Any local resident can point out the old barn in whose practice ring the family rehearsed on their white horses, chosen because they are easy for the performers to see. The mother of the family was descended from one of the last jesters of the English court.

Henderson's first hotel, now known as the BECK HOUSE, built in 1825 by Lewis Reavis, stands on Young St.

On the courthouse lawn is a marker to the memory of Leonard Henderson, for whom the town was named.

Right from Henderson on State 39, a sand-clay road, is WILLIAMSBORO, 7 m., whose few remaining houses, like its associations, are linked with the past. At the close of the 18th century Williamsboro was a thriving community. From 1820–40 it contained the finest race track in the State. It was just S. of one of the best fords across the Roanoke River, used by wild animals in their migrations;

Indians who found good hunting had called the place the Lick, but the first settlers, arriving about 1740, discovered so many hazelnut trees bordering the stream that they named their settlement Nutbush.

In 1779 Judge John Williams gave all this land to his son-in-law, Robert Burton, who changed the name to Williamsboro. In 1789 Burton had the town chartered, 15 prominent men being appointed to serve as trustees. They laid out the present Main St. 90 ft. wide, crossing the Townsville Road at right angles, and sold lots for six pounds sterling each, the purchasers agreeing to build houses; 75 lots were sold, but only a few houses were built.

Williamsboro was at one time suggested as the site of the State capital, to replace Hillsboro. At another time it received two votes as the proposed seat of the State university, but it was considered too far N. The present TOWN SPRING was originally called Nutbush Mineral Spring.

Here is the SITE OF THE SNEED MANSION HOUSE, built by the Sneeds on one of the early lots. It remained a popular gathering place, especially for members of the legal profession, until about 1860. When court was in session at Oxford, judges, lawyers, and "all that could" came here for relaxation, cockfighting, horse racing, hunting, dancing, card playing, and drinking. This gave rise to the expression "court adjourned to Sneed Mansion House."

Springer College was established here before 1770. It burned in 1830. Williamsboro Academy, under the direction of John Hicks, opened its classes on June 5, 1805. The present building of ST. JOHN'S EPISCOPAL CHURCH was erected during the latter part of the 18th century. It is claimed that brick for the foundation was brought from England. Funds have been raised (1936) to restore this structure.

The present LE MAY PLACE is the house occupied by Bishop John Stark Ravenscroft in 1828.

CEDAR WALK, at the end of a lane on the S. side of Main St., is one of the oldest houses in Vance Co. As Blooming Hope it was the Burton home, built in 1750 by Hutchins Burton for a boarding school. Burton hanged himself from the attic stairway. To this day any unusual noise is attributed to Hutchins Burton's ghost.

1. Left from Main St., at a point half a mile beyond the lane to Cedar Walk, on a dirt road to the SITE OF MONTPELIER, 1 m., home of Judge John Williams. Here about 1757 he conducted a law school said to have been the first such school in North Carolina. The house burned in 1894.

2. Left from Main St. at the Island Creek Baptist Church on a dirt road to BURNSIDE, site of the home in 1760 of Col. Menucan Hunt, first State Treasurer. The present house, on the S. side of Flat Creek, built by Dr. Thomas Hunt, son of Menucan Hunt, has wide plank wainscoting.

3. Right from Williamsboro on a dirt road to the REMAINS OF OAKLAND, 1 m., the summer home, about 1820, of "lordly" Governor (1802-05) Turner. Only the four chimneys remain standing.

At 9.5 m. on State 39 is the DAVE GLOVER PLACE (L), built about 1800 by Dr. Phil Thomas.

TOWNSVILLE, 15 m. (244 pop.), was named for Capt. Joseph Townes, donor of land for a railroad station, though the official spelling now omits the

NORTH CAROLINA

"e." Here is the NUTBUSH PRESBYTERIAN CHURCH, whose congregation was organized before 1754. The present building was erected in 1805. This is one of the white churches that John Chavis, Negro slave, teacher, and preacher, frequently visited between 1809 and 1832.

At **28 m.** on US 1 is BEARPOND.

Left from Bearpond on a gravel road is GILLBURG, **2 m.**, site of the plantation owned by John D. Hawkins in 1820. Some of the old stone slave houses are still standing, though the home of Hawkins was burned in 1905.

At **30 m.** is the ZEB VANCE HIGH SCHOOL (L), named for Governor Vance, who is said to have given a $5 bill to every child named for him, until their number became too great. North Carolina has many citizens who bear the name of Zebulon Vance.

At **30.5 m.** (R) stands KITTRELL COLLEGE (Negro).

KITTRELL, **31 m.** (350 alt., 220 pop.), lies in the midst of flowering fields and rows of evergreens belonging to the CONTINENTAL PLANT NURSERY. The gardens surround the village.

Right from Kittrell on the unpaved Lynback Road to Ruin Creek, **2 m.**, SITE OF POPCASTLE INN, a tavern and gaming house operated from Colonial days until about 1860. Local legend says that the immense log and stone structure, now gone, was built by a European nobleman, a political refugee, but that its second owner, a pirate of great wealth who called himself Captain Pop, gave the inn its name. Gaming pits, a race track, and a bar attracted local gamblers. The captain is said to have buried bags of gold in the neighborhood before his arrest and execution. Records reveal that one William Penner was licensed to operate a tavern here in 1800.

At **33 m.** are the rock pillars (L) that once supported iron trestles of the SAL Ry. over the Tar River. Masons were brought from Scotland in 1840 to build these trestles for the Raleigh and Gaston Ry. At the time it was credited with being the highest railroad bridge in the world. Since the present bridge is higher than the original bridge, the stone pillars are no longer used.

At **35 m.** US 1 crosses TABBS CREEK, a tributary of the Tar, on which John Mask Peace, first known white settler of the region, resided in 1713.

FRANKLINTON, **40 m.** (432 alt., 1,320 pop.), is a cotton textile and lumber mill town whose business district is crowded, sunbaked, and unpretentious. One of the mills manufactures turkish towels. The town is the chief shipping point in Franklin Co. for cotton and fancy bright-leaf tobacco.

Left from Franklinton on State 56 is LOUISBURG, 10 m. (375 alt., 2,182 pop.), seat of Franklin Co. The town dates from 1758. Situated at the "old fords of the Tar" River, it was named in 1764 in memory of the capture of the French fortress at Louisburg, Nova Scotia, by American forces in 1745. The main street follows the old highway from Philadelphia to New Orleans once traveled by John Marshall and other notables. One of the last remaining bands of Tuscarora Indians in North Carolina was exterminated in 1725 at the junction of Lynch's Creek and the Tar River, 4 m. NW. of Louisburg. Skeletons of many of these Indians have been found nearby.

Lumber is the principal manufactured product, from 20 to 30 million ft. being shipped annually.

Louisburg is the birthplace of Edwin W. Fuller, author of *Angel in the Cloud and Other Poems* and *Sea Gift* (published 1873), the latter a novel once so popular at the University of North Carolina that it was known as the Freshman's Bible.

LOUISBURG COLLEGE, situated in a grove of oaks on the summit of the highest hill in town, is a standard coeducational junior college. Chartered in 1855, it was privately owned until 1907, when it was given to the North Carolina Methodist Conference by Benjamin Duke, heir of Washington Duke, into whose possession it had come in 1891. From 1902 to 1931 the college was restricted to the education of girls. Under a plan inaugurated in 1935, students are admitted at reduced fees in consideration of their performing work about the plant.

The MARKER AND DRINKING FOUNTAIN on Courthouse Square was erected by the North Carolina Division, United Daughters of the Confederacy, in 1923 "in appreciation of the fact that the first flag of the Confederacy, 'The Stars and Bars,' was designed by a son of North Carolina, Orren Randolph Smith, and was made under his direction by Catherine Rebecca (Murphy) Winborne. Forwarded to Montgomery, Ala., Feb. 12, 1861. — First displayed in North Carolina at Louisburg, March 18, 1861." Smith's portrait, by Mrs. Marshall Williams of Faison, N.C., hangs in the Governor's mansion in Raleigh.

1. Left from Louisburg **5 m.** on State 561 is the JOHN ALLEN PLACE, where Smith lived when the flag was displayed. This house, one of the show places of the country, contains many pieces of old furniture and interesting relics.

2. Right from Louisburg **1 m.** on State 39 to GREEN HILL HOUSE, where in 1758 Bishop Coke held the first North Carolina Methodist Conference. The structure is still in good condition.

3. Left from Louisburg on State 39–59 at **2 m.** is the junction with a dirt road; on this road is the point where Lynch Creek enters Tar River, **4 m.**, site of the hanging in 1767 of Major Lynch, a British officer commissioned to collect taxes in the frontier Colonies. Because a mob summarily carried out the sentence of a mock court, the term "lynch law" is believed by some to have had its origin here. It is also contended, however, that the term was derived from the proceedings of Judge Charles Lynch, who in 1782 was given immunity by an act of the Virginia Assembly for having illegally fined and imprisoned certain Tories in 1780 (*see Cheraw, S.C.*).

A bridge now spans Lynch Creek near the spot where until a few decades ago stood the oak tree from which Major Lynch was hanged.

YOUNGSVILLE, **46 m.** (451 alt., 395 pop.), is a small village, L. of the highway, with unpaved bumpy streets. Prior to its incorporation in 1875, the town was called Pacific.

WAKE FOREST, **50 m.** (386 alt., 1,527 pop.), is a small community centered by one block of business buildings, with streets bordered by dwarf magnolias and shrubs around old houses that harmonize with the ivy-grown buildings on the wooded campus of WAKE FOREST COLLEGE (Baptist) in the heart of the village. The thousand young men, many of whom arrive in collegiate old cars overflowing with tennis racquets, study lamps, and radios, bring very different equipment from that used by the 16 original students of Wake Forest Institute, chartered in 1833 and opened in 1834. Then an axe and a hoe were required in addition to "two sheets and two towels."

The early school was established by an act that provided for "a college in the Forest of Wake." Wake Co. was heavily wooded and students had to help clear the site. The region is still noteworthy for its fine trees.

The college, which dates from 1838, occupies a 25-acre campus. Its 13 buildings are set among magnolias, oaks, maples, elms, and cedars, giving the impression of an old English park. A border of young long-leaf pines rises above the low rock wall surrounding the entire college green. Besides offering liberal arts courses, the college maintains schools of law and medicine.

In addition to 200 acres in the vicinity, Wake Forest College owns other property of interest. The CALVIN JONES HOUSE, on the western edge of the campus, was built sometime before 1820 on the site of present Wait Hall, where it stood until about 1834. While Dr. Calvin Jones was its resident, he entertained the distinguished people of the day. Dr. Jones owned the tract on which the college stands, having bought it in 1820 from Davis Battle, who probably built the house, which is still in an excellent state of preservation.

The NORTH BRICK HOUSE, built in 1838 by C. W. Skinner just off the northern edge of the campus, has served as the home of President Samuel Wait (1834–45), President William Hooper (1845–49), and Prof. W. G. Simmons.

The SOUTH BRICK HOUSE, also well preserved, was built S. of the campus in 1838 by the Reverend Amos J. Battle.

US 1 between Wake Forest and Raleigh is much traveled by

students going to the city for recreation. Even the college dances are held in Raleigh. In 1936 the student body succeeded in gaining permission to give dances on the campus, but members of the church were so loud in their disapproval that the students voted to relinquish the privilege rather than risk a schism.

At **54 m.** US 1 crosses the narrow and muddy Neuse River, whose falls some 2 miles to the W. operate a cotton mill.

At **57 m.** is the CHEVIOT HILLS GOLF COURSE.

The SITE OF A TAVERN kept by Isaac Hunter in 1788 is at **60 m.** By order of the North Carolina Convention the State capitol was to be ten miles from this point.

At **61 m.** is CRABTREE CREEK, flowing through a wild cool setting of thick green vegetation and tall trees.

At **62 m.**, in suburban Raleigh, is a store (L) where native pottery from the vicinity of Sanford is displayed.

RALEIGH, **66 m.** (363 alt., 37,379 pop.), State capital (*see N.C. GUIDE*).

Railroad Stations. Seaboard Air Line R.R., Southern Ry., and Norfolk Southern R.R., Union Station, Dawson and Martin Sts.; Seaboard Orange Blossom Special, Johnson St.

Points of Interest. State Capitol (*see illustration*), Hayward Mansion, State Supreme Court Building, Birthplace of Andrew Johnson, Shaw University, N.C. State College of Agriculture and Engineering, and others.

Section 18. Raleigh to South Carolina Line, 114 m.

South of Raleigh US 1 swings into the rolling eastern slopes of the thickly wooded Piedmont Plateau and runs through farming country. Cotton, corn, and tobacco are the predominant crops N. of Moore Co. South of Little River the highway skirts a region of peach orchards. This section is "in the clay," its sandy red soil being particularly adapted to fruit growing. Loblolly pine and scrub oak, intermingled with gum, maple, and poplar, are the chief native growths of the Sand Hills, which geologists believe may have been a prehistoric ocean beach.

US 1 turns W. in Raleigh and follows Hillsboro St., becoming at **3 m.** a four-lane highway.

MEREDITH COLLEGE, **3.5 m.** (R), is a Baptist school for girls with a four-year course.

METHOD, **4 m.** (446 alt., 300 pop.), an unincorporated Negro village (L), owes its growth to a Negro educator, merchant, and leader, Berry O'Kelly (d. 1932), who founded the school here that bears his name. Three large brick buildings and a church are included in the plant, the pupils coming from the surrounding country in school busses.

The STATE FAIR GROUNDS, **5 m.** (R), are thronged with approximately 250,000 people each year during the third week in October when, under the auspices of the Board of Agriculture, the State of North Carolina holds its fair. A metal grandstand and concrete bleachers, race tracks, agricultural exhibit buildings, machinery sheds, stock barns, offices, and a hospital are included in the equipment.

The STATE HIGHWAY SHOPS, **5 m.** (R), have a supply depot, garage, and repair shop. Here is the training ground of the State highway police.

At **8 m.** US 1 reaches the outskirts of the village of Cary.

Right from this point on US 70 to the NATHANIEL JONES HOUSE, **2 m.**, a short distance (L) from the highway. The recently discovered diary of Mrs. Nancy Anne Jones, widow of Nathaniel Jones, describes a historical incident of which several differing accounts have been given. The mistress of this house on the old Durham Highway, main thoroughfare of the central section of the State, was accustomed to having distinguished guests. Many travelers between Raleigh and the University of North Carolina at Chapel Hill stopped here, always certain of a hospitable welcome and the famous Jones mint julep. Statesmen, scholars, and soldiers were among her guests; by accident, however, according to the story, one hot summer day in 1838 found the household somewhat unprepared for guests.

The arrivals were Governor Edward B. Dudley of North Carolina and his colleague, Pierce Mason Butler of South Carolina. They were led into the parlor and, after some delay, presented with tall frosted glasses of julep topped with mint. For some reason there was a long delay before the second round arrived and, while members of the household were absent, the maid, Lany, heard the Governor of North Carolina say, "It's a damned long time between drinks," and his companion echo, "Damn long!"

The scandalized maid hurried off to report this to her mistress and the household was thrown into consternation by this seeming reflection on its hospitality. In spite of their efforts to keep the scandal secret, the story leaked out and today the North Carolina Governor's remark is hoary American folklore.

Another version of the origin of the remark has been handed down in the family of John Motley Morehead, Minister to Sweden during the Hoover administration. Morehead's grandfather was Governor of North Carolina in the early 1840's, when a political offender — a white man, not a Negro, as some versions give it — escaped from South Carolina, seeking refuge in the State to the north. Governor J. H. Hammond, a Democrat, asked through the usual legal channels for the man's return. Governor Morehead, a Whig, refused extradition, in part because of the intercession of influential friends of the fugitive.

After much futile correspondence the two officials agreed to meet with their staffs and legal advisers for a personal conference. The place chosen was on the common State Line, not far from Charlotte, N.C. During the discussion Governor Hammond became much excited and finally announced that further refusal on the part of North Carolina would result in his sending a military force across the border to seize the fugitive.

"Now, sir," shouted the Governor of South Carolina, crashing his fist upon the table, "what is your answer?"

"My reply, sir," answered the Governor of North Carolina with great deliberation, "is this: It's a damned long time between drinks."

This unexpected answer had the effect of relieving the tension of the situation, even though it did not immediately settle the dispute. In the atmosphere of tolerance that was created the two Governors were able to talk dispassionately and eventually to reach a settlement satisfactory to both States.

CARY, 8.5 m. (496 alt., 900 pop.), is a farming community with a few tourist camps. The village, which dates from about 1852, was founded by A. Frank Page, father of Walter Hines Page (1855–1918), author, editor, and Ambassador to Great Britain during the World War. The BIRTHPLACE AND HOME OF WALTER HINES PAGE (*private*) is across the railroad tracks from US 1, half a block from Schoolhouse St. The two-story white Colonial dwelling stands in a grove of elms, surrounded by an old picket fence. The story is told that Page as a boy of 12 walked the railroad tracks 8 miles to Raleigh to hear President Andrew Johnson speak.

Right from Cary at a brick filling station on the Reedy Creek Road to an unpainted schoolhouse, 2 m.; R. from this school through a pine forest, where dogwood and other shrubs grow in a tangle of wild phlox and columbine, to the old COMPANY MILL, 2.5 m. Walter Hines Page laid some of the scenes of his novel, *The Southerner*, in this neighborhood. The old mill that appears in the story was owned by the author's grandfather and was operated as a powder mill during the Civil War. Standing on the bank of Crabtree Creek beside a dam, the structure is in good condition, its overshot wheel intact after 100 years. The millstone, however, lies crumbling on the floor.

Through the woods in front of the mill are marks of an old trail, probably not Cornwallis' route to Hillsboro, as local legend says, since maps fail to bear out the supposition; more likely it is part of the old Ramsgate Road cut by Governor Tryon on his way to quell the Regulators. Boy Scout cabins and a swimming pool now occupy the space in the woods about the mill. The site is part of CRABTREE CREEK PARK, a 60,000-acre national recreation and demonstration area.

APEX, 16 m. (504 alt., 863 pop.), received its name in the early 1870's when a survey for the Raleigh & Augusta Ry. showed it to be the highest point on the right-of-way between Norfolk and Sanford. The railroad was later absorbed by the Seaboard Air Line. The town gained some attention, after North Carolina had adopted prohibition in 1907, through the activities of the Baldwin gang, which used the place as headquarters for distributing liquor run in from "wet" Virginia by a fleet of fast automobiles. Once a tobacco market, Apex is now only a trading center for the neighboring farm section.

MERRY OAKS, 24 m. (245 alt., 179 pop.), is a rural settlement in the red clay belt, named for the forests of majestic oaks that dominate the region. Inhabitants believe that early settlers held merry gatherings under them.

At **26 m.** the route crosses the HAW RIVER, which cuts down through the north central part of fertile Chatham Co., across a hilly and broken region where the hills attain the elevation of small mountains and the scenery takes on a rugged aspect seldom found in the Piedmont. This is a region of swift-flowing streams, Rocky River, Robinson Creek, and Bear Creek furnishing power for many small mills that grind the large quantities of wheat grown here. US 1 here passes through cotton growing country, but this represents the agricultural interest of only a small strip of Chatham.

MONCURE, 27 m. (145 alt., 144 pop.), is a farming village in a cotton, tobacco, and grain-growing region.

At **27.5 m.** US 1 crosses DEEP RIVER, which flows from the E., a narrow stream winding its tortuous way through green valleys. Its high abrupt banks in places become hanging cliffs with a drop of 100 ft. or more. Deep River is bordered by productive bottom lands, much of the area being covered with oak and pine forests. Rabbits, squirrels, and birds, as well as larger game, make this region a favored hunting ground.

Deep River flows into the Haw River a mile S. of Moncure, their confluence forming the Cape Fear River.

LOCKVILLE, **41 m.**, formerly known as Ramsey's Mill, was the scene of a British encampment after the Battle of Guilford Courthouse. General Cornwallis' troops remained here only long enough to build a bridge across Deep River.

At **42 m.** the highway crosses a boundary line that was in part erased in 1907 when Lee Co. was finally created from Chatham, Harnett, and Moore Cos. Known as the LORD GRANVILLE LINE, this boundary was famous from the beginning of the settlement, since it was the generally accepted line separating the Scottish Highlanders in Cumberland Co. from the English.

Established in 1746, the line marked the extent of the grant given Lord Granville by King George II. From the Virginia boundary it ran S. to parallel 34° 35′ longitude, the old line continuing to divide Moore Co., formed in 1734, and Chatham Co., formed in 1770. It is still the boundary line between several counties lying to the E. of Lee Co.

Although the line was evidently determined by chance, it separates the rich clay hills of the northern part of what is now Lee Co. from the sandy lands of the long-leaf pine belt to the S. The Lord Granville Line is still well known to the older inhabitants, being recognized in old records and title papers of this region.

From the days when William Byrd wrote *The History of the Dividing Line*, through the years when citizens waged local battles for a unit of government whose seat should be within a half-day's journey of every settlement, the establishing of lines and boundaries has been an important matter to the people of the State. Even today disputes over local boundaries, those between farms and pasture lands, for example, are among the chief matters coming up in county courts.

SANFORD, **46 m.** (359 alt., 4,253 pop.), seat of Lee Co., is on the edge of the pine belt bordering the Sand Hill section of the State. The trading center for four adjacent counties, Sanford has several blocks of business section, somewhat smoky and dusty because of trains, and the cotton mills huddled close together near the railroad crossing. Loads of tobacco and cotton en route to the warehouses give the streets more animation during autumn and early winter. Wide streets bordered by attractive homes standing on well-kept lawns characterize the residential section.

Sanford is in the heart of the pottery district extending through Lee and Moore Cos., where descendants of the Staffordshire potters who settled here 200 years ago continue this craft. The NORTH STATE POTTERY is one of the largest and best known in North Carolina. Smaller potteries, operated by the old time kickwheel and using mule-power grinding mills, are in the vicinity. Here is the HOME OF THE LATE CHARLES D. McIVER, founder of the Woman's College of the University of North Carolina at Greensboro.

STATE CAPITOL, RALEIGH, NORTH CAROLINA

STATE HOUSE, COLUMBIA, SOUTH CAROLINA

NORTH CAROLINA

The town was settled by English Protestants, French Huguenots, and Scottish Presbyterians, the latter predominating in rural districts over the county.

At **47.5 m.** is the junction with a country road.

Right on this road to the old BUFFALO PRESBYTERIAN CHURCH, **100 yds.**, the white building gleaming through a grove of fine oaks on the site of the first church, organized in 1796. It was the farthest N. of the churches formed by the Scottish settlements on the Cape Fear River and its tributaries.

CAMERON, **57 m.** (300 alt., 300 pop.), is one of the largest dewberry markets in the world. The community hums with activity while this crop is being marketed during the first weeks of May. The town ships by truck and rail to northern markets an average of 60,000 crates of berries yearly. Since legalization of alcoholic beverages, the demand has increased and prices have risen.

At **61 m.**, along the side of the highway (L), is VASS (317 alt., 602 pop.), likewise a dewberry market. The town, which has a cotton mill and a furniture factory, grew up in the 1870's when logs were floated down Little River, thence by the Cape Fear River to Wilmington. The place was known as Winder until 1907, when the present name was adopted to honor a railway executive.

At **62 m.** the route crosses LITTLE RIVER, leaving the comparatively level lands of upper Moore Co., where the surface is usually wet, orange clay, and entering the dry, white rolling ridges of the Sand Hills. South of Little River is an area with many peach orchards. Forests here are thinner, and trees seem shorter than those in more northerly regions of the State. Short-leaf North Carolina pines give way to the lighter green, long-leaf variety. Sand dunes, long since left bare by the sea, are covered with the pines. Everywhere is evidence of the planting of long-leaf pines to increase their number.

The region abounds with fox, raccoon, opossum, squirrel, rabbit, quail, and dove. Many deer stray into this region from the Fort Bragg Game Refuge. Several non-resident sportsmen maintain private game preserves in this area.

LAKEVIEW, **63 m.**, is an unincorporated village of filling stations, tourist camps, and picnic grounds lining US 1 and overlooking small CRYSTAL LAKE, beyond which, on a sloping green hill, is a white-painted resort hotel. There are no bath houses.

In the section to the E. is the U.S. military reservation at FORT

BRAGG, largest field artillery reservation in point of acreage in the Nation (*see N.C. GUIDE*).

At **72 m.** is SOUTHERN PINES (519 alt., 1,500 pop.), whose golf courses, with those of nearby Pinehurst (*see N.C. GUIDE*), attract the foremost professionals and amateurs of the country. The atmosphere is unusually mild, dry, and invigorating, average winter temperature being 55° and snow very rare. In the winter season the town's normal population swells to about 5,000. *Gymkhanas* (tournaments) are among the winter diversions; there are facilities for riding, tennis, archery, and other outdoor sports.

Southern Pines centers around the landscaped railway station. Broad St. runs parallel with the railroad tracks, the two-way boulevard being separated from them by a parkway with magnolia trees, pines, and blossoming shrubs. Here are gift shops, book stores, newsstands, specialty shops, sand-clay tennis courts, and a motion picture theater. In the early years of the town, which was incorporated in 1887, 20 public-spirited women with the tradition of prim New England gardens behind them organized a Village Improvement Society to remove stumps from this main street.

Exploitation of the climatic conditions, coupled with the adaptability of the Sand Hills to peach-growing, eventually helped to develop this region of pine barrens into an asset to the State. The original settlers, who arrived in 1774, cultivated the creek bottoms; among these immigrants were Flora Macdonald, Scottish Jacobite heroine, who appears in many songs and stories, and her husband, who returned to England in 1779. As the descendants of the early immigrants increased in number the fertile sections were too small to support them and many left, parts of the area reverting to near-wilderness. Hillsides were clothed with blackjack oak and second-growth pine, the "spindling successors of one of the noblest hardwood forests of America."

Later lumbering was the chief industry until the timber was exhausted. Then railroads stood idle for a time for lack of freight. Planters tried growing cotton, then tobacco; peach growing proved the solution of the problem.

The writers' colony of Southern Pines claims as its founders James Boyd, author of *Drums*, a historical novel with a North Carolina setting, and his wife, who induced Katherine Newlin Burt, the novelist, and Struthers Burt, novelist and essayist, to join them.

NORTH CAROLINA

Other members of the colony are Lawrence B. Smith, author of hunting and fishing stories; Walter and Bernice Gilkyson, short story writers; and Almet Jenks and Maude Parker, contributors to national magazines.

ABERDEEN, 76 m. (500 alt., 1,382 pop.), is a trading center and shipping point for the growers of tobacco, vegetables, and fruit of this section of the Sand Hills. The town has made little attempt to attract tourists.

Aberdeen is the present home of the Page family, A. F. Page, a miller by trade and father of Walter Hines Page, having emigrated from Wake Co. and built a dam and lake W. of the town. This family built the railroad line that is now part of the Norfolk Southern. Originally called Blue's Crossing for a family of turpentine manufacturers and railroad builders, the town became known as Aberdeen when it was incorporated in 1893. Many of the early settlers of the region were Scottish. Aberdeen Creek was known as Drowning Creek in early days.

As in most of these peach-growing regions, local housewives who wish to buy fruit for home canning are offered shipped products from other States, at almost prohibitive prices. Practically their only glimpse of native fruit comes from loaded trucks speeding to northern markets.

Left from Aberdeen on a paved route, the old Pee Dee Road, to the old BETHESDA CHURCH, standing in BETHESDA CEMETERY, approached through a wrought-iron arched gateway, 1 m. (*admission by permission of Mrs. Belle Pleasants, whose residence (R) is 100 yds. from church*).

Old Bethesda Church, a rectangular white clapboard structure with cupola and spire, erected in 1850, preserves its old slave gallery intact. At the end of the Civil War a part of General Sherman's army encamped in and around it.

With a congregation organized in 1790 by the Philadelphia Presbytery, the first church, built in that year, was little more than a brush arbor standing in the 50-acre tract granted by King George III to John Patterson in 1766. Rose bushes near the church are said to have grown in the yard of the Patterson home, which is no longer standing. Early services were held in two languages because many Scottish settlers spoke only Gaelic. A church built in 1832 served until the present building was erected.

The congregation has long since outgrown the austere little structure. Members have been worshipping for years in a much larger brick structure in Aberdeen. Only on Homecoming Sunday, usually the first Sunday in October, is Old Bethesda used, though occasionally special exercises are held there. On this day some former members and their families travel great distances for the reunion. Arriving in automobiles, and wearing clothes in the latest modes, homecoming throngs step back in spirit to the generation to which the church belongs. They sing old hymns to the accompaniment of a hand-pumped organ. Former pastors and members speak to the assemblage. Then family picnic baskets yield a feast of fried chicken, potato salad, pickled peaches, and an imposing array of pies, among other delicacies. Reminiscences begun around the picnic cloth continue throughout the afternoon as the older people walk about the churchyard.

The TOMB OF WALTER HINES PAGE bears a slab of gray granite inscribed with his name and the dates: August 15, 1855–December 21, 1918. Page, who became ill at his post in London during the closing weeks of the World War, was rushed to his home in Pinehurst, where he died shortly afterward. His body, originally placed in the new cemetery to the S. of the church, was moved across the narrow road and placed under a clump of trees that is surrounded by a low rock wall.

Beneath the cedars in the older part of Bethesda Cemetery, behind the church, lie crumbling, crude, and brown-stained monuments to early settlers. One is inscribed:

"1798
HERE LIES THE
CORPS OF ISBEL
BUCHAN
MEMO-MENTO"

Another reads:

"In Memory of
COLIN BETHUNE
(an honest man)
a native of Scotland
by accident, but a citizen of
the U. S. from choice
who died
March 29, 1820
Aged 64 years.
His dust must mingle with the
ground
Till the last trump's awakening
sound
It will then arise in sweet
surprise
To meet its saviour in the
skies."

PINEBLUFF, 80 m. (307 alt., 289 pop.), which failed to prosper after its establishment as a winter resort, now presents a somewhat deserted appearance. A few scattered houses, many of them winter residences, occupy the wide streets. Since there is no business district, the village resembles a rural community. Promoters erected a large hotel, which was later unprofitably converted into a club offering accommodations to northern visitors. Since 1935 it has been used as a sanatorium for chronic alcoholics.

At **84 m.** US 1 crosses the LUMBER RIVER and runs through the Sand Hills into the North Carolina and South Carolina flatlands. Unlike most of the Sand Hills, this is a region of dark pine forests and darker cypress swamps; the cypresses are draped in vines and Spanish moss. It has been called "a shadowy underworld, lost to the sun; a world of sorrowful twilight, remote, unreal, and lifeless," silent except for the chattering of blackbirds, the caw of distant crows, and the roar of motor cars on the highway.

HOFFMAN, **88 m.** (335 alt., 569 pop.), is in a low and sparsely settled section of the Sand Hills where flowers and shrubs bloom throughout the winter. The village, named for a large landholder in this region, was settled by Scottish-Irish, German, and Swiss immigrants. Cotton and corn are grown here, but peaches are the chief product. A large platform where this fruit is sorted stands close to the SAL Ry. track. A sand-clay road leads into the orchards E. and W. of the platform. Several modern dwellings, two stores, a filling station, and the small houses occupied by Negroes who work in the orchards compose the village.

MARSTON, **92 m.** (335 alt., 125 pop.), lies in the peach-growing section of the Sand Hills where the soil is also adapted to such crops as melons, peanuts, and sweet potatoes. Negroes make up almost half the population.

ROCKINGHAM, **102 m.** (211 alt., 2,906 pop.), seat of Richmond Co., lies on a pleasant plateau surmounting a hill. Established in 1785, it was named for the Marquis of Rockingham, who befriended the Colony before the Revolutionary War. Many of the inhabitants are descendants of original settlers, and the corporate limits of the town are practically the same as when it was laid out.

Although Rockingham has retained the air of another generation, it has modern facilities and wide well-paved streets. It lies in a rich agricultural region where corn, tobacco, melons, and garden produce are grown. The county has a million peach trees. Cotton nevertheless constitutes 75 percent of the output of the farms, and cotton raising is a "Negro-and-mule" job.

Rockingham is also an industrial center. The 10 mills in the region employ white operatives exclusively. Their work ends on Friday, and they have normally spent most of their money by Saturday afternoon, when certain streets of Rockingham are given over to the Negroes.

The Negro population of the Rockingham area is almost equal to the white. Since the Negroes live largely on the cotton plantations, where the land is level, the rows are long, and the summer sun is scorching, public opinion in Rockingham is agreed that part of the town should be theirs one day a week. Very few of them fail to be in Rockingham on Saturday. White people by common consent usually stay off the streets the Negroes frequent for trading, gossiping with their friends from other plantations, and learning to imitate the urban Negroes. The carnival spirit prevails as entire families stroll about in their best clothes, perhaps stopping for crackers, a box of sardines, and a bottle of pop at some cafe where a blaring radio has replaced the old-fashioned phonograph. But there is a serious side to the occasion. All these Negroes are sharecroppers; in cotton-picking time they must learn the price of cotton and the prices other planters are paying for labor, so they can hold their own in bargaining.

RICHMOND COUNTY COURTHOUSE stands upon a beautifully landscaped bluff E. of the business district. In the public square is a CONFEDERATE MEMORIAL erected in 1930 by the United Daughters of the Confederacy.

US 1 runs southward, E. of and parallel with Pee Dee River, to the South Carolina Line, **114 m.**

SOUTH CAROLINA

N.C. Line — Cheraw — Camden — Columbia — Aiken — Ga. Line, **171 m.** US 1.

The highway between Cheraw and Columbia is paralleled by the Seaboard Air Line Ry., and between Columbia and Batesburg by the Southern Ry.
Route paved throughout.
Accommodations of all kinds available at short intervals, with hotels chiefly in cities.

Section 19. *North Carolina Line to Columbia,* **96 m.**

US 1 traverses the central section of South Carolina, an area of deep sandy ridges with sparse and stunted vegetation. Short-leaf pine and blackjack oak are the chief trees. For years this was the most poverty-stricken section of the State, redeemed only by the fall-line cities and the few towns that were settled mainly as resorts. Now many acres are devoted to profitable orchards and fruit farms.

The highway crosses the Big Pee Dee River, passing through an old covered bridge, the only one on US 1. Each piece of wood was cut and numbered, its place being determined in advance of the building. During the extreme high water of the spring floods the bridge is impassable.

CHERAW (Ind., *fire town* or *place of the tall grass*), **10 m.** (145 alt., 3,575 pop.), was settled by Welsh emigrants from Pennsylvania in 1735. The town was carefully planned and remains beautiful today. Its distinctive charm is created by its division into large blocks with broad streets. Each street is planted with four rows of shade trees.

The large number of trees in Cheraw is owing to an old town law that required anyone seen intoxicated on the street to go to the woods, bring back a tree, and plant it.

The first white settlers in the area made their homes at the head of navigation on the Big Pee Dee River. The land they occupied formerly belonged to the Cheraw Indians, hence the name of the town. When upper South Carolina was divided into districts, the section in which the town was situated became the District of the Old Cheraws.

The term "lynch law" is said to have originated at Cheraw during Revolutionary times (*see also Louisburg, N.C.*). Col. Charles Lynch of Lynchburg, Va., had been named Judge Advocate to serve at courts-martial for Gen. Nathanael Greene, whose camp was nearby. So arbitrary were some of the decisions of Colonel Lynch that the expression came to indicate the passing and execution of sentence without trial.

Capt. Moses Rogers, commander of the *Savannah*, which in 1819 completed the first trans-Atlantic crossing under steam, came to live in Cheraw after the *Savannah* was destroyed by fire. He commanded a steamer plying up and down the Big Pee Dee River between Cheraw and Georgetown during the days when this was an important river-shipping point for both North and South Carolina. In 1823 he built his own steamer, the *Great Pee Dee*, but on the first voyage down river he contracted yellow fever and died aboard ship. The GRAVE OF CAPT. ROGERS is in the St. David's Episcopal Churchyard. River freighting was a prosperous business at the time, a total of 135,000 bales of cotton being shipped from the town in 1825.

Old ST. DAVID'S EPISCOPAL CHURCH, 1st and Church Sts., named by early Welsh settlers for the patron saint of Wales, was built between 1770 and 1775. In the churchyard are buried soldiers of seven American wars. The church was used by British soldiers as a smallpox hospital in the Revolutionary War, and 50 of those who died here are buried in one grave in the yard. Also in the churchyard is a CONFEDERATE MONUMENT, one of the first erected.

Baptist and Presbyterian congregations of the community, about 1820, disputed over which was to hold services in St. David's Church. Once when the Baptists were holding services there, the Presbyterians loaded and fired an old Revolutionary cannon, to the consternation of the Baptist preacher, who hurriedly dismissed the congregation. Later the Episcopal Church claimed the building, and the Presbyterian minister, who was responsible for the cannon episode, wrote: "While the lion and the unicorn were fighting for the crown, up came the puppy dog and knocked them both down."

The OLD MARKET HALL, Market and 2nd Sts., built in 1836 for the town hall, is now used as the city court.

The MCKAY HOUSE, Kershaw and 3rd Sts., an ante-bellum home, was built in 1822. Here Lafayette was entertained in 1825 when he visited Cheraw.

The HARTZEL HOME on McIver Ave., built in 1790 of hand-hewn lumber, is of southern Colonial design. It was used as personal headquarters by General Sherman in 1865.

A sign (L) indicates the entrance to the 700-acre CHERAW STATE

PARK (*free*). The main road diverges into walks and drives through the wooded hillsides and valleys. A 10-acre lake, cabins, a barbecue pit, camping grounds, fishing, boating, and swimming attract tourists to the park. The 5,148 acres of the adjoining CHERAW RECREATIONAL AREA are now being developed. Around a 300-acre lake, camps of various sizes are to be built, planned to provide suitable recreational facilities for tourists, social service groups, clubs, and the like. A wildlife sanctuary at the head of the lake and a game preserve are also on the program. There will probably be a small up-keep fee for the use of this area.

From PATRICK, **24 m.** (223 alt., 250 pop.), is shipped more tar, rosin, pitch, and turpentine than from any other manufacturing point in the State. One of its three naval stores plants is the largest of its kind in South Carolina.

At HIGHTOWER, **29 m.**, is the junction with the Ruby-Hartsville Road.

Right on this improved road at **5 m.** a dirt road leads (R) to SUGAR LOAF and HORSESHOE MOUNTAINS, two curious formations. Sugar Loaf, cone-shaped, is probably the highest sand mountain of its shape harboring a growth of timber.

At **36 m.** is the intersection with State 95.

Right on State 95 is the newly planted pine forest of the SAND HILL AGRICULTURAL DEMONSTRATION PROJECT, **9 m.** (L). At **10 m.** (R) is the SAND HILL NURSERY.

McBEE, **38 m.** (473 alt., 500 pop.), is a fruit growing and shipping center.

At **44 m.** is the ford on the old INDIAN TRAIL crossing BIG LYNCHES RIVER, which divides Chesterfield and Kershaw Cos. A peculiarity of the three channels of the Big Lynches is that in the E. and W. channels the water flows southward toward the junction with the Big Pee Dee, while in the middle channel it flows northward to connect with the E. channel.

A POTTERY PLANT (R) a few hundred yards W. of the bridge, produces hand-made flower pots, bowls, pitchers, jugs, and churns from a fine clay found near the Big Lynches. The proprietor often takes time to demonstrate the dexterous coordination of hands with the turns of the potter's wheel required in the formation of pleasing shapes.

BETHUNE, **45 m.** (476 alt., 522 pop.), a shady and restful town, has a hotel and tourist cabins.

Kershaw Co., organized in 1798 and named in honor of Col. Joseph Kershaw, a Revolutionary leader and founder of Camden, has an area of 673 sq. m. Its northern part belongs to the Piedmont Plateau, with red hills, red clay sub-soil, and outcroppings of superior granite. A fine grade of cotton is produced in the county. The middle region is in the Sand Hill Belt, a part of the Coastal Plain, and is adapted to the culture of peaches and grapes. The southern part, in the river terrace region of level, rich, alluvial land, is subject to occasional overflow in the river valleys. In this region are large and excellent plantations. US 1 follows the border of the fall-line through slightly rolling lands, with occasional settings of pecan orchards.

At **61 m.** (L) is the CAMDEN AIRPORT.

CAMDEN, **64 m.** (222 alt., 5,183 pop.), a winter resort (*see S.C. GUIDE*).

Railroad Stations. Southern Ry., E. DeKalb St.; Seaboard Air Line Ry., Gordon and Chestnut Sts.

Points of Interest. Pantheon; Courthouse, Presbyterian Church (*see illustration*), and Monument to DeKalb, all designed by Robert Mills; "King" Haigler Weathervane; Iron Man; and others.

The FOREST TREE NURSERY, **67 m.** (*open*), jointly maintained by the State and Federal Governments, edges the highway (L). This is the first and smaller of the experimental projects in this State to conserve lands through reforestation. The larger plant was established near Georgetown in 1934. These nurseries utilize the services of the Civilian Conservation Corps. In 1935, 15 million forest tree seedlings were here made available for planting 15 thousand acres of denuded lands.

A dirt road leads from the nursery grounds.

Left on this road to an INDIAN MOUND, **1 m.**, about 30 ft. high and 75 ft. square at the base. Some excavations have been made.

From the basin of the Wateree, **68 m.**, US 1 climbs to a high ridge of the Sand Hills. On both sides lie troughs and crests of ancient shore lines with their growths of scrubby blackjacks and stunted pines. Here and there among the ranges are ponds fed by springs or wet-weather streams. Dotted about are the cabins of the real Sand-Hillers, hybrids often of Negro, Indian, and white strains. In the past these people, like the blackjacks and the pines, have barely managed to exist on what seemed to be nature's waste lands. The unpainted cabins that lie in coves between the ancient sand dunes are unequipped with modern conveniences, not even stoves for cooking. Many of the inhabitants are victims of pellagra. In recent years, however, science has discovered the potential values of these barren sands; new fertilizing formulas introduce inert plant foods, with the result that various commercial crops — grasses, grains, peaches, and grapes — are now being produced.

The SAND HILL EXPERIMENT STATION (R), **81 m.** (*open*), is a joint Federal and State agency, under immediate control of Clemson College, seeking through research and practical experimentation to improve the productivity of lands of this region. The plant, established in 1926, has 887 acres of sand lands, excellent buildings, and a chemical laboratory. The experiments cover horticulture, dairying, field crops, and soil fertility. Field and laboratory experiments and cooperative experiments with farmers in other sections, are carried on. This station has already done much toward making the desert bloom. Along the highway orchards of peaches and grapes, producing luscious fruit, are evidences of the beginning of the conquest of this desert.

At **91 m.** is the junction with a dirt road.

Right on this road to a large WHOLESALE MULE MARKET, **1 m.**, which supplies from six to eight thousand mules a year to concerns in three States. The stock is bought from country dealers in the mid-western stock-raising States.

An almost unbroken line of residences flanks the highway for some distance N. of Columbia, on the western edge of Richland Co. The county was founded in 1785, and within its area anything from the finest cotton to the finest peaches, berries, melons, grains, and grasses can be produced.

COLUMBIA, **96 m.** (312 alt., 51,581 pop.), State capital (*see S.C. GUIDE*).

Railroad Stations. Southern Ry. and Atlantic Coast Line R.R., S. Main St.; Seaboard Air Line Ry., Gervais and Lincoln Sts.; Columbia, Newberry & Laurens R.R., 630 Wayne St.

Points of Interest. State House (*see illustration*), Confederate Monument, Statue of Washington, Trinity Church, University of South Carolina, Governor's Mansion, Woodrow Wilson Home, and others.

Section 20. *Columbia to Georgia Line,* **75 m.**

US 1 between Columbia and Aiken continues to follow the fall-line, the demarcation between the Piedmont and Coastal Plain areas of South Carolina. Owing to the dry, sandy nature of the soil, for many years the chief vegetation of this Sand Hill section consisted of scrub oaks and stunted pines enlivened occasionally by blue lupine or other small, hardy flowers.

When Washington traveled over this route in 1791 he commented: "The whole road from Augusta to Columbia is a pine barren of the worst sort, being hilly as well as poor." Today instead of pine barrens there are peach orchards, grape vines, pecan groves, acres of ferny asparagus, cotton, corn, and numerous vegetable patches. Unsightly posters and signs rather than the land provoke unfavorable comment today from travelers.

US 1 runs westward from Columbia on Gervais St., crossing the CONGAREE BRIDGE, completed in 1927, below the junction of the Saluda and Broad Rivers. Named in honor of the Battle of Lexington, Lexington Co. is primarily an agricultural region of small farms and little tenancy. Early settlers were mostly Germans, industrious, thrifty, and cooperative.

NEW BROOKLAND, 1 m. (243 alt., 1,722 pop.), is largely a residential town, being rapidly built up by people who commute to Columbia daily for work in the cotton mills.

US 1 crosses the neck of HORSE SHOE POND, 2 m. (R), notable for the fresh-water sponges on its bottom. It is said to dry up every seven years. Recently, owing to flocks of wild ducks that stop here when immigrating, the pond has been put under protection of the State Game Warden.

The GREEN HILL TOURIST CAMP, 3 m., occupies the unmarked site from which Sherman's artillery shelled Columbia on February 16, 1865.

LEXINGTON, 12 m. (359 alt., 1,152 pop.), is largely residential. On the eastern approach is a unit of a large MILL system (*open to public*).

At the intersection of US 1 and State 6 in Lexington is a MONUMENT to the soldiers, sailors, and marines of the World War.

1. Right on State 6 to LAKE MURRAY DAM, 5 m., one of the largest earthen dams in the world.

2. Left on State 6 is the village of RED BANK, 4 m., which has a TEXTILE PLANT (*open to public*), producing high grade prints and employing 400 to 500 people. At 9 m. is a KAOLIN MINE.

SOUTH CAROLINA

Between Lexington and Batesburg US 1 continues along a thin strip of the Sand Hill, with the Piedmont on one side and the Coastal Plain on the other; Lexington Co. has parts of the three distinct areas into which the State is divided and its natural resources are consequently diversified. This county contains more than half of Lake Murray; granite, the only mineral of commercial importance, is quarried at Cayce; boxes, baskets, brick, fertilizer, flour, caskets, monuments, cotton goods, and cottonseed oil are manufactured; in addition large quantities of lumber are cut.

The ever-present quantities of vegetables, grain, berries, melons, peaches, and pecans brought from Lexington Co. to the Columbia curb market have given rise to the saying that "Lexington County feeds Columbia."

At LEESVILLE, **29 m.** (656 alt., 1,340 pop.), is a casket factory. The division between Leesville and Batesburg is negligible; a joint public school is on US 1 between the two towns.

BATESBURG, **31 m.** (660 alt., 2,839 pop.), has the highest elevation in the county. A casket factory is operated here also.

The course of US 1 between Batesburg and Augusta cuts through a corner of Saluda Co., skirts the edge of the one-time prominent town of MONETTA, **37 m.**, and traverses the W. central Sand Hills of Aiken Co. North of Aiken, the county seat, the hills are steep and the scenery picturesque. Along the way are occasional handsome old country homes, some of which cater to tourists.

Aiken Co. was formed from Barnwell, Edgefield, Lexington, and Orangeburg Cos. in 1872, and is one of the largest and most noted in the State. The soil is a light friable, varying from a light sandy to a deep fertile loam. The main products are asparagus, cotton, corn, melons, oats, sugar cane, and fruits. Large annual shipments of hogs, chickens, peanuts, and potatoes are made. Lumbering is a major industry. Here are kaolin mines and many textile mills.

AIKEN, **59 m.** (527 alt., 6,025 pop.), tourist resort (*see S.C. GUIDE*).

Points of Interest. Handsome homes, including Edgewood and Let's Pretend.

HORSE CREEK VALLEY, which US 1 traverses S. of Aiken, has sacrificed much scenic beauty to industrial development. Between a point 4 miles N. of Aiken and Hamburg runs a zone of fine sedimentary clays 6 miles wide with beds 5 to 45 ft. deep. There is a reserve, according to the U. S. Geological Survey, of 120 million tons of high grade kaolin and the largest and purest sedimentary clay deposit in the United States. About 30 mines and 7 refining plants are regularly in operation, employing 1,200 or more people. Throughout the valley is a network of textile mills.

The toes of each town in this valley seem to tread upon the heels of the next, and the distinct limits of the many-operation corporations are difficult to define.

At WARRENVILLE, 64 m. (222 alt., 300 pop.), is the intersection with a good unpaved country road.

Right on this road is GRANITEVILLE, 2 m. (215 alt., 2,560 pop.), where William Gregg, called the father of southern cotton manufacturing, established the Graniteville mill in 1848. From the first this factory made money, and it was operated successfully throughout the Civil War. Gregg came to South Carolina from what is now West Virginia in 1824. Within ten years he amassed a substantial fortune as a watchmaker and silversmith in Columbia. He then moved to Edgefield, where he became interested in a small, struggling cotton factory, Vaucluse, which, with his brother-in-law, he bought and put on a paying basis. He moved his residence to Charleston in 1843, becoming a partner in a jewelry business there but continuing his interest in cotton manufacture. He interested Charleston capitalists in the idea of southern cotton manufacturing and was able in 1845 to secure the charter for his Graniteville mill, capitalized at $300,000.

Gregg had definite economic theories which he both published and practiced. He believed that plants should begin with adequate capital, be self-sustaining, and have a surplus over local needs, which would make for a sounder system. He traveled extensively in New England and European textile centers and wrote articles for the *Charleston Courier* which were collected and published in pamphlet form.

On the same road is VAUCLUSE, 5 m. (289 alt., 900 pop.), where today there is still a unit of the Graniteville company mills.

In LANGLEY, 67 m. (172 alt., 1,688 pop.), are several kaolin plants.

BATH, 69 m. (170 alt., 1,250 pop.), has textile mills and clay mines.

HAMBURG, 75 m., once an important town of the Southeast, is now a mere hamlet on US 1 on the South Carolina side of the Savannah River. It was the northwestern terminal of the Charleston-Hamburg Line of the South Carolina R.R. Over this, one of the early American railroads, the locomotive, *Best Friend*, on alternate days struggled to pull its load.

SOUTH CAROLINA

In times when the value of bank notes was questionable, scrip from the old Hamburg Bank was readily accepted. During the Reconstruction period the Hamburg Riot of 1876 started the chain of events leading to the Red Shirt organization and the restoration of white supremacy in the State. At **75 m.** is the Georgia State Line, the Savannah River, which is crossed on a free bridge.

GEORGIA

S.C. Line — Augusta — Waycross — Fla. Line, **222.5 m.** US 1.
Paved surface throughout. Cattle and pigs a hazard.
Hotel and tourist accommodations vary from poor to excellent.

Section 21. South Carolina Line to Florida Line, 222.5 m.

In its 222.5-mile course in Georgia, US 1 S. of Augusta passes through only one town, Waycross, with a population exceeding 2,500. The highway traverses a rural section that is the locale of two outstanding works of modern fiction: Erskine Caldwell's novel, *Tobacco Road*, from which the record-breaking play was adapted; and Caroline Miller's Pulitzer Prize novel of 1933, *Lamb in His Bosom*. In the extreme southern part of the State, US 1 skirts the Okefenokee Swamp, a favorite laboratory for naturalists.

Between Augusta and Louisville the highway follows an old Uchee Indian trail, which later became a stagecoach route. Before the Civil War this region was a part of the old plantation belt, slave labor being abundant to cultivate the large farms. Charm and mellowed grace linger about the old homes, some of which date back almost to the Revolution, but more in evidence is the unpainted shack of the sharecropper, with sagging porch and paneless windows.

Winding through the low red clay hills, US 1 bisects fields of white cotton, which grows to a height of about 3 ft. In late August and September, groups of barefoot Negroes, with red bandannas or wide straw hats on their heads and burlap sacks slung from their shoulders, bend low over the stalks and pick the soft staple from the boll. When the sacks have been filled, the contents are dumped on large sheets at the end of the rows.

Between the fields of cotton, grain, sugar cane, and peanuts are farmhouses, some of them shakily balanced on rock supports. Here and there are wells with windlasses and oaken buckets, rusty plantation dinner bells on tall poles, and bee-martin gourds swinging from crosspieces on tall posts. These gourds furnish a nesting place for the small martins that keep the hawks away from the chickens. Frequently the porches are boarded up to hold the loose cotton that is piled there until enough for a bale has been picked. Instead of planting grass on their lawns, the housewives sweep the yards clean with a bundle of small branches; but even the shabbiest house is brightened

PRESBYTERIAN CHURCH, CAMDEN, SOUTH CAROLINA

TURPENTINE DISTILLERY, GEORGIA

OLD SLAVE MARKET, LOUISVILLE, GEORGIA

SOUTHERN GEORGIA PLAINS

with petunias, zinnias, and geraniums growing in the yards and in tin cans on the porches.

A measure of prosperity is reflected in new houses, fresh paint, and new farm implements. Gleaming against the sky from the roofs of many houses and barns are new lightning rods, some adorned with glittering colored balls, others in three-branched effect like the devil's fabled pitchfork, all evidences of faith in the shining, twisted strands of metal running down into the earth.

Since cotton is still the principal money crop, Georgia farmers suffered from the low price cotton brought for many years; five-cent cotton spelt ruin to them. Even when the Federal Government pegged the price to 12 cents through loans, and though it sometimes rose to 15, returns did not always meet production costs.

Below Swainsboro US 1 stretches through the Piney Woods or Wiregrass section, which is pervaded by a strange silence and an air of remoteness. The last part of Georgia to be developed, it was opened in the mid-19th century by small-scale farmers from the Carolinas, who were attracted by the lumber of the pine forests. Relatively few Negroes live in this country, and the land is worked by independent owners whose obscure heroism is celebrated by Caroline Miller's *Lamb in His Bosom*.

The towns have developed somewhat in recent years, since tobacco has been grown on a commercial basis. The production of cigarette tobacco on a large scale was introduced into Georgia after 1915 as a means of crop diversification in the pine barrens section because of the impoverishment of the soil by the growth of cotton. In 1936 the planter received approximately 21¢ a pound for his tobacco.

As a result of better drainage and improved sanitation, malaria and hookworm, which were prevalent in the lower part of the State, are to a great extent under control.

AUGUSTA, 0.5 m. (143 alt., 60,342 pop.), winter resort (*see GA. GUIDE*).

Railroad Station. Southern Ry., Atlantic Coast Line R.R., Georgia R.R., Charleston & Western Carolina Ry., Georgia & Florida R.R., and Central of Georgia R.R., Union Station, Walker St., opposite Barrett Plaza.

Points of Interest. The Hill, University of Georgia School of Medicine, Junior College of Augusta, Paine College (Negro), Haines Institute (Negro), Cotton Exchange, Ware's Folly, Meadow Gardens, and others.

Startling religious signs mark the highway near Augusta. These thickly clustered signs were erected personally by David Brinkman, a young evangelist of that city. Most of the texts give admonitions disconcerting to the motorist: "Prepare to Meet Thy God," "After Death the Judgment," and "Because There is Wrath, Beware."

At **15 m.** is the junction with the Bath Road.

> Right on this road is BATH, **0.5 m.** (400 alt., 17 pop.), a small village, formerly known as Richmond Bath, which was settled in the early 19th century as a summer resort because the cold, clear water of the spring supposedly possessed medicinal properties. During ante-bellum days this retreat of wealthy planters was celebrated for its old mansions and bountiful hospitality. When malaria in low-lying Burke Co. caused "third-day chills and fever" many families fled here for safety.
>
> Most of the old homes have been burned; only the decaying MANSE and the well-preserved PRESBYTERIAN CHURCH remain. The white clapboard church was designed by the architect, James Trowbridge of Boston, and built about 1820. The pulpit and pews were made by hand, and in the NE. side of the church is the old slave gallery with its side entrance. The original bell hangs in the square steeple.
>
> For eight years, beginning in 1843, the Reverend Frank R. Goulding served as minister; in the manse next door, now crumbling and weather-beaten, he wrote *Young Marooners*, and tried to perfect a sewing machine before Howe patented his invention. He failed, however, because he did not place the eye of the needle near its point.
>
> In the churchyard is the BATH CEMETERY, its oldest stone bearing the date September 20, 1816.

At **31.3 m.** (L) is the ABRAHAM (or ABRAM) BEASLEY PLACE (*private*), an excellent example of the pioneer Georgia home, probably built soon after the Revolutionary War. There is no proof of the exact date because all Jefferson Co. records were destroyed by Union troops during the Civil War. The old house, now in a state of disrepair, is of the "dog-trot" type, an evolution of the earliest log house. The two rooms are connected by a roof that covers an open space known as a "breezeway" or "dog-trot." It is built of heavy hand-hewn timbers held together by wooden pegs. The great logs were crudely squared and evened, the beam running along the roof of the front porch being a solid piece of timber 60 ft. long. The house is occupied by descendants of the original owner.

WRENS, **33.3 m.** (468 alt., 1,085 pop.), was established in 1884, when the tracks of the Augusta Southern R.R. were laid. The founder, **W. J.** Wren, inherited the land from his grandfather, John

Wren, who, according to local tradition, had acquired it in exchange for two blind horses. Though predominantly agricultural in its interests, the town has several planing mills, a flour mill, and a cotton gin.

At the eastern edge of town stands POPE HILL (*private*), a house erected about 1850, where Jefferson Davis as a prisoner of Union forces was allowed to stop for breakfast. The exterior is covered with wide clapboards painted white; although the front has been considerably altered by the addition of a porch and porte-cochère, the outlines of the original small stoop can still be seen in the paneling on both sides of the front door. Until the railroad was built, the residence served as an inn and a relay station where stagecoaches changed horses.

Wrens was a boyhood home of Erskine Caldwell, who is known for *Tobacco Road, God's Little Acre,* and numerous short stories, including *Kneel to the Rising Sun,* all dealing with the tenant farmer. With his father, a Presbyterian minister, Caldwell visited the country people throughout the section, and noted the manner in which the sharecroppers live. When challenged for his presentation, Caldwell replied: "It is no more obscene than life." Most Georgians, however, contend that the conditions described are less general than his work implies.

Tobacco Road is the name of a dirt road that runs along a ridge from northern Georgia to a point on the Savannah River below Augusta. Over this road tobacco was hauled in mule-drawn hogsheads to the port where it was loaded on boats.

At **35 m.** (R) is the OLIPHANT HOME (*private*), a plantation house with slave quarters, built between 1820 and 1830. The master's house is a story-and-a-half structure of wide clapboards with a center hall flanked by two high-ceiled rooms; later rooms have been added on each side of the front porch. The kitchen, originally standing some distance from the house, has been moved nearer the back porch. From the rear of the big house a lane leads between the double row of slave cabins, which are sagging and weather-worn but held intact by their massive stone chimneys. The old gin house still remains on the plantation. Although Sherman's men burned nearby houses on their March to the Sea, they left this place unharmed because, the story is told, the mistress of the Oliphant house was courteous to the Federal soldiers and had food prepared for them.

At 42.3 m. (R) is the J. J. Norton home, known as the OLD WHIGHAM PLACE (*private*). An original grant in the possession of the Whigham family shows that the land was owned by that family in 1790, and it is believed that the house was built shortly afterward. A gaunt, high-standing frame structure, it lacks the grace of the Greek Revival, the predominant architectural style of the better houses of the Old South. A one-story porch juts from the front, and a kitchen ell from the side. Massive end chimneys dwindle to narrow, tall flues above the roof. After having remained in the hands of the Whigham family until 1910, the place became a pecan market catering to the tourist trade.

At 46.3 m. (L) is the GOBERT HOUSE, built between 1796 and 1800 by Benjamin Gobert, a political refugee from France. The one-storied frame house is of comfortable appearance, with a steeply sloping shingled roof, and double doors opening on the wide front porch. The interior has wide clapboard ceilings, and chair moldings about the wall. Only the main part of the house and a few old magnolia trees are still standing.

LOUISVILLE, 48.2 m. (337 alt., 1,650 pop.), seat of Jefferson Co., was for a time Georgia's capital. Having been at Savannah, the seat of government was moved temporarily to Augusta when Savannah fell into the hands of the British. Louisville was laid out in 1783 on a thousand-acre tract purchased by the State. The first statehouse was completed in 1796 in time for a session of the legislature, and the last session held there was in 1805, after which Milledgeville became the capital. The COUNTY COURTHOUSE, built from materials of the statehouse, now occupies the statehouse site.

On Broad St., at a point where two Indian trails intersected, stands the old SLAVE MARKET (*see illustration*), built in 1758 before Louisville was founded. Hand-hewn posts support the roof, which is approximately 20 ft. square. The market bell, which had been sent in 1772 to a convent in New Orleans as a gift from the King of France, was captured by pirates and sold at Savannah, where it was bought for the Louisville market. In addition to giving notice of slave sales, it warned settlers of Indian attacks and called them together for sheriffs' sales after the incorporation of Jefferson Co. This is said to be the only slave market in the South still standing as originally built.

In front of the courthouse, facing E. Broad St., stands the YAZOO FRAUD MARKER, indicating the place where the Yazoo papers were burned on February 15, 1796, after an impressive ceremony in the presence of the Governor and members of both houses. Speculative companies had bought from Georgia 15,500,000 acres of land, lying in the present States of Mississippi and Alabama, for less than two cents an acre. A state-wide wave of indignation caused the passage of a legislative act to rescind the sale and to destroy all records of the transaction.

Tradition has handed down a dramatic story of the event. While the crowd stood with uncovered heads, a white-haired man, known to no one present, galloped up, dismounted, and proclaimed that he had come to see justice done. Saying that no earth-born fire, but rather fire from heaven, should destroy the works of iniquity, he drew a sunglass from his pocket and held it over the pile of wood that had been assembled until smoke began to rise. Then he vanished, and was seen no more.

One of the landmarks of Louisville is the old GARVIN HOME (*private*), corner E. 8th and Screven Sts., which was built by Dr. Philip Scott about 1840. The house, constructed on square lines with veranda columns rising to a second-story roof, has now fallen into decay. About it stood many outbuildings and slave cabins, and interspersed with tall trees were quantities of mimosa, flowering pomegranates, and figs.

In the Louisville City Cemetery, on W. 7th St., is a tall granite monument marking the GRAVE OF HERSCHEL V. JOHNSON, Governor of Georgia, a superior court judge, and candidate in 1860 for the Vice-Presidency of the United States.

Near the cemetery is a small granite marker on the SITE OF LOUISVILLE ACADEMY, chartered in 1796; it was one of the earliest educational institutions in the State.

At frequent intervals along the highway or in the small towns are cotton gins, barn-like structures usually made of wood or corrugated sheet iron. (The word "gin" is a corruption of the word "engine", which was applied to Eli Whitney's invention.) In the fall, wagons and trucks filled with cotton stand in line before each of the large gins, and the wagons are driven in turn under the metal suction pipe that draws the cotton into the gin. There, by means of rollers or saws, the white lint is separated from the seed; the lint is then compressed by power presses, covered with jute bagging, and fastened with steel bands. The seeds are blown through pipes into a seed house, from which they are sold to refineries for use in cooking oils and other kitchen products. The hulls and the "cake" from which the oil is pressed are sold in large quantities for cattle feed and fertilizer. After baling, the cotton is stored in warehouses until it is sold.

SWAINSBORO, 78.7 m. (350 alt., 2,422 pop.), seat of Emanuel Co., was incorporated in 1854. Advantageously situated at the intersection of US 1 and US 80, the town is expanding rapidly, and many new stores, public buildings, and residences have been erected. Among the industrial plants of the town are sawmills, planing mills, cotton gins, turpentine stills, machine shops, and warehouses. Hogs, chickens, turkeys, and goats are marketed in large numbers.

Emanuel County was created in 1812 and named for David Emanuel, Revolutionary soldier and Governor of Georgia. Covering 1,000 square miles, it is so large that its citizens often speak of it as the State of Emanuel. Its rolling terrain is particularly suited to the growing of cotton, bright-leaf tobacco, sweet potatoes, corn, nuts, sugarcane, hay, and velvet beans. This variety makes possible a four-year program of crop rotation promoted by the county. The area also produces large quantities of naval stores.

LYONS, 107.6 m. (275 alt., 1,445 pop.), seat of Toombs Co., was chartered in 1897. Tobacco, cotton, and corn are cultivated on the surrounding farms, and timber lands are extensive in the area.

The big-stemmed Jersey potato is raised here in large quantities for the New York market. New Jersey formerly supplied the market with this product. Later Maryland, farther S., realized that it could raise these potatoes and, because of its earlier spring, reach the market before New Jersey. Virginia in turn superseded Maryland, and now Georgia has entered the competition. This variety of sweet potato, though akin to the yam, is stringy and not a favorite with Georgians.

Left from Lyons on a dirt road is the STATE PENITENTIARY, 17 m. This model prison was constructed under supervision of the P.W.A. for the State and the Prison Commission of Georgia. Outwardly this massive but dignified white concrete structure with modern lines has the appearance of a handsome manufacturing plant or office building. With a frontage of 1,020 ft. and a depth of 842 ft. it contains eight units and can care for 2,000 prisoners. Above the two fluted columns of the simple but substantial entrance is a panel in bas-relief by Julian Harris, sculptor, portraying various activities, including industrial phases of work in which the prisoners engage. The units on the right are for white prisoners and those on the left for Negroes. Centering around the central tower on the upper floors are cell blocks of a maximum degree of security. Ranging outward from these are cells of varying degrees of security, approaching minimum security in those farthest away from the center. Young boys throughout are segregated from the more hardened criminals.

Much care has been taken in the design of the kitchen with its cold storage facilities and laundry equipment. There are four mess halls for the prison population, two for Negro and white help, one for the guards, and one for the warden and his staff. Placed strategically about the various units are sleeping quarters, accommodating 75 guards, in close contact with the warden's office and signal room. There are two large recreation fields for exercise under close supervision.

Since the prison is almost completely isolated, the plant was designed as a self-contained unit. There is ample storage space not only for daily but also for emergency needs. Spare parts for all mechanical equipment are kept in stock. Engines and dynamos are so placed that they will be entirely separate and safe from the approach of any of the inmates. Among the equipment are a telephone system, a signal system, and a siren whistle to be used in the event of an escape.

There is a 980-acre tract of land, surrounding the prison and adjoining the old State prison farm, for cultivation in food crops by the prisoners. In a rear unit are machine shops where the convicts can learn trades.

The plans and specifications of the building were reviewed by the U.S. Bureau of Prisons, and the building is said to be one of the most modern of its kind. Over a period of years the State is to pay 70 percent of the cost, the Federal Government giving 30 percent. The building has been erected at a cost of $1,281,980; equipment will bring the total to $1,500,000.

BAXLEY, **138.4 m.** (210 alt., 2,122 pop.), seat of Appling Co., is a town of neat homes, good churches, and the usual small-town business houses. Being in a section that was developed late, it was not incorporated until 1875. In recent years, however, good transportation facilities have made it a marketing and shipping center. The county now produces lumber, tobacco, naval stores, pecans, and syrup, as well as garden plants and evergreen shrubbery.

Two warehouses provide ample marketing facilities for the tobacco growers of the surrounding district. During the market season, which lasts for three or four weeks in late summer, the farmers bring their golden aromatic leaves to the red brick or corrugated metal warehouse, where they pile them neatly on the floor. The sharp odor is stifling in the sweltering air of the warehouse. As the auctioneer goes from pile to pile, he rapidly calls prices in a staccato manner unintelligible to the layman, and the buyers signal their competitive bids. When the season is over, buyers move on to the North Carolina markets, and the people of the town settle down again after the period of bustling activity.

The turpentine stills are also of interest. Resin from the slashed pines is here converted into hard rosin and crude turpentine. A large copper kettle of crude resin is heated gradually, and the hot vapors escape through the condensing worm, which is cooled by a stream of water. The unpainted frame sheds are crowded with barrels of amber-colored rosin, and the loading platforms are gummed with resin drippings.

The dross, chips of pine wood covered with inflammable rosin, is gathered and sold for kindling. With a few handfuls of dross and a few fat pine splinters, the poorest wood and hardest coal can be made to blaze quickly.

Caroline Miller was living here in a small green cottage when she wrote *Lamb in His Bosom*. With no formal education beyond high school training and with a background limited to Georgia, she set about writing a novel of her own section. Bumping over the country roads in her little car, she bought chickens, eggs, and vegetables from the farmers to enable her to talk with them. Mrs. Miller was about 30 years old and the mother of three small sons when she received the 1933 Pulitzer Prize for her first published work.

Southern Georgia is not a rich man's country and the farmer is the backbone of the area. In the latter part of the 19th century the forests of this section were devastated by the lumber industry, but now the once barren cut-over pine land, ugly with decaying stumps, has been developed into farms. The recent drainage of stagnant water and sluggish streams has added much to the healthfulness of the section.

ALMA, 156.7 m. (195 alt., 1,234 pop.), is the seat of Bacon Co., an agricultural area with the crops and industries characteristic of this section.

As the highway approaches Waycross, the farmhouses become neater, many being painted and provided with electric lights. Each has its flower plot in front, vegetable garden to the side or rear, some pecan trees for nuts and shade, and a few cattle to provide milk and beef for home consumption.

Throughout the Wiregrass section the poorer tenant farmers are often satisfied with the "piney woods" cattle and razorback hogs, inferior animals that are allowed to roam and graze as they please. Through the efforts of the State Department of Agriculture and other agencies, the farmers are being encouraged to improve their livestock by proper breeding, care, and sanitation. When a traveler complains

GEORGIA

of the pigs in the road, a south Georgian may answer proudly, "Yes, but look how nice and fat they are. You don't puncture your tires the way you did when you ran over a razorback."

HEBARDVILLE, 180.4 m. (148 alt., 309 pop.), centers around the CYPRESS CO. MILL, which has a daily sawing capacity of 150 thousand ft. Timber is cut from the nearby cypress swamps and hauled by rail to this place, where it is sawed and planed.

WAYCROSS, 183.4 m. (140 alt., 18,063 pop.), a fairly new town, is given an appearance of age by the large oaks that grow along its streets. This clean and well-paved city has a progressive appearance, to which the trim parks lend dignity. The city owes much of its development, as well as its name to its being at the converging point of nine railroads and five highways.

In 1818 settlers began to claim the land near Kettle Creek, now a part of Waycross, and wherever they settled, they built blockhouses and fortifications for protection against the Indians. By 1825 the land had been acquired from the Indians and was granted to individuals under a lottery system. The land lottery system originated in Georgia in the early 19th century after the disposal of the lands lying W. of the Chattahochee River. Staking the future of Georgia on people instead of on lands, the officials of the State determined that land should be disposed of in small tracts free of charge. Governor Troup expressed the policy in these words: "Men and the soil constitute the strength and wealth of the nations, and the faster you plant men, the faster you can draw on both." According to this policy the land was surveyed and charted into parcels, generally of 212.5 acres, and offered to the public through lotteries, each citizen having one chance and heads of families, two chances. Since there were more citizens than parcels of land in every lottery, many people drew blanks.

As late as 1870, however, the town was merely a railroad junction with 50 inhabitants and a few scattered houses; but within the span of one generation it has become an important trading and commercial center of southern Georgia. Because the early settlers were very religious, some people have insisted that the name means Way of the Cross. When Frank L. Stanton, Georgia poet and journalist, visited the town in 1888, it was considered the holiest place in the State. He wrote of it that the citizens went to church "six days a week and six times on Sunday." Attendance at a Trinity Methodist Church service inspired him to write his poem, *The Love Feast at Waycross*. Today 15 white and 24 Negro churches provide places of worship.

Throughout a belt 75 miles wide, beginning at Savannah and running through Waycross to Bainbridge, bee culture has come to be so extensive that Georgia leads the South in the production of honey. The blossoms of the tupelo tree provide a heavy amber-colored honey, and the small white blooms of the gall-berry bushes give a clear, almost white, variety. The Waycross industry is owned by J. J. Wilder, who has 8,500 colonies of bees in 300 apiaries.

Among the industries of the city are the production of naval stores and the marketing of furs brought from the Okefenokee Swamp; the city has two planing mills, a pecan-crushing plant, two tobacco warehouses, and a casket factory. Local tobacco growers take their tobacco leaves to the two large warehouses to be hung on long racks to dry; in the 1935–36 season, 3 million lbs. brought $826,000 to Waycross.

The Georgia Hide and Fur Co. is the largest exporter of furs and alligator hides in the State. Among the skins are those of bear, wildcat, otter, raccoon, opossum, skunk, and muskrat, the prices ranging from $1 for the wildcat to as much as $50 for the otter. Most of these pelts are obtained from the Okefenokee in the winter by the same trappers who hunt for alligator hides in the summer. The alligator hides are marketed at prices ranging from 75c for two-foot hides to $4.80 for six-foot hides.

The MUNICIPAL ROSE GARDEN, on Plant Ave. between State and Gilmer St., is well cared for by the Waycross Rose Society and the Park and Tree Commission. The average yearly temperature of 65° permits flowers to bloom the year around.

The ATLANTIC COAST LINE R.R. SHOPS, on US 1 at the southern limits of the city, are the largest shops of this company. Covering many acres of land and representing an investment of $3,000,000, the shops employ hundreds of skilled mechanics and laborers. In connection with the shops is a diversion yard, where numerous fruit and vegetable cars are sent for icing and rerouting. Cars of cattle from southern ranges and products of southern fields are shipped from here to the markets of the Nation.

Right from Waycross on State 50 is WINONA PARK, **3 m.**, which contains a large lake surrounded by tall pines. With its beautiful winding drives it is a popular recreation center for the citizens of Waycross.

GEORGIA

The varied types of soil of this section produce corn, sugarcane, peanuts, beans, cantaloups, watermelons, pecans, grapes, peaches, and pears. The pineapple-pear, which has a sweet taste somewhat like that of the pineapple, is considered best for canning.

RACEPOND, **203.4 m.**, is a station on the Atlantic Coast Line R.R. It is said that the settlement received its name from the race track built around a cypress pond. During the Seminole War, soldiers were sent here to capture the Indians who had hidden in the great swamps of the Okefenokee. Having much leisure, the soldiers built the race track to enable them to race horses for their own amusement.

FOLKSTON, **218.2 m.** (80 alt., 506 pop.), seat of Charlton Co., is the home of Dan Hebard, who controls the Hebard Lumber Co.

Right from Folkston on an unnumbered dirt road that runs into the OKEFENOKEE SWAMP (*see Side Route 4*).

At **222.5 m.** US 1 crosses the ST. MARY'S RIVER, which is the Florida Line.

FLORIDA

Ga. Line — Jacksonville — New Smyrna — Fort Pierce — West Palm Beach — Miami — Key West, **568 m.** US 1, US 1-Alt., and State 4.

Florida East Coast Ry. between Ga. Line and Florida City and Atlantic Coast Line R.R. between Ga. Line and Miami parallel route.
Hard surfaced; few curves. Cattle a hazard, especially at night. Dangerous railroad crossings near Jacksonville.
Accommodations of all kinds, chiefly in cities.

Section 22. Georgia Line to Jacksonville, 37.9 m.

Between the St. Mary's River and Jacksonville US 1 passes over the eastern edge of the Trail Ridge, the watershed of the peninsula, for approximately eight miles. From here the Ridge section slopes into the flat woods area of northeast Florida. Few people live in this section of the State, and except in the three small towns, few houses are seen along the route. There are dense hammock lands along the river at the northern end of the route, and evergreen pinelands border the highway.

From the white concrete bridge spanning the ST. MARY'S RIVER, 0 m., an excellent view is afforded of the deep narrow stream and its wooded banks. All types of bay vegetation grow along the water's edge, the sweet and black gum, magnolia, swamp holly, poplar, several varieties of oak, elm, ash, willow, cedar, and some slash pine. Bamboo vine, yellow jessamine, Virginia creeper, and wild grape enmesh the trees and cling to some of the shrubs and underbrush. Here mistletoe is found clinging to the black gum, and palmettos grow in profusion. Prickly ash, elbow, and hurrah bushes are common. Flood tides have cut deeply into the high banks of the river and many of the trees droop precariously over the water.

Usually the St. Mary's is a peaceful little stream exhibiting temperament only in swirls and eddies as it twists and turns through the semitropical forest; but after a period of rains the river becomes a raging torrent lashing at the trees and shrubs along its banks. During these times the normal depth of eight ft. at the bridge increases to 18 or 20 ft.

The drab coffee-colored water was formerly in demand by the masters of four-riggers and tramp steamers docking at Fernandina,

FLORIDA 253

because of the length of time it retained its flavor when placed in casks. Regular trips up the river were made by ship chandlers to obtain the water, which sold for one cent per gallon.

Several hundred feet from the bridge a HUGE ARCHWAY has been erected by the Jacksonville Motor Club. The name "Florida" appears at the apex cast in iron. Just S. of the archway (R) is a small granite MONUMENT commemorating Robert E. Lee; the bronze plaque states that this highway, here called the Dixie, is dedicated to his memory.

CRYSTAL SPRINGS, **0.1 m.** (L), a popular picnic and camping ground, is named for a small sulphur spring. The same telltale white film and odor indicating the presence of this mineral, are found at many Florida springs. A large tourist camp occupies nearby grounds. A PRODUCE INSPECTION STATION is beside the highway; all produce entering the State must pass inspection.

In places along the route clay is seen in the otherwise sandy loam. Dense growths of oak, gum, bay, and hickory, with the usual lesser types of hammock vegetation, shade the road. Here and there are pine thickets and cypress ponds. The undergrowth of the drier regions consists of saw palmetto, gall-berry, and wire grass. At the forest's edge are many native grasses and herbs. Wild flowers grow profusely in all seasons of the year. A dense section of flat pinelands is passed, in which many of the trees have been "streaked" for the extraction of turpentine. Several large stills are in the vicinity, though none of them is seen from the highway.

HILLIARD, **7 m.** (66 alt., 312 pop.), is a village serving a considerable rural area in which the livelihoods of the inhabitants are derived chiefly from the production of naval stores, from truck farming, and from timber cutting. The town has been a trading post since the early 1800's but there was little growth until the present highway was built.

The construction of a large mill here in 1881 by the Hilliard and Bailey Lumber Co. was also of importance. The place was named for one of the firm's members. At that time the Savannah, Florida & Western R.R. connected the place with Kings Ferry, where the timber, cotton, and other products of the area were shipped N. by boat.

Consisting mainly of a group of filling stations, a few homes, and stores, Hilliard caters to the thousands of tourists who pass through here annually. Since the repeal of prohibition several merchants in the town have profited by the sale of alcoholic beverages, Hilliard being the nearest village on this heavily traveled highway to Georgia which is legally a dry State.

The King's Highway, once a post road between New Smyrna and Savannah, Ga., passed near here; between this point and Jacksonville US 1 follows the old route.

Except for an occasional filling station, few signs of habitation are seen S. of the town, the entire region being a monotonous stretch of flat woods. Even flat woods, however, have their charm, for the pines are richly colored in deep green and dark brown, and the moist coolness of these trees enriches the air with a pleasant fragrance. Had Caroline Miller lived here, the setting for *Lamb in His Bosom* would have required little change.

CALLAHAN, 18 m. (20 alt., 637 pop.), a compact rural town, derives its revenue from the chicken farms and sawmills nearby. Truck farming is the major industry of the back country. Settled early in the 19th century by traders and farmers from southern Georgia, Callahan's growth is restricted by its nearness to Jacksonville, though the latter city provides a ready market for the former's produce. Callahan is one of the two incorporated municipalities in Nassau Co. The town shows an urban aspect, having modern homes, stores, and hotels.

Pine thickets prevail S. of Callahan but scrub oak and bay vegetation are occasionally seen. White enameled wire or picket fences have been erected along the highway at the edges of the many small brooks and streams to safeguard motorists.

At 20.5 m. (R) is a large outdoor swimming pool drawing the patronage of Callahan residents.

Much of this land is under State forest service protection and occasional watchtowers are visible from the highway. For nearly 15 miles the route is bordered by tall broom grass, which is used by the natives in making crude brooms. Commercially this type of broom grass is used as a filler in regular brooms, and two factories in Jacksonville buy thousands of pounds of it annually.

At 24.6 m. double railroad tracks are crossed (*no watchman or signal lights*).

DINSMORE, 25.5 m. (26 alt., 178 pop.), is the popular dairying center for Jacksonville. Large pastures with dairy herds are seen N.

FLORIDA

and S. of the town. Massive oaks and magnolias shade the highway, softening the prosaic appearance of the scattered homes, stores, and gasoline service stations. Several roadside inns specialize in preparing chicken dinners.

The number and frequency of houses and truck farms become greater as Jacksonville is approached.

JACKSONVILLE, **37.9 m.** (26 alt., 129,549 pop.), largest city in the State (*see FLA. GUIDE*).

Railroad Station. Atlantic Coast Line R.R., Seaboard Air Line Ry., Southern Ry., Florida East Coast Ry., Union Terminal, 1000 W. Bay St.

Points of Interest. Naval Stores Yard, Municipal Docks, Cotton Compress, Municipal Power Plant, Hemming Park, Confederate Park, Memorial Park, Municipal Zoo, and others.

Caution. Six railroad tracks cross US 1 a block within the city limits (*no watchman or signal lights*).

Section 23. *Jacksonville to New Smyrna*, **112.7 m.**

The northern part of this section of US 1 traverses much unimproved pine land, interrupted by occasional marshes and cypress hammocks; the cabbage palm abounds in the regions around rivers and creeks where the undergrowth is sometimes dense and impenetrable, suggesting the more luxuriant tropical jungles of the section farther S. Below the imaginary frost line at Daytona, the tall feathery Australian pine is frequently used for windbreaks and hedges, and for roadside planting.

US 1 swings SE. from Jacksonville to St. Augustine on the coast; below that point it follows the coast line of the mainland though seldom in sight of the ocean because of the barrier reefs and sandbars. Florida East Coast and Flagler are almost synonymous names. Henry M. Flagler was one of John D. Rockefeller's closest business associates in the Standard Oil business for more than 40 years; about 1883 he became interested in Florida as a potential resort area and shortly afterward bought the little railroad connecting Jacksonville and St. Augustine. In 1886 he built the Ponce de Leon Hotel in St. Augustine. Gradually buying up little logging railroads and extending his lines under the name of the Florida East Coast Railway, he reached Palm Beach in 1892, Miami in 1896 and Key West in 1912, establishing palatial hotels along the coast at intervals.

Development of the area was slow, however. Palm Beach attained a kind of aristocratic prestige after a time but rail service to the south was so slow that only those with plenty of time to spare thought of going down the coast for recreation. Even when the World War began the population of Miami was only about 6,000 and, except for a few wealthy sportsmen, winter visitors were chiefly elderly people who were trying to escape from the cold of the north. Miami Beach was a sandspit reached by motorboat; the few bathers undressed behind the half open walls of a little deserted shack or on the open beach.

The World War industrial boom and the difficulties in the way of foreign travel after the war started the tourist flow to south Florida; the discovery of vitamins and the place of fruit and vegetables in the year-round diet stimulated the agricultural exploitation of the southern section for winter fruit and vegetable growing. Then someone discovered the new Eldorado — the value of Florida real estate — and the new gold rush was on, with Miami as the shining goal; people poured in by train, steamer, and automobile, on muleback and on foot. Fortunes were made and lost, but the State gained 50 percent in population between 1920 and 1930.

From the business section of Jacksonville, US 1 crosses the St. John's River on the municipally owned toll bridge, and continues through the South Jacksonville suburban section, with tourist camps strung out along the roadside.

At **8 m.** (R) are the BOWDEN FREIGHT YARDS OF THE F.E.C. R.R. Fifty miles of tracks at this point, used for the storage, the transfer, and the icing of freight shipments, will hold over 2,000 cars.

BAYARD, **19.5 m.** (25 alt., 225 pop.), is a small settlement at the junction of US 1 and the old St. Augustine road (formerly US 1).

Between Bayard and St. Augustine the highway closely parallels the F.E.C. R.R. All section houses are painted bright yellow with green trim.

In the spring the marshes beside the highway here are blue with iris, a plant considered sacred by the Indians, who also used the roots medicinally. On high ground beside the road grows the vine of the passionflower, so called by Spanish missionaries because to them the bloom symbolized the passion of Christ. In the center of the blossom is a cross; the stigmas, they said, represented the nails, the anthers the wounds and the rays of the corona the crown of thorns. This native flower is commonly called the maypop; its succulent, edible

ON A FLORIDA BEACH

BISCAYNE BAY, MIAMI, FLORIDA

FLORIDA 257

fruit grows to the size of a hen's egg and is in some cases highly perfumed.

At **40.8 m.** (R), at the city limits, are the F.E.C. R.R. SHOPS AND ROUND HOUSES. Opposite (L) is the ST. AUGUSTINE GOLF LINKS, an 18-hole course at which, for years, Johnny Farrell, has been the professional during the winter months.

ST. AUGUSTINE, **41.2 m.** (7 alt., 12,111 pop.), oldest city in United States (*see FLA. GUIDE*).

Points of Interest. Fort Marion, City Gates, Old Spanish Treasury, Plaza and Old Slave Market, Museum of Natural History, old houses, and others.

Ponce de Leon landed in this vicinity in 1513, and a permanent settlement was made by Menendez in 1565. Many present-day citizens of St. Augustine are descended from early Spanish settlers, and from Minorcans who came over during the English period. Hotels and buildings have various types of architecture, including Spanish, Moorish, and American Colonial. Many of the old streets are very narrow, Treasury Street being only 7 ft. wide. Prior to 1910, St. Augustine was the leading resort of Florida; today the city still derives its principal revenue from the tourist trade, though Florida East Coast Railway pay rolls and the fishing and shrimping industry also help to support the community. An effort is being made to restore the old city to its appearance in the early Spanish period.

Right from the Plaza on King St., passing the Ponce de Leon Hotel, Flagler's first hotel venture, and crossing the San Sebastian River Bridge; three blocks W. of the river, L. on US 1.

At **42.2 m.** is a sharp turn (L), from which the highway swings southward through pine flat woods and scrub palmetto land, with a slight rise when it crosses Moultrie Creek.

MOULTRIE, **47.2 m.** (500 pop.), was named for John Moultrie, Lieutenant Governor of Florida during the English period, who built a large stone mansion on his plantation, Belle Vista, near here. In 1784, with many other British settlers, he left Florida and moved to the Bahamas.

Right from Moultrie on a dirt road, the Upper Moultrie Road, through a dense and confusing pine woods with many trails. (*Trip should not be made without a guide.*) The SITE OF FORT PEYTON is at **1.5 m.** A marker (L), off the trail **0.8 m.**, indicates the spot where Osceola, the great Seminole leader, was captured. Approaching Fort Peyton under a flag of truce in October 1837, Osceola and his warriors were captured by General Jesup who was reprimanded for violating the truce but he defended himself by pointing out that Osceola had already broken a treaty. It is said that Osceola, perceiving that he was trapped, folded his arms scornfully and remained mute. In company with Coacoochee he was imprisoned in Fort Marion and later taken to Fort Moultrie at Charleston, S.C., where he died.

Although nothing remains of the old wooden fort and blockhouse, erected in 1836, a marker has been placed on the site. William Tecumseh Sherman of Civil War fame was stationed here as a lieutenant during the last days of the Seminole War.

South of Moultrie the highway continues through an almost uninhabited district of pine flat woods.

BUNNELL, 72.7 m. (23 alt., 671 pop.), is a small settlement in the heart of the Flagler County potato-growing area. The chief industry of the town is the canning of potatoes too small for ordinary shipment. A more unusual industry, however, is the exporting of palmetto buds; more than 350,000 of these are shipped annually to churches throughout the Nation to be used as Easter decorations.

Left from Bunnell on State 72 is FLAGLER BEACH, 8 m., a small but popular bathing and fishing resort.

KORONA, 78.2 m. (31 alt., 150 pop.), is a farm settlement established in 1912 by a number of Polish families. The 56 families still use their native language and retain many Old World customs.

At Korona is a junction with the old Dixie Highway (US 1-Alt.). The route follows the old Dixie Highway, which branches L. at Korona and R. at a fork at 80.3 m.

At 85.2 m. are the RUINS OF ANACAPE (TISSIMI) MISSION, approximately 50 yards L. of the highway and almost hidden from view in an undergrowth of weeds and vines. This mission was reputedly built by Franciscan friars about 1655, as one in a chain of 44 missions. It was destroyed by the English in 1706, but later rebuilt and used as a sugar mill during the British occupation of Florida (1763–83).

At 86 m. is the junction with a shell road.

Right on this road are the NATIONAL GARDENS, 3.5 m., with a 280-acre peat deposit of superior grade. The facilities of this small farm project include a nursery and a coquina quarry, the products from which are used in development of the enterprise.

A turn of the highway (R) reveals wide stretches of salt marsh.

At 86.1 m. is TOMOKA RIVER, named for the Indians who formerly occupied this territory. Alligators sun on the banks of the stream,

FLORIDA

while cranes and pelicans are seen occasionally. Black bass, perch, and bream are caught in large numbers.

SUNSET PARK, 87.2 m., has two small inns where boats can be rented for fishing.

At 88.2 m. are INDIAN BURIAL MOUNDS, from which the Smithsonian Institution has excavated a number of skulls and other bones. South of this point the highway is continuously arched with intermingling branches of trees that grow on both sides of the road. The Halifax River (L) is occasionally seen through the trees.

ORMOND, 92 m. (6 alt., 1,517 pop.), is a quiet, conservative city with limited accommodations. The well-kept lawns and gardens of its estates and homes are the pride of the winter residents. The town was established in 1873 by the Corbin Lock Co. of New Britain, Conn., as a resort for employees threatened with tuberculosis. Originally called New Britain, the town was renamed in 1880 in memory of Capt. James Ormond, a local plantation owner who had been killed by a runaway slave.

The ORMOND TROPICAL GARDENS (*open daily, adm. 25¢*), off Division St., W. on Granada Ave., a privately owned 116-acre tract, contain more than a quarter of a million tropical and subtropical plants.

Left from Ormond, across a long, wooden bridge spanning the Halifax River, is ORMOND BEACH, 0.4 m., resort that was the winter home of the late John D. Rockefeller. The oil magnate's estate, THE CASEMENTS, (R) at the end of the bridge, is small, with a house notably unpretentious. Guards formerly stood at all entrances and gardeners were busy all day long on the landscaped grounds.

Opposite The Casements is HOTEL ORMOND (*open Dec.–March*), a rambling wooden structure painted bright yellow and green, after the fashion of all F.E.C. Ry. buildings. The building of the hotel was begun in 1875 by John Anderson and Joseph Price, pioneers in the beach development; it was later sold to Henry M. Flagler, who enlarged the structure to its present size.

A tennis tournament, to which America's leading amateurs are invited, is held annually upon the four fine courts of the hotel.

Adjacent to the hotel are the ORMOND BEACH GOLF LINKS, John D. Rockefeller's favorite course, where he appeared daily to play a round of golf or to dispense dimes.

In keeping with the usual charges that prevail at Ormond Beach, the fees for the course have been set at $2.50 per day, with "slight" advances during the tournaments that are held here each winter and attended by America's leading golfers.

In front of the hotel and paralleling the river runs the JOHN ANDERSON HIGHWAY, a winding, wooded roadway that affords fine views of the Halifax. Many of the older estates of the city are here.

East of the Ocean Shore Blvd. at Granada Ave. is the HOTEL COQUINA, a large, expensive hostelry built in modified Spanish style, its walls covered with coquina. It is an imposing building on the very edge of the sea. The two sections of the hotel are connected by an arched bridgeway, under which cars pass to one of the hotel entrances.

A ramp leads from the end of Granada Ave., the main street of Ormond Beach, to the hard-packed sands (R) over which at low tide motorists can drive to DAYTONA BEACH, 5 m. A sign advises against driving N. because of the soft sand generally encountered between this point and Flagler Beach.

At Ormond the old Dixie Highway (US 1-Alt.) runs straight ahead, following the river; the newer and wider roadway, the new Dixie Highway, is reached by turning R. from the town center two blocks and L. on Ridgewood Ave. The routes unite in Daytona Beach.

On the alternate route is HOLLY HILL, **94.9 m.** (7 alt., 1,146 pop.), a suburb of Daytona Beach; it was so named because of the abundance of holly that formerly grew here. The town site is a part of the old Turnbull land grant.

Right on 11th St., across the railroad tracks, to the HOLLY HILL JUNGLE GARDENS (*open daily, adm. 25¢*), **1 m.**, which reputedly contain the largest planting of Easter lilies in North America. There are seven solid acres of magnificent blooms, producing annually 45,000 bulbs.

DAYTONA BEACH, **97.7 m.** (7 alt., 16,598 pop.), year-round resort city (*see FLA. GUIDE*).

Airport. Sholtz Field, 2.5 m. W. of city on US 92, Fla. 21; Eastern and National Air Lines.

Points of Interest. Speed Course, Casino Burgoyne Civic Center, International Temple of Speed, Bethune-Cookman College for Negroes, Burgoyne Home, and City Island.

The old Dixie Highway (US 1-Alt.) and US 1 unite in Daytona Beach.

Daytona Beach, successful as both a summer and winter resort, was originally called Daytona for Mathias Day of Ohio, who founded the city in 1871. It first attracted Nation-wide attention by automobile speed tests on the beach in the early years of the 20th century. The city is almost entirely dependent upon its tourist trade, though the cultivation of bulbs and citrus groves in the environs also supplies some income.

Southward along the east coast grows the coontie or comptie plant. The roots of the plant provide sago starch from which the Seminoles

FLORIDA

and the white pioneers made bread when cornmeal was not available. Flour is made by pounding the root in water. A fine white sediment settles in the bottom of the bowl; and the water and the roots are removed. The sediment, dried, is the desired flour. The Indians regarded the coontie as sacred to the Great Spirit, and used it during the feast at their annual Green Corn Dance.

PORT ORANGE, 103.1 m. (12 alt., 678 pop.), organized in 1861, was originally included in the Turnbull land grant. In the early part of the 19th century the fertile soil of this section produced sugarcane and indigo, which were in great demand in the markets of Europe. During the Seminole War the pioneers in this area were forced to abandon their homes and flee.

Although the citrus industry, to which the town owes its name, is still of some consequence to the community, it has been superseded in recent years by the shrimping industry and the cultivation of oyster beds that lie offshore in the broad expanse of the Halifax River.

There is exceptionally fine fishing here, both from the old bridge that crosses the river and from boats that can be rented at the wharves.

During the Seminole War the Battle of Dunlawton was fought along the river front of Port Orange. The defenders, refugees from the neighboring plantations, under General Putnam, were forced to withdraw from the vicinity, and the Indians under King Philip destoyed the old sugar mill and nearby settlements.

Right from Port Orange on Herbert St., following markers to the ruins of the old DUNLAWTON SUGAR MILL (*open 6 a.m.–6 p.m., adm. 25¢*), the building of which was reputedly begun during English occupation; it was later destroyed, rebuilt, and improved many times. It is known to have been used as late as 1880, and is one of the largest coquina ruins in the district. Two tall chimneys rise above the trees, but the walls of the once important mill are now overrun with vines. Most of the machinery remains in place, coated with rust, but imposing.

During the Civil War Edward Archibald McDonald, who established the settlement, transported water from the Halifax River and used the kettles of the mill to make salt for the Confederate forces.

At **104.1 m.** is ALLENDALE, a small residential village strung out along the highway and the river; it has an inn and the usual assortment of gas stations and tourist homes.

At **104.6 m.** is Ross Bay, an arm of the Halifax River popular as a fishing place (*boats for hire*). In season the marshlands and mangrove swamps provide excellent duck, marsh hen, and reedbird hunting.

At **106.2 m.** (R), S. of Spruce Creek Bridge, is TURNBULL CASTLE, a large frame house overshadowed by tall pines, cedars, and oaks. Its foundations are believed to have been used for the home of Dr. Andrew Turnbull, since it is known that this plantation at one time belonged to the developer of New Smyrna.

The highway at this point turns E. and is built upon shell-marl land, as is evidenced by the exposure of oyster shells along the shoulders of the road, from which have grown the gnarled old trees that shade the highway on the outskirts of New Smyrna.

NEW SMYRNA, **112.7 m.** (10 alt., 4,149 pop.), a little town built upon the ruins of one of Florida's oldest settlements, stretches for 4 miles along the W. bank of the North Indian River. Enormous liveoaks, magnolias, and bay trees shade the residential and business houses, mainly of post-Victorian frame construction. Most of the business district lies near the highway, and the better residential section along the winding river, but a few homes have been built W. of US 1.

The first known settlement on the site of New Smyrna was the Indian village of Caparaca. The Spanish missionaries were here in 1696 when the Mission of Aticuimi was founded, a century before those of California. In 1767 Dr. Andrew Turnbull brought 1,500 colonists to Florida. About 1,200 were from the Island of Minorca, S. of Spain; the others were Italians and Greeks. The British Government furnished a sloop of war and 4,500 pounds sterling bounty to promote the settlement. Lord Grenville, English Secretary of State, was a partner in the undertaking, which had many other powerful backers. Grants covering more than 100,000 acres of land were made to the colony. Though the colonists found pioneering in Florida anything but idyllic, they accomplished a great deal in the nine years of the life of the settlement. An intricate system of canals drained the rich hammock land, and the indigo raised in the fertile soil found a good market in England.

Many of the settlers died; dissatisfaction was high and troops were brought in to keep the colonists in control. Charges and countercharges against administration of the colony were made by those friendly to the English Government and those opposed to it. When a new Governor of Florida was appointed in 1776 the remaining colonists were permitted to leave the settlement and they migrated to St. Augustine, where their descendants still form a part of the population.

FLORIDA

New Smyrna changed little until 1803, when Spanish grants of land were given to the Martin and Murray families. From that time on, through periods of Seminole raids and blockade-running in the Civil War, the town has made slow progress. During the last 30 years it, like other east coast cities, has had stimulation from the advent of the railroad, the completion of the Intracoastal Waterway, and highway improvements.

Citrus groves, packing plants, and the shops of the F.E.C. Ry. provide the chief sources of income here, though the fishing and shrimping industries furnish employment for a large number of residents.

The old FORT, Hillsboro St., between Washington and Julian Sts., was discovered and partly unearthed in 1854. Buried under a shell mound, the blocks of coquina are generally believed to have been the foundation of a home intended for Lord Hillsborough, begun at the time of the founding of the city in 1767 by Dr. Turnbull.

The TURNBULL CANAL, in places dug through solid coquina, extends 4 miles W. from the boat slip on the river's edge and is still used for drainage purposes. The canal is about 10 ft. wide and 10 deep; the section that flows through the center of town is covered by sidewalks and street intersections.

The CITY ZOO (*free*), on Lytel Ave. between Palmetto and Live Oak Sts., contains a small collection of native birds, alligators, and other fauna.

The YACHT CLUB, a Spanish-type, stuccoed building on an island in the Indian River opposite the Fifth St. Bridge, annually holds regattas for sail and motor boats.

The ANGLERS CLUB, opposite Washington St., on the tip of a large island in the river, is the headquarters of an active fishing and boating organization holding annual meets (*Nov.–April*). Ways and ample docking facilities are provided for small river and ocean craft.

In New Smyrna on Wayne Ave. and fronting on the river is the INDIAN RIVER DUDE RANCH, which has a main building and a number of rustic cottages, a large stable, a swimming pool, and a boathouse.

The INDIAN RIVER SCHOOL, an expensive boys' preparatory institution, is under separate management, but occupies ranch buildings and uses ranch facilities.

Left on Washington St. is CORONADO BEACH, **1.5 m.**, reached by way of a roadway that traverses and connects several small islands built up by the mangroves that grow so prolifically in the Indian River opposite the city. The roadsides have been adorned with palms, flowering shrubs, and Australian pines. From the drawbridge an excellent and unobstructed view of the river is presented. In the broad expanse of the river annual sail and motor boat regattas are held.

Across the bridge (R) is a low bluff known as DUMMITT'S MOUND, in reality an old Indian shell mound, named for Capt. D. D. Dummitt, New Smyrna's first port collector, who at one time lived on top of the bluff.

Beyond the peninsula, Flagler Ave. leads to a ramp that descends to the beach (*bathing and boating facilities*). The beach southward is frequented by fishermen seeking redfish, better known as channel bass, some of which weigh 40 pounds.

The PONCE DE LEON LIGHTHOUSE (L) marks the entrance to the inlet of the same name.

At the river's edge is MASSACRE BLUFF, site of the massacre in 1835 of a number of French sailors by Seminole Indians.

Right from the beach on Flagler Ave. to TURTLE MOUND, 6 m., for centuries a familiar landmark to sailors. Rising 50 ft. above the beach and called the Mount of Surruque by the Indians, it was charted on maps of Florida as early as 1562. Spanish galleons stopped here for repairs, wood, and water. Turtle Mound has been preserved by the Florida State Historical Society. A fishing camp and picnic grounds are provided on the lagoon side of the mound. At 12.5 m. a COAST GUARD STATION faces the ocean. So narrow is the peninsula at this point that the rear door of the station opens on a lagoon of the Indian River.

Section 24. New Smyrna to Miami, 247.2 m.

This stretch of the highway borders the Intracoastal Waterway, which separates the Florida mainland from the Atlantic Ocean. Numerous side roads from US 1 lead across bridges and causeways to outlying peninsulas and keys where facilities for fishing and surf bathing are available. The foliage becomes more luxuriant and tropical S. of the picturesque Indian River.

Between Fort Pierce and Palm Beach the highway runs through a series of modest coast towns; between Palm Beach and Miami, Florida's "Gold Coast," landscaped estates and many nurseries line the highway, and add to the floral beauty of the region.

South of New Smyrna, the highway winds through dense palmetto growth known as the TURNBULL HAMMOCKS, once broad cleared acres of fertile soil.

A barrier of pines and cabbage palms obscures MOSQUITO LAGOON (L), but the numerous signs advertising camps and boats for hire and "Tom, Dick and Harry's" camps attest the popularity of fishing at the end of the many winding sand trails that run down toward the sea.

OAK HILL, 12 m. (18 alt., 457 pop.), is a small citrus-packing village.

At 14 m. the highway curves (R) across a lowland meadow and crosses a new concrete railroad overpass. Descending, the roadway follows a fill barely three feet above the water level, and traverses part of a vast salt marsh, where grasses are gathered and shipped for use as broom fillers.

Small creeks twist between the islands of palms, cypresses, and sweetgums. Throughout the spring months the marsh is an undulating field of yellow sunflowers; during September it is pink with rosemallow. In early morning and late afternoon, flocks of ibises, cranes, and other water birds feed along the causeway and in the marshes. Kingfishers sit on telephone wires, ready to make sudden plunges for minnows.

At 16 m. the highway enters a short stretch of hammock where tall cabbage palms predominate. The white bud of this native palm, cooked or raw, is considered a great delicacy. When the bud is out, however, the tree dies. Commanding features of the landscape are the rows of tall, dark green Australian pines that line the highway, forming windbreaks for adjoining citrus groves.

MIMS, 27.8 m. (487 pop.), is a small cluster of houses around a packing plant.

At 29.5 m. the highway climbs another new concrete overpass, offering a sweeping panorama of a long, palm- and pine-bordered sound known as INDIAN RIVER. In the distance (R) the river broadens to its greatest width, 7 miles, and the shore of Merritt Island is dimly revealed. The FEDERAL RADIO STATION (R) broadcasts hourly weather reports for airplane guidance.

TITUSVILLE, 32.5 m. (14 alt., 2,089 pop.), seat of Brevard County, was named for Col. H. T. Titus, an early resident who was an antagonist of John Brown in the days of "Bleeding Kansas." Louis Coleman, one of the pioneer settlers, owned the Sand Point lands in North Titusville that the agent of Henry M. Flagler once sought to purchase. Coleman put too great a price on the property and the proposed Flagler development took place at Palm Beach instead.

Between the highway and the river is the SAND POINT IMPROVEMENT PROJECT, which now contains a yacht basin, a swimming pool, a diving tower, a ball diamond, tennis courts, and a dirt track for auto or pony races. The 67-acre park and recreation center is reclaimed swampland, a mosquito-control as well as a beautification project. Oleanders and hibiscus plantings surround the 19th century frame houses and boom-period stucco buildings, which line the west bank of the Indian River.

The city's industrial plants include five citrus-packing houses; the State's largest BARREL FACTORY, whose products are used by the fish and vegetable shippers of the Indian River country; and a CRABMEAT PICKING AND PACKING PLANT on the CITY PIER (*open*).

Left from Titusville on State 119, crossing Indian River Bridge to the first road L.; L. here, passing a heavy live-oak hammock with the appearance of a park, to the old DUMMITT GROVE, **8 m.** Part of it is said to be the oldest living citrus grove in Florida, having been planted about 1830. Its trees still bear fruit. Since the death of Capt. Douglas D. Dummitt, the founder, there have been many successive owners, including the Italian Duke of Castalucci, who built the present octagonal house, still called the DUKE'S CASTLE.

Between Titusville and Indian River the highway is bordered with tall oleanders.

INDIAN RIVER CITY, **36.3 m.** (19 alt., 120 pop.), frequently called Clark's Corner, is a community with several Spanish-type houses, and with gas stations, a lunchroom, and a post office in a natural park facing the widest part of the Indian River.

South of Indian River City the highway is slightly elevated and parallels Indian River; it is shaded by the growth of tall palms and pines. Palmetto thickets, low shrubbery, and scrub pine (R) add to the beauty of the water views.

At **44.6 m.** is a junction with the old Dixie Highway, which follows the shore of the Indian River through Cocoa and Rockledge, rejoining US 1, the express highway, near Bonaventure Station; L. here.

COCOA, **51.7 m.** (26.5 alt., 2,164 pop.), is a tourist city and a citrus center. Fruit trees in nearby hammocks are said to have borne since 1868. The serenity of palm- and shrub-darkened residential sections contrasts with the scattered business section, which appears to cover too large an area. Incorporated in 1895, Cocoa is an outgrowth of Rockledge. It was named for the nut palm that grows in the vicinity, one of the most graceful of palms, its trunk curving upward to the great clusters of nuts at the top.

Fishermen, casting from the platforms at the sides of the Indian River Bridge, make numerous catches of salt-water fishes, among

FLORIDA

which the shark is not uncommon. Schools of porpoise roll through the water, and pelicans are often seen to drop vertically and snatch fish from the water.

Good fishing is found in the quiet waters of the Indian and Banana Rivers, in the surf along the beach, off the coast (*boats for hire at city dock, foot of King St.*), and in the fresh waters of the upper St. John's River and its lakes.

Woodlands W. of the city offer a variety of game, and LAKE POINSETT provides good bass fishing (*boats and guides available*).

Left from Cocoa, across a free bridge, is MERRITT, **1 m.**, on Merritt Island. This island, stretching along the coast for 42 miles and varying in width from 9 miles to a strip barely wider than the road, is named for an adventurous Spanish grandee of the early 19th century.

1. Left from Merritt on a narrow paved road are INDIANOLA, **3 m.**, COURTENAY, **5 m.**, and ORSINO, **15 m.**, all citrus-growing communities.

2. Right from Merritt on a winding paved road through many groves and past deserted houses to GEORGINA, **5 m.**, with old churchyard burial grounds; LOTUS, **9 m.**; TROPIC, **15 m.**; and across Banana River Bridge (*toll 25¢*) to INDIALANTIC BEACH, **21 m.**

3. Left from Merritt, then R., crossing a narrow causeway to COCOA BEACH, **9 m.**, offering beach motoring, surf bathing, and beach or pier fishing.
Left here on the shell and marl road, passing through wild and tangled growth to ARTESIA, **17 m.**, and CANAVERAL HARBOR, **18 m.**, proposed in 1925 as a harbor for Orlando. CAPE CANAVERAL (Sp., *reedy point*), **23 m.**, was noted in 1513 by Ponce de Leon, who called it Cape of the Currents. It appeared as Canaveral on LeMoyne's map of 1564. Menendez was wrecked here in July 1572 and walked to St. Augustine, arriving in the late fall. He saved himself from capture by the Indians by telling them that a large Spanish force was following him. Canaveral's first lighthouse, built in 1847 and in time endangered by encroaching seas, was replaced in 1868 by the present TOWER. The light, flashing every minute from its 139-ft. height, is visible for 17 nautical miles.

ROCKLEDGE, **53.2 m.** (29 alt., 551 pop.), an oak- and palm-shaded city that is one of the oldest resorts on the east coast, was named for the ledge of coquina, rising from 3 to 20 ft. above the river, on which it is situated.

BONAVENTURE, **56 m.** (16 alt.), is a small settlement of citrus growers and farmers. At **57.8 m.** the alternate route unites with US 1.

At **59 m.** the shore line of the Indian River is irregular and the banks are often relatively high. Small pine- and palm-studded peninsulas jutting into the river create lagoons reflecting everchanging sky colors and cloud formations. The early name for the river was Ais (Ind., *deer*). The Ais Indians who occupied this area antedated other Florida tribes.

EAU GALLIE, **68.9 m.** (19 alt., 871 pop.), named by W. H. Gleason with a combination of French and Indian words meaning rocky water, is on the coquina shores of the Indian and Gallie Rivers, opposite the mouth of the Banana River. Shortly after the Civil War Gleason had been appointed to make a topographical and agricultural survey of the Florida peninsula to ascertain whether it was suitable for Negro colonization; finding that the natural resources of the country required capital and skilled labor for successful development, he reported adversely. In 1866 he settled in the district.

River traffic once flourished here; in 1890 all material for Flagler's Royal Poinciana Hotel was brought by rail to this point where it was trans-shipped for carriage to Palm Beach by water. A State agricultural college established nearby in 1874 was one of several institutions later merged to form the University of Florida, now at Gainesville.

Left from Eau Gallie on State 101 across the Indian River are EAU GALLIE BEACH, 2 m., and the CANOVA OCEAN FISHING PIER.

At the east end of the bridge is the junction (L) with a paved road leading to MATHER'S BRIDGE, 4 m., beyond the Banana River, another favorite fishing place.

South of Eau Gallie the highway runs along the high river bank, affording a view of the river to the MELBOURNE BRIDGE and beyond.

MELBOURNE, **73.5 m.** (22 alt., 2,677 pop.), named by a native of Australia for the town of his birth, contains buildings more rococo in style than are those of the Indian River towns to the N. There is an 18-hole GOLF COURSE (*open; greens fee $1.50; special weekly, monthly, and season rates*).

More than 100 varieties of fresh- and salt-water fishes are caught near here. Artificial lures are favored for all types of fishing (*information, tackle, guides, and boats available at docks*).

Right from Melbourne on State 24 to CRANE CREEK, 3.5 m., where workers of the Smithsonian Institution excavated mastodon remains now on exhibition in Washington, D.C.

MALABAR, **79.9 m.** (26 alt., 138 pop.), consists of several white families and a Negro colony working at the sawmill W. of the railroad.

GRANT, 85.2 m. (11 alt., 209 pop.), is the site of a factory that manufactures small hydroelectric plants for homes.

Here the highway penetrates several palm jungles, giving emphasis to the increasingly tropical nature of the flora. Frequent views of Indian River reveal sand bars swarming with herons and other waterfowl.

MICCO, 89 m. (25 alt., 274 pop.), consisting of many old houses, each with its sulphur-water artesian well, derives its name from the Seminole word for chief.

At 91.5 m. is the SEBASTIAN CREEK BRIDGE, a concrete span replacing the narrow wooden bridge that proved the Waterloo of southern Florida's most notorious band of desperados. It was on this site that in November 1924 the nucleus of the Ashley gang — John Ashley, Hanford Mobley, Ray Lynn, and Bob Middleton — met death in battle with deputy sheriffs. Fleeing their haunts after 14 years of bank robbing, high jacking, rum running, and bootlegging, these four members of the gang were stopped at the bridge by a red lantern and a chain, and shot when they resisted arrest.

The white sandy plot (R) is the SITE OF A FISHING CAMP used prior to 1890 by Grover Cleveland, E. C. Ballard, and others. Although their winter homes were in Eau Gallie, they came here by boat to take advantage of the excellent fishing grounds. South of this bridge the highway parallels Indian River for 4 miles.

Across Indian River (L) is Sebastian Inlet, providing a channel between the ocean and the river. This inlet was dredged by the united efforts of nearby communities.

SEBASTIAN, 93.9 m. (21 alt., 386 pop.), in a beautiful area, was one of the first trading posts on the east coast. River steamers formerly stopped at the foot of Main St., where some of the pilings of the old dock are still visible. The street was first cleared to facilitate the hauling of wood to steamers for fuel.

Sebastian is on the side of a ridge that slopes to the Indian River. Practically every residence has a view of the water. The town having no water system, each house has its own artesian well; the water is impregnated with sulphur.

Henry M. Flagler is reputed to have negotiated for a site near here, as well as in Titusville, for the proposed resort hotel before his railroad reached this point, but was unable to obtain a clear title.

Across the river (L) is PELICAN ISLAND, a Government bird sanctuary in which thousands of white pelicans and terns spend the winter months.

The drying nets, fish docks, and crab-picking shacks, hanging precariously over the waters of Indian River (L), are in distinct contrast with the neat cottages and landscaped lawns that line the opposite side of the highway.

WABASSO, 98.9 m. (20 alt., 300 pop.), probably named by Guale Indians who migrated here from Ossabawa, near Savannah, Ga., is a small community sustained by its fishing industry, citrus groves, packing houses, and a sawmill.

At 100.6 m. the highway swings away from the Indian River to enter an area devoted largely to the citrus industry.

GIFFORD, 104.6 m. (19 alt., 500 pop.), was named for F. Charles Gifford, who is credited with having selected the site for Vero Beach. It is said that he held up the extension of the F.E.C. Ry. by placing an excessive price on his land. In retaliation, the railroad started a small town exclusively for Negroes and named it for him. The railroad was built around the Gifford holdings, and Gifford is now the Negro section of Vero Beach.

At 106.8 m. both sides of the highway are lined with rows of towering Australian pines, which form an attractive entrance to Vero Beach from the north and protect the citrus groves (L).

VERO BEACH, 107.1 m. (19 alt., 2,268 pop.), seat of Indian River County, was about 1882 selected as a townsite by W. H. Gifford, because of the fertility of the soil in the area. The present town extends across the Indian River (known as the Narrows at this point) to the Atlantic Ocean. Vero Beach is a citrus shipping point and popular with winter visitors.

The skeletal finds of Dr. Sellards (1916) were made in the Van Valkenburg's Creek area in the western part of the village during a canal excavation. Parts of human skeletons of some antiquity were uncovered here and the probable age of the Vero Beach man became the subject of much speculation and controversy.

POCAHONTAS PARK, 14th Ave. and 21st St., offers recreational facilities and is a tourist center.

Left two blocks E. of the center of town onto an avenue lined with royal palms, hibiscuses, and oleanders; beyond a drawbridge over the Intracoastal Waterway is the ocean shore. There is excellent fishing at this point (*boats and guides available*). A CASINO (*open Nov.–May*) faces the ocean; beyond it are many private estates.

At **109 m.** US 1 crosses one of several drainage canals that carry the overflow from bottom lands lying W. of the road. These canals and lateral ditches are part of the Indian River Drainage District projects, covering more than 50,000 acres. The drained lands produce pineapples and winter vegetables.

At **109.7 m.** (L) are the McKEE JUNGLE GARDENS (*adm. $1, children under 14 free; guides for parties*), covering 80 acres. They were opened in 1931 by Arthur G. McKee, an Ohio industrialist who, during many years of world travel, had become interested in tropical plant culture. McKee made the gardens in a desire to create an area of outstanding beauty. From a virgin tract of jungle growth he cleared away only the trees and underbrush necessary for the successful propagation of 2,500 different species of tropical and subtropical plants; along winding paths now grow thousands of rare and exotic plants, gathered from every corner of the globe. In the jungle depths are many valuable varieties of orchids, ferns, and flowering vines. Growing in the pools and lagoons are water lilies, some with pads large enough to support a child. Of special interest are the bougainvillea glade, the azalea garden, the mirror pool, the watery maze, and the cathedral aisle leading to the lower glen. The pools are fed by an artesian well. Alligators, peacocks, parrots, and other jungle inhabitants are on display and native birds have found the garden a place of sanctuary. A large enclosure contains a number of monkeys.

In the heart of the garden a Seminole Indian village has been built with thatched huts that are open at all times to those of the race who may care to visit here.

FORT PIERCE, **122 m.** (24 alt., 6,376 pop.), seat of St. Lucie County, was named for the fort built on the site in 1838 as a link in the chain of east coast fortifications to protect settlers from the Indians. The site was doubtless selected because the St. Lucie Inlet afforded easy communication by water with the North. Despite the Indians, white settlers remained in the area to cultivate pineapples and garden truck. Some citrus groves were set out.

The blight and freeze of 1898 proved a serious setback to farmers and grove owners here, but today citrus-growing remains one of the principal industries.

Fort Pierce is the most important shipping point between Jacksonville and Miami. The city is the transfer point for large cargoes of citrus, vegetables, fish, lumber, and some phosphate. It is also the receiving point for incoming cargoes of general merchandise to be distributed along the central east coast. A new $100,000 pier with refrigerated citrus-shipping facilities is leased by the Bull Steamship Lines, which provide five weekly freight sailings to Baltimore and New York.

One of the principal tourist attractions is fishing. Snook, trout, channel bass, and numerous other salt-water fish are caught from boats in the Indian River channel, off the jetties at the inlet, along the causeway, and from the pier. In nearby back-country streams black bass, perch, and other varieties abound.

An annual Washington's Birthday event is the gathering of the "old timers" from the lower Indian River section, who swap yarns of the old days. A record of these recollections has been kept for a number of years.

At Fort Pierce is the junction with State 140.

Left from Fort Pierce on State 140, passing the SITE OF FORT SANTA LUCIA. Menendez left a garrison here in 1568, but the Indians killed so many of the soldiers that the survivors mutinied and abandoned their fortifications, fleeing northward to St. Augustine.

This narrow though well-paved road parallels Indian River for its entire length, affording fine views. Along it are some of the best citrus groves of the Indian River country. JENSEN, 15 m., is a small resort for tourists and sportsmen. At 15.5 m. R. to RIO, 17.5 m., and the junction with US 1 (*see below*).

WHITE CITY, **126.9 m.** (32 alt., 670 est. pop.), the second largest community in St. Lucie Co., was settled shortly after the Chicago World's Fair of 1893 by a number of Danish people from Chicago who became interested in the opportunities for citrus cultivation in this area after reading a series of articles on the raising of citrus fruits, written by a Danish newspaper man covering the fair. The citizens named their principal street Midway, commemorating the main street at the Chicago Fair.

White City derives a substantial income from citrus and truck farming. Two asparagus ferneries are also in the vicinity.

Between White City and **129.9 m.** US 1 is bordered (L) by the JENSEN SAVANNAH, a low grassy plain, in which are lakes, ponds, creeks, runs, and branches of the St. Lucie River. This wild country, full of game, birds, and fish, is so low that most of it is under water after a heavy rain. Guides should be used by those

THE GATES AT WESTOVER, VIRGINIA

OKEFENOKEE SWAMP, GEORGIA

FLORIDA

unfamiliar with the area (*guides and boats available at Jensen or Stuart*).

At **139.1 m.** is the St. Lucie River, the eastern section of the CROSS-STATE WATERWAY. This route affords water passage for ships and yachts of 6-foot draft or less, from the Atlantic Ocean, by way of the St. Lucie Canal, Lake Okeechobee, and the Caloosahatchee River, to the Gulf of Mexico (*see FLA. GUIDE*).

STUART, **140.1 m.** (14 alt., 2,070 pop.), the principal community in Martin Co., built on the St. Lucie River, near the inlet of the same name, is a quiet town of importance only because of the exceptional fishing in its vicinity (*guides available for hunting and fishing on the Jensen Savannah*).

Right from Stuart on the N. fork of the St. Lucie River to the GILSON SLIDE RULE FACTORY, **3 m.** Besides making straight rules for various purposes, the factory grinds circular rules and calculators, and prints books of instruction on their uses.

At **154.1 m.** picturesque HOBE SOUND is seen (L), surrounded by Australian pines. This body of water, a part of the Intracoastal Waterway, is noted for its good fishing. Its name was apparently derived from Jobe (Sp., *Jupiter*). In 1682 Johnathon Dickenson and a number of others were shipwrecked about 5 miles above Jupiter Inlet, and were captured by Indians who took them S. to the inlet, which the aborigines called Hoe Bay.

At **156 m.** the highway runs on high ground furnishing a delightful view of the sound across a wide rolling, treeless country.

For about 5 miles the highway parallels the ocean, permitting an almost unobstructed view of the varicolored waters.

At **163 m.** parking space has been provided for cars, between the highway and the high bank of the beach. This spot, popular for surf fishing, is used largely by residents of West Palm Beach.

At **165 m.** (R) is a small stone monument commemorating the so-called "Celestial Railroad" that connected Jupiter with the vanished settlements of Neptune, Mars, Juno, and Venus. Juno, at the northern end of Lake Worth, was the seat of old Dade Co. from 1889 to 1899, but declined in importance when the seat was transferred to Miami. The railroad was abandoned in 1894, when the through line from Jacksonville was opened by Henry M. Flagler.

At **167 m.** (L) is the 18-hole SEMINOLE GOLF CLUB (*private*).

Right of the highway at **169 m.** is KELSEY CITY (470 pop.), built during the boom. When it was incorporated in 1923, the citizens spent a considerable amount of money promoting it as the future "largest industrial city in the South," but it became a tiny suburb whose residents commute to West Palm Beach.

RIVIERA, 174.2 m. (19 alt., 1,629 pop.), on the western shore of Lake Worth (*three tourist camps, trailer space, and cabins*), has a colony of Conchs, a people of Spanish, English, Negro, and Indian blood, named for the shellfish they are said to eat. Early in the 19th century a group of English fishermen established a colony on the Bahama Islands; intermarried there with Negroes and Spaniards; then moved, in 1900, to Singers Island on Lake Worth opposite Riviera, where they intermarried with a nearby band of Seminoles. When a tropical hurricane destroyed their settlement in 1919, they moved to their present home L. of US 1. These people have dark skins, kinky hair, thick lips, and broad features of Negroes. Although the men confine their activities to fishing, the women and children weave palmetto baskets, and make flowers and trinkets from fish scales.

WEST PALM BEACH, 178.9 m. (20 alt., 26,610 pop.), a resort (*see FLA. GUIDE*).

Railroad Stations. Seaboard Air Line Ry., Tamarind St. between Evernia and Datura Sts.; Florida East Coast Ry., 5th St. and Railroad Ave.

Airport. Eastern Airlines, Municipal Airport, 5 miles W. of city on Southern Blvd. Taxi fare 50¢, time 15 min.

Ferries. West Palm Beach to Palm Beach, fare 5¢.

Points of Interest. Dockmaster's Home, Ada L. Saunders' Museum, Elisha N. Dimick Monument, and others.

West Palm Beach, founded in 1893 by Henry M. Flagler, is a commercial and resort city, stretching for eight and a half miles along the west shore of Lake Worth.

Left from West Palm Beach on Lakeview Avenue across Lake Worth bridge to a narrow island, on which at **1 m.** is PALM BEACH (14 alt., 1,836 pop.), one of the most fashionable winter resorts in America (*fishing, bathing; prices increased during winter*). Around the shores of Lake Worth are palatial villas, elegant hotels and cottages. Several of the ornate buildings here were designed during the boom period by Addison Mizner; a number of beautiful modern homes have been built recently. On the grounds of the Royal Poinciana Hotel is a rare TAMARIND TREE. The PALM BEACH ART CENTER (*free*) on Main St. exhibits the work of contemporary artists. One of the show places is WHITE HALL, the former home of Henry M. Flagler (1830–1913), whose business was a partnership in the Standard Oil Co., and hobby was making Florida a winter resort.

FLORIDA

LAKE WORTH, 185.9 m. (21 alt., 5,119 pop.), received its name from the lake that stretches along its eastern edge. This body of water, 18 miles long and separated from the ocean by a narrow strip of land, is actually a lagoon; it was named for Maj. Gen. William J. Worth, in charge of the American force in the last days of the Seminole War.

Municipally owned ice, cold storage, electric light, and water plants pay most of the cost of operating the village.

The municipal 18-hole GOLF COURSE in on the lake front at the foot of Lucerne Ave. (*greens fee, 75¢*). On the ocean front is the Lake Worth CASINO (*dancing and swimming*), reached by a bridge.

LANTANA, 188.2 m. (11 alt., 253 pop.), named for a shrub with dense spikes of red and white flowers that grows wild here, has as its principal attraction a large OSTRICH AND ALLIGATOR FARM (*open daily, adm. 25¢*), near the northern city limits. Here are exhibited alligators of all ages, ranging from those just hatched to one veteran said to be more than 400 years old. In addition to crocodiles and ostriches, the farm has monkeys, lemurs, kangaroos, and snakes.

BOYNTON BEACH, 192.2 m. (19 alt., 1,053 pop.), a trading center, stands on a sandy ridge in an area of rich farm lands. An exceptionally fertile soil, composed of marl, muck, and sand, extends westward from the town limits to the Everglades. Many Finnish farmers have settled here.

DELRAY BEACH, 196.8 m. (20 alt., 2,706 pop.), is a tourist resort and center of an area producing beans, peppers, tomatoes, fruits, peanuts, and sugar cane. Here is a settlement of Michigan farmers of German ancestry. A large PIGEON-BREEDING PLANT furnishes squabs for the Palm Beach market. West on Atlantic Ave. is the DELRAY CLUBHOUSE and 9-hole GOLF COURSE (*open*). At Atlantic Ave. and the coastal canal is the CITY PARK (*picnic and recreation grounds, shuffleboard courts, and card pavilions*). At the eastern end of Atlantic Ave. and Ocean Blvd. is the DELRAY PAVILION AND POOL (*small fee*). Fronting the ocean at this point is a mile-long municipal beach (*surf fishing; boats rented for deep-sea fishing*).

In Delray is JOURNEY'S END, home of the writer, Nina Wilcox Putnam. Its doors, windows, and grillwork were salvaged from the old Royal Poinciana Hotel in Palm Beach. Mrs. Putnam, assisted by her husband and son, did much of the construction work.

Left from Delray Beach on Atlantic Ave. to the SUNKEN GARDENS, 1.8 m. (*open daily, adm. 35¢; guides*). Here is grown a variety of floral curiosities, including the dainty lipstick flower, the silk-cotton tree, the pelican flower, the jackfruit tree with fruit sometimes 40 pounds in weight, and more than 2,000 other plants.

At **2 m.** is the town of GULF STREAM, a small village centering about the wealthy GULF STREAM CLUB (*private*) and its 18-hole golf course lying between the boulevard and the coastal canal. North of the golf course, side roads leading from the boulevard are lined with tall Australian pines, coconut palms, and pink and white oleanders. Clumps of royal and cabbage palms grow near the fairways. On a side road W. of the club are the POLO FIELDS, where, in 1936, Serge Mdivani was killed. Winding in and out among the trees and shrubbery are bridle paths leading to the stables, maintained primarily for the polo ponies.

At **201.6 m.** is the junction with an asphalt road.

Right a short distance on this road is YAMATO, settled by Japanese who grew tomatoes and pineapples until 1926, when they sold their property to real estate promoters and moved to other sections of the State. All that remains of the village is a small store and an unused freight station.

BOCA RATON (Sp., *rat's mouth*), **205 m.** (17 alt., 784 pop.), is a small resort. Its name was first applied to an inlet just S. of the city limits. Left of US 1, about half a mile SE. of the town hall, is the BOCA RATON CLUB (*private*), which has a limited membership of wealthy people. Additions have been made to the club building, originally designed by Addison Mizner as an inn. It now contains 605 rooms, five patios, an outdoor swimming pool, and a ballroom. A cut has been dredged to connect Lake Boca Raton with the ocean and allow yachts to moor at the club wharves. The club maintains a golf course, gun traps, and a riding stable.

DEERFIELD, **207.5 m.** (15 alt., 1,556 pop.), a farming town where quantities of beans and peppers are grown, was originally named Hillsboro, but adopted its present name about 1907 when deer were plentiful in the vicinity. Negroes, who settled here to work in the now extinct pineapple-growing industry, still form two-thirds of the population. Many have prospered as landowners.

POMPANO, **213.7 m.** (15 alt., 3,000 pop.), originally a small village on the ocean, moved several miles inland to its present site, after suffering much damage in the 1928 hurricane. An engineer surveying here for the railroad was delighted by the flavor of a fish served him at dinner. When he learned that the fish was called pompano and abounded in the waters opposite this site he put "Pompano" on his map as the village's name. Although pompano

FLORIDA

also known as butterfish, are rare and are considered a luxury in other parts of Florida they breed offshore at this point, feeding on the shellfish, and can be caught with rod and reel, though a net is usually employed. The meat is fine-flaked, with a delicate flavor.

In spite of the town's name, gardening is of first importance here. During the winter months, when beans and green peppers are harvested, New York vegetable buyers come here to purchase crops. The town's small crate factories, vegetable-packing platforms, express loading platforms, and railroad offices, ordinarily deserted, then become centers of activity; on every street corner groups of farmers, buyers, and merchants gather to discuss the latest market quotations on vegetables.

Left from Pompano on a paved road at **3.7 m.** is HILLSBOROUGH LIGHTHOUSE on Hillsborough Inlet, named for the Earl of Hillsborough who owned large Florida grants during English occupation. Human bones excavated here are said to be pirate remains.

The Hillsborough light completed in 1907, a 5,500,000 candlepower light and one of the most powerful on the South Atlantic coast, marks the northern limit of the Florida Reef, an underwater coral formation paralleling the lower part of the east coast of Florida.

North of the light is the HILLSBOROUGH CLUB, a semi-private club-hotel.

At **217 m.** (R) are recently abandoned rock pits containing sky-blue water that contrasts vividly with the uncompromising white of the unweathered limestone borders.

At **217.3 m.** is the ornate gilt gateway (L) of the LION FARM (*adm. adults 35¢, children 15¢*), where lions are bred for zoos and circuses. Most of the beasts live in unfenced grottos surrounded by water-filled moats, across which they are afraid to venture.

FORT LAUDERDALE, **222.1 m.** (10 alt., 9,222 pop.), is the seat of Broward Co. and a favorite headquarters of winter yachtsmen. It was built on the side of an abandoned military outpost called by the same name and established in 1837 during the second Seminole War.

Fort Lauderdale is the home of Katherine Rawls, an Olympic swimming champion.

The Indians believed the NEW RIVER, 75 ft. deep and bisecting the city from E. to W., was created in a single night. Geologists explain that the stream was probably an underground river, suddenly exposed when surface rock crumbled during an earthquake. The river is as black and as deep now as when it was filled with alligators;

but today its dark surface mirrors the white paint, mahogany, and gleaming brass of pleasure boats.

More than 100 miles of natural and artificial waterways wind through Fort Lauderdale; some were built to aid commerce and agriculture, while others were intended to add to the charms of boom-time subdivisions, whose empty artificial islands and unfinished Venetian bridges now stand deserted.

COLEE MONUMENT, in a little wooded park at Tarpon Bend in the New River, marks the site of the old fort. Here, in the heart of COLEE HAMMOCK, now a prominent residential section, occurred a massacre of whites (1842) by Seminole Indians under the leadership of Arpeika (*Sam Jones-be-Damned*).

Youthful Crop-ear Charlie, a member of Arpeika's tribe, had been friendly with the white people. Caught while trying to warn his benefactors of the plans he had overheard, he was bound to a tree and forced to witness the slaying of the whites. Afterward his tribe punished him by cropping his ears, upper right and lower left; depriving him of his name and identifying family colors; and exiling him, with only a hunting knife and a few rags, in the Everglades. He was told that after seven years he might approach the camp and ask for another trial. Seven years later, in June, at the time of the Green Corn Dance, when the annual council again sat to pass on violations of tribal laws, warriors examined him and decided that he could live near the tribe, but he could not marry nor could he eat, sleep, or hunt with his people. He still was denied his Indian name and tribal dress. No member of the tribe was allowed to mention his name, but answered all questions about him with "I don't know anything." Crop-ear Charlie lived to be more than a hundred years old, dying in a little shack near the present town of Dania.

Near Las Olas Blvd. is the HOTEL AMPHITRITE, built in the remodeled superstructure of a passenger steamship that the 1934 hurricane obligingly moved across the river and beached on this convenient spot.

U.S. COAST GUARD BASE No. 6, at Las Olas Beach, is an outgrowth of one of the houses of refuge that the Federal Government constructed in 1888 at intervals of 25 miles along sections of the lower Florida coast. At that time the coast was poorly charted and unprotected. Built to shelter shipwrecked sailors, these structures were used by travelers and by the local populace during hurricanes.

FLORIDA

Beginning at Fort Lauderdale, the old Dixie Highway follows the CAPRON TRAIL, built during the Seminole Wars; it was cut bit by bit through the native jungle, later becoming a 16-mile wagon road to Miami. Having served its purpose — that of enabling the soldiers to cut off the flow of supplies from the Seminoles, which were being imported from Cuba — the Capron Trail was abandoned at the end of the war and, in most places, became obliterated. Consequently, travel between Palm Beach and Miami, until the establishment of the railroad in 1896, was very difficult. The traveler had either to go by boat or to walk 66 miles along a lonely beach. If he chose to walk he usually accompanied the postman who carried the mail from Palm Beach to Miami on foot and he paid five dollars for the privilege. Only the postman knew the trail. Hidden at the numerous inlets, the mail carrier had boats in which he ferried his companions across.

At **224.1 m.** is the intersection with a new rock road.

Left on this road **3 m.** is PORT EVERGLADES, marine shipping point for Broward Co., with a fine harbor. The new harbor, built in a shallow lagoon known during boom times as Lake Mable, was created by the opening of a deep exit to the ocean. With a 35-ft. depth, Port Everglades is a port of call for large passenger vessels, and its freight traffic has increased in recent years.

At **225.1 m.** (L) is a BANYAN TREE advertised as the "million-dollar tree." This amazing native of East India has a large smooth trunk and horizontal limbs from which it sends down slender, vine-like branches that take root in the ground and develop into secondary trunks attached to the parent and forming in time a whole grove. A boom-time yarn relates that a tourist offered the owner a million dollars for the huge tree, provided that it could be transplanted to his northern estate and persuaded to survive the cold.

DANIA, **227.4 m.** (12 alt., 1,674 pop.), a tomato-farming center, is in an area known during the Seminole Wars as Five Mile Hammock. Of the many Danish families who migrated to Dania in 1896, and subsequently named the town, little trace remains today.

South of the business district is Davie Road, paved but unmarked.

Right on this road is a SEMINOLE INDIAN RESERVATION, **4 m.**, where Indian affairs for the entire State are managed. The office of the Indian agent is in a big, gray, frame house with a high gable roof. Its bleak unimaginative architecture contrasts sharply with the styles common in southern Florida.

The dozen or so small, white, one-room-and-porch houses of the Seminoles here are totally unlike the palmetto-thatched huts used by the Indians in the Everglades, and here are no banana plants, jungle stockades, or misspelled signs to attract the attention of passing strangers. The reservation has a business-like air; here the Seminole works and lives normally; he is not on parade with alligators and rattlesnakes as in the amusement areas of Miami and St. Petersburg. Jobs are provided for the Indians who live here permanently or for as long a time as they desire. The school offers both general education and simple vocational training.

The first modern Seminole church (Baptist) was built by the Indians at the reservation with contributed materials, and dedicated in the summer of 1936. In charge of the ceremonies was an Indian from Oklahoma named Holy Canard, who passed out printed business cards to the effect that he held a formal commission from the President as "principal chief of the Creek Nation." Church officials include Pastor William King and Deacons Jim Gopher and Willie Jumper.

DAVIE, 8 m., a conservative, year-round farming community rarely visited by tourists, is in the rich muck lands that skirt the edge of the Everglades.

At 17 m. are the FLAMINGO CITRUS GROVES (*open*), yielding more than 72 varieties of tropical fruit. Many tropical plants are on display in the nearby botanical gardens.

HOLLYWOOD-BY-THE-SEA, 230.1 m. (7 alt., 1,674 pop.), built in 1921 by a California developer, Joseph W. Young, is directly on the ocean shore, where the city owns nearly 6 miles of public beaches.

RIVERSIDE MILITARY ACADEMY, a large privately-owned military school, housed in a boom-time hotel, holds winter terms here and fall and spring terms in Gainesville, Ga.

HOLLYWOOD BEACH HOTEL, a large, many-towered structure, at the eastern terminus of palm-bordered Hollywood Blvd., is a complete resort city under one roof. Near the ocean is the municipally-owned BATHING CASINO, with three bathing pools, two for children and one for adults, in which some nationally famous swimmers have been trained.

The HOLLYWOOD GOLF AND COUNTRY CLUB, on 17th Ave., is maintained for the guests of the Hollywood Beach Hotel; the ballroom of the club house has a glass dance floor and a removable ceiling.

The MUNICIPAL GOLF COURSE is W. of 36th Ave.

OJUS, 233.9 m. (13 alt., 600 est. pop.), was incorporated as a town in 1925 but soon acquired so many debts that it was forced to give up its corporate existence.

The one industry is the MAULE OJUS ROCK PLANT, mining limestone that is used in building and road construction.

FLORIDA

Across the highway (R) is GREYNOLDS PARK in an area of abandoned rock pits. Above stone-block walls rises a castellated observation tower; this structure, of native rock with a ramp spiraling to the top, was patterned after an Aztec temple. Inside the park, an area of sweeping green lawns surrounds a stone pavilion that harmonizes architecturally with the English type stone cottage of the caretaker. To the W. are picnic grounds in a native hammock, and large groves of glossy Caribbean pines.

NORTH MIAMI BEACH, 236 m. (500 est. pop.), was formerly named Fulford for an early settler. It is said the town changed its name in the hope of becoming a railway terminal for Miami Beach, which has no such facilities.

At the traffic light is the junction with Golden Glades Road, also called Sunny Isles Road.

Left on this causeway road, crossing salt marshes to the ocean and SUNNY ISLES CASINO, 2 m. This building stands at the junction of the Golden Glades Road and State 140, the latter winding southward along the ocean beach.
There are many beautiful homes in this section. Near the Sunny Isles Casino is a new fishing pier (*nominal charge*).
Right on State 140; at BAKER'S HAULOVER, 3.7 m., a bridge that crosses an outlet to upper Biscayne Bay where a long stone jetty extends into the ocean. The jetty is a popular fishing place.

At 237 m. is the junction with a paved road, a remnant of the old East Dixie Highway, heavily traveled during the boom, but seldom used today.

Right on this road is ARCH CREEK NATURAL BRIDGE, 0.5 m., carved out of native oolitic rock and used for passage since early Spanish days. A hundred years ago it was part of the Capron Trail. Over it passed soldiers to end the long, bloody Seminole War, which the Indians and their allies were prolonging by successfully landing supplies and contraband from Cuba in southern Florida. At the SE. end of the bridge, a quiet place with great vine-clad oaks, stood the stone house and mill of Luis, part Indian and part Cuban, who served as agent in the transactions. Here was fought one of the battles of the war.

At 237.2 m. US 1 crosses Arch Creek as it flows through a pleasant meadow.

At 241.1 m. is the northern rim of Miami (*see illustration*).

At 242.1 m. US 1 broadens, following Biscayne Boulevard.

MIAMI, 247.2 m. (10 alt., 110,637 pop.), winter resort (*see FLA. GUIDE*).

282   U. S. ONE

Railroad Stations. Seaboard Airline Ry., 2210 NW. 7th Ave.; Florida East Coast Ry., 200 NW. 1st Ave.

Airports. Pan American Airways, Inc., 2500 S. Bayshore Dr., Miami; 5.5 m., taxi fare, 50¢, time 15 min. Eastern Air Lines, NW. 36th St. at Miami Springs, 7 m., taxi fare $1.50, time 30 min. Planes for local or short trips, at Chalk's Flying Service, County Causeway; Viking Airport, Venetian Causeway.

Steamship Piers. Clarke Steamship Co., Pier No. 2, foot of NE. 10th St., Clyde-Mallory Steamship Co., Pier No. 2, foot of NE. 10th St.; Merchants and Miners Trans. Co., Pier No. 1, foot of NE. 12th St.; Munson Steamship Line, Pier No. 3, foot of NE. 9th St.; Peninsular & Occidental Steamship Co., Pier No. 2, foot of NE. 10th St.

Points of Interest. Aquarium, Old Fort Dallas, Lummus Park, Musa Island Indian Village, Pirate's Cove, Croton Gardens, Ten Million Dollar Hen Hotel, and others.

Section 25. *Miami to Key West, 170.2 m. State 4A.*

Ferries. Between Lower Matecumbe and Grassy Key and between Vaca and No Name Key; infrequent service. Inquire at Miami Motor Club for schedules and to make reservations; $2 to $4 for car and its passengers. Bridges under construction will be completed in spring of 1938.

Observe speed limits on bridges.

State 4A, an extension of US 1 known as the Oversea Highway, is the only route running down over the curving chain of coral islands at the southern end of Florida. For a few miles south of Miami it runs through resort suburbs of that city; it then traverses the yellow-green savannas whose flatness is broken only by occasional hammocks and clumps of mangrove. Herons and cranes feed in the drainage ditch beside the highway and far overhead float a few hawks. The route leaves the mainland, running for more than 100 miles across small keys, which, except in two places, are tied together by bridges. These breaks will eventually be spanned.

The bridges are so long that at times it seems as though the route were running over the sea itself; to the right is an arm of the Gulf of Mexico, to the left is the Atlantic Ocean. In the clear shallow waters beneath the bridges are seen spreading sea fans and fish — among them the blue mass of the tentacled man-of-war — and on the horizon the emerald dots of scattered islands.

East from the City Hall, **0 m.**, in Miami on Flagler Ave.; R. on S. Miami Ave., which State 4A follows.

SOUTH MIAMI, **9.8 m.** (1,160 est. pop.), formerly called Larkins for an early storekeeper, was given its present name the day after he died. Large packing houses, characteristic of many in this vicinity,

FLORIDA

handle tomatoes, truck crops, and citrus. South of the city limits are (L) abandoned oolitic rockpits, now filled with clear greenish-blue water and often used as swimming pools by small fry.

In KENDAL, **11.5 m.** (13 alt., 300 est. pop.), a small citrus-growing settlement, are the COUNTY HOME and COUNTY HOSPITAL.

PERRINE, **17 m.** (13 alt., 800 pop.), was named for Dr. Henry Perrine, a botanist who obtained a Government grant in 1835 for experimentation with tropical plants. Dr. Perrine introduced the sisal (*Agave rigida*), popularly miscalled the "century plant," which now has spread over south Florida.

PETERS, **18 m.** (13 alt., 175 est. pop.), is named for Tom Peters, a pioneer tomato grower, who in pre-railroad days ran a mule tramline to Cutler, from which he shipped his produce N. by boat.

At **20 m.** is the junction with Mainland Drive.

Right on this paved road to the TROPICAL MONKEY JUNGLE (*adm. 25¢*). Java monkeys run wild in a gumbo-limbo hammock; it is the visitors who are caged. Monkeys, even though eager for peanuts, will not enter the screen-guarded pathways for fear of being trapped. The tribe unites, when new monkeys are added to the colony, and drives them away. Some varieties of monkeys and apes are kept in cages.

GOULDS, **22 m.** (12 alt., 326 pop.), is at the northern end of an area with large citrus groves.

PRINCETON, **24 m.** (12 alt., 255 pop.), was originally called Modello. Here several Princeton graduates started a lumber mill in 1905, and put up a huge sign, *Princeton*. Although repeatedly removed, the sign always reappeared, and the F.E.C. Ry. finally adopted the name.

1. Right from Princeton on the Coconut Palm Road to REDLAND FARM LIFE SCHOOL, **2.3 m.**, which collects its pupils from a large area.

2. Left from Princeton on this road to the ALLSPATTAH (Ind., *alligator*) GARDENS, **2 m.**, where, in winter, several acres of sweet peas are in bloom.

At NARANJA (Sp., *orange*), **25 m.** (150 pop.), the road is built across an old rock pit now filled with water. A float for swimmers is moored to the northern bank of the pit.

At **26 m.** is the junction with Newton Road.

Left on this road to FENNELL ORCHID JUNGLE, **0.5 m.** (*open daily during winter blooming season, adm. 25¢; guides*), a commercial orchid nursery. Hundreds of orchids, native and exotic, have been acclimated on hammock trees. *Cattleya* *guatemalensis*, a beautiful orchid blooming high in live-oaks, is grown in quantities.

HOMESTEAD, 30.2 m. (9 alt., 2,319 pop.), is the commercial center of an agricultural area specializing in winter fruit growing. With the coming of the railroad in 1904, Homestead, so named because its original settlers were homesteaders, developed rapidly from a primitive backwoods town into a modern community. A large tract N. of the town is being planted (1938) with 25,000 mahogany trees.

JOHNSTON'S PALM LODGE (*free*), Avocado Road and Krome Ave., owned by Col. H. W. Johnston, the Burbank of South Florida, contains one of the largest collections of tropical plants and trees in the country. There are 267 different kinds of jellies and marmalades on sale.

The SUBTROPICAL EXPERIMENT STATION, on Waldin Drive, conducts experiments in the raising of citrus fruits, avocados, and winter vegetables under subtropical conditions.

A large AVOCADO GROVE is on Waldin Drive. The Homestead Avocado Exchange has shipped about 2,000 carloads of the product in one season.

COCOLOBO CAY CLUB, on an island in Biscayne Bay opposite Homestead, is owned by a group of wealthy anglers. It was one of the haunts of Black Caesar, the pirate.

FLORIDA CITY, 31.7 m. (10 alt., 452 pop.), where royal palms grow in rows on the main street, was incorporated in 1913. It was first called Detroit, but the name was changed when the post office department objected.

Right from Florida City on State 205 to ED'S PLACE (*free*), 1 m., containing monolithic garden furniture and large novelties carved by its owner from local oolite. This granular variety of limestone is composed of small round concretions and resembles fish roe in appearance.

At 14 m. is ROYAL PALM STATE PARK (*free*), where a 4,000-acre tract of dense hammock is preserved in its native state by Florida's women's clubs. It is within the borders of the proposed Everglades National Park. The 260 varieties of native plant life include tall palms, great oaks — many of which harbor orchids — and 31 varieties of ferns, some 27 ft. high. Here the strangler fig and morning glory grow to giant size. Here live multicolored butterflies, including the sleeping *Heliconia*. The area is a bird sanctuary; the giant ibis and pink flamingo live among 150 other species of birds.

PARADISE KEY, within the park, consists of 300 acres of jungle botanically similar to those of the West Indies. Here are native royal palms more than 100

FLORIDA

feet tall; rare orchids, air plants, vines, and water plants of many kinds, including the Egyptian lotus.

ROYAL PALM LODGE (*meals and rooms; picnic grounds free*) is open the year around.

Proceeding W. through the park is a road, built along one of the many drainage canals. The banks (R) are covered for nearly 35 miles with buttonwood trees, gallberry and elderberry bushes. Beyond are thick mangrove islands and cypress hammocks; L. are small patches of cornfield and road construction-camp shacks.

In some places are great expanses of dead mangrove trees, their trunks twisted and denuded of foliage. These are reminders of the devastating hurricane that visited this region September 3, 1935.

Cars can follow the road past BEAR LAKE, a desolate body of water about a mile wide and nearly two and a half miles long. This lake is full of many kinds of fishes, whose fins are seen cutting the surface of the water early in the morning and in the late afternoon.

The beautiful flamingo formerly existed here in such large numbers that it was killed, picked, and salted down as food, chiefly for use on sailing ships. Those remaining in the park are now given protection.

Cranes, herons, raccoons, skunks, otters, brown bears, and wildcats all inhabit the lake area, secure in their isolation.

Great alligators are occasionally visible, their snouts barely above the water. They are also seen sunning themselves on muddy banks.

South of Florida City the highway runs for 10 miles through desolate swamps where dense mangrove patches stretch claw-like roots into the water, gathering sediment that in time will form new land.

At **43.5 m.** the road slopes toward CARD SOUND BRIDGE, which stretches between the mainland and the northernmost of the group of coral islands extending 140 miles into the sea and forming a dividing line between the Atlantic Ocean and the Gulf of Mexico.

The largest, Key Largo, has the usual southern Florida palmetto and scrub flatwoods but S. of it the vegetation is increasingly tropical. The islands are narrow and level, and the vast blue expanse of the sea sweeps to the horizon. Tropical water birds are innumerable. Palms, gumbo-limbo, and golden fig and lime trees grow from coral crevices so glaringly white that it is painful to look at them without tinted glasses. The keys are divided into two groups, the Upper and the Lower. North of Bahia Honda they are coral reefs; south of it they are oolitic.

It is difficult to determine the total area of the islands, some of which are very irregular in shape. The total land area of all probably does not exceed 60 square miles; most of them do not rise more than 6 feet above sea level.

The most important products of the keys are limes, the juiciest and largest grown in Florida. The main occupations of the people have always been fishing, sponging, and farming.

At **44 m.** (R) is SMITTY'S HOUSEBOAT, moored near the center of Card Sound Bridge, and at **44.7 m.** (L) is PELICANS ROOST at the end of the bridge (*boats and tackle available at both places*).

KEY LARGO (Sp., *long*), the northernmost island (320 pop.), is about 30 miles long and at most 1.5 miles wide. Its elevation is greater than that of the other islands in the chain, and it has perhaps the most fertile soil.

At **49.6 m.** is the junction with an unpaved road.

Left on this road to the northern shore, where is the ANGLERS' CLUB CAMP, 5.8 m., owned by a wealthy group. Offshore here is a group of three large and several small islands. These are not, however, the northernmost of the keys; the chain extends N. along the coast for 50 miles.

Among the islands immediately N. of Key Largo — of which Old Rhodes, Elliott, and Sand Keys are the largest — the point of chief interest is BLACK CAESAR'S ROCK (*accessible only by boat*), a tiny island between Old Rhodes and Elliott Islands.

This place was the stronghold and hiding place of Black Caesar, the gigantic chief of an African tribe, who had been captured by a slave trader; during a hurricane off the Florida coast Black Caesar, with a number of others, escaped and reached shore safely. He and his followers built a boat of the wreckage they found and became pirates. His tremendous strength and natural ferocity made him feared along the entire coast. Needing a place to lie in wait for prey and to make repairs on his boat, Black Caesar chose this island among the keys as his stronghold.

To facilitate the removal of the barnacles from the bottom of his ship, Black Caesar had a large iron ring fastened in the coral rock off the western shore of the island. A block-and-fall was rigged to the masthead, the rope being reeved through another block hooked to the ring; the crew hauled on the rope until the vessel lay on her side. After one side had been scraped, the other was treated in the same manner. It is said that Black Caesar also used this method to screen his boat from view when there were pursuers, and to lie in wait for possible victims. The boat would be canted enough to hide the mast in the tree tops. When danger was past or when prey was near enough to be pounced upon, a slackening of the line would soon right the boat to an even keel.

When in time Blackbeard joined Black Caesar, the two became the terror of the region. Blackbeard added to his ferocious appearance by wearing a long black beard braided into many tails, which he looped over his ears. There is little doubt that when they boarded a vessel they seemed like devils from "a hell of their own," as Blackbeard himself boasted. Both pirates met violent deaths while plying their trade.

At this junction the appearance of the key begins to change. Here rolling hammock land contains tall growths of feathery-leaved wild

FLORIDA

tamarind, gumbo-limbo — conspicuous by reason of its red bark, madeira, dogwood, crabwood, great bird fig, and sapodilla. Wild grapevines cover entire trees, often hiding the identity of the support. Day glories and moonvines are everywhere, and the shoulders of the highway are colored with wild flowers. There are few houses along the road, but trails lead through thick hammocks to the ocean and to farms and groves.

The rolling hammock land is soon left behind, and lime groves line the highway. Unkempt vegetation, left for windbreaks, makes it difficult for persons accustomed to the methodically planted citrus groves to recognize the groves as such. Here, on the upper keys, lime trees grow in leafmold and thin soil; farther S. where dirt becomes scarce the trees seem to flourish equally well in rock crevices.

At **56.8 m.** are MABLE'S PLACE and KEY INN (*lodging and meals*).

KEY LARGO STATION, **59.1 m.** (50 est. pop.), was formerly a station on the Florida East Coast Ry., which connected Key West with the mainland. This once-celebrated oversea section was built in 1911, the first train running over the route January 22, 1912. At Key West passenger cars were shunted on tracks of seagoing ferryboats, which carried them to Havana, 90 miles away; thus travelers could step into a Pullman in New York and step out of it in Cuba. Uninterrupted service was maintained from 1912 until September 2, 1935, when the great hurricane destroyed more than 40 miles of track. The F.E.C. Ry. decided against rebuilding the damaged tracks and roadbed, and discontinued service below Homestead, on the mainland. The dismantling of the line is now complete, the right-of-way having been acquired by the Florida State Road Dept. for this highway. The ferry service to Cuba is now carried on through Fort Lauderdale (*see Section 24*).

There is a large LIME PACKING HOUSE (R) near the old station.

At **61.1 m.** (L) is LARGO GARDEN, a refreshment stand built in a beautiful grove having many different kinds of plants. Coral boulders mark the shoulders of the road here.

NEWPORT, **63.8 m.**, is a small settlement of Negroes employed in nearby groves.

ROCK HARBOR, **66 m.** (12 alt., 131 est. pop.), is a tiny village with a 30-foot OBSERVATION TOWER (L) over its post office. The tower is a square stucco structure anchored by cables to bedrock; from its railed upper platform is a view of the Atlantic, Florida Bay, and the Gulf. Eastward is the ocean shore, where are racks for fish nets. All around the tiny settlement are extensive lime groves that bear through most of the year; to the W. is a mango grove.

At **66.8 m.** is MAC'S PLACE, where cabins, sea foods, gasoline, and boats are available. Sportsmen starting out to catch bonefish often buy supplies here.

TAVERNIER, **73.1 m.** (10 alt., 91 est. pop.), takes its name from a stream that winds past the lower end of Key Largo. The French pronunciation of the word has been lost, the natives pronouncing it as though it rhymed with beer.

This waterway is supposed to have been a favorite hiding place for Tavernier, lieutenant of Jean La Fitte, the pirate who was, in 1814, promised 30,000 pounds sterling and a commission in the Royal Navy if he would assist the British operations against New Orleans. Instead La Fitte offered his information and aid to the Americans, whom he and his men served in the Battle of New Orleans. After he was pardoned by President Madison, La Fitte resumed his piracy near the present site of Galveston. When a naval expedition was sent against him for attacking American property, he sailed away. Neither his destination nor his fate is known.

Brought into existence as the southernmost railway stop on Key Largo, Tavernier was just a railroad station until O. M. Woods acquired holdings during the boom days, built a lumber shed, a moving-picture theater and other facilities. Few of the inhabitants live along the highway, but roads lead to homes along the shores.

At Tavernier are some of the storm-proof houses built along the keys by the American Red Cross and the F.E.R.A. Constructed entirely of reinforced concrete, these homes are anchored to bedrock; the massive effect is emphasized by heavy wooden storm shutters and the huge slabs of masonry that form the roofs.

At **73.7 m.** is a CAMP on Tavernier Creek, where boats are available for fishing in the ocean or the bay.

At **73.8 m.** is the northern end of PLANTATION KEY, named for pineapple and banana plantations that flourished in the past. This island was first settled by Bahamans who migrated from Key Vaca and Indian Key in search of farm land; from the 1870's until shortly after the beginning of the present century, it was a very prosperous area. From the road it looks almost uninhabited, but in reality there are many homes, hidden behind the hammocks.

Palms on the lower part of the key show many evidences of the 1935 hurricane, the center of which cut a devastated path at this point.

At **78.6 m.** is SNAKE CREEK, scene of one of the major washouts of the '35 hurricane. The RAILROAD TRESTLE (R) was temporarily rebuilt after the storm for the removal of stranded railroad cars.

WINDLEY ISLAND, **78.9 m.**, was named for an old settler. At the foot of the bridge (L) is the CROOKED DOOR, a camp with boats for hire and bait for sale. Much fine-grained Windley Island coral rock has been used for interior trim in building construction.

A broad expanse of low prairie (L) was the SITE OF THE WORLD WAR VETERANS CAMP NUMBER ONE, one of the three camps destroyed by the 1935 hurricane with many fatalities. A few yards down the road (R) are rock quarries, from which derricks lift huge blocks of coral limestone. The rock has a texture suitable for limited use in sculpture; when treated, it can be used for tiles.

At **80.1 m.** is WHALE HARBOR. Across Whale Harbor extended another railway fill similar to that at Snake Creek, where today bent, twisted rails, swept 50 yards from their bed, are testimony to the hurricane's violence.

UPPER MATECUMBE KEY (Sp., *bent bushes; pron. matty-cum'-bee*), **81.6 m.**, is famous among fishermen. On the ocean front, tabbed without much originality by the sun-baked natives as "Millionaire's Row," are many attractive homes and private fishing lodges.

ISLAMORADA (Sp., *purple isle; pron. i-la-mo-rah'-do*), **82.5 m.** (10 alt., 180 est. pop.), stands in the interior of the key, with flat, scrub palm country surrounding it. It was through the efforts of Henry M. Flagler that the Matecumbe Keys became popular among sportsmen; this place was established by him as a station for the convenience of fishermen. A group of boatmen and skilled guides live near the former station.

At **84.5 m.** is a ferry slip (*gasoline, refreshments, and boats available*).

Left from the extreme southern shore of Upper Matecumbe is TEA TABLE KEY, **1 m.** (*accessible only by boat*), so named because of its flat terrain. Between 1839 and 1840 it was used as one of several bases for naval vessels engaged in Seminole War operations.

Southwest of Tea Table Key and L. of the bridge is INDIAN KEY, **2 m.** It is accessible only by water, but can be approached from all sides. This feature, combined with its fertile acreage, led to its use as a trading post from the time the first Spaniards bartered with the Indians.

The island, containing only 12 acres, was first settled by Capt. Jacob Houseman, of Staten Island, N.Y., as a base for wreckers. In 1838 Dr. Henry Perrine, a botanist of note, landed here with his family to experiment with the growing of tropical plants imported from Yucatan. On the morning of August 7, 1840, the settlement was attacked by 200 Indians; Dr. Perrine and 12 others were killed. The Perrine family, whom the doctor had hidden in a turtle pen beneath the pier, and several others were finally rescued by a Government cutter. Today nothing remains of the settlement except a brick cistern and the gravestone of Captain Houseman.

When the Indian Key massacre was reported, Government troops were sent to quell the uprising. With the help of an escaped Negress who had been held in slavery by the Indians, the entire band of Caloosas with the exception of a few braves who were out hunting, was captured and sent to prison. Fearing revenge for having led the soldiers into the Everglades on the trail of the killers, the former Negro slave left her home and moved to Key West, where she lived to be more than 100 years old.

The inhabitants of the Matecumbe Keys have many superstitious beliefs. One is that sheepshead, a fish with large strong teeth, after feeding on barnacles of copper-sheathed wrecks, become poisonous, and that persons eating such fish die soon afterward.

In the Bay of Florida, 2 miles W. of the southern tip of Upper Matecumbe, is LIGNUM VITAE KEY, on which grows lignum vitae, a very heavy hardwood found nowhere else on the Florida Keys.

LOWER MATECUMBE, 87.9 m., is the site of two of the three World War veterans camps that were swept away by storm in 1935.

At 92.3 m., conspicuously marked at the lower end of this island, is the FERRY SLIP, where automobiles trundle on ferries for the 14-mile crossing to Grassy Key. On these boats excellent meals are served, with turtle steak a favorite dish. The ferries follow a protected waterway, well inside the line of keys, and are never out of sight of the railway viaduct.

The name of GRASSY KEY, 105 m., southern terminus of the ferry, is said to have been derived from an old settler, not from the nature of its grassy growth. The island is two and a half miles long.

CRAWL KEYS, 107.5 m., was named for the sponge and turtle pens, called crawls by the native fishermen. The word is believed to be a corruption of "corral" (*stock pen*).

Right from Crawl Keys is BAMBOO KEY, 1 m., a small irregularly shaped island that is supposed to have fewer mosquitoes than the other keys. This has been attributed to the presence of a parasitic plant, *Cuscuta umbalata*, that thrives on the island. Actually, however, the properties of this odoriferous plant as a mosquito eradicator have not been proved.

At **109.5 m.** is the junction with an unpaved road.

Left on this road to a large emergency landing field, **1 m.**, on land near the ocean shore.

KEY VACA (Sp., *cow*), **110.4 m.**, is thought to have been so named because of the cattle that roamed on it at one time.

At **117 m.** on Key Vaca is the one-story SOMBRERO LODGE, a well-appointed hotel with five large wings.

The keys here were, in the middle of the last century, the scene of an unusual industry. The *beche de mer*, a sea-slug, was salted down for export to the Orient, where it is considered a delicacy.

MARATHON, **118 m.** (7 alt.), is the only settlement of any consequence on this key. A clubhouse owned by Miami sportsmen is recognized by its 30,000-gallon water tank.

The road leading to the ferry landing is well marked.

South of Key Vaca is BOOT KEY HARBOR, graveyard of a number of boats used in constructing the railway, and sunk in these waters when their usefulness ended. In the collection of old craft is virtually every kind from side-wheeler to barge.

Visible from the ferry is what was once the longest railway bridge in the world crossing ocean waters — PIGEON KEY VIADUCT, extending 7.6 miles between tiny Pigeon Key and Duck Key.

South of here the geology of the archipelago changes. From this point to Dry Tortugas all islands are of white oolite with a tangle of mangroves whose roots stabilize old islands and build new ones, simply by retaining the mud washed in by tides. These lower keys have a very scant covering of topsoil, and for that reason have not yet attracted farmers. It has been found, however, that lime trees will grow in the crevices of the limestone; tomatoes, okra, melons, and similar produce grow in the few inches of topsoil, accumulated bit by bit as the mangrove and buttonwood deposit their rich mold. Papayas grow wild here, bearing a small, sweet fruit.

NO NAME KEY, **132.1 m.**, is the western terminus of the ferry. The scenery on No Name Key, with pines and palmettos, suggests certain sections of northern Florida, but sapodilla trees are evidence of the subtropical climate.

At **132.2 m.** (R) is NO NAME LODGE, a fishing resort.

BIG PINE KEY, **135 m.**, contains a grove of comparatively large Cuban pines at the place where topsoil is thickest. Cranes and herons are numerous.

At **136.2 m.** is the junction with a hard-surfaced road.

<small>Left on this road to BIG PINE INN, **7 m.**, a quiet hotel with chicken dinners, rooms, and fishing boats.</small>

BIG TORCH KEY, **137.6 m.**, was so named because of the quantity of torchwood on the island. This wood is so resinous that a torch made of it will burn twice as long as does one of pine.

At **139.6 m.** is MIDDLE TORCH KEY. Here, in addition to torchwood, grows the soapberry tree. For years natives have used the soapberry for catching fish — by hand. The seeds are crushed into a gelatinous mass in calm water, when they release a toxic substance that stupifies fish swimming near it. While the substance can be used for cleansing, it is not commonly utilized for that purpose.

RAMROD KEY, **139.9 m.**, has a post office with a picturesque old muzzle-loading cannon.

SUMMERLAND KEY, **142.1 m.**, has excellent farm land. Extensive lime groves are cultivated here and many tropical fruits are raised for northern markets.

At CUDJOE (contraction of *Cousin Joe*) KEY, **144.3 m.**, pigeons are often seen flying over the road or feasting on the berries of the poison-wood tree. When bruised, the tree exudes a gum that blackens the trunk. It is one of the first to grow on cut-over and burnt hammock land.

SUGAR LOAF SOUND, off SUGAR LOAF KEY, **147.7 m.**, is the site of successful sponge-culture experiments. Here sponges are grown from cuttings and cultivated. The name of the key is derived from the sugar-loaf pineapple formerly cultivated on its soil.

PIRATE'S COVE FISHING CAMP, **149.1 m.**, is one of the best known resorts on the lower keys. During the 1935 hurricane many of its buildings were demolished; the place has been rebuilt on a smaller scale with more secure construction.

SADDLEBUNCH KEY, **155.4 m.**, is an island attractive because of Gandolphe Creek, where mangroves are reflected in clear water. Mangrove and buttonwood line the road, with flat expanses beyond them.

TINY BIRD KEY, **160.2 m.**, is little more than a mangrove swamp, named for the sooty terns that abound under protection of the National Park Service.

GEIGER KEY, **160.6 m.**, is another of the small islands named for an early settler.

FLORIDA

On BOCA CHICA KEY (Sp., *little mouth*), **162.5 m.**, the smooth recently built highway is at times less than 75 ft. from the sea.

At **165.7 m.** (R) is BOCA CHICA FISHING CAMP.

At **167.4 m.** (R) is a BOTANICAL GARDEN with many kinds of tropical plants.

At **168.6 m.** the highway forks, providing two routes leading into KEY WEST, **170.2 m.** (6 alt., 12,831 pop.).

Airports. Miami-Key West Airways, at Yacht Basin, two blocks from center of city; taxi 25¢ per passenger; Pan-American, Roosevelt Blvd., 3 m., taxi 50¢.

Piers. Gulf side of island for P. & O. Steamers to Tampa & Havana.

Information Service. Hospitality House, Elks Lodge Bldg., Duval St.; House Dept., W.P.A. Bldg., Eton St.

Key West, seat of Monroe Co., and the southernmost city of the United States, covers an entire subtropical coral island, one mile wide and half a mile long. Coco-palms flourish, and Spanish limes, dates, pomegranates, and sapodillas grow wild. The place was called Cayo Hueso (*bone key*) by Spanish explorers as early as the 16th century because many human bones were found here.

The island was granted, in 1815, by Ferdinand VII to Don Juan Pablo Salas as a reward for military service. It was not settled until 1822, when it became a naval base of the United States.

About half the inhabitants are descendants of white people of British birth who came here from Virginia, New England, and the West Indies; about one-quarter are descendants of Cubans and Spaniards; and roughly one-sixth are Negroes who have lived — or whose parents lived — in Bahama or the West Indies. The population is bilingual, speaking both Spanish and English.

The earliest businessmen of the island were pirates; the first legal business to develop was wreck salvaging. So many ships were wrecked on the nearby reefs and so rich were the cargoes that, in 1846, a time of unusually severe storms, $1,600,000 worth of shipwrecked property was brought in. The establishment of the lighthouses gradually ruined this source of income. Some return of prosperity came during the Civil War when naval activity increased. After the beginning of the Cuban revolution in 1868 Cubans, many of them cigar makers, came to Key West; in 1874 a modern cigar factory was established, becoming the nucleus of an industry that gave the city its next wave of prosperity. Sponge fishing also became important. In time labor troubles in the cigar industry increased, and by 1906 the business began to move away to Gulf coast cities. In the meantime the place had begun to lose its importance as a supply station for coal-burning ships. The opening of the Florida East Coast Ry. in 1912 gave another economic reprieve, but the effect was only temporary as practically all the cigar factories had left and the sponge-fishing industry had declined. Another blow came in 1925 when the Federal Government reduced the size of the army base; in 1932 the naval base became inactive and the Coast Guard headquarters was transferred to St. Petersburg. The city is the locale of Ernest Hemingway's novel, *To Have and Have Not*.

In 1934 the Governor of the State placed the affairs of the county in the hands of the F.E.R.A., which began the rehabilitation of the city by developing it as a winter resort. The whole place was cleaned up; streets and promenades were landscaped, modern facilities were installed, new buildings were erected, and charming old ones were repaired. A yacht basin and other tourist attractions were developed. During the first resort season more than 35,000 visitors arrived, about 3,000 remaining throughout the winter.

The SPONGE DOCK, foot of Grinnell St., is one of the busiest spots on the island. The auction here is worth seeing.

In the TURTLE CRAWLS, N. end of Margaret St., are often seen specimens hundreds of years old and weighing several hundred pounds. Boats that come to the adjacent dock frequently bring in large jewfish, sharks, and the like. Near the crawls are a canning plant and a turtle-soup factory. The butchering takes place shortly after noon nearly every day.

In the OPEN-AIR AQUARIUM, foot of Whitehead St., are many brilliantly colored tropical fishes.

FORT TAYLOR, entered from Angela St., has played an important part in the history of the city since its foundations were laid in 1845.

The ERNEST HEMINGWAY RESIDENCE (*private*), corner of Olivia and Whitehead Sts., was built shortly after the Civil War.

From KEY WEST LIGHTHOUSE (*open dawn to sunset*), corner of Whitehead and Division Sts., is an exceptional view of this and nearby islands. Aviaries on the grounds hold hundreds of tropical birds.

The BAHAMA HOUSES stand close together, the Bartlum residence on Eaton Street and the Roberts home on Williams Street. The former was first built on Green Turtle Key, Bahama Islands, by Capt. Joe Bartlum in the early part of the 19th century; when the family in the early thirties decided to move here, the house was taken apart, loaded aboard a schooner, and rebuilt on its present site. The Roberts place was likewise brought from the Bahamas. These houses are constructed entirely of white pine and, though unpretentious, have a simple dignity and an air of comfort. They differ from most Key West buildings in having low ceilings, but are like them in having delicate balustrades on the porches and large shuttered openings.

SIDE ROUTE 1
MAINE

Perry — Quoddy Village — Eastport, **7.3 m.** State 190.
Two-lane tar-surfaced roadbed.

State 190 runs close to the shore of Passamaquoddy Bay, which, in sunlight, is intensely blue; beyond the islands dotting the water rise the hills of New Brunswick. This route is particularly delightful in the early morning, when the thumping of motorboats and the tangy aroma of drying fish are reminders of the area's fishing activities.

State 190 branches SE. from US 1 at Perry (*see Section 7*), **0 m.**
At **0.7 m.** is the junction with a gravel road.

Left on this road is PLEASANT POINT, **2 m.**, a 100-acre reservation established about 1822 and occupied by 300 Passamaquoddy Indians. The State appoints an agent to supervise the business affairs of the reservation, but the Indians elect their own governor and may send a member of the tribe to represent them before the legislature. Houses on the reservation are of modern camp type, and there is a fully equipped elementary school.

These Indians had accepted Roman Catholicism before there was extensive white settlement in the State; though they are devout communicants, they retain some of their primitive ceremonies. After a conventional church wedding in the little brick church, for example, the dark-skinned, sleek-haired Passamaquoddies dance to the beating of drums and the chanting of old songs. Discarding ordinary dress, which differs little from that of the white people living around them, they don ancient costume and headdress, and paint their faces. They welcome visitors to these affairs and appreciate applause. While they do not make friends easily, once their shyness has worn off they belie their reputation for taciturnity and are excellent story-tellers. The Passamaquoddies do some farming and occasionally work on the road but their livelihood is derived chiefly from fishing.

From the time of the Revolution, the men have been active in military service; many joined the northern troops in the Civil War. In the INDIAN CEMETERY (R), at the top of the hill near the entrance to the reservation, is a monument to Moses Neptune, killed at the Argonne in 1918, and another to the memory of Charles Nola, who was posthumously awarded the *Croix de Guerre* for remarkable courage and tenacity during the World War in defending an advance post until he was killed. Most of the graves are marked by small wooden crosses with carved inscriptions.

A DAM, a part of the discontinued Passamaquoddy Project, has been built between Pleasant Point and Carlow Island.

At **4.2 m.** State 190 crosses a bridge to Moose Island. A short distance south of the bridge is QUODDY VILLAGE, in which 250 New

England youths are learning (1938), in a National Youth Administration experiment, to choose careers compatible with their talents and abilities.

The boys occupy 120 temporary cottages, nine permanent houses, the apartment buildings, the barracks, and the mess halls formerly used by the laborers and engineers employed on the gigantic tidal project to harness the high tides of the Bay of Fundy. The youths have their own municipal government, run a newspaper, and do all the maintenance and service work.

EASTPORT (*see illustration*), **7.3 m.** (80 alt., 3,466 pop.), with its neighbor Lubec, has long been important in the fishing industry, though it is now less so than formerly. Fishing, like agriculture, has fallen on evil days. Centralized control of the marketing end of the business, the use of the high-powered beam trawlers that destroy millions of young fish, pollution of the streams in which the fish formerly spawned, and other factors have reduced many of the fishermen to abject poverty.

In this area the most valuable fish are cod, haddock, cusk, hake, pollock, halibut, and herring; the small herring are canned as sardines. Sardine canning began in Eastport about 1875 and since that time the women of the town, young and old, drop whatever they are doing, seize their aprons and knives, and rush to the factories when the siren announces a new catch. The old folk speak of sardines as "little fish biled in ile."

The once worthless herring scales have become a valued by-product of the industry, now being carefully gathered for the making of an essence used to give iridescence to artificial pearls. Two plants here manufacture the product.

The town was settled in 1780 but European traders were here a hundred years earlier. The port had considerable prosperity after the passage of the Embargo Act of 1807, becoming the center of extensive two-way smuggling operations. The British ignored these activities until after 1812 when war was declared; in July 1814 they captured the town, confiscating several vessels that were about to sail, loaded with contraband.

The SITE OF FORT SULLIVAN, erected in 1808 for the protection of the settlement, is on a high ledge behind the Shead Memorial High School; from the ledge is a magnificent view of the coast and islands.

The GEORGE PEARSE ENNIS ART SCHOOL (*open*) is on High St.

opposite Boynton St. Artists visit Eastport each summer because of striking coast views and in spite of the fogs that are frequent in August.

The EASTPORT COUNTRY CLUB INN, on the outskirts of the city (*open*), maintains a 9-hole golf course.

Yachting and fishing are popular forms of recreation (*boats for hire*). CAMPOBELLO ISLAND (*see Side Route 2*) is visible from the waterfront.

SIDE ROUTE 2

MAINE

Whiting to Lubec (Treat's and Campobello Islands), **11 m.** State 189.

Two-lane gravel road.

State 189 runs through an area that demonstrates why "rockbound" always precedes mention of the coast of Maine; on the mainland are high cliffs, the land rises abruptly from the rivers and bays, and the offshore islands are rugged. The area is particularly fascinating to inlanders because both the villages and the people have distinctive characteristics, developed by long contact with the sea. The weathered wharves and canning factories are the center of interest to visitors, as well as the centers of community life.

State 189 branches NE. from US 1 at Whiting (*see Section 1*), **0 m.**, crossing Orange River.

At **1.6 m.** (R) is a free camp site.

At **5.7 m.** is the West Lubec post office.

1. Left from West Lubec post office on a gravel road, along which are shafts of abandoned lead mines, is NORTH TRESCOTT, **5.5 m.** (20 alt.; Trescott Town, 365 pop.), on a point of land formed by the Cobscook River and an arm of Cobscook Bay.

COBSCOOK FALLS, visible at the road's end, are formed by high tides rushing with tremendous force through a narrow gut.

2. Right from West Lubec post office, on State 191, is CUTLER, **14.1 m.** (60 alt.; Cutler Town, 492 pop.), a farming and fishing community on a horseshoe-shaped harbor. The town with its irregular coast line has numerous picnic grounds and camping spots.

At **9.8 m.** is the junction with a local road.

1. Left on this road, known as the North Lubec Road, which has many excellent views as it runs along a narrow neck of land that extends into Cobscook Bay. NORTH LUBEC, **3 m.** (80 alt., Lubec Town), gained notoriety from the Jernegan gold swindle (1896–98). Jernegan, pastor of a local church, claimed he had perfected a method of extracting gold from sea water by electrolysis. A stock company was formed and much stock sold throughout the country. A plant was erected on the shore; divers were sent to the bottom and came up bringing small quantities of gold. Large crews of workmen were imported and operations went on for a few months until Jernegan, having collected a considerable sum of money, disappeared.

2. Right on the local gravel road is WEST QUODDY HEAD, **8 m.** (40 alt.), the most easterly point of the United States, where a Coast Guard station and a

lighthouse are maintained. From this point the high cliffs of Grand Manan Island are visible on a clear day.

LUBEC, 11 m. (80 alt.; Lubec Town, 2,983 pop.), had greatly increased activity from the beginning to the discontinuation of the Passamaquoddy Power Project. It is a picturesque seaside village with beautiful views of surrounding bays and coves.

CHALONER TAVERN, Main and Cleaves Sts., formerly a stage line terminus, has been used as a public house since 1804. Chaloner's, the Golden Ball, and Stearns' were the taverns in this harbor town in an earlier day when illicit border trade was profitable. Flour, bought in Canada for $4 a barrel, sold here for $8. Smuggling was rampant. Vessels hailing from Lubec or nearby towns took out papers for Spain or Portugal, sailed instead to some Canadian port where sugar, molasses, flour, and rum were loaded, and returned with full cargoes. At any time of night innkeepers might be awakened by furtive knocks upon their doors.

The GOLDEN BALL, now the Comstock House, is on Pleasant St. It is said the tavern keeper had a special room for deserting British sailors whom he recognized by their sea-soaked clothing, for they usually swam ashore. Generally they had money and he was glad to aid them in boarding a coaster at nearby ports. The story is told of an English officer who, looking for a hideout, was tossed into the street when he displeased the innkeeper. The keeper's daughter went to the officer's assistance and later they were married.

Most of the old houses here face E., according to the early custom.

On TREAT'S ISLAND (40 alt., Lubec Town), in Cobscook Bay, reached from Lubec by ferry, considerable construction was done in connection with the Passamaquoddy Tidal Project. The dam was to have run directly across the island.

A large granite shaft near the center of the island is in memory of Col. John Allen, Indian Superintendent for the Eastern District during the Revolution, who was chiefly responsible for keeping the Passamaquoddy Indians on the side of the colonists. Colonel Allen conducted a trading post on this island.

CAMPOBELLO ISLAND (Ital., *beautiful meadow*), though Canadian soil, is reached by a few minutes ferry ride across Lubec Narrows. The SUMMER HOME OF PRESIDENT FRANKLIN D. ROOSEVELT, 1.5 m. from the ferry, a large red house, is visible from the road. There is good fishing from the island, and the 30 miles of improved roads winding over it and passing many beautiful summer homes, provide magnificent panoramic views of the sea and the Maine coast.

SIDE ROUTE 3

VIRGINIA

Richmond to Westover, **25.6 m.** State 5.

Well-paved route; no accommodations.

East from the capitol, **0 m.**, in Richmond on Broad St. (*see Section 15*); L. from Broad St. on 21st St. to Main St.; L. from Main St. on Lester St., which becomes State 5; this road follows the N. bank of the James River, winding through delightful woods and fields that are, or once were, parts of the historic estates that line the river banks. In the spring the wayside is rich with blossoms; in the fall, red, brown, and yellow leaves lend color. In the woods are deer and other game, but strangers are warned against attempting to hunt because here, as in most of Virginia, the woods and fields are privately owned.

At **8.7 m.** (R) is an entrance to the RICHMOND NATIONAL BATTLEFIELD PARK (*see VA. GUIDE*). In the park is FORT HARRISON, one of the principal Richmond defenses in the Civil War before it fell on September 29, 1864. The earthworks are particularly well preserved.

Not far E. of Fort Harrison on the river bank is the site of VARINA, the estate to which John Rolfe brought his Indian bride Pocahontas after their marriage in 1614 and where they lived until their departure for England in 1616. John Rolfe is thought to have made his experiments with tobacco here, attempting to cultivate a plant stronger in taste and less bitter than that grown by the Indians at the time, in order to compete with the better grade tobacco the Spanish were sending to Europe. In less than five years after he started this work the colonists had given up their search for precious metals in favor of tobacco raising, which netted them more wealth than the gold of which they had dreamed.

At **13.7 m.** (R) are large gates marking the entrance to CURLES NECK, now a private estate with its own race track, owned by a northern sportsman, but formerly a Colonial estate that was the home of the radical young Nathaniel Bacon, who led an uprising in 1676 to secure popular control of the Colonial government. Governor Berkeley had failed to act to protect the settlements from Indian attacks; Bacon and his followers formed an unauthorized force against the

Indians and succeeded in dispersing them. Bacon was making progress toward reforming the government when he was stricken with fever and met a premature death (*see VA. GUIDE*).

Curles Neck was later owned by Richard Randolph, whose grandson was John Randolph of Roanoke.

MALVERN HILL, **17.1 m.** (R), is crowned by a comfortable old farmhouse on the site of the Colonial home of the Cocke family. Lafayette camped here in July and August of 1781, while watching for Cornwallis. On the north side of the hill McClellan, retreating from before Richmond in July 1862, was attacked by Lee, whom he repulsed, and fell back to Harrison's Landing on the James River (*see VA. GUIDE*).

East of Malvern Hill US 1 runs along TURKEY ISLAND, a former estate of William Randolph, founder of the numerous American clan of Randolphs. A dirt road branches at **19.3 m.**

Left on this road **2 m.** is the SITE OF THE FOREST, home of the widow, Martha Wayles Skelton, who was here married to Thomas Jefferson on January 1, 1772. It is said that the honeymoon journey to Monticello was a hard one, with Jefferson having to lead the horses through snowdrifts on the road.

At **21.3 m.** is the junction with a dirt road.

Right on this road is SHIRLEY, **1.8 m.** (*gardens open weekdays, adm. 50¢; house open only during annual April Garden Week*). The estate was patented by Maj. Edward Hill and descended to his granddaughter, Elizabeth Hill, who became the wife of John Carter, son of "King" Robert Carter, in one of those marriages carefully planned by the bustling agent of Lord Fairfax to bring under his control more rich Virginia acres than he was able to patent in his own name. Anne Hill Carter, a granddaughter of John and Elizabeth Hill Carter, was here wooed and married by "Light Horse Harry" Lee; the couple became the parents of Robert E. Lee.

The house, built about 1740 by "King" Carter for his son and daughter-in-law, is a three-story brick structure with porticoed entrances and gabled roof. The third story was added some time after the lower floors were built. The house stands clear of shrubbery on a lawn that slopes to the river; the two unusually large outbuildings that held the plantation offices and kitchens stand at equal distances from the corners of the N. entrance. The interior is not symmetrical. The door leads directly into a room that occupies more than a quarter of the main floor and holds a three-story staircase. In this entrance hall is an oil portrait of "King" Carter, elegant in a bright red coat and looking, in spite of his Colonial finery, like a prosperous modern businessman. Portraits of other Carters and of Hills line the halls, as they do the walls of the parlor (L). In the parlor is an oil portrait of Edward Hill, who died about 1740; he lived in an older house, long ago destroyed, situated a short distance from the present building. Over the

VIRGINIA 303

fireplace are fine pastel profiles of a younger Robert Carter and his wife, drawn by Saint-Memin. The room also holds some rare old books, among them an early edition of *Tristram Shandy*. The house is owned by Mrs. M. C. Oliver, a lineal descendant of John and Elizabeth Carter.

At **22.5 m.** on State 5 is the junction with a dirt road.

Right on this road **1 m.** is the HOPEWELL FERRY (*leaves the N. bank on the half-hour and the S. bank on the hour, 7 a.m.–6 p.m.; fee 65¢*).

At **23.9 m.** (L) is a dirt road entrance to a U.S. FISH HATCHERY. East of this entrance are small farms and open fields. There is a junction at **25.6 m.** with a dirt road, the entrance lane to Westover.

Right on this road **0.3 m.** are the gates to BERKELEY (*house and grounds open daily; adm. 50¢*). The approach to this old home of the Benjamin Harrisons is a long dirt lane, flanked by a small wood and fields. The large brick house has suffered externally from renovations, but is now in the hands of Malcolm Jamieson, who is gradually restoring it to its former appearance for preservation as a museum; the ugly porches and porticoes will be removed, since they did not belong to the early house; the pink paint is to be scraped from the brick walls; the former arched doorways at the ends of the central hall will be replaced to match the central arch of the hall. The detached brick buildings at the ends that served as offices and kitchens are still intact.

The interior of Berkeley has suffered fewer changes than has the exterior, though partitions have been added between the arches at either side of the central chimney that separates the front and back parlors. The woodwork is delicately fluted. During the restoration of the walls of the front parlor a piece of the rough plaster was exposed and on it was found "B. Harrison" in large script surrounded by scrolls and flourishes. Which Benjamin Harrison left his mark is a matter of conjecture because there have lived here Benjamin Harrison, Attorney General and Treasurer of the Colony; Maj. Benjamin Harrison, member of the House of Burgesses; and Benjamin Harrison, member of the Continental Congress and signer of the Declaration of Independence. It might well be the last, because the old Signer was a man given to occasional whimsical fancies; it was he who shocked Philip Fithian, the serious young tutor of Councillor Carter's children, by refusing to discuss the serious aspects of the first Continental Congress, which he had attended as an observer, and showing more concern over a bet that Virginia girls excelled those of Pennsylvania in beauty.

Opposite the parlor on the river front of the house is a large dining room and behind it is a staircase with a broad landing, where, according to tradition, a plantation orchestra sometimes played during dinner.

In this house was born the Signer's son, William Henry, who became ninth President of the United States and grandfather of another Benjamin Harrison, the twenty-third President.

The grounds drop in three terraces to the river, but little of their former state is apparent.

The main dirt road continues past the entrance to Berkeley to the mansion of the neighboring WESTOVER, **2.1 m.** (*gardens open weekdays; adm. $1*). This old place (*see illustration*), in some ways the most interesting along the James River, was built by William Byrd about 1735 on land inherited from his father, who was a member of the Virginia Council and a businessman who had built up a fortune in the Colony. This fortune had enabled the elder William Byrd to send his children to England for their educations; young William Byrd associated there with the gentry, studied law, traveled, and learned to enjoy the life of a modern young man of his day. At the age of 28 years he was still in London when his father died in December 1704; he returned immediately to America and soon married and attempted to take a place in Colonial affairs. He came into disagreement with Governor Spotswood, however, and finally left for England, where he stayed for five years, strengthening his connections with those who played an important part in Colony affairs. During this period his first wife died, and when he finally returned to the Colony in 1726 he brought with him a wife born in England. A few years later he built Westover.

The original house was burned twice in the next few years but was rebuilt each time along the original lines; that built in 1750 stands today, and is considered one of the most beautiful examples of Georgian architecture in America. It is a three-story brick structure, the third story created by the tall hipped roof with four slender dormers on each front. Two slender chimneys rise higher than the ridge at each end. Low separate outbuildings stood at the sides; the one to the E., destroyed during the Civil War, has been replaced by one of ungainly proportions with a gambrel roof, in contrast with the sweeping lines of the outbuilding to the W. In recent years these outbuildings have been connected with the main structure by pavilions. Of particular interest are the high stoop with its broad flight of steps, the delicate ornamentation of the entrance, whose broken-scrolled pediment is considered one of the finest in America, and the arched heading of the windows.

The interior of the house has been much changed; in it is furniture that was brought from Czechoslovakia by the present owner, Richard Crane, who was attracted to the place in part by the beautiful view of the river. The library of William Byrd, the finest in the country in his day, was sold long ago.

Attention of visitors is drawn first to the beautiful wrought-iron gates in the iron fence that encloses a small area in front of the N. entrance; these simple barred gates are topped by gateheads of elaborate pattern enclosing the cypher of the builder. On either side are heavy posts bearing clumsy stone eagles that look as though they were trying to fly with clipped wings. Finials on the posts, breaking the fence at intervals, are of different patterns. These gates are duplicated at each end of the shallow ellipse, formed by tall tulip poplars, between the house and the river. West of the house lie beautiful old formal gardens, fragrant with the odor of boxwood. Where the paths meet in the center is the GRAVE OF WILLIAM BYRD, builder of the house, marked by an ornate monument with a florid epitaph. The guide explains that Byrd himself wrote this epitaph, but authorities disagree with this statement.

Tunnels running underground to the river bank are a reminder that the house was built at a time when there was always danger of Indian attack and a need for secret exits.

SIDE ROUTE 4
GEORGIA

Folkston to Okefenokee Swamp, **10 m.**

An unnumbered dirt road branches W. from US 1 (*see Section 21*) at Folkston, Ga., **0 m.**; on this is CAMP CORNELIA, **10 m.**, situated on Trail Ridge, which forms one of the boundaries of the OKEFENOKEE SWAMP (120 alt.). At Camp Cornelia is an old camp belonging to the Hebard Lumber Co. From this point a trip can be taken up SUWANEE CANAL, an old drainage canal, into the interior of the swamp.

Permission to enter the swamp is required, and can be obtained from Camp Cornelia at Folkston or the refuge headquarters at Waycross.
Guides necessary; can be hired in Folkston at hotel; service $5 a day, boats extra, depending on size.
Transportation furnished by guides; small motorboats, bateaux, or duck punts.
Clothing, hunting or fishing togs, or any old clothes.
Equipment for overnight trip obtained from guides at reasonable cost.
Accommodations crude.
Best Season, late fall, winter, or early spring, because flies, mosquitoes, and other insects are numerous in warm weather.
(Since the Okefenokee is bisected by dense cypress growths, passage from one side to the other is difficult. An entrance from the W. up the Suwanee River to Billy's Island can be made from Fargo.)

For the biologist and naturalist a trip into the Okefenokee Swamp (*see illustration*) is one of the most interesting that can be taken in Georgia, not only because of the jungle-like beauty of the semitropical growth but because of the many species of plant and animal life rarely found anywhere else. The total area of the swamp is 475,450 acres, of which 296,000 acres are now owned by the U.S. Bureau of Biological Survey. To date 288,000 acres have been developed as a refuge for wild animal and bird life.

The Okefenokee Swamp is larger than the State of Rhode Island. Extending from a few miles S. of Waycross to an ill-defined termination in Florida several miles S. of the Georgia Line, it is roughly 45 miles long and 35 miles wide. Its name (Ind., *Owaquaphenoga, trembling earth*) was given when it was the hunting grounds of the Lower Creeks and Seminoles.

In this weird intricate area, large bodies of water stretch through labyrinths of giant moss-covered cypress trees. White and golden water-lilies, locally called "bonnets," purple water hyacinths, and other flowering plants form bright varicolored splashes against a silver-gray gently-swaying screen of Spanish moss. The great expanse of swamp, with cypress and tupelo trees growing out of the water, is broken by many acres of submerged trembling earth called "prairies," which are covered with a heavy growth of yellow-eyed marsh grass. The monotony of the scene is broken by "houses," the name given to clumps of bushes and trees growing on more solid areas. The prairies are threaded by a maze of water runways, which lead from lily-covered cypress bogs to alligator holes. The swamp is further broken by several lakes and islands and is drained by two rivers.

A motorboat can be taken up the slow-moving water of the old drainage canal, which is bordered by tall tupelo, Dahoon holly, and cypress trees draped with Spanish moss. The holly has an abundance of bright red berries, but the leaf is rounded like that of the live-oak and lacks the usual spines. The water of the canal is clear but dark brown, being colored by decaying vegetable matter. At the end of the canal is CHASE PRAIRIE, navigable only by the duck punts, small and narrow shells that are pushed with long poles by guides who stand near the sterns. The poles, usually about 15 ft. long, have three prongs with which the submerged masses of vegetation are grasped. The punts are shallow, drawing only four inches of water, for there are many grassy stretches to be skimmed; they are narrow, so that they can thread their way between the enlarged tupelo roots and the cypress knees, which are enlarged roots projecting above the water.

Other prairies are Grand, New Territory, Durdkin, and Carter's. GRAND PRAIRIE, which covers 50 square miles and is perhaps the largest, contains Gannett Lake, Buzzards' Roost Lake, Coward Lake, Seagrove Lake, and many smaller "bays" and water holes.

Swamp "houses" are built and bogs are extended in a strange manner. A phenomenon, known locally as a "blow-up," occurs when gases formed beneath the water by decaying vegetable matter force masses of vegetation, sometimes 100 ft. square, from the bottom of the water. The surface of the mass, resembling muck, rises several inches above the surrounding water, and in time is covered with grass, briars, small bushes, and water weeds. When it has accumulated this débris, the entire mass either sinks again, pushed down by the growing cypress roots, or floats until caught by a clump of trees. During the floating period this earth-raft collects seed from cypress and other trees and in time develops into a "house." Thus "houses" are formed from above and below, many never becoming stable but swaying and trembling under ordinary weight. From the soggy turf grows an impenetrable undergrowth of berries, smilax, and muscadines.

Across Chase Prairie is FLOYD'S ISLAND, on which is a camp house belonging to Mr. Hebard, who comes in every year for a hunting trip. Here as Mr. Hebard's guest, Samuel Scoville of Philadelphia has spent much time studying the wildlife of the Okefenokee and hunting particularly for the ivory-billed woodpecker, generally regarded as an extinct species but reported to have been seen by the natives of the swamp. Constant warfare on snakes during the last 30 years has greatly reduced their number. Although reptiles are undoubtedly present, only an occasional rattler or moccasin is found, and many explorers have made several excursions into the swamp without seeing a snake.

Floyd Island was named for Gen. John Floyd, who in 1813 was commissioned to drive the Indians from the larger islands within the swamp. It is one of more than 35 flat, white sand islands of the swamp that differ little from the surrounding mainland. They are carpeted with saw palmetto, huckleberries, blueberries, gall-berries, sedges, and various small herbs. The sandy interior supports a growth of long-leaf and slash pine, but in the more fertile hammocks along the margins grow live-oak, water oak, magnolia, bay, and sweetgum trees. Some of the islands are surrounded by bogs of muck and moss that are dense enough to walk upon. Here are found great numbers of the spotted, greenish pitcher plants, growing to the unusual height of three feet. These pitcher plants ensnare small flies into their tube-like leaves by means of a sweetish liquid. The plant then imprisons them with a projecting flap, and after they are drowned in the liquid, it digests them. Flowers that give variety to the waterways are the blue-flowered pickerel weeds, "maiden canes," purple water-shields, and dainty white floating hearts.

Other habitable islands are Honey, Bugaboo, Billy's, and Cow House. To these islands a few hardy settlers ventured and made a hard living by marketing lumber and pine resin and by raising cattle. BILLY'S ISLAND, named for Billy Bowlegs, a Seminole chief, is the largest of these, four miles long and one mile wide. For two generations it was the home of the Jackson Lees, for many years the only white family to dwell in the interior of the area. Theirs was the frontier life of the early colonists, totally without neighbors or ordinary necessities; although 15 children were born, no doctor ever visited the island. When timber crews first came into the swamp the Lees tried life outside, but returned within a year, homesick for the peaceful existence on Billy's Island. For a short time this island was the site of a thriving lumber camp, with a store, school, and motion picture house, but it is now almost deserted. COW HOUSE ISLAND was named during the Civil War; when Federal troops were approaching the swamp in search of supplies, the farmers drove their cattle to the island to hide them from the enemy.

No large streams flow into the Okefenokee, but two rivers have their headwaters in the interior. The St. Mary's winds eastward to the Atlantic Ocean, and the Suwanee, made famous in song by Stephen C. Foster, drifts SW. to empty into the Gulf of Mexico. As the Suwanee River courses through the swamp, patches of dense shade and brilliant sunshine dapple the dark cypress-stained water. Since the swamp is well drained, the water is not stagnant but perceptibly in motion, the current being strongest in the runways that cut through the "prairies."

An eerie stillness pervades the swamp, broken occasionally by the splashing of waterfowl, the songs of thousands of birds that make it their sanctuary, the bellowing of alligators, the hooting and screeching of owls, the calls of animals, or a faint, rumbling sound. No one knows the cause of this rumbling, called by natives the "booming of the swamp."

Waterfowl and birds of many species abound here. Ducks of many varieties, black, mallard, buck, and canvasback, migrate here in winter. The wood duck, Wilson's snipe, green-winged teal, killdee, and hooded merganser are found in lesser numbers. In flight, the rare and picturesque white sandhill or whooping crane makes a perfect cross against the sky. Many native and migratory birds, robins, cardinals, woodpeckers, ruby-crowned kinglets, red-winged blackbirds, and brown-headed nuthatches, give color and music. Other varieties are the barred owl, catbird, red-tailed hawk, marsh hawk, Ward's heron, kingfisher, and the pied-bill grebe.

Alligators, some of them eight feet in length, are found in the deeper pools of the prairies and in the many lakes. A familiar sound through the swampland is the deep-throated bellowing of these saurians, which are generally harmless unless provoked into an attack. Since they help keep the mud from accumulating on the lake bottoms and build wallows that are inhabited by fish, they are unmolested except by the trappers who market their hides in Waycross.

Native trappers hunt deer, panthers, bear, and wildcats, and trap otters, raccoons, and round-tailed muskrats for their pelts, which they market in Waycross. These trappers serve as guides for hunters who find on the islands a big-game sport in the chase of the Florida bear, the largest mammal of the swamp. The hunts are often held at night as communal affairs, the men of the surrounding farms bringing their hounds and joining in the pursuit. Strange little Le Conte frogs and pocket gophers are among the animal life of the swamp.

In the water are found more than 30 species of fish, among which are warmouths, stump-knockers, sand-flirters, trout, mudfish, catfish, jackfish, and large-mouthed bass. The rare rainwater fish (*Leptolucania ommato*) is among the many varieties of tiny subtropical fish.

There is a legend that some Indian hunters, lost in the swamp, saw an island and pressed toward it. At last, fainting from exhaustion and hunger, they sank to the ground on it. A group of beautiful women suddenly appeared and told them to go no farther. Though warning the enraptured hunters of fierce husbands who killed intruders, the women were compassionate and placed delicious fruits, marsh eggs, and corn pones before the men. Being shown a path by which they could return safely to the settlement, the hunters went unwillingly, resolving to return with a large force and win these mysterious beauties for their wives. But no sooner did they set foot on the path than the women vanished. Every later effort to find these "daughters of the sun" failed. The island, hidden in the center of the swamp, was never seen again.

Okefenokee remains a wilderness in spite of repeated efforts to reclaim it. Fifty years ago a large corporation with steam shovels and dredges dug miles of canals, the plan being to drain the swamp into the St. Mary's River and, after taking the rich timber, to turn the great prairies into farm lands. After more than a million dollars had been spent, the corporation became insolvent and abandoned the project.

The next effort was made by the Hebard Lumber Co., which forced into the swamp a railroad built bridge-fashion on piling with branch lines leading to the principal islands and "bays." For several years the work continued, but in time the mill was shut down because of the great expense of cutting and shipping the timber. The railroad is now a skeleton of rotting cross ties and piling.

Geologists say that the Okefenokee was once a salt-water sound that became shut off from the ocean by a barrier reef now called Trail Ridge, and that in its earlier stages it probably resembled the much younger Dismal Swamp of North Carolina and Virginia and the Everglades of Florida. Swallowing up the concerted efforts of men to conquer it, it stands virtually as it was in Colonial days, when the Seminoles, driven by the white men, retreated into the heart of the great swamp and stole like shadows over the trembling earth.

ANNUAL EVENTS ALONG US 1

January, National Motorcycle Race, Daytona Beach, Florida.
January, Artists and Writers Golf Tournament, Palm Beach, Florida.
January, Open Golf Championship, Miami, Florida.
January, Country Club Amateur Championship, Miami, Florida.
January, All States Card Club Luncheon, Miami, Florida.
January, Men's Amateur Golf Championship, Coral Gables, Florida.
January, State Trap Shooting, Daytona Beach, Florida.
January, Beaux Arts Black and White Costume Ball, Miami, Florida.
January, Left Handers' Golf Championship, Coral Gables, Florida.
January, Women's Title Holders Golf Championship, Augusta, Georgia.
January, Automobile Exhibition, Portland, Maine.
January, St. Cecilia Ball, Charleston, South Carolina.
January 1, Saddle Horse Association Indoor Show, Philadelphia, Pennsylvania.
January 1, Orange Bowl Football Game, Miami, Florida.
January 1, Mummers Parade, Philadelphia, Pennsylvania.
January, first Monday, Bachelor's Cotillon (second), Baltimore, Maryland.
January, second week, Rhode Island Department of the American Legion Ice Carnival, Providence, Rhode Island.
January, second week, Providence Festival Chorus Mid-Winter Concert, Providence, Rhode Island.
January, last week, Mercer County Agricultural Show, Second Regiment Armory, Trenton, New Jersey.
January–April, Dog Races, West Palm Beach, Florida.
January–May, Garden Season, South Carolina.
February, Four Ball Golf Tournament, Coral Gables, Florida.
February, Dixie Amateur Golf Championship, Miami, Florida.
February, Miami-Biltmore Mixed Foresome Medal Play Tournament, Coral Gables, Florida.
February, Glen Curtis Golf Tournament, Miami Springs, Florida.
February, Pirates of Penzance Operetta, "Grito de Baire" (Cuban Patriotic Day), Key West, Florida.
February, Art and Artists' Exhibit, Miami, Florida.
February, Rose Ball, Lake Worth Casino, Lake Worth, Florida.
February, International Boat Races, Daytona Beach, Florida.
February, Romany Chorus Outdoor Concert, Palm Beach, Florida.
February, National Moth Boat Races, Melbourne, Florida.
February, All State Day, Lake Worth, Florida.
February, Rotary Senior Golf Tournament, Daytona Beach, Florida.
February, Frostbite Dingy Races, Miami, Florida.

February, National Championship Stock Car Races, Daytona Beach, Florida.
February, Winter Carnival, Camden, Maine.
February, Eastern Dog Club Show, Mechanics Building, Boston, Massachusetts.
February, Chinese New Year Celebration, Philadelphia, Pennsylvania.
February, Bok Award Presentation, Philadelphia, Pennsylvania.
February, Tropical Fiesta, Hollywood, Florida.
February 13–14, Outboard Motor Regatta, New Smyrna, Florida.
February 15, "A Day in Spain," St. Augustine, Florida.
February 16, Lithuanian Day Festivities, St. Alphonsus Church, Baltimore, Maryland.
February 22, Helen Doherty Milk Fund Charity Ball, Coral Gables, Florida.
February 22, "Old Timers" Annual Picnic, Ft. Pierce, Florida.
February 22, Washington's Birthday Yacht Club Regatta, Palm Beach, Florida.
February 22, International Music Festival, Symphony Hall, Boston, Massachusetts.
February 23–29, "La Semana Alegre" (Week of Joy), Key West, Florida.
February, first Saturday, Boston Athletic Association Games, Boston Garden, Boston, Massachusetts.
February, first week, Dog Show, Fifth Regiment Armory, Baltimore, Maryland.
February, first week, New England Sportsmen's and Boat Show, Mechanics Building, Boston, Massachusetts.
February, first week, Winter Sports Carnival, Providence, Rhode Island.
February, third week, National Horse Show, Philadelphia, Pennsylvania.
February–May, Thursdays at 8 p.m., Bond Astronomical Club Meetings, Harvard University, Cambridge, Massachusetts.
March, Cineraria Show, East Rock Park, New Haven, Connecticut.
March, Mid-Winter Sailing Regatta, Miami, Florida.
March, Cotton Ball, Lake Worth Casino, Lake Worth, Florida.
March, Miami-St. Petersburg Yacht Race, Miami, Florida.
March, International Four Ball Championship Tournament, Miami, Florida.
March, South Atlantic States Tennis Tournament, Augusta, Georgia.
March, National Golf Tournament, Augusta, Georgia.
March, Sand Hill Garden Club Tour, Augusta, Georgia.
March, Women's Invitation Tournament, Augusta, Georgia.
March, Bowdoin College Interscholastic Track Meet, Brunswick, Maine.
March, High School Championship Basketball Tournament, Bangor and Lewiston (alternately), Maine.

ANNUAL EVENTS ALONG US 1

March, Massachusetts Horticultural Society Spring Flower Show, Mechanics Building, Boston, Massachusetts.
March, Charity Horse Show, Philadelphia, Pennsylvania.
March, Motorboats and Sportsmen's Show, Philadelphia, Pennsylvania.
March, Amateur Field Trials, Camp Lee, Petersburg, Virginia.
March 17, Evacuation Day Ceremonies and Parade, South Boston, Massachusetts.
March 25, Maryland Day.
March 30, Pioneer Visitors and State Club Night, Miami, Florida.
March, first or second week, Southern Conference Basketball Tournament, Raleigh, North Carolina.
March, second week, Exhibition of Works by the Blind, Philadelphia, Pennsylvania.
March, last week, Flower Show, Philadelphia, Pennsylvania.
March, River Revelry Celebration, Fort Lauderdale, Florida.
March–April, Seminole Sun Dance, Palm Beach, Florida.
March or April, Easter Sunrise Service, Coast Guard Academy Bowl, New London, Connecticut.
March or April, Easter Sunrise Service, East Rock Park, New Haven, Connecticut.
March or April, Easter Monday Egg Hunt, East Rock Park, New Haven, Connecticut.
March or April, Easter Flower Show, East Rock Park, New Haven, Connecticut.
March or April, Easter Sunrise Services, Ribaut Monument, Jacksonville, Florida.
March or April, Metropolitan Opera Company, Lyric Theatre, Baltimore, Maryland.
March or April, Easter Sunrise Service, Municipal Stadium, Baltimore, Maryland.
March or April, Chickering Anniversary Concert, Jordan Hall, Boston, Massachusetts.
March or April, Easter Sunrise Service, Elizabeth, New Jersey.
March or April, Easter Sunrise Services, Philadelphia, Pennsylvania.
April, International Moth Class Regatta, Daytona Beach, Florida.
April, Miami Beach Pro Tennis Championship, Miami, Florida.
April, Seminole Sun Dance, Palm Beach, Florida.
April, Boys' Club Marathon Race, Portland, Maine.
April, Maine Open Handicap Golf Tournament, Brunswick, Maine.
April, Maryland Daffodil Society Daffodil Show, Community Center, Guilford, Maryland.
April, Horse Races, Bowie, Maryland.

April, Hutchinson Horse Show, Kentucky Riding Academy, Harrison, New York.
April, Exhibition of School Children's Art Work, Swarthmore, Pennsylvania.
April, Federation of Flower Clubs Flower Show, Providence, Rhode Island.
April, Deep Run Hunt Race Meet, Curles Neck, Richmond, Virginia.
April, Kennel Club Show, Richmond, Virginia.
April, Fairfax Hunt Horse Show, Alexandria, Virginia.
April 14, Pan-American Day, Miami, Florida.
April 19, Patriot's Day Marathon and Ceremonies, Boston, Massachusetts.
April, first Saturday, Junior Point-to-Point, Worthington Valley Course, Baltimore, Maryland.
April, first week, Ice Carnival, Carlin's Park, Baltimore, Maryland.
April, first week, Women's Mid-South Championship Golf Tournament, Southern Pines, North Carolina.
April, first week, City Baseball Championship, Philadelphia, Pennsylvania.
April, second Saturday, My Lady's Manor Point-to-Point, Monkton, Maryland.
April, second week, National Homes Show Week, Fifth Regiment Armory, Baltimore, Maryland.
April, third Saturday, Grand National Point-to-Point, Hereford, Maryland.
April, last Saturday, Maryland Hunt Cup Point-to-Point, Worthington Valley Course, Baltimore, Maryland.
April, last week, Boston Symphony Orchestra Pension Fund Concert, Symphony Hall, Boston, Massachusetts.
April, last week, Pennsylvania Relays Carnival, Philadelphia, Pennsylvania.
April or May, Garden Week, Virginia.
April–May, Tours of Maryland Gardens and Homes, Federated Garden Clubs of Maryland.
April–May, daily except Sundays, Pimlico Race Track Spring Meeting, Old Pimlico Road, Baltimore, Maryland.
April–May, Azalea Festival, Charleston, South Carolina.
April–September, Major Leagues Baseball, Fenway Park or National League Field, Boston, Massachusetts.
May, State Intercollegiate Track Meet, Maine.
May, Bird Dog Field Trial, Bangor, Maine.
May, Skeet Shooting, New Haven Gun Club, New Haven, Connecticut.
May, Iris Shows, East Rock Park, New Haven, Connecticut.
May, University of Maryland Pony Show, College Park, Maryland.
May, Novelty Park Club Marathon, Pawtucket, Rhode Island.
May, Interscholastic Track Meet, Providence, Rhode Island.
May, Horse Races, Narragansett Park, Pawtucket, Rhode Island.
May, All States Card Club May Breakfast, Miami, Florida.

ANNUAL EVENTS ALONG US 1

May, Iris Field Day, New Jersey College of Agriculture, New Brunswick, New Jersey.
May, Long Island Sound Yacht Racing Association Opening Regatta, Rye, New York.
May, Hobby League Show and Exhibition, Philadelphia, Pennsylvania.
May, Auto Races, Langhorne, Pennsylvania.
May, Harrison Horse Show, Kentucky Riding Academy, Harrison, New York.
May, Lawridge Horse Show, Port Chester, New York.
May, Preakness Day, Pimlico Race Track, Baltimore, Maryland.
May, Pimlico Race Track Special Stake Races, Baltimore, Maryland.
May, Azalea Show, Towson Nurseries, Baltimore, Maryland.
May, Catholic Sodality Union Rally, Fifth Regiment Armory, Baltimore, Maryland.
May, Dixie Handicap, Pimlico Race Track, Baltimore, Maryland.
May, Baltimore Spring Handicap, Pimlico Race Track, Baltimore, Maryland.
May, Fete of Lights, Maryland Institute Art Ball, Baltimore, Maryland.
May, McDonogh School Horse Show, Reisterstown Road, Baltimore, Maryland.
May, Girl Scouts' Garden Tour, Baltimore, Maryland.
May, Mary Washington (mother of George Washington) Mother's Day Celebration, Fredericksburg, Virginia.
May, Spring Races, Media, Pennsylvania.
May, May Day Celebration, Swarthmore College, Swarthmore, Pennsylvania.
May, Flower Show, Raleigh, North Carolina.
May 5, Pioneer Day Dinner, Miami, Florida.
May 11, Powder House Day Pageant (based on Revolutionary War episode), New Haven, Connecticut.
May 16, Moore Park Play Day, Miami, Florida.
May 30, Memorial Day Exercises, Lansdowne, Pennsylvania.
May, first Sunday, Boston Music School Settlement Concert, Jordan Hall, Boston, Massachusetts.
May, first week, Ringling Brothers-Barnum and Bailey Circus, Boston Garden, Boston, Massachusetts.
May, first week, Noncompetitive Boston Music Tournament, Steinert Hall, Boston, Massachusetts.
May, first week, Handicraft Club Exhibit, Providence, Rhode Island.
May, first week, Horse Show, Essex Troop Armory, Newark, New Jersey.
May, first week, Longwood Gardens Pageant, Kennett Square, Pennsylvania.

May, first week, National Music Week Oratorio by Handel Choir, Peabody Conservatory of Music, Baltimore, Maryland.
May, first week, Tulip Show, Community Center, Guilford, Maryland.
May, first week, Musical Festival, Lansdowne, Pennsylvania.
May, second week, Federation of Music Clubs Music Week Festival, Providence, Rhode Island.
May, second week, Garden Club Flower Show, Third Presbyterian Church, Newark, New Jersey.
May, second week, Philadelphia on Parade, Philadelphia, Pennsylvania.
May, second week, Dewey Day Celebration, Navy Yard, Philadelphia, Pennsylvania.
May, second Wednesday, Women's Civic League Flower Mart, Washington Monument, Baltimore, Maryland.
May, second week, Folklore Festival, Philadelphia, Pennsylvania.
May, third week, Germantown May Market, Philadelphia, Pennsylvania.
May, third week, Flower Mart, Rittenhouse Square, Philadelphia, Pennsylvania.
May, last week, Students' Exhibition Concerts, Peabody Conservatory of Music, Baltimore, Maryland.
May 30, Launching of Flower "Ship" on the Delaware in Memory of Deceased Naval Veterans, Philadelphia, Pennsylvania.
May or June, City Golf Tournament, Augusta, Georgia.
May–June, nightly at 8 p.m., "Pops" Concerts by members of the Boston Symphony Orchestra, Symphony Hall, Boston, Massachusetts.
May–June, Saturdays, College Crew Races, Charles River, Massachusetts.
May–September, Water Sports and Fishing, South Carolina.
June, Boston National Home Show, Mechanics Building, Boston, Massachusetts.
June, Skeet Shooting, Great Eastern States and National Telegraphic Championship, Remington Gun Club, Inc., Lordship, Connecticut.
June, Greenwich Country Club Golf Championship, Greenwich, Connecticut.
June, Pony Show, Harford County Fair Grounds, Bel Air, Maryland.
June, Westchester County Horse Show, Port Chester, New York.
June, Outdoor Archery Tournament, California Road, Port Chester, New York.
June, Providence Festival Chorus Concert, Providence, Rhode Island.
June, Westchester County Horse Shows, Port Chester, New York, and Westchester Country Club, Rye, New York.
June, American Yacht Club Invitation Overnight Cruise to New London, Rye, New York.
June, Residents' Amateur Golf Championship, Maine.
June, Maryland Yacht Club Opening, Baltimore, Maryland.

ANNUAL EVENTS ALONG US 1

June, Peony and Rose Show, Horticultural Hall, Boston, Massachusetts.
June, Longfellow Garden Club Display, Portland, Maine.
June, Arundel Garden Club Exhibition, Portland, Maine.
June 9, Memorial Day, Petersburg, Virginia.
June 13, Festival of St. Anthony of Padua, Baltimore, Maryland.
June 14, Flag Day Celebration, Betsy Ross House, Philadelphia, Pennsylvania.
June 17, Bunker Hill Day Celebration, Boston, Massachusetts.
June, first week, Greenwich Kennel Club Dog Show, Greenwich, Connecticut.
June, first week, Clothes Line Art Exhibition, Philadelphia, Pennsylvania.
June, first week, Wissahickon Day, Riders and Drivers Meet, Philadelphia, Pennsylvania.
June, first week, Field Mass for Police and Firemen, Philadelphia, Pennsylvania.
June, second week, Historical Pageant and Fête, Old Swede's Church, Philadelphia, Pennsylvania.
June, third week, State Women's Amateur Golf Title Play, Providence, Rhode Island.
June, third week, American Legion and Auxiliary Pageant, Longwood Gardens, Kennett Square, Pennsylvania.
June, third week, Yale University Commencement, New Haven, Connecticut.
June, last week, Opening of Robin Hood Dell Symphonic Season, Philadelphia, Pennsylvania.
June, last week, Freshman, Combination, and Junior Varsity Crew Races, New London, Connecticut.
June, last week, Yale-Harvard Baseball Game, Mercer Field, New London, Connecticut.
June–August, Rose Show, East Rock Park, New Haven, Connecticut.
June–August, Music Hill Concerts, Greenwich, Connecticut.
July, Automobile Races, Folly Beach, South Carolina.
July, Yacht Regatta, Boothbay Harbor, Maine.
July, Maryland Yacht Club Regatta, Baltimore, Maryland.
July, Municipal Music Festival, Druid Hill Park, Baltimore, Maryland.
July, Miller Memorial Race, Gibson Island Club, Baltimore, Maryland.
July, Horse Races, Old Orchard Beach, Maine.
July, Yacht Regatta, Kennebunkport, Maine.
July, Yacht Regatta, Harpswell, Maine.
July, Casco Bay Regatta, Chebeague Island, Maine.
July, State Champion Trap Shoot, Maine.
July, Horse Show, Westchester-Biltmore Country Club, Purchase, New York.
July, Race Week, Larchmont Yacht Club, Larchmont, New York.

July, Display of Roses, Roger Williams Park, Providence, Rhode Island.
July, Fairfield County Hunt Horse Show, Westport, Connecticut.
July 3–4, Volusia County Frolics, Daytona Beach, Florida.
July 4, People's Regatta, Schuylkill River, Philadelphia, Pennsylvania.
July 4, Independence Day Celebration, Philadelphia, Pennsylvania.
July 4, Cla-na-Gael Athletic Games, Philadelphia, Pennsylvania.
July 4, Scottish Games Association National Competition, Greenwich, Connecticut.
July 5, Dog Show, Progressive Dog Club, Larchmont, New York.
July, fourth week, Joint Farmers' Convention and 4-H Clubs Meeting, Raleigh, North Carolina.
July (odd years), Portland-Halifax Yacht Race, Maine.
July–August, Horse Races, Bel Air, Maryland.
August, Children's Gardens Exhibition, Horticultural Hall, Boston, Massachusetts.
August, Horse Show Association of Maryland Show, Baltimore, Maryland.
August, State Tennis Championship, Portland, Bar Harbor and Squirrel Island (alternately), Maine.
August, Portland-to-Monhegan-Island Yacht Race, Maine.
August, Flower Exhibition, Machias, Maine.
August, Open House Day, Wiscasset, Maine.
August, Summer Visitors' Day, Maine.
August, Portland-to-Peaks-Island Swim Contest, Maine.
August, Three-Quarter Century Club, Maine.
August, American Yacht Club Invitation Cruise Day, Rye, New York.
August, Championship Tennis Tournament, Augusta, Georgia.
August, All States Card Club Birthday Party, Miami, Florida.
August, State Championship Skeet Shoot, Maine.
August, Open Amateur Golf Championship, Maine.
August, Art Exhibition, Old Lyme, Connecticut.
August, Hamburg Fair, Lyme, Connecticut.
August, Massachusetts Horticultural Society Midsummer Exhibition, Horticultural Hall, Boston, Massachusetts.
August 10, Biennial Celebration of the Battle of Stonington (next in 1939), Stonington, Connecticut.
August, third week, Grange Fair, Old Lyme, Connecticut.
August, third week, New London County 4-H Fair, North Stonington, Connecticut.
August, fourth week, Watch Hill Beach Club Water Carnival, Watch Hill, Rhode Island.
August, last week, Tennis Tournament, Lansdowne, Pennsylvania.
September, Debutantes Ball, Raleigh, North Carolina.
September, National Tobacco Festival and Pageant, South Boston, Virginia.

ANNUAL EVENTS ALONG US 1

September, Cedar Point Race, Gibson Island Yacht Club, Baltimore, Maryland.
September, Horse Show, Greenwich, Connecticut.
September, Guilford Fair, Guilford, Connecticut.
September, Grange Horse Fair, Old Saybrook, Connecticut.
September, Grange Fair, North Stonington, Connecticut.
September, Topsfield Fair, Treadwell Farm, Topsfield, Massachusetts.
September, Horse Races, Suffolk Downs, East Boston, Massachusetts.
September, Bird Dog Field Trials, Damariscotta, Maine.
September 6, Lafayette Day Celebration, Independence Hall, Philadelphia, Pennsylvania.
September 12, Defender's Day, Baltimore, Maryland.
September 13, Westchester Kennel Club Dog Show, Westchester-Biltmore Country Club, Purchase, New York.
September, daily except Sundays, Horse Races and Fair, Timonium, Maryland.
September, first Monday, Middle States Regatta, Philadelphia, Pennsylvania.
September, second week, Massachusetts Horticultural Society Late Summer Exhibition, Horticultural Hall, Boston, Massachusetts.
September, fourth week, Endicott Cup Golf Tournament, Providence, Rhode Island.
September, fourth week, Rhode Island Women's Golf League Tournament, Providence, Rhode Island.
September, last week, State Fair, Trenton, New Jersey.
September or October, State Fair, Richmond, Virginia.
October, Harford County Fair, Bel Air, Maryland.
October, Chrysanthemum Field Day, New Jersey College of Agriculture, New Brunswick, New Jersey.
October, Food Fair and Better Homes Exposition, Philadelphia, Pennsylvania.
October, Opening of Philadelphia Forum Season, Philadelphia, Pennsylvania.
October, Massachusetts Horticultural Society Fruit and Vegetable Exhibition, Horticultural Hall, Boston, Massachusetts.
October, State Dog Show, Portland, Maine.
October, Horse Races, Laurel, Maryland.
October, Virginia Fox Hunters' Association Annual Trials, Petersburg, Virginia.
October 10, "Grito de Yara" (Cuban Cry for Freedom), Key West, Florida.
October 11, Pulaski Memorial Day, Baltimore, Maryland.
October 12, Columbus Day, Baltimore, Maryland.

October 12, Columbus Day International Marathon, Port Chester, New York.
October 12, Columbus Day Celebration, Philadelphia, Pennsylvania.
October 27, Navy Day Celebration, U. S. Submarine Base, Groton, Connecticut.
October 27, Navy Day, Open House at Navy Yard, Philadelphia, Pennsylvania.
October, last Sunday, Holy Name Society Rally, Fifth Regiment Armory, Baltimore, Maryland.
October, first week, Dahlia Show, Vincent Dahlia Farm, Baltimore, Maryland.
October, first week, Market Day and Country Fair, Lansdowne, Pennsylvania.
October, first week, Electric and Radio Show, Philadelphia, Pennsylvania.
October, first week, Dog Parade ("Mutt Show"), Philadelphia, Pennsylvania.
October, first week, Rhode Island Golf Association Invitation Tourney, Providence, Rhode Island.
October, second week, Philadelphia Orchestra Symphonic Season Opening, Philadelphia, Pennsylvania.
October, second week, Fox Hunt, Rose Tree Fox Hunting Club, Media, Pennsylvania.
October, third week, State Fair, Raleigh, North Carolina.
October–November, Thursdays at 8 p.m., Bond Astronomical Club Meetings, Harvard University, Cambridge, Massachusetts.
October–November, Professional Football Games, Fenway Park, Boston, Massachusetts.
October–May, Sundays at 3 p.m., Old South Forum, Old South Meeting House, Boston, Massachusetts.
October–May, Sundays at 8 p.m., Ford Hall Forum, Boston, Massachusetts.
October–May, Sundays at 3:30 p.m. and 8 p.m., Thursdays at 8 p.m., Public Library Lectures and Concerts, Boston, Massachusetts.
October–May, Sundays at 10:30 a.m., Community Church of Boston, Symphony Hall, Boston, Massachusetts.
October–May, Fridays at 2:15 p.m. and Saturdays at 8:15 p.m. (except when on tour), Boston Symphony Orchestra, Symphony Hall, Boston, Massachusetts.
November, Junior Air Meet, Fort Lauderdale, Florida.
November, Chrysanthemum Show, East Rock Park, New Haven, Connecticut.
November, Equestrian Sports Field Day, Augusta, Georgia.
November, Slash Pine Festival, Waycross, Georgia.
November, Open Golf Tournament, Augusta, Georgia.

ANNUAL EVENTS ALONG US 1

November, Poultry Show, Portland, Maine.
November, Pomological Seed Exhibit, Maine.
November, Food Exhibition, Portland, Maine.
November, Salon of Allied Arts Exhibition, Boston, Massachusetts.
November, World's Championship Rodeo, Boston Garden, Boston, Massachusetts.
November, Automobile Show, Mechanics Building, Boston, Massachusetts.
November, Automobile Show, Fifth Regiment Armory, Baltimore, Maryland.
November, Horse Races, Bowie, Maryland.
November, Kennels Club Dog Show, Philadelphia, Pennsylvania.
November, Thanksgiving Day, Santa Claus and Santa's Son Parade, Boston, Massachusetts.
November, Thanksgiving Day Toyland Parade, Philadelphia, Pennsylvania.
November, daily except Sundays, Pimlico Race Track Fall Meeting, Baltimore Maryland.
November, first week, Chrysanthemum Show, Providence, Rhode Island.
November, first or second week, Amateur Field Trials, Camp Lee, Petersburg, Virginia.
November, second week, Automobile Show, Philadelphia, Pennsylvania.
November, third week, Food Show and Better Homes Exposition, Providence, Rhode Island.
November, last week, Food Show, Fifth Regiment Armory, Baltimore, Maryland.
November, last week, Army-Navy Football Game, Philadelphia, Pennsylvania.
December, All-American Air Meet, Miami, Florida.
December, State Grange Meeting, Boston, Massachusetts.
December, Handell and Haydn Society's "The Messiah," Symphony Hall, Boston, Massachusetts.
December, Battle of Trenton Celebration, Trenton, New Jersey.
December, "The Nativity," Christmas Pageant, Lansdowne, Pennsylvania.
December 24, Christmas Eve Celebration, Beacon Hill, Boston, Massachusetts.
December 24, Christmas Eve Carol Singing, Philadelphia, Pennsylvania.
December 24, Christmas Ball, Philadelphia, Pennsylvania.
December 31, Sounding of Liberty Bell at Midnight, Philadelphia, Pennsylvania.
December, first Monday, Bachelor's Cotillon, Baltimore, Maryland.
December or January, National Winter Sports Exposition, Boston Garden, Boston, Massachusetts.
December–March, Tuesdays at 8:15 p.m., National Hockey League, Boston Garden, Boston, Massachusetts.

December–March, Horse Races, Hialeah Race Track, Miami, Florida.
December–April, Dog Races, Jacksonville, Florida.
December–April, Dog Races, Miami and Hollywood, Florida.
December–May, Jai Alai, Miami, Florida.
December–March, Dog Racing, Miami, Jacksonville, and West Palm Beach, Florida.

INDEX

INDEX

	PAGE		PAGE
Aberdeen, N. C.	227	Arlington National Cemetery	185
Abnaki Indians	26, 36	Arnold Arboretum	63
Accotink, Va.	189	Arnold House	69
Adams, G. J.	10	Arnold Tavern, Site of	70
Agricultural Demonstration Project	233	Artesia, Fla.	267
		Asbury, Francis	167, 197, 208
Agricultural Experiment Station	180	Ashland	213
Agricultural Research Center	176	Ashland, Va.	199
Aiken, S. C.	237	Ashley Gang	269
Airports		Augusta, Ga.	241
Newark	129	Avocado Grove	284
Washington	187	Avondale, Pa.	148
Airway Radio, Elizabeth	130	Avongrove Consolidated School	148
Ais Indians	268		
Alabama, The	79	Babcock Burial Ground	88
Alexandria, Va.	187	Babcock House	87
Allendale, Fla.	261	Bacon, Nathaniel	301
Allen Place	218	Bahama Houses	294
Allis House	100	Bailey Island	37
Allspattah Gardens	283	Baker's Haulover	281
Alma, Ga.	248	Baldpate Hill	58
Alna Meeting House	30	Baltimore, Md.	168
Ammemdale Normal Institute	175	Bamboo Key	290
Anacape Mission, Ruins of	258	Bangor, Me.	16
Anacostia River	181	Baptist Church, East Greenwich	68
Anchor and Hope Farm	156	Baptist Church, Easty Lyme	94
Andrew Jackson, The	91	Barbour's Heights	77
Annie, The	92	Barney's Point	10
Antietam Soldier	87	Batesburg, S. C.	237
Anvil Tavern	146	Bath, Ga.	242
Apex, N. C.	222	Bath, Me.	32
Applecrest Farm	53	Bath, S. C.	238
Appomattox Manor	204	Battlefields	
Appomattox River	204	Bladensburg	182
Apponaug, R. I.	67	Drewry's Bluff	203
Aquia Church	193	Great Swamp Fight	110
Aquia Creek	192, 193	Spotsylvania	196
Arch Creek Natural Bridge	281	Yellow Tavern	201
Arlington	185	Baxley, Ga.	247
Arlington Memorial Bridge	185	Bayard, Fla.	256

Bayonne Bridge	129
Beal, Aunt Peggy	11
Beal, Barney	10
Beals	10
Beals Island	10
Bear Lake	285
Bearpond, N. C.	217
Beasley Place	242
Beaver Tail Light	78
Beck House	215
Beckwith House	94
Bedford High School	110
Bel Air	190
Bel Air Academy	163
Bel Air, Md.	162
Belfast, Me.	19
Belgrade, The	12
Bellamy, Samuel	8
Belmont	171
Belt Boulevard	202
Berkeley	303
Berkeley, Md.	159
Berwyn, Md.	178
Best Friend	238
Bethel Presbyterian Church	162
Bethesda Church	227
Bethune, S. C.	233
Biddeford, Me.	40
Big House	175
Big Lynches River	233
Big Pee Dee River	231
Big Pine Key	291
Big Torch Key	292
Bill Memorial Library	93
Billy's Island	308
Bingham, William	14
Birmingham Manor	176
Black Caesar	286
Black Horse Inn	143
Black Horse Tavern	97
Black Mansion	14
Black Point	39
Blackstone Memorial Library	103
Bladensburg, Md.	181–3
Blaisdell House, Belfast	19
Blaisdell House, Winterport	17
Boardman House	47
Boca Chica Key	293
Boca Raton, Fla.	276
Bok, Mary Louise	20
Bolton Priory	117
Bonaventure, Fla.	267
Bonhamtown, N. J.	132
Bonnet Point	79
Boot Key Harbor	291
Boston, Mass.	62
Botanical Garden, Fla.	293
Botanical Museum, N. Y.	120
Boulevard Bridge	202
Bourne Mansion	42
Boxford, Mass.	59
Boydton Plank Road	206
Boynton Beach, Fla.	275
Brandywine Baptist Church	145
Branford, Conn.	103
Branford Point	103
Breakheart Reservation	60
Brent, Giles	192
Brent, Margaret	192
Brewer, Me.	15
Bridgeport, Conn.	108
Bridges, H. Styles	4
Broadway	122
Brocklebank House	58
Brompton	196
Bronx Park	120
Brook Hill	202
Brown House	114
Brunswick, Me.	33
Bryn Athyn, Pa.	138
Bucknam House	12
Buffalo Presbyterian Church	225
Bull Garrison House, Site of	74
Bunnell, Fla.	258

INDEX

	PAGE		PAGE
Burlingame Reservation	86	Cascade Trail	170
Burnham Tavern	9	Casco Bay	35, 36, 37
Burnside	216	Casco Castle, Ruins of	35
Burr House	109	Case House	75
Bush Homestead	115	Casements, The	259
Bushnell, Cornelius Scranton	100	Casey House	77
Bushnell, David	98	Castello Family	215
Byram Point	113	Cedar Knoll	117
Byram River	113, 115	"Celestial Railroad" Monument	273
Byrd, Col. William	304, 199, 207, 209	Central State Hospital	206
		Chadd's Ford Junction, Pa	146
Calais, Me	2	Chadd's Ford, Pa	145
Caldwell, Erskine	240, 243	Chaloner Tavern	300
Calkins Tavern	94	Chamberlain, Gen. Joshua	16
Callahan, Fla	254	Champlain, Samuel de	3, 22, 31
Calvert, George, Lord Baltimore	150	Charles River	62
Calvert, Leonard, Lord Baltimore	192	Charlestown, R. I.	85
Calvert Mansion	181	Chase Prairie	306
Cambridge, Mass.	62	Chavis, John	214–5, 217
Camden Bowl	21	Cheraw Indians	231
Camden, Me.	20	Cheraw, S. C.	231
Camden, S. C.	234	Cheraw State Park	232-3
Cameron, N. C.	225	Cherryfield, Me.	12
Campbell Monument	105	Cheverus, Father Jean de	27
Camp Cornelia, Ga.	305	Chillicote House	16
Campobello Island	298, 300	Choate House	59
Canaveral Harbor	267	Chopowamsic Creek	192
Canova Ocean Fishing Pier	268	Chopowamsic Park	191
Cape Canaveral	267	Christ Church, Stratford	107
Cape Neddick	45	Cilley House	24
Capitol, The	187	Clapp House	28
Capron Trail	279, 281	Clark's Point	7
Capture of Breakfast Hill, Site of	48	Clark Tavern	106
		Clay House	19
Cardiff, Md.	160	Cliff Island	37
Card Sound Bridge	285	Clifton Heights, Pa.	140
Carlton Bridge	31	Clifton Park	168
Carroll Place	213	Clinton, Conn.	98
Carson House	73	Closet Hall	116
Carter, "King" Robert	302	Clough, Capt. Samuel	29
Cary, N. C.	222	Coast Guard Academy	94

U. S. ONE

	PAGE
Coast Guard Stations	
Great Wass Island	11
Indian River	264
Las Olas Beach	278
Narragansett	80
Point Judith	81
Cobb, Col. David	13, 14
Cobbs Hall	205
Cobscook Falls	299
Cock and Kettle Inn	54
Cocoa Beach, Fla.	267
Cocoa, Fla.	266
Cocolobo Cay Club	284
Coggeshall House	71
Colcord, Lincoln	18
Colee Hammock	278
Colee Monument	278
Cole, Goody	50
College Bridge	133
College Park, Md.	179
Collingwood	187
Colonial Heights, Va.	205
Colonial Village	111
Columbia Falls, Me.	11
Columbia, Me.	12
Columbia, S. C.	235
Comedy	110
Conanicut Island	77
Concord Meeting House	144
Concordville, Pa.	144
Congaree Bridge	236
Congdon House	67
Congregational Churches	
Boxford	59
Ellsworth	14
Greenwich	113
Guilford	101
Hampton	50
Madison	100
Massachusetts	64
Old Lyme	95
Old Saybrook	97

	PAGE
Orange	105
Saco	40
Scarboro	38
Wells	44
Weston	111
Westport	110
Connecticut College	94
Connecticut River	96
Conowingo Dam	156
Conowingo, Md.	154
Convent of Holy Angels	125
Cooper House	75
Cooper, James Fenimore	116
Coronado Beach, Fla.	263
Coronation Rock	86
Coronet, The	34
Cos Cob, Conn.	112
Courtenay, Fla.	267
Cowesett, R. I.	67
Cow House Island	308
Crabtree Creek Park	222
Cram, Ralph Adams	53
Crane, Col. John	6
Crane Creek	268
Cranston, R. I.	66
Crawl Keys	290
Cromwell, Oliver	60
Crozet, Col. Claude	202
Crystal Springs	253
Cudjoe Key	292
Curles Neck	301
Curry, John Steuart	110
Custis, George Washington Parke	185
Custis, Mary Ann Randolph	186
Cutler, Me.	299
Damariscotta, Me.	26
Dania, Fla.	279
Danish Village	39
Dante Orphanage	144
Danvers State Hospital	60

INDEX

	PAGE		PAGE
Darien, Conn.	111	Dummitt's Mound	264
Darlington, Md.	159	Dumpling Pond	112
Davenport Memorial Museum.	32	Dunes Club	80
Davie, Fla.	280	Dunlawton Sugar Mill, Ruins of	261
Davis, Jefferson	12, 243	Dunstan, Me.	40
Day House	31	Dutch Gap, Va.	203
Daytona Beach, Fla.	260	Dutch Island	77
Dearborn, John	48	Eagle Island	37
Dearborn, Samuel	48	Earle, Alice Morse	78
Dedham, Mass.	63	Eastern Point	92
Deep River	223	East Greenwich Academy	69
Deer Creek	159, 160, 161	East Greenwich, R. I.	67
Deerfield, Fla.	276	East Haven, Conn.	104
Deer Isle	22	East Holden, Me.	15
Delaware and Raritan Canal	134	East Lyme, Conn.	94
Delaware River	134, 135	East Machias, Me.	6
Delray Beach, Fla.	275	Eastport, Me.	297
Dennys River	5	East River, Conn.	100
Dennysville, Me.	5	Eau Gallie, Fla.	268
Desert of Maine	35	Ebenezer Academy, Site of	207
Devil's Basin	57	Eddy, Mary Baker	25
Devil's Foot Rock	72	Ed's Place	284
Devon, Conn.	107	Eels House	106
Dewitt, Va.	207	Eight-Sided House	181
Dexter House	66	Eldredge House	67
Dinsmore, Fla.	254	Eldredge Memorial Fountain	69
Dinwiddie, Va.	207	Elizabeth, N. J.	130
District of Columbia Workhouse	190	Elizabeth River	130
Dix Memorial Park	16	Elkridge, Md.	170
Dochet Island	3	Ellsworth, Me.	13
Dockray House	83	Elmfield	52
Dodge Homestead	53	Elnathan Street House	104
Dole House	56	Ennis Art School	297
Doswell, Va.	198	Episcopal Chapels	
Drewry, Capt. A. H.	203	Falls River	53
Drewry's Bluff, Battle of	203	Portsmouth	47
Dublin, Md.	160	Episcopal Memorial Church,	
Duck Hole	100	Ogunquit	44
Dueling Ground, Bladensburg.	**183**, 24	Everett, Mass.	62
Duke's Castle	266		
Dumfries, Va.	191	Fairfield, Conn.	108
Dummitt Grove	266	Fairfield Memorial Library	109

	PAGE		PAGE
Fairlea Farms	105	Hill	92
Fair of the Iron Horse	169	Knox	17
Fairview, N. J.	126	Philip Kearny	78
Falls River Falls	53	Taylor	294
Falmouth Foreside, Me.	36	Forts, Sites of	
Falmouth Town Forest	36	Christanna	207
Falmouth, Va.	194	Machias	7
Faulkner's Island	100	Mansfield	88
Fennell Orchid Jungle	283	New Casco	36
Field House	19	Peyton	257
Finley, Rev. Samuel	152	Santa Lucia	272
First Church, Lynnfield	60	Sullivan	297
First Church, Milford	106	Washington	122
Fisher's Island	91	Forty-Fifth Parallel Marker	4
Five Elms	42	Foster, Benjamin	7, 9
Five Forks	206	Foster's Rubicon	9
Flagler Beach, Fla.	258	Foxborough State Hospital	63
Flagler, Henry M.	255, 259, 269, 274, 289	Frankfort, Me.	17
		Franklin, Benjamin	48, 74, 99, 110
Flamingo Citrus Groves	280	Franklin Ferry House	78
Florida City, Fla.	284	Franklinton, N. C.	217
Floyd's Island	307	Fredericksburg	**194**, 195
Flying Cloud, The	91	Freeport, Me.	34
Flying Place	10	Frenchtown, R. I.	71
Folkston, Ga.	251	Fresh Air Farm	164
Fones, Daniel	71	Friendship, Me.	25
Fordham University	121	Friends' Meeting Houses	
Fore River	37	Deer Creek	158
Forest Hill, Md.	161	East Greenwich	69
Forest Tree Nursery	234	Oxford	149
Fort Everglades, Fla.	279	Friends' Meeting House, Site of,	
Fort Hale Park	104	Nottingham	149
Fort Lauderdale, Fla.	277	Frisbie Homestead	102
Fort Lee, N. J.	124	Frisbie House	103
Fort Neck Lot	86	Frost House	42
Fort Pierce, Fla.	271	Fuller's Tavern	63
Forts		Fullerton, Md.	168
Belvoir	189		
Bragg	225–6	*Galena, The*	92
Greble	77	Galilee	81
Griswold	93	Gardiner House	78
Harrison	301	Garrison Cove	39

INDEX

	PAGE		PAGE
Garrison Island	26	Greenbelt, Md.	178
Garvin Home	245	Greene, Gen. Nathanael	68, 71
Geiger Key	292	Greene Homestead	68
General Stanton Inn	85	Greenfield Hill, Conn.	110
Georgetown, Mass.	58	Green Hill House	218
George Washington Bridge	122	Greenwich, Conn.	113
Georgia Penitentiary	246–7	Greenwood, R. I.	66
Georgia, The	32	Gregg, William	238
Georgina, Fla.	267	Greynolds Park	281
German Meeting House	25	Griswold House	94
Gerrish House, Site of	55	Groton, Conn.	93
Gifford, Fla.	270	Groton Long Point	92
Gilbert, Raleigh	31	Groton Monument	93
Gillburg	217	Grove Beach	98
Glebe, The	74	Guale Indians	270
Glover Place	216	Guast, Pierre du	3
Gobert House	244	Guilford, Conn.	100
God's Little Acre	243	Gulf Stream, Fla.	276
Goethals Bridge	129	Gum Tavern, Va.	198
Golden Ball, The	300	Gunpowder Falls	167
Gorges, Fernando	31	Gunston Hall	190
Gorton Pond	67		
Gouldsboro, Me.	13	Hackensack River	127, 128
Goulds, Fla.	283	Hale, Edward Everett	84
Governor Ames, The	25	Halethorpe, Md.	169
Governor Dummer Mansion	57	Half-Way House	203
Governors, N. C. and S. C.	221–2	Halifax River	261
Grand Prairie	306	Hall Houses	102
Grange Hall, Holden	15	Hall of Fame, N. Y. U.	121
Graniteville, S. C.	238	Hamburg, S. C.	238
Grant, Fla.	269	Hamilton, R. I.	77
Grant, Gen. U. S.	198, 204, 205	Hamilton's Crossing	196
Grassy Key	290	Hammonasset River	99
Graves House	100	Hammonasset State Park	99
Graystone, N. C.	213	Hampden Highlands, Me.	16
Great Captain's Island	113	Hampden, Me.	16
Great Chimney House	84	Hampton Falls	51
Great Pee Dee, The	232	Hampton, N. H.	49
Great Republic, The	90–91	Hancock, Me.	13
Great Swamp Fight, Site of	110	Hanover, Va.	200
Great Wass Island	10	Harford Baptist Church	161
Green Bank Farm	148	Harlem River	121

	PAGE		PAGE
Harrington, Me.	12	Homestead, Fla.	284
Harrison, Benjamin	303	Hoodoo Marker	165
Hartzel Home	232	Hopewell, Va.	204
Haunted House, Hampton	50	Horse Creek Valley	237
Haversham Corner	87	Horseshoe Mountain	233
Haviland Inn	116	Horse Shoe Pond	236
Haw River	223	Horticultural Station	177
Hazard Castle	80	Housatonic River	107
Hazard House, Narragansett	79	*House that Tutt Built, The*	12
Hazard House, Sugar Loaf Hill	83	Howland House	68
Hazard Memorial Library	82	*How the Women Went from Dover*	49
Hazard, Thomas	83	Hubbell House	110
Head Tide, Me.	30	Hudson River	122
Hebardville, Ga.	249	Hunnewell House	38
Hedgerow Theater	142	Hunting Creek	187
Helme House	74	Hunts River Bridge	71
Hemingway, Ernest	294	Hutchinson River	118, 119
Henderson Marker	215	Hutchinson River Parkway	115, 118
Henderson, N. C.	213	Hyatt Manor	181
Henricopolis, Site of	203	Hyattsville, Md.	181
Henry, Patrick	**200**, 199	Hyland House	101
Hermitage Golf Club	202		
Herring Run Park	168	*Increase, The*	45
Hickory Hill	200	Indialantic Beach, Fla.	267
Hicks House	137	Indian Burial Grounds	85, 259, 296
Higgins Beach	38	Indian Key	289
Hightower, S. C.	233	Indian Lake	6
Hill Burying Ground	56	Indian Maid Mill	85
Hill, Gen. A. P.	206	Indianola, Fla.	267
Hilliard, Fla.	253	Indian River	265
History of the Dividing Line	209	Indian River City, Fla.	266
Hive of the Averys, Site of	92	Indian River Dude Ranch	263
Hobe Sound	273	Indian River School	263
Hockomock Bay	30	Indians	
Hoffman, N. C.	229	Abnaki	26, 36
Hogshead Point	100	Ais	268
Holden, Me.	15	Cheraw	231
Holland House	84	Guale	270
Holland Tunnel	120	Lenape	137
Holly Hill, Fla.	260	Narragansett	70, 79, 86, 90
Hollywood-by-the Sea, Fla.	280	Niantic	86
Holy Ghost and Us Society	33	Passamaquoddy	296

INDEX

	PAGE		PAGE
Pequonnock	108	Jonesport, Me.	10
Pequot	86, 91, 110	*Jonny-Cake Papers*	83
Red Paint	24	Journey's End, Boxford	59
Sasco	108	Journey's End, Delray Beach	275
Seminole	264, 278	*Journey to the Land of Eden*	207
Siwanoy	117	Judson House	107
Susquehannock	187	Jungle Gardens, Holly Hill	260
Tuscarora	218		
Indian Trail	61	Kaolin Mine	236
International Bridge	2	Kavanaugh Mansion	27
Ironworks		Kellogg, Harold	58
Bath	32	Kelsey City, Fla.	273
Pembroke	4	Kelsey-Highlands Nursery	59
Ironworks House	61	Kelsey Point	98
Islamorada, Fla.	289	Kendal, Fla.	283
Isle au Haut	23	Kennebec River	31
Islesboro	19	Kennebunk, Me.	41
Ivy Mills, Pa.	144	Kennett Square, Pa.	147
		Kent County Courthouse	69
Jackson, Thomas "Stonewall"	197	Kent County Jail, First	70
Jacksonville, Fla.	255	Kent County Jail, Second	69
Jamaica Pond	63	Kentish Artillery Armory	67
Jameson's Tavern	34	Kentish Guards Armory	68
James River	203	Key Largo	285, 286
Jarrettsville, Md.	161	Key Largo Station, Fla.	287
Jay, John	116	Key Vaca	291
Jeff Davis Trail	12	Key West, Fla.	293
Jefferson, Thomas	188, 302	Kidd, Captain	37
Jennersville, Pa.	149	Kiddie Keep-Well Camp	131
Jensen, Fla.	272	Kimball Bird Sanctuary	86
Jensen Savannah	272	King Homestead, Scottow's Hill	39
Jersey City, N. J.	127	King House, Saco	40
Jerusalem, Md.	166	Kingsville, Md.	166
Jerusalem Mills	166	King Tom Farm	86
Jewell Island	37	Kittrell, N. C.	217
Johnson House	19	*Kneel to the Rising Sun*	243
Johnston's Palm Lodge	284	Knox State Arboretum	24
Jonesboro, Me.	9	Korona, Fla.	258
Jones House, Cary	221		
Jones House, Portsmouth	47	Laddin's Rock	112
Jones House, Wake Forest	219	Lafayette Elm	42
Jones, Ichabod	6	Lafayette House	41

	PAGE		PAGE
Lafayette, Marquis de	78, 152, 159, 171, 202	Boxford	59
		Camden	20
La Fitte, Jean	288	East Machias	6
Lakeland, Md.	179	Ellsworth	14
Lake Lucerne	15	Fairfield Memorial	109
Lake Murray Dam	236	Hazard Memorial	82
Lake Poinsett	267	Port Chester	114
Lake Saltonstall	103	Providence	66
Lakeview, N. C.	225	Taylor Memorial	148
Lake Worth, Fla.	275	Topsfield	58
Lamb in His Bosom	240, 248	Wiscasset	29
Lancaster House	38	Lighthouse Point	104
Langhorne, Pa.	136	Lighthouses	
Langley, S. C.	238	Faulkner's Island	100
Lansdowne, Pa.	139, 140	Hillsborough	277
Lantana, Fla.	275	Key West	294
Lapidea Manor	142	Owl's Head	22
Larchmont, N. Y.	117	Point Judith	81
Larkin House	47	Ponce de Leon Inlet	264
Larrabee Garrison House, Site of	43	Rockland	21
Latrobe, Benjamin H.	170	Stonington	90
Latter-Day Saints	10	Stratford Point	108
Laurel, Md.	172	Lignum Vitae Key	290
Lawrenceville, Va.	207	Lincoln, Abraham	205
Laysville, Conn.	94	Lincoln, Gen. Benjamin	5
Lee, Capt. Samuel	102	Lincoln University	149
Lee, Gen. Robert E.	186, 195, 198, 205, 253	Linden, N. J.	130
		Lindsey Tavern	43
Lee, "Light Horse Harry"	302	Lion Farm	277
Lee-Payson-Smith House	28	Lippincott House	12
Leesville, S. C.	237	Little Captain's Island	113
Leiper, Thomas	142	Little Gunpowder Falls	165
Le May Place	216	Little River	225
Lenape Indians	137	Lockville, N. C.	223
Lenape Monument	137	Longwood Gardens	146
Leon, Ponce de	257	Longwood Village	147
Lexington, S. C.	236	Lord Granville Line	223
Liberty, The	3	Lord House	42
Libraries		Lord's Point	91
Bel Air	163	Loring Garrison, Site of	36
Bill Memorial	93	Lorton, Va.	190
Blackstone Memorial	103	Lotus, Fla.	267

INDEX

	PAGE		PAGE
Louisburg College	218	Markham, Pa.	144
Louisburg, N. C.	218	Marston, N. C.	229
Louisville Academy, Site of	245	Marye's Heights	195–6
Louisville, Ga.	244	Maryland Canal	155
Love Feast at Waycross, The	250	Mason-Dixon Line	150
Lower Matecumbe	290	Mason House	3
Lubec, Me.	300	Mason Island	91
Lucerne-in-Maine	15	Mason Monument	92
Lumber River	229	Massacre Bluff	264
Lyme Art Gallery	96	Massacre Pond	39
Lynch, Col. Charles	**218**, 231	Mather's Bridge	268
Lynch Creek	218	Matunuck Beach	84
Lynnfield, Mass.	60	Matunuck Point	84
Lynn Reservoir	60	*May Night*	95
Lyon House	113	McBee, S. C.	233
Lyons, Ga.	246	McIntire Garrison House	45
		McKay House	232
Macdonald, Flora	226	McKee Jungle Gardens	271
Machias, Me.	7	Meddybemps Lake	4
Machiasport, Me.	6	Media, Pa.	143
Machias River	8	Melbourne, Fla.	268
Machias-Whitneyville R.R.	7	Melchers, Gari	194
Madison, Conn.	100	Merchant's Hope Church	205
Madison, Dolly	199	Meredith College	220
Magraw, Rev. James	152	Merrimac River	56
Mahlon Stacy Park	134	*Merrimac, The*	203
Maine State Prison	24	Merritt, Fla.	267
Malabar, Fla.	268	Merry Oakes, N. C.	223
Malden, Mass.	61	*Message from the Sea*	97
Malvern Hill	302	Methodist Church, East Greenwich	70
Mamaroneck, N. Y.	116		
Mansion House	81	Method, N. C.	220
Manson, N. C.	212	Miami, Fla.	281
Man Without a Country, The	84	Mianus, Conn.	112
Marathon, Fla.	291	Micco, Fla.	269
Marches Tavern	56	Middleburg, N. C.	213
Margaretta, The	7, 9	Middlesex County Tuberculosis Hospital	131
Marie Antoinette House	29		
Marine Historical Museum, Mystic	91	Middle Torch Key	292
		Milbridge, Me.	13
Marine Museum, Penobscot	18	Milestones	48, 59, 99, 109
Market Hall, Cheraw	232	Milford, Conn.	105

Millay, Edna St. Vincent	22, 56
Miller, Caroline	240, 248
Miller Tavern	19
Mims, Fla.	265
Minnieville, Va.	190
Mizner, Addison	274
Mogg Megone	39
Momauguin Point	104
Moncure, N. C.	223
Monetta, S. C.	237
Monitor, The	100, 203
Monkey Jungle	283
Monocacy, Battle of	164
Montpelier, Md.	173
Montpelier, Site of	216
Montpelier, Thomaston	23
Monument Park	125
Monuments	
Carter Jackson	74
"Celestial Railroad"	273
Civil War, Saugus	61
Civil War, Topsfield	58
Colee	278
Confederate, Cheraw	232
Confederate, Rockingham	230
Groton	93
Lenape	137
Mason	92
Mesheck Weare	52
Peace	58
Ponus	111
Province of Maine	45
Soldiers'	61
War Memorial	133
Washington	187
Washington Masonic	187
William Campbell	105
World War, Lexington	236
World War, Ridgefield	125
Moonstone Beach	84
Moose Hill, Conn.	102
Moose Hill, Mass.	63
Morris Cove	104
Morris, Robert	135
Morrisville, Pa.	135
Morsemere, N. J.	125
Morton, Pa.	140
Mosquito Lagoon	264
Mosquito Mountain	17
Mother Bailey House	93
Mother Brook	63
Moulton, Gen. Jonathan	50
Moultrie, Fla.	257
Mount Agamenticus	45
Mount Battle	21
Mount Vernon	187, 186
Mount Waldo	17
Mount Welcome	154
Mousam River	41
Mt. Carmel Church	198
Muirkirk, Md.	174
Mule Market	235
Mystic, Conn.	91
Mystic River	62
Napatree Point	88
Narragansett Baptist Church	78
Narragansett Church, Wickford	76
Narragansett Indians	70, 79, 86, 90
Narragansett, R. I.	79
Narraguagus River	12
Naranja, Fla.	283
National Battlefield Park, Richmond	301, 203
National Gardens	258
National Military Cemeteries	
Arlington	185
Marye's Heights	195
National Military Parks	
Fredericksburg	196
Spotsylvania	196
Negro Foot	199
Nellie Chapin, The	10
Nequasset Meeting House	31

INDEX

	PAGE		PAGE
Newark, N. J.	129	North Miami Beach, Fla.	281
New Brookland, S. C.	236	Northport, Me.	20
New Brunswick, N. J.	133	North State Pottery	224
Newburyport, Mass.	57	North Trescott, Me.	299
New Canaan, Conn.	111	North Yarmouth Academy	35
Newcastle, Me.	27	Norwalk, Conn.	111
New England Rarities	39	Nottingham Lots	149, 151
New Haven, Conn.	104	Nottingham, Pa.	149
New Jersey College for Women.	133	Nottoway River	207
New Jersey College of Agriculture	133	Nutbush Presbyterian Church..	217
		Nut Plains, Conn.	102
New Jersey Reformatory	131		
New London, Conn.	94	Oakford, Pa.	138
Newport, Fla.	287	Oak Hill, Fla.	265
New River	277	Oak Hill, Me.	38
New Rochelle, N. Y.	117	Oak Hill, Va.	205
New Smyrna, Fla.	262	Oakland	174
New Wife and the Old, The	50	Oakland, Remains of	216
New York City	119	O'Brien, Capt. Jeremiah	7, 9
New York University	121	Occoquan, Va.	190
Niantic Indians	86	Octorara	153
Niantic River	94	Octoraro Creek	153
Nickels House	27	Ogunquit, Me.	44
Ninigret, Thomas	86	Ojus, Fla.	280
Noank, Conn.	92	Okefenokee Swamp	305, 251
Noblesboro, Me.	26	Old Fork Church	198
No Name Key	291	Old Lyme, Conn.	95
Nonesuch River	38	Old Man of Seabrook	54
Norlina, N. C.	210	*Old Narragansett*	78
Noroton, Conn.	111	Old Saybrook, Conn.	96
Norsemen	53	Oliphant Home	243
North Attleboro, Mass.	64	Olney	164
North Bergen, N. J.	126	Opera House, Camden	20
North Brick House	219	Orange, Conn.	105
North Burial Ground	66	Orange River	5
North Edgecomb, Me.	29	Ormond Beach, Fla.	259
North Hampton, N. H.	48	Ormond, Fla.	259
North Haven, Me.	22	*Orphans of the Storm*	117
North Hill	48	Orr's Island	37
North Indian River	262	Orsino, Fla.	267
North Kingstown Beach	71	Osceola	257
North Lubec, Me.	299	Otis House	19

U. S. ONE

	PAGE		PAGE
Owl's Head, Me.	22	Penobscot River	15, 16
Oxford, Pa.	149	Pequonnock Indians	108
Oxford Valley, Pa.	136	Pequot Hill	92
		Pequot Indians	86, 91, 110
Page, Walter Hines	228, 222, 227	Pequot Path	89
Palisades, N. J.	125	Perio's Point	11
Palisades, The	122	Perkins Cove	44
Palm Beach, Fla.	274	Perley-Hale-Perkins House	59
Palmer House	90	Perrine, Dr. Henry	290
Palmer Northrup House	72	Perrine, Fla.	283
Paradise Key	284	Perry Hall Mansion	167
Parker River	57	Perry Hall, Md.	167
Parson Capen House	58	Perry, Me.	4
Parsons' Cause	200	Perry, Oliver Hazard	83
Passagassawakeag River	18	Perry, Samuel	84
Passaic River	128	Petersburg, Va.	206
Passamaquoddy Bay	296	Peters, Fla.	283
Passamaquoddy Indians	296	Peterson House	33
Passamaquoddy Project	296, 300	Pettaquamscutt Park	80
Pataganset Lake	94	Pettaquamscutt Rock	74
Patapsco River	169	Petuquapaen, Site of	112
Patapsco State Park	170	Peyton's Ordinary	193
Patrick, S. C.	233	Philadelphia, Pa.	139
Patuxent River	173	Phillips House	73
Pawcatuck, Conn.	89	Phipps Point	30
Pawcatuck River	88	Phips, Sir William	30
Pawtucket, R. I.	65	Picture Rocks	7
Peace Dale, R. I.	82	Pidge Tavern	65
Peaks Island	37	Pierce House	47
Pearl of Orr's Island, The	37	Pigeon Key Viaduct	291
Peck Tavern	95	Pillings Pond	60
Pee Dee River	230	Pinebluff, N. C.	228
Pelham Manor, N. Y.	117	Pine Grove Cemetery	59
Pelican Island	270	Pine Ridge, Pa.	142
Pelicans Roost	286	Pinkney House, Site of	163
Pembroke, Me.	4	Pirate's Cove Fishing Camp	292
Pennamaquam River	4	Piscataqua River	46, 47
Penn's Neck, N. J.	134	Piscataway, N. J.	132
Penn's Treaty with the Indians	141	Pitcairn, John	138
Pennsylvania Training School	143	Plantation Key	288
Penn, William	135, 137, 146	Playland, Rye	116
Penobscot Bay	18, 22	Pleasant Point, Me.	296

INDEX

	PAGE		PAGE
Plum Beach	77	*Progress to the Mines*	199
Plummer House	38	Prospect, Me.	17
Plymouth Church, Milford	106	Prout's Neck	39
Pocahontas	193, 203, 301	Providence, R. I.	65
Pocahontas Park	270	Pulaski Skyway	127
Poe, Edgar Allen	121	Putnam, Gen. Israel	113, 115
Poe Park	121	Putnam, Nina Wilcox	275
Pohick Church	189	Put's Hill	113
Point Judith	81	Pyle Blacksmith Shop	144
Pompano, Fla.	276	Pylesville, Md.	160
Ponus Monument	111		
Popcastle Inn, Site of	217	Quakers	49, 69
Pope Hill	243	Quaker Whipping Stone	55
Popham, George	31	Quantico Marine Base	191
Popham, Sir John	31	Quiambog Cover	91
Poplar House	212	Quidnesset, R. I.	71
Poplar Mount	212	*Quimby's Spiritual Science Healing Disease*	25
Poquonock Bridge	92	Quoddy Village	296
Port Chester, N. Y.	114	Quonochontaug Beach	87
Port Deposit, Md.	155	Quonset Point	72
Porter's Landing	35		
Portland, Me.	37	Racebrook Country Club	105
Port Orange, Fla.	261	Racepond, Ga.	251
Portsmouth, N. H.	47	Race Tracks	
Post Road	47, 66, 115	Bowie	173
Pot Boils, The	194	Laurel	171
Potomac Path	189	Rahway, N. J.	131
Potomac River	185	Raleigh, N. C.	220
Potowomut, R. I.	70	Ramrod Key	292
Potter Houses	83	Randolph-Macon Men's College	199
Potter Pond	83	*Ranger, The*	7
Powder House	64	Rappahannock River	194
Presbyterian Churches		Raritan River	132
Bath	242	Red Bank, S. C.	236
Elizabeth	130	Red Beach, Me.	3
Hyattsville	181	Redland Farm Life School	283
Nottingham	149	Red Paint Indians	24
West Nottingham	152	Relay, Md.	169
Priest Neale's Mass House	160	Revere, Paul	47, 89
Primitive Culture, Museum of	82	Rhodes	8
Princeton, Fla.	283	Rhodes Tavern	177
Princeton University	133		

	PAGE		PAGE
Richard's Oak	152	Sachem's Head	102
Richardson House	136	Saco, Me.	40
Richmond, Va.	202	Saddlebunch Key	292
Ridgefield, N. J.	126	Salem Chapel, Site of	208
Ridgeway, N. C.	211	Salisbury, Mass.	55
Rigbie, Col. Nathan	159	*Sally, The*	29–30
Rio, Fla.	272	Salt Island	98
Rippon Lodge	191	Saltpeter Lot	67
Rising Sun, Md.	151	Sanborn, Franklin B.	53
Riverdale, Md.	181	Sandford, Rev. Frank W.	33
River Road	170	Sand Hill Cove	81
Riverside Military Academy	280	Sand Hill Experiment Station	235
Riviera, Fla.	274	Sand Hill Nursery	233
Roaches Run Sanctuary	187	Sand Point Improvement Project	265
Roanoke River	209	Sanford, N. C.	224
Robbinston, Me.	4	Saponey Church	207
Roberts, Kenneth	42	Sasco Indians	108
Robinson, Edwin Arlington	30	Saugus Center, Mass.	60
Robinson, Hannah	78, 73	Savannah River	239
Rockefeller Institute for Medical Research	133	*Savannah, The*	232
		Saxon Woods Park	115
Rockefeller, John D.	259, 255	Scallop Shell	81
Rock Harbor, Fla.	287	Scarboro Marshes	39
Rockingham, N. C.	229	Scarboro, Me.	38
Rockland, Me.	21	Scarborough Beach	80
Rockledge, Fla.	267	"Scotch" Boardman House	60
Rockport, Me.	21	Scotchtown	199
Rodman House	82	Scottow's Hill	39
Roger Williams Park	66	Scott, Winfield	207
Roosevelt Park	131	Seabrook, N. H.	53
Rose Garden, Waycross	250	Seacoast Mission Ship	11
Rose Tree Hunt Club	142	*Sea Gift*	218
Ross Bay	261	Searsport, Me.	18
Rossburg Inn	180	Sebastian Creek Bridge	269
Rowlandsville, Md.	154	Sebastian, Fla.	269
Royall Garrison House, Site of	36	Seminole Indian Reservation	279
Royal Palm State Park	284	Seminole Indians	264, 278, 279
Ruggles House	11	Sheepscot River	27
Rundlett May House	47	Shelter Harbor	87
Russell House, Site of	103	Sherman, William Tecumseh	258
Rye, N. H.	48	Shiloh, Me.	33
Rye, N. Y.	115	Shirley	302

INDEX 341

	PAGE		PAGE
Siwanoy Indians	117	St. Ignatius Roman Catholic Church	161
Slave Market, Louisville	244	St. James Episcopal Church	132
Smith, Capt. John	188, 193	St. John's Church, Kingsville	165
Smith House	72	St. John's Episcopal Church, Williamsboro	216
Smith's Falls	154		
Snake Hill	126	St. John's River	256
Sneed Mansion House, Site of	216	St. John's Roman Catholic Church, Jersey City	127
Snowden	194		
Snowden Mansion	172	St. Joseph's Villa	201
Somerville, Mass.	62	St. Louis School for Boys	40
South Anna River	198	St. Lucie River	272, 273
South Brick House	219	St. Mary Episcopal Church	36
South County Barn Museum	76	St. Mary's Manor	137
Southerner, The	222	St. Mary's River	251, 252
Southern Pines, N. C.	226	St. Mary's Roman Catholic Church	160
South Freeport	35		
South Hill, Va.	208	Stockton Springs, Me.	18
South Langhorne, Pa.	136	Stokes Estate	159
Spotsylvania, Va.	196	Stone Ranch Military Reservation	94
South Lynnfield, Mass.	60		
South Miami, Fla.	282	Stonington, Conn.	89
South Norwalk, Conn.	111	Storer Garrison House	43
South Walpole, Mass.	63	Storer House	42
Spite House	21	*Story of a Sandpile*	59
Spotsylvania Court House, Battle of	196, 197	*Story of Kennett*	146
		Stow, Capt. Stephen	106
Spotsylvania Tavern	197	Stowe, Harriet Beecher	37
Spotsylvania, Va.	196	St. Patrick's Church, Providence	66
Sprague Memorial Park	81		
Springfield Meeting House	140	St. Patrick's Roman Catholic Church, Newcastle	27
Sproul Astronomical Observatory	141		
		St. Paul's Church, Hutchinson River	118
Stafford Courthouse	193		
Stamford, Conn.	112	St. Paul's (Old Narragansett) Church, Site of	73
Stanton House, Clinton	98		
Stanton, Joseph, Jr.	87	Stratford, Conn.	107
Starr House	102	Stratford Point, Conn.	108
Statue of Columbus	66	Strathaven	142
St. Augustine, Fla.	257	St. Stephen, N. B.	2
St. Croix River	2, 3, 4	Stuart, Fla.	273
St. David's Episcopal Church	232	Stuart, Gen. J. E. B.	201
Stephenson Tavern	18		
Stevens Farm	99		

U. S. ONE

	PAGE		PAGE
Stuart, Gilbert	77	Thomaston, Me.	23
Submarine Base, Groton	93	Thomas Viaduct	169
Subtropical Experiment Station	284	Thompson House	104
Success	153	Thornburg, Va.	197
Sugar Loaf Hill	83	Thornton Academy	40
Sugar Loaf Mountain	233	Thornton, William	188
Sugar Loaf Sound	292	Tiny Bird Key	292
Sullivan, Me.	13	Titusville, Fla.	265
Summerland Key	292	Tobacco Auctions	
Sunday Night at Seth Parker's	10	Baxley	247
Sunken Gardens	276	Henderson	214
Sunken Road	195	South Hill	208
Sunset Park	259	*Tobacco Road*	240, 243
Suntaug Lake	60	*To Have and Have Not*	294
Surveying School, M.I.T.	6	Tome, Jacob	155
Susquehanna and Tidewater Canal	157	Tomoka River	258
		Toonerville Trolley	117
Susquehanna River	156	Topsfield, Mass.	58
Susquehannock Indian Fort, Site of	154	Toughkenamon, Pa.	148
		Tower Hill House	81
Susquehannock Indians	187	Towers, The	80
Suwanee Canal	305	Townsville, N. C.	216
Swainsboro, Ga.	246	*Tragedy*	110
Swarthmore, Pa.	141	Treat's Island	300
Swedenborg, Emanuel	138	Trenton, N. J.	134
Sword of Truth and the Harbinger of Peace, The	10	Triangle, Va.	191
		Tropical Gardens, Ormond	259
Sylmar	150, 151	Tropic, Fla.	267
		Tucker Mansion	29
Tavernier, Fla.	288	Tuck Memorial House	50
Taylor, Bayard	147–8, 146	Turkey Island	302
Taylor House	42	Turnbull Canal	263
Taylor Memorial Library	148	Turnbull, Dr. Andrew	262
Taylor River	51	Turnbull Hammocks	264
Tea Table Key	289	Turner House	70
Telegram Marker	175	Turnpike Lake	63
Telegraph Road	197	Turtle Mound	264
Temple Lutheran Church Recreation Center	140	Tuscarora Indians	218
Ten Rod Road	73	Underwood Spring	36
Thames River	93	Union Canal	157
Theater-by-the-Sea, Matunuck	84	Union River	14

INDEX

	PAGE		PAGE
Unitarian Church, Kennebunk	41	Washington Masonic Memorial	187
University, New York	121	Washington Monument	187
University of Maryland	179	Washington State Normal School	7
Updike House	76	Watch Hill, R. I.	88
Upper Matecumbe Key	289	Waterloo, Md.	171
Varina	301	Waycross, Ga.	249
Vass, N. C.	225	*Way Down East*	117
Valley Forge	117	Weare, Mesheck	52
Vance High School	217	Wedding-Cake House	43
Vance, Zebulon Baird	214, 217	Weems, Parson Mason Locke	190
Van Horn's Tavern	176	Wells Beach	44
Varnum House	68	Wells, Me.	43
Varnum Memorial Armory	68	Wellswood Inn	52
Vaucluse, S. C.	238	Wepawaug River	105
Vero Beach, Fla.	270	Wequetequock, Conn.	89
Veterans Camp, Site of	289	West, Benjamin	140, 141
Views Afoot or Europe Seen with a Knapsack and Staff	148	Westbrook, Conn.	98
		Westerly, R. I.	87
Vinalhaven, Me.	22	West Grove, Pa.	149
Vines, Richard	8, 40	West Lubec, Me.	299
Wabasso, Fla.	270	West Mystic, Conn.	92
Wager Weeden Watering Place	84	West Nottingham Academy	151
Wakefield, R. I.	82	Weston, Conn.	111
Wake Forest, N. C.	219	Weston, Hannah	10
Waldoboro, Me.	25	Westover	304
Waldo, Gen. Samuel	25	West Palm Beach, Fla.	274
Waldo-Hancock Bridge	18	West Pembroke, Me.	4
Waldo Patent	25, 23	Westport, Conn.	110
Walker-Gordon Farm	134	West Quoddy Head, Me.	299
Walking Purchase	137	Whale Harbor	289
Ward, Gen. Andrew	102	Whale Rock Light	79
Warfield, Va.	207	Whaling Museum	90
War Memorial Boulder	60	Wheeler Park	130
Warren, Me.	25	Wheelwright, Rev. John	44
Warrenville, S. C.	238	*Whidaw, The*	8
Warwick, R. I.	66	Whigham Place	244
Washington Academy	6	White City, Fla.	272
Washington Bridge	107	Whiteford, Md.	160
Washington, D. C.	184	White Hall	274
Washington, George	122, 125, 187–8, 189, 194	White House, Belfast	19

	PAGE		PAGE
White House, The	183	Wood House	28
White Oak Primitive Church	195	Woodlawn	188
White Plains, Battle of	118	Woolwich, Me.	31
Whitfield House	101	*Wreck of Rivermouth, The*	51
Whiting, Me.	5	Wrens, Ga.	242
Whitneyville, Me.	9	Wright Homestead	99
Whittier, John Greenleaf	52, 39, 49, 50, 51	Wright House, Ridgefield	125
		Wright's Lookout	7
Wickford, R. I.	75	Wrightstown, Pa.	137
Wilcox Tavern	87		
Williamsboro, N. C.	215	Yacht Club, Rockland	22
Williams, Roger	70, 73	Yamato, Fla.	276
Willow Dell	84	Yarmouth Church, Site of	36
Wilson's Mill	159	Yarmouth, Me.	35
Windley Island	289	Yazoo Fraud	244–5
Windmill Cottage	67	Yeadon, Pa.	140
Winona Park	250	Yellow Tavern, Battle of	201
Winterport, Me.	16	Yellow Tavern, Va.	201
Winthrop, John	60, 104	York Institute	40
Winthrop, John, Jr.	70, 71, 96	York Island	37
Wiscasset, Me.	27	Youngsville, N. C.	219
Wise, N. C.	210		
Wolf Stones	89	Zenger, John Peter	118
Woodbridge, Va.	191	Zoological Park, New York	120
Woodcock House	63	Zoo, New Smyrna	263